Nietzsche's System

Nietzsche's System

John Richardson

OXFORD
UNIVERSITY PRESS

OXFORD
UNIVERSITY PRESS

Oxford   New York
Auckland   Bangkok   Buenos Aires   Cape Town   Chennai
Dar es Salaam   Delhi   Hong Kong   Istanbul   Karachi   Kolkata
Kuala Lumpur   Madrid   Melbourne   Mexico City   Mumbai   Nairobi
São Paulo   Shanghai   Singapore   Taipei   Tokyo   Toronto

and an associated company in Berlin

First published in 1996 by Oxford University Press, Inc.
198 Madison Avenue, New York, New York 10016

First issued as an Oxford University Press paperback, 2002

www.oup.com

Library of Congress Cataloging-in-Publication Data
Richardson, John, 1951–
Nietzsche's system / John Richardson.
p.   cm.
Includes bibliographical references and index.
ISBN 0-19-509846-3; 0-19-515595-5 (pbk.)
1. Nietzsche, Friedrich Wilhelm, 1844–1900. I. Title.
B3317.R45   1966
193—dc20   95-11857

2 4 6 8 9 7 5 3 1

Printed in the United States of America
on acid-free paper

To My Mother and Father

PREFACE

My aim is to offer a systematic reading of Nietzsche's thought—a reading that is conservative in its method and approach, but that tries thereby to capture better the radical lessons in his thought. I suppose, conservatively, that Nietzsche's writings do articulate a system of claims, and that he still aims these claims to be true. I try to render this system with a conceptual specificity and clarity that are at least cousins to those practiced by analytic philosophers. But I also try to adapt these standards to do full justice to the extraordinary content of his claims—a content so radical that it revises the very type of truth it purports to have.

I present this project in detail in the Introduction. Here let me mention some procedural and technical points.

Most of my references to Nietzsche are to work—abbreviated to the familiar English-translation codes given in the Bibliography—and section number; for example, BGE1. Further letters refer to prefaces, forewords, and so on, again according to codes supplied in the Bibliography; for example, BGE/P. An intermediate roman numeral refers to a chapter or part with separately numbered sections; for example, TI/I/1. Exceptions to this policy are P&T and PortN, which I cite by page number; for example, P&Tp5. Sometimes I also add a page number for works (BT, UM, PTAG) with very long sections; for example, BT1p33. In EH I cite the chapters discussing Nietzsche's earlier works, using those works' abbreviations; for example, EH/BT/1.

Where I cite or quote writings Nietzsche did not complete (or approve) for publication, I supply the year of composition in brackets; for example, WP957 [1885]. I do this both (1) to alert the reader that these passages may have a different evidential status (see the Introduction) and (2) to locate them chronologically against Nietzsche's finished writings (whose years of composition are given in the Bibliography), so allowing speculations about *shifts* and *stabilities* in his views. Lists of passages are ordered chronologically (and not, for example, by section number in WP).

In German, I have worked from the *Kritische Studienausgabe*, ed. Giorgio Colli and Mazzino Montinari (Berlin: de Gruyter, 1980). When a passage is not in one of the English translations listed in the Bibliography, I cite this edition by volume, then give the notebook number followed by the entry number in brackets; for example, KSA/10/12[39]. The last two numbers, together with the year I also supply, allow the passage to be located as well in the *Kritische Gesamtausgabe* (by the same editors).

I have generally begun with the translations by Kaufmann and Hollingdale, but then revised them—sometimes extensively—for the sake of greater literalness and greater consistency in rendering philosophically relevant terms. In some cases—for example, in my efforts to render *wollen* as '(to) will'—this leads to a certain awkwardness. But such strictness seems called for by this book's project and approach—indeed by *any* effort to place Nietzsche's concepts carefully.

The assumption is not that Nietzsche uses his terms precisely and consistently, so that they might be (straightforwardly) defined. His working vocabulary is vast, his use of words fluidly inventive. Yet some words come to him persistently, recurringly—and they come to him in certain (evolving) relations to one another. These relations form the skeleton of his philosophical thought, and to study them closely we need to deal carefully with his words.

Therefore, my intent has been to translate Nietzsche's key terms consistently, by the same English words everywhere, according to a table of equivalences I give in the Appendix—*except* where I supply (in the quote) the German in brackets. Cases in which an English word renders more than one German word are marked in the Appendix by asterisks. (So with these exceptions, and the errors I've no doubt made, the German can be inferred from the English.)

Except for its occurrence in '*Übermensch*', I have consistently rendered *Mensch* by 'human being' rather than 'man', contrary to the practice of Kaufmann and Hollingdale. I have also, however, preserved Nietzsche's exclusionary use of 'he' for the anonymous human being. This policy has an obvious appropriateness when translating Nietzsche, but I have also followed it myself. The available devices for avoiding that use not only seem awkward, but clash gratingly with the Nietzschean viewpoint this book tries to enter. See § 3.4.2 on the issue of a 'male bias' in Nietzsche's philosophy.

Most of my immediate debts in writing this book originated in a discussion group Roy Sorensen organized for it in summer 1992. Its participants were Raziel Abelson, Chauncey Downes, Jim Dwyer, Ken Gemes, Frances Kamm, Brian Leiter, and Roy Sorensen—I hope and feel I've learned something from each. Brian Leiter's written comments at the time, and our later conversations, were especially helpful. Ken Gemes has given me exceptionally valuable written and oral comments on a more recent draft. I've profited over the years from talking about Nietzsche with Graham Parkes. And I am grateful to a former student, Stephen Miller, both for comments and for help with the manuscript.

New York   J. R.
June 1995

CONTENTS

Nietzsche's System

INTRODUCTION

This book's project is to show that Nietzsche has a metaphysics—to show it by presenting, in conceptual and argumentative detail, a metaphysical system that both fits and clarifies what he says (writes). Such a project might seem perverse, but would be so only, I think, if it had the intent or effect of diminishing Nietzsche. My aim, at least, is otherwise: to show the great interest and fruitfulness of his thought, precisely *as a* metaphysics.

This result, of course, depends on what I mean by 'metaphysics'. Let's begin with this: concretely, it's that historical series of philosophical systems that preceded Nietzsche, and that he complains so emphatically against. These philosophies are (broadly) metaphysical, by being organized systematically around a (more narrowly) metaphysical core. I proceed on a guiding assumption about this substantive core: that it consists in an account of the 'essence' or 'being' of things, so that 'metaphysics' is equivalent to 'ontology'. Differently put, metaphysics tries to see and describe things in an aspect that is not only true of them but also (somehow) basic to them—prior even to all the other true ways we can view them. And metaphysics needs system, because it needs to show how these primary truths reach out into all those other views, in a way that helps us see that, and how, they're true. So, to begin with (I'll gradually add to this list), metaphysics claims a (1) *systematic* (2) *truth* (3) about *essence*. Such were the ambitions or pretensions of Nietzsche's predecessors.[1] How much does he share with them, and where and how does he break from them?

1. The full metaphysical structure, which I attribute to Nietzsche, appears most clearly and completely in Plato and Aristotle; I develop the comparison with Plato in chapter 2.

It's plausible to think this problem central for understanding Nietz-sche—a key test for any reading of his writing. It examines an aspect that he himself puts great weight on and that bulks very large in his self-conception: he purports (often) to stand outside or after that long tradition, at deepest odds with it; he emphatically attacks system, truth, and essence.[2] He is, as I put it, *hypercritical:* he argues the null positions in both epistemology (skepticism: no truth) and ontology (nihilism: no being). Moreover, it is in taking these positions that he has seemed so preeminently prescient a prophet of the modern (or now postmodern) age, to so many who count (post)modernity to lie in just such a break. Derrida and others have drawn from his denial of metaphysics (and truth in general) a radical lesson about philosophy's proper goals and style.[3] Others reject that lesson but also attribute it to him.[4] Have they rightly read Nietzsche's position here? Despite his own professions, and despite the very common view, it is problematic whether he breaks from those predecessors at all so deeply or decisively. Interpreters have often stressed this problem.[5]

My response to this central problem will be conservative—though by it I hope to capture more cogently the radical force Nietzsche's thought otherwise has. I try to present his thought as a system of views organized around an ontology: an interpretation of the being or essence

2. See notes 12–14 in this Introduction.

3. Derrida (1976, 19) qualifies the point: "Radicalizing the concepts of *interpretation, perspective, evaluation, difference,* . . . Nietzsche, far from remaining *simply* (with Hegel and as Heidegger wished) *within* metaphysics, contributed a great deal to the liberation of the signifier". Kofman (1993, 121) speaks of "the radical novelty and originality of Nietzsche's thought and project, which aims to burst the bounds of metaphysical thought". Rorty 1989, 98: "Nietzsche was not only a non-metaphysician, but an antimetaphysical theorist."

4. Habermas 1990, 85–86: "Nietzsche had no choice but to submit subject-centered reason yet again to an immanent critique—or to give up the program entirely. Nietzsche opts for the second alternative: He renounces a renewed revision of the concept of reason and *bids farewell* to the dialectic of enlightenment."

5. Haar 1985, 7: "Here we have the supreme perplexity that can remain at the horizon of our own interrogation: in what sense does Nietzsche 'overcome' the metaphysics that he combats?" Danto 1965, 80: "There is a crucial tension throughout Nietzsche, between a free-wheeling critic, always prepared to shift ground in attacking metaphysics, and a metaphysical philosopher seeking to provide a basis for his repudiation of any such enterprise as he is practicing." Compare Lyotard 1991, 28–29. We'll soon see how deconstructionists also find such a tension. See also the references in n. 19. Of course, Nietzsche interpreters often define metaphysics differently than I have (and will). So Clark (1990, 21) notes how deconstructionists seem to take metaphysics as *any* claim to truth; by contrast, she takes it to claim an a priori truth about things-in-themselves and argues that Nietzsche rejects it in favor of a neo-Kantian empiricism (206). Since I take metaphysics to involve a claim about essence (whose implications will be developed shortly), I give it a much richer content than mere truth claiming; but I try to show how Nietzsche can make claims about essence, even while rejecting the thing-in-itself and while appealing to (hoping for) empirical supports.

of things. I try to lay out this ontology and show how it fits and even shapes his other main thoughts, including those that seem to renounce any such metaphysical intent. To be sure, it fits the latter only by being a new kind of metaphysics: by making changes in those central notions of system, truth, and essence. Nietzsche's metaphysics is different not just in content but in form—in the very *type* of truth it claims. But I argue that these revisions keep him still clearly within the traditional project.

This different type of metaphysics Nietzsche has also affects the way he has it: his new type of truth requires a new type of grasp or understanding. It does not require that the whole system of views be laid out methodically in the manner of this book. It may even discourage the philosopher from so baring himself, even to himself: the unity of his thought should be generated from the system of his unconscious drives and attitudes and can be vitiated by overexplicitness. So, in mapping Nietzsche's thought, we are charting structures he often preferred *not* to discover or express; to an extent, his thought fills out this system despite his own conscious efforts.[6] This explains (I think) some of gap between this book and Nietzsche's texts.

Deconstructionists might also embrace this task—but with a quite different purpose than mine. For of course they don't exempt Nietzsche, either, from their deconstructive baring of metaphysical roots. His grammar and concepts inevitably give him such roots: the very need for expression in language subverts anyone's effort to state an antimetaphysical lesson.[7] By contrast, I try to show that Nietzsche's lesson is itself a metaphysical one after all. But I don't take this as a deflating move: I try to show his metaphysics as, in many respects, a novel and sophisticated one that can make plausible claim to improve on all previous such systems. And I try to show that it is in relation to this metaphysics that we get our best grasp of the force and interest of his other main views: for example, eternal return, the master/slave contrast, becoming, and even those hypercritical views that seem to preclude metaphysics. The new that's best in him is his reworking and advancing of thoughts framed long before him.

6. GM/P/2: "we [philosophers] may not make single errors or hit on single truths. Rather do our thoughts, our values, our yeses and nos and ifs and buts grow out of us with the necessity with which a tree bears its fruit". See also BGE6. KSA/13/11[410] [1887–88]—a draft for TI/I/26 quoted in the following text—continues: "Perhaps one may guess, by a look beneath and behind this book, which systematizer it is with difficulty avoiding—myself". Another motive for not systematically presenting his truths is suggested by HH/I/178, 199. See the Preface for my procedures and policies in the translations and citations from Nietzsche.

7. Yet this inexpressible lesson can still be learned, they think, by the work of uncovering those roots. Derrida—soon after the line quoted in the following text—begins: "Therefore, rather than protect Nietzsche from the Heideggerian reading, we should perhaps offer him up to it completely, underwriting that interpretation without reserve" (1976, 19). See how he continues.

Other interpreters have read him this way.[8] The most important such account is Heidegger's reading of Nietzsche as "the last metaphysician",[9] but this is rendered suspect by Heidegger's interest in placing Nietzsche at the end of (but still within) a tradition first superseded by Heidegger himself. By contrast, I have quite different motives in stressing Nietzsche's links with the tradition. But I proceed directly against Derrida's advice (1976, 19): "To save Nietzsche from a reading of the Heideggerian type, it seems that we must above all not attempt to restore or make explicit a less naive 'ontology'".[10]

I hope that even some who don't and won't think Nietzsche so traditional can still find uses for my account. Those who approve the antimetaphysical break (they think) he makes may wish to sharpen their sense of just what this break involves, by seeing him sketched as if he never made it. Others, who regret his (apparent) asystematicity and suspect that it leads him into inconsistency, may wish to judge whether his views can hang together, even if he himself never meant them to. For such readers, this book might be useful as an experimental effort to give conceptual specificity to what a 'Nietzschean system' (even if not Nietzsche's own) might be. Indeed, at many points this is all I can claim myself, since I often push for specificity beyond what can be found in Nietzsche's words: the system this book sketches is, in its details at least, a construction on and beyond what he says, and an effort to use, to think productively with, the ideas he leaves us. The boundary between these projects of describing and developing is, inevitably, very hard to draw, but I propose that the main lines of what follows *do* match the deep structure of his thought.

My project offers a further, more concrete advantage: the chance to approach Nietzsche and his issues in a way more like that we already practice, and not to feel it necessary to turn at once so drastically away from our familiar philosophical procedures (as, for example, Derrida seems to do). It lets us hear him, at least at our start, as using language with the same straightforward intent as thinkers before him have done; it encourages us to try to give a definiteness or precision as philosophical terms to the words he most often uses to state his views. It encourages us to unfold his views methodically out of that metaphysical core.

8. E.g., Kaufmann 1974, 211ff.; Schacht 1983, 187ff.
9. See Heidegger 1979–87, 3:8, for example.
10. I should make explicit what I hope will be evident below, that this orientation against Derrida and other 'postmodernists' is partly a device of presentation and is consistent with trying to learn from them in important ways. Because my reading of Nietzsche is informed by such lessons, it sketches an ontology 'in the neighborhood' of postmodernism itself. Some of that movement's radical ideas find conceptual and argumentative specificity when located as elements in this embracing Nietzschean system. And, I argue, these ideas are also rendered more coherent in another way: by being freed from the self-undermining paradoxes involved in a 'perspectivism' that casts away all claim to a privileged truth.

My suggestion is not, that this ontology 'grounds' those other views in a fully architectonic way, as the first, most certain truths, from which further views are inferred and by which they're justified. I take it not to be a necessary condition for 'metaphysics' that the ontology be claimed true a priori; my attribution of a metaphysics to Nietzsche must not be taken this way. In his case, the system is offered as a hypothesis to be tested and (he hopes) progressively confirmed in experience. Hence the evidence lies at the periphery to the system and runs in from there, through decreasingly specific accounts of the data, to the central ontology—rather than from an ontology proven first, up to the detailed implications it supports. And yet, although Nietzsche denies his ontology the evidentiary primacy usual in metaphysics, the ontology keeps another traditional priority: it supplies the concepts and structures for all his more concrete efforts to describe that experiential data; indeed, it even helps to determine what that data shall be.[11] For this reason, it remains apt to present Nietzsche's system from the center out, beginning with the abstract ontology and seeing how it organizes and infuses his other thoughts.

This guiding project also serves as an excuse or vehicle for treating an array of other philosophical concerns. As is obvious enough, I reflect on the network of issues Nietzsche himself confronts and weigh his decisions on them; I try, as mentioned, to use his ideas to think better on these issues. Any effort to interpret any philosopher had best have this topical intent as well: to help us face the problems themselves, in new light by way of this thinker. But our project—looking for a metaphysics in Nietzsche—makes us traverse an unusual range of such problems. In seeking a metaphysics, we seek an ontology that infuses the full variety of the philosopher's other views, and with Nietzsche this variety is especially great. We have to pursue him into a representative sample of his strikingly diverse concerns.

Moreover, since we're seeking a metaphysical *system*, we'll also be considering these issues in a special regard: in their interconnectedness, in how they support and sustain one another. I do not dwell single-mindedly on any by itself but (I hope) needn't therefore be superficial. Another sort of depth is achievable, by seeing how issues bear and reverberate on one another, and how certain choices on some issues fit with, prompt, and support certain choices on others. Metaphysics makes system a virtue, contrary to the tendency of analysis, which breaks a problem into ever finer parts and then absorbs itself in these. This book tries to celebrate that other philosophical virtue, by showing how Nietzsche, its apparent archenemy, might have valued and practiced it, too, and in an attractive and viable version.

11. I develop Nietzsche's epistemology in § 4.5; I compare his 'empiricism' to that we can find in Aristotle (where its presence proves that there can be a 'metaphysics' grounded in 'experience').

A point I've already touched on may make this approach seem perverse. Don't all Nietzsche's railings against his philosophical predecessors throw the burden of doubt heavily against any such account of his thought? Isn't this break among the most vivid impressions one gets from his writing? He expresses those hypercritical—skeptical and nihilist—views as a rejection of all his predecessors' 'metaphysics'.[12] He denounces their effort at systems; in *Twilight of the Idols:* "I mistrust all systematizers and I avoid them. The will to a system is a lack of integrity" [TI/I/26].[13] And he attacks their claim to a privileged truth about essence; in *Beyond Good and Evil:* "[A philosophy] always creates the world in its own image; it cannot do otherwise" [BGE9].[14] So it seems the suggestion that he even might have such a theory ought to be dismissed out of hand.

But other evidence supports this approach. Consider the dramatic ending to the last note in (the posthumously assembled nonbook) *The Will to Power: "This world is the will to power—and nothing besides!* And you yourselves are also this will to power—and nothing besides!" [WP1067: 1885] Such remarks do seem to announce an ontology—a truth about the essence of things.

To be sure, these remarks are more common in Nietzsche's notes (his *Nachlass*) than in his books, which has led some interpreters to question his commitment to them. Doesn't Nietzsche's choice not to publish his most explicitly ontological thoughts, together with the way he abandons the project of systematically presenting his ideas (as a book to be called *The Will to Power*), show that he decides *against* rendering his thought in this metaphysical way?[15] Indeed, it might show that he decides not to present his thought this way, or even to think it out for himself thus methodically and systematically. As I've already noted, this could be because he thinks its deep structural unity is (properly and healthily) a product of mainly unconscious processes and is best left in that implicitness. So, although I try to show that there are enough refer-

---

12. BGE2 contrasts metaphysicians with "a new species of philosophers" Nietzsche hopes will arrive. BT/ASC/7: "so that perhaps, as laughers, you may some day send all metaphysical comforts to the devil—metaphysics in front!" See also WP1048 [1885–86] and WP462 [1887].

13. D318: *"Beware of systematizers!* — There is a play-acting of systematizers: . . . they will to impersonate [*darstellen*] complete and uniformly strong natures."

14. WP625 [1888]: "The demand for an *adequate mode of expression* is senseless: it lies in the essence of a language, a means of expression, to express a mere relationship— The concept 'truth' is *nonsensical*".

15. The case against (relying on) the notebooks is well stated by Magnus (1986, 1988b), who claims that "without the *Nachlass* it is virtually impossible to read eternal recurrence and will to power as first-order descriptions of the way the world is in itself" (1988b, 233); he points out that WP1067 [1885], quoted in the text, was eventually discarded by Nietzsche.

ences to will to power (and allied notions) in what Nietzsche chose to publish to render the notebooks not anomalous, I also try to justify attributing the power ontology to him even apart from his explicit statements of it, by showing how well the rest of his thoughts can be clarified by being organized systematically around this partly concealed core.[16]

I investigate how far this 'power ontology' can be reconciled with the several types of passages that seem to count against it. Now, indeed, the very diversity of Nietzsche's writings and the apparent contradictions among them in themselves pose a challenge to this approach. Anyone struggling with his writings will find it hard to keep confident that all Nietzsche says articulates a coherent overall view. Part of the problem is just that his views evolve—a complication we familiarly meet in other thinkers, too. We can also cope with this familiarly, by focusing our attention on 'the mature Nietzsche': his writings (published and not) from the time of *The Gay Science* on.[17] But this won't solve the larger problem—for even within this period, indeed even within single works, he says (apparently) contradictory things on many large issues. Surely any single rendering of his thought, even in some period, would have to contradict many passages. This already suggests that Nietzsche might have goals that are drastically different from those in the metaphysical tradition, for which such inconsistency would be a quite cardinal flaw. Moreover, there are specific remarks that seem to weigh directly against such a reading. Some of these I've just mentioned, for instance, Nietzsche's frequent attacks on metaphysicians, which often dispute their basic methods or goals—above all, their systematic effort to state essential truths. Other remarks suggest a positive alternative to such metaphysics, an alternative that Nietzsche and his interpreters often sum up in the title *'perspectivism'*.

It is this perspectivism that poses the main challenge to the suggestion that Nietzsche has a metaphysics or ontology. As with metaphysics, we can give perspectivism a first, approximate sense: that (not just belief

16. I allow that it's important to be aware which quotations are from texts Nietzsche completed for publication, which not. It's partly to flag this difference that I append the year to all quotes of the latter sort. See further the Preface on translations and citations.

17. So the pivotal year would be 1881, in which he 'experienced' eternal return and began writing *The Gay Science*. Of course, the nature of Nietzsche's development is disputed; see the account by Heidegger (1979–87, 1:154, 201–2, 2:107) and the very different one by Clark (1990, 95ff.). I give no sustained review of his development, though § 4.3.3 sketches his evolution on the topic of truth. If the power ontology is really basic in his later works, it will be the crucial dimension for evaluating how far his views change. And we find important anticipations of this ontology very early on. Hence I often supplement prime evidence from the later period, by citing anticipations in the earlier works. See the chronology of Nietzsche's writings, by approximate date of composition, in the Bibliography.

and appearance but) *truth* and so *being* are perspectival, or different for different perspectives; thus there's no way that the world, or any of its parts, is 'in itself' or 'objectively'. There's no truth or being *simpliciter*, only the 'true-for' and 'is-for'. Interpreters often find such a view in Nietzsche and take it to show that his claims about will to power are intended with a drastically different force than apparently parallel claims made within the tradition. A remark often and aptly cited occurs at BGE22: having characterized the physicist's account of the world as "interpretation, not text", and sketched his alternative vision of this world as will to power, he concludes, "Supposing that this also is only interpretation—and you will be eager enough to make this objection?—well, so much the better."[18]

It's clear enough that Nietzsche is, in some sense, a perspectivist. So our task is to see whether and how his apparent metaphysics—his teaching of the will to power—can be reconciled with his perspectival critique. Just what does the latter involve? And how much 'metaphysical force' must we strip from that teaching to render it consistent with that critique? In fact, the tension we find here holds also between the perspectivism and all of Nietzsche's other positive views insofar as he promotes these as truer than what we believed before. In particular, that claim seems to undermine the status not just of his ontology but of his values: of the new ideal he presents and preaches, apparently as something much more than just what his single perspective prefers.

Interpreters of Nietzsche have often noted this crucial problem.[19] We can distinguish two main types of solutions they have offered for it. Each reconciles Nietzsche's (apparent) metaphysics and perspectivism, by weakening one or the other side of this tension or opposition. A more conservative approach gives primacy to the metaphysics; a more radical one gives primacy to the perspectivism.[20]

The *two-level response* holds that Nietzsche's perspectivism is generated by his metaphysics, and doesn't apply back to it so as to call its

---

18. WP418 [1883]: "One seeks a picture of the world in that philosophy in which we feel freest; i.e., in which our most powerful drive feels free for its activity. This will also be the case with me!"

19. Nehamas 1985, 2: "Faced with this dilemma, some authors choose to emphasize what they consider Nietzsche's 'positive' views and to overlook his perspectivism and its apparent implications. Others, by contrast, concentrate on the perspectivism and ignore such views or construe them negatively". Sometimes the issue is posed as a tension between Nietzsche's will to power claims and his supposed nihilism; Schacht (1973) and Solomon (1973a) put it this way, the latter with his focus on values. Wilcox (1982) discusses the tension between Nietzsche's cognitivist and noncognitivist expressions, again particularly about values; Westphal (1984) also states the problem in these terms.

20. This contrast doesn't coincide with that between 'analytic' and 'Continental' interpreters, because, for example, Danto and Nehamas belong to the radical camp, but Heidegger (as we've seen) belongs to the conservative.

status into question.[21] This reading tries to insulate the metaphysics from the perspectivism; it limits the latter's scope, to apply not at the level of being or essence but at a 'lower', contingent level. Nietzsche's position would be that because 'what is' really does have this (abstract) character of will to power, perspectivism holds for all of its other (more concrete) features: 'what is' has no other reality than will to power; everything else is true of it only 'for a perspective'. Of course, this first response needs to show just how Nietzsche's will to power doctrine could generate a perspectivism that applies in this limited way.

The *perspectivist response* maintains that this perspectivism does apply to the teaching of will to power, and indeed to all of Nietzsche's philosophical claims.[22] This reading suggests that the perspectivism is his most basic thought—perhaps also his most vital lesson for our age. That will to power teaching is just the proverbial ladder we cast away once we've used it to boost ourselves up to see the truth of perspectivism. Nietzsche would then be offering all that he says with a force that is radically different from that of thinkers before him. When he says that the world and we are will to power, when he preaches Dionysus as a higher ideal than Christ, he wouldn't intend these positions to be any truer than their opposites; he'd be offering them as 'just his perspective'. This second response needs to show how these positions could then have as strong a claim to our attention as Nietzsche thinks: What interest can we have in his perspective if it's no truer than any other?

My own response has more affinity with the first of these alternatives, though it seeks a route between the two. Unsurprisingly, we find that both terms have to be understood differently—more complexly and also more 'weakly'—than we've so far done. Nietzsche's thought includes both a metaphysics and a perspectivism, once these are more complexly grasped. But I argue that the metaphysics is basic: it's an ontology *of* perspectives.

We can get a first sense of this by recalling a familiar objection against the (generic) perspectivist: that he contradicts himself insofar as he imputes a nonperspectival truth to his perspectivist thesis itself.[23] Our

21. I take Schacht to be stating such a view when he distinguishes (1973, 79) "two sorts or orders of values"; see also his 1983, 202. Danto (1965, 222) suggests it when he says: "Apart from the bare *assertion* of power striving, there appears to be little one can say about the world which is not interpretation"; elsewhere (1965, 77, 230) he seems to favor a more thoroughly perspectivist reading.

22. Nehamas 1985, 80: "Construed in this manner, the will to power is not a general metaphysical or cosmological theory. On the contrary, it provides a reason why no general theory . . . can ever be given." So, too, Thiele 1990, 33. And see Strong 1988, 220; Kofman 1993, 142. Such readings of Nietzsche often align him with postmodernism.

23. Familiarly, such problems are raised by Plato's critique—in the *Theaetetus*—of Protagoras' relativism. Other interpreters have compared Nietzsche's difficulty to the liar's paradox: Kaufmann 1974, 204ff.; and Danto 1965, 230.

problem is an ontological version of this; it begins with the question, What are these 'perspectives'? Mustn't any perspectivism characterize in some way the viewpoints to which it relativizes truth and being? Mustn't it say that there *are* perspectives and that *we* are (or have) perspectives? And won't this look very much like an account of at least one (basic) type of thing there objectively is and that we objectively are? It seems that a perspectivist will have trouble avoiding ontological claims in defending or even presenting his view; indeed, that there's no (determinate) view there without some such clarification.[24]

Moreover, Nietzsche's own positing of perspectivism takes a quite different form from such a reluctant filling out. He explains what he means by these 'perspectives' with great emphasis: they are wills to power, in a sense he tries to develop or analyze. He goes further: he asserts that we and indeed all things are basically such perspectives, such wills to power. Many of his more detailed accounts of persons—his elaborate psychological insights—presuppose this claim; his diagnoses are framed from a vocabulary that reflects it. He considers this way of understanding things original to himself, he takes it to be one of his major thoughts, and he often uses it to generate or justify his perspectival critique. By contrast, it's much less common for him to apply the latter back to the will to power teaching; BGE22 is an unusual case. Indeed, if we do so apply it and see that teaching as 'just a perspective', won't this erase the chief reason he gives us for accepting the perspectivism at all? Doesn't the latter take both its sense and its justification from the ontological claim? Kicking away the ladder, we lose the only support we had for that position.

These points again favor the approach I take: to begin by supposing that Nietzsche does intend his will to power teaching to be a 'transperspectivally true' account of the being or essence of things. He does not, to be sure, claim that it *must* be true this way. He doesn't purport to derive and establish this account of reality a priori; he suggests it as a best-so-far explanation of our experience. So he describes this claim as a hypothesis to be tested [BGE36]. The following may be viewed as an extended attempt at such testing, both of the claim's capacity to play the role of an ontology underlying Nietzsche's thought and of its plausibility in itself. Let me preview the overall way I proceed with this project.

1. Being   In chapter 1, I lay out Nietzsche's notion of will to power in all its metaphysical abstraction, but also in its richness of structural detail. I think this structure hasn't yet been adequately analyzed by Nietzsche's interpreters: the teaching says far more about what things in

---

24. These problems are the worm in postmodernism—at least as this position is prevalently *received* from Derrida and other sources. In finding a Nietzschean system that avoids these problems, we find a view very much like this postmodernism, but more coherent.

general (and we in particular) 'are' than is usually supposed. In turn, this closer analysis allows us to more closely track the systematic implications of that 'power ontology'. For example, the basic possibilities for human life will be the basic forms our will to power can take; so we better understand Nietzsche's sense of the familiar master, slave, and overman by seeing how these human types can be unfolded from the power ontology. More abstractly, Nietzsche's basic valuative contrast between active and reactive and his analyses of what persons and societies are both need to be grasped in terms of will to power. Even his perspectivism—in this first look chapter 1 takes—can be seen as issuing from that metaphysical view.

In laying out this power ontology and seeing how the active/reactive contrast modulates it, we uncover another basic structural feature of Nietzsche's metaphysics, allowing us to add to the list already begun: surprisingly and even paradoxically (to us), it conceives of (4) essence (or being) as *differentially realizable*. Although all things are essentially wills to power, they can 'realize' this essence more or less well and can 'be' will to power more or less fully or adequately. So the power ontology is gradational and, with these grades, is infused with *values*. This further feature also has familiar precedents in the metaphysical tradition.

2. Becoming   This attribution of an ontology to Nietzsche—this claim that he has a theory of being—might seem inconsistent with one very relevant set of evidence: his attacks on the very notion of 'being'. He frequently insists that the world is 'not being but becoming'. I therefore try to show, in chapter 2, how my reading can explain and indeed illuminate such remarks: by developing how they express merely the temporal aspect of that power ontology, the way it says we and other beings are 'in time'. Nietzsche's insistence on 'becoming' is not a denial of all ontologies but a key premise in one ontology. This brings out yet another traditional structural feature of this ontology, its conception of (5) essence as *temporally specified*. As we unfold Nietzsche's temporal views, we rehear or revise our first statement of the power ontology: this temporal aspect recasts the structures of chapter 1. As we follow out the implications for persons and societies, our first account of these is improved as well. For example, we now see how the three basic human types are also three different ways of living through time; such restatements give us a fresh approach to ideas that are by now overly familiar.

Because my aim is to examine Nietzsche's continuities and breaks with the metaphysical systems before him, it makes sense to select a representative member of that past tradition for more detailed comparisons. My choice here is an obvious one. Nietzsche often presents his ideas as diametrically opposed to Plato's, depicting Plato as (roughly) a first and worst case of that misguided tradition, indeed its founder. In particular, Nietzsche presents his ideas as reversing the priority Plato gives to being over becoming. So it's natural to pursue those detailed comparisons, by relating Nietzsche's temporal views to Plato's. This will show, on the one hand, that his vehement attacks on Plato are interlaced with crucial agreements, even on temporal points. We see that these attacks, read in isolation, overstate how far he breaks from Plato, especially in portraying himself as renouncing all ontology. On the other hand, our better grasp of these links and agreements with Plato brings into sharper view the ways Nietzsche's temporal thought really is radical, contrary not just to Plato but to our own natural assumptions. What Nietzsche shares with Plato gives sense and value to his radical thought beyond him. So we see past the too-common presumption that any Platonic or metaphysical remnant in Nietzsche must be a flaw or limitation.

3. *Value*   The perspectivist reading of Nietzsche denies him not only a metaphysics but also (what we might call) any 'posited values', that is, values he proposes as true. By contrast, my conservative reading portrays the perspectivism as subordinate to, and insulated from, a system of such values, along with (ontological) facts. In chapter 3 I focus on this valuative aspect of his thought. In particular, I examine how the values that infuse his metaphysical-temporal views generate and justify his estimations and rankings of persons. Nietzsche's power ontology projects a certain 'human ideal'—the overman—as well as a sense in which this ideal is our 'good'. This is one more way his metaphysics is traditional: by (6) grounding an *ethics*. Of course both the force and content of Nietzsche's values are in some ways radically new; he famously proclaims this in announcing himself 'beyond good and evil'. But again we find that these breaks become clearest and most compelling when we plot them against certain continuities.

The way Nietzsche's values do break from morality in their content raises a troubling worry against them, however: they seem to allow or even advocate a quite intolerable injustice. This problem arises for both his politics (his account of an ideal society) and his ethics (his advice on how to treat individual others). His ideal society seems repellently inegalitarian; his ideal person seems a predator out to dominate others, unrestrained by any moral scruples. Doesn't Nietzsche commend an aggressive, competitive stance toward others, quite incompatible with those personal connections—love, friendship, cooperation—we value most? And don't these warped values show up, too, in his infamous views about women? Such worries bar many readers from accepting Nietzsche's values or even taking them seriously. And if such values indeed issue out of the power ontology, these problems reflect on the latter as well. Another task of chapter 3 is to weigh how far his values conflict with our deeply rooted attachments here.

4. *Truth*   In chapter 4 I return to address more directly the basic puzzle of this book: whether Nietzsche really does have a metaphysics, or whether the perspectivism that issues from the power ontology turns

back on it to undermine its claim to be true, revealing it, too, as 'just a perspective'. My opening, two-level insulation of ontology from perspectivism is surely too simple and artificial a device to stand in the end. I try to replace it with something more satisfactory: when we see better what truth and perspectivism are (for Nietzsche), we find them compatible after all.

So when we look with more care at his views about truth, we see how he treats it as the object of a social-historical drive: the 'will to truth'. This drive's historical depth has laid into its object—into the notion of truth—a great complexity of aspects or criteria. Once we also improve our grasp of Nietzsche's perspectivism, we see that although it's inconsistent with (renders unsatisfiable) some of truth's criteria, it fits very well with others. This lets us locate a 'perspectival truth' that Nietzsche highly esteems: as the goal of a later stage of the will to truth that he embraces and preaches. Indeed, this reveals a last structural feature of his metaphysics: (7) it *justifies its own activity*, or truth thinking more generally, as (even) the highest human good.

All of this runs against the common picture of Nietzsche as antirational, antitheoretical; his break turns out to be not in the value he places on insight and truth but in his analysis of what these involve. He revises what it is to be 'in the truth'. Thus he joins cause in a will to truth descended from that in the metaphysical tradition, and furthers it. He joins in the project of metaphysics, in the full sense: he claims a (1) systematic (2) truth about (3) essence, an essence or being that is (4) temporally specified, but above all (5) differentially realized, generating values that ultimately (6) ground an ethics, in which (7) the metaphysical project itself gets ranked highest. So we can apply to him—not in criticism but in welcome—these words from BGE20: "the most different philosophers fill out ever anew a certain basic schema of possible philosophies. Under an invisible spell, they always revolve once more in the same orbit; however independent of one another they may feel themselves with their critical or systematic wills, something within them leads them, something drives them in a determinate order, one after the other".

1

BEING

This chapter's title expresses my working hypothesis that Nietzsche has a metaphysics or ontology—a 'theory of being'. My task here is to see to what extent the will to power thesis, by playing this role, can explain and clarify the other main elements in his thought. This *'power ontology,'* as I call it, explains those other main ideas not by serving as a first truth from which they're derived but by offering a conceptual structure embedded in them: Nietzsche thinks his other thoughts *in its terms.*[1] In seeing how this is so, we take a first overall look at a Nietzschean system of views.

So I begin § 1.1 with an account of will to power itself. I try to strip the notion of the misleading connotations it initially bears for us and to present it in the abstractness that fits it for its metaphysical role. But this abstractness permits, and that role also requires, that the concept have a structure we can clearly delineate—will to power is not a 'cosmic force' in quite so mysterious a way as we sometimes suppose. By piecing together Nietzsche's scattered accounts, we discover the richness and concreteness of his vision here, which will allow the notion to infuse, and thus clarify, most of his other main views.[2]

As anticipated, we'll eventually see that Nietzsche offers his ontology with a somewhat different force than philosophers commonly do,

1. So the order of my presentation is not the order of our knowing, for Nietzsche; this ontology mustn't be taken as an a priori foundation.
2. Other developments of such an ontology include Heidegger 1979–87, 1:193ff. (for example); Schacht 1983, 212ff.; Lampert 1986, 245ff.

and for reasons connected with its very content. Roughly, this ontology implies a perspectivism, which reaches back to affect in certain ways the status of that ontology itself, changing how we're to hear or understand it. In chapter 4 I examine what type of truth Nietzsche still values and claims for his principal thoughts, including this ontology. But first we need to equip ourselves with more of the content of his thought, material that is best unfolded in unqualified assertions, as of 'objective facts'. So I adopt the strategy described in the Introduction. I temporarily insulate the will to power ontology from the perspectival critique, presenting the former as intended with the same 'dogmatic' force as the doctrines of Nietzsche's predecessors. I present these two thoughts as applying at different levels: things 'really are' will to power and really do have whatever structural features this implies, whereas all their other properties are true of them only relative to some perspective.[3]

Among the structural features of will to power itself, two are of special importance. In § 1.2 we'll see in a preliminary way just how that ontology produces or involves the perspectivism—how the latter can be read as taking its character and its limits from the metaphysical view. Much of the rest of this book weighs whether this two-level reading does justice to the way Nietzsche means his perspectivism. And in § 1.3, almost as crucially, we'll see how that ontology is infused with *values*— since the essence it describes is one that can be better or worse 'realized'. Wills to power occur in two fundamental forms: 'active' and 'reactive'; the contrast between these projects the basic dimension of Nietzsche's values. His metaphysical ranking of this pair will ramify up into the diverse array of his more particular evaluations.

I then, in § 1.4, focus attention on a particular type of will to power: the human; we see how the ontology supports a certain psychology, in Nietzsche's analysis of the person as a synthesis or construct out of many such wills. Moreover, this person is also (and needs also to be understood as) a part in a still more encompassing synthesis, his society or people. These dual analyses, together with that basic valuative contrast between the active and reactive, lead Nietzsche toward a basic *typology* for persons: the familiar 'master', 'slave', and 'overman', though he names them with many more terms than these. He distinguishes them as characters in a saga about our society's history and also as phases in an ideal psychological biography. In § 1.5 we'll see how these stories about these types are rooted in that will to power metaphysics; we then grasp these familiar ideas both freshly and with more rigor, seeing the deeper logic to Nietzsche's conception of them.

---

3. The rest of this book examines the various ways this two-level account (an idealism nesting in a realism) needs to be re-understood, before finally–in § 4.5–showing how the boundary between ontology and perspectivism can be collapsed.

1.1 The metaphysics of will to power

In his early manuscript on the first philosophers, Nietzsche speaks of "a metaphysical doctrine, which has its origin in a mystical intuition and which we meet in all philosophies, together with ever-renewed attempts to express it better—this proposition that 'all is one'" [PTAG3p39: 1873]. And we meet it, apparently, in Nietzsche himself. He says many times, in many ways and many contexts, that things are will to power [*Wille zur Macht*].⁴ Let's begin with this familiar core to his philosophy, with what I've called his 'ontology' or 'metaphysics': this is his account of what the world most basically 'is'. Here, as later with the hackneyed contrast between master and slave, we must work to reach beneath the level of grasp with which long familiarity has left us content, just as Nietzsche himself must struggle to free his terms from the complex layers of meaning deposited by earlier philosophers. What is this 'power' that things essentially will? Does it encompass all and only what that word (or the German *Macht*) refers to in everyday use? How do things 'will' this power? Is it in just the way we usually think we ourselves will? Or, as could rather be expected, does Nietzsche intend more precise and idiosyncratic senses for such basic terms in his thought? We must hope indeed for senses precise enough to support the use we shall see he will make of these terms, in laying out his own values, as well as in many others of his most distinctive views. And if we do discover an articulable and complexly structured point here, we'll have found an important general way he resembles his metaphysical predecessors.

When we first hear Nietzsche's claim, and as long as we allow our

---

4. Kaufmann (1974, 200), in his helpful history of Nietzsche's approach to his mature use of the concept, cites TSZ/I/15 as its first published appearance; TSZ/II/12, a fuller account, says (through Zarathustra saying what life itself says): "Only where there is life is there also will: not will to life but—thus I teach you—will to power!" Here and often elsewhere the point is restricted to 'life' (e.g., BGE13, GS349, WP254 [1885–86]); Nietzsche's main interest is of course in *human* will to power. But he extends this 'power biology' or 'power psychology' into a 'power ontology' in many other places; see especially BGE22, BGE36, WP1067 [1885], WP634 [1888], and WP692 [1888]. (Note also here WP582 [1885–86]: "'Being'—we have no other representation of it than as *'living'*—How can something dead 'be'?") There are many less-explicit statements of such a 'global' view, such as references to "the absolute homogeneity of all happening" [WP272: 1887] and "a *power-willing* occurring in all happening" [GM/II/12]. My project below will be to show how often this power-ontological vision of the world is implicit in what Nietzsche says. It's worth noting that he makes his point (whether about life or being) using each of the traditional terms usually translated 'essence': *Wesen* (in BGE259, GM/II/12, WP693 [1888]) and *Essenz* (BGE186). See again the Introduction on the complaints that Nietzsche's notebooks give (a) the only evidence for a power ontology, and (b) evidence that can be discounted.

understanding of it to be guided by his terms' surface suggestions, we suppose he is speaking of a human willing that aims at power over other persons as its ultimate end. That is, we take him to be saying that all people 'first' or 'basically' want power—which we interpret as political, economic, or personal rule over others—and that with a view to this they then adopt their distinctive behaviors, as different routes toward a single end. His point seems to be that as a matter of psychological fact a condition of authority over other persons is our 'highest end', all our other goals being chosen and pursued only as means to this. His position seems analogous to psychological hedonism, only substituting this power for pleasure.

This reading finds support not merely in the sound of his phrase. Some of Nietzsche's own remarks encourage it, including his attacks on psychological hedonism and the way he proposes his own view as a substitute for it.[5] And many of Nietzsche's more casual readers have taken his will to power thesis in this way. In turn, this reading has important implications for the way one interprets his values, as grounded in that thesis. Because he seems to fix level of power as the true standard for value, this reading suggests that the Nietzschean ideal will be (only) such individuals as Napoleon. It encourages the comparison of Nietzsche with Plato's Callicles and Thrasymachus, and perhaps even the suspicion that he wasn't very much misappropriated by the Fascists.[6] In short, this intuitive grasp of his notion of power underlies several important grounds for aversion to Nietzsche.

This simple reading seems less common today than it once was.[7] But although many now see its inadequacy, I think it hasn't yet been replaced with a full enough positive conception of the will to power. We must work to grasp this notion, and other Nietzschean ideas, on the basis of his most grounding, philosophical remarks. We must build strictly from these our understanding of comments couched in more ordinary terms and not immediately read the latter in an ordinary way. Or at least we should once fully attempt to develop his meaning this way. As we follow this route, we discover (I hope) a more subtle and even plausible view.

More particularly, we discover that the natural analogy to psychological hedonism (taking this with a familiar notion of pleasure, as ex-

5. See GM/III/7, TI/I/12, WP688 [1888], WP702 [1888]. Nietzsche accepts psychological hedonism in *Human, All Too Human* (I/18, 103–4).

6. So says Stern; see n.30 in this chapter.

7. Kaufmann (1974, 180) shows that Nietzsche did indeed use 'power' to mean 'worldly power' in early writings, such as UM, but that this use was abandoned. Haar 1985, 8: "We must accordingly discard from the very start, as a great misconception, any interpretation of the Will to Power that is *solely* psychological or anthropological."

plained in § 1.1.1) is misleading in several respects. To begin with, 'will to power' is most basically applied not to people but to 'drives' or 'forces', simpler units which Nietzsche sometimes even calls 'points' and 'power quanta'.[8] These are the simplest 'units' of will to power, or the simplest beings that are such will; we grasp Nietzsche better if we begin with these and only later make the complex extension to persons. This breadth of his use of the phrase already suggests that we mustn't hear 'will' with the narrowly human referent it most connotes.[9] Indeed, we'll see he believes that our usual notion of the will is not just too narrow— it's not even true of us; he'll claim that precisely because we are constituted out of drives or forces, we don't 'will' anything in the way we ordinarily suppose. But these points are best postponed until we attempt the extension to persons.

Turning for now to the other term, 'power', we see that this, too, must be read with a special sense. That broad application of 'will to power' again shows that power can't be so distinctively human an end as the political and economic domination that first come to mind. Indeed, power will be a quite different type of end from such domination, or from pleasure. It can't be a highest end in the familiar way pleasure is for psychological hedonism, because neither drives nor their ends of power are as completely homogeneous as this would require them to be. We must come to see several connected points here. Drives pursue distinctive activities not chosen as means to the end of power. And 'power' doesn't name some determinate state describable without reference to those activities—in the way that 'pleasure' is usually presumed to name a specific experience, the same for all. This means that power is 'individuated', necessarily different in content in different wills; this grounds the familiar individualism in Nietzsche's values. Together, these points make the structure of his theory quite different from psychological hedonism, so that indeed its effect is less to supply a new end than to introduce a new telic structure, in place of that most natural to us.

8. Already in BT1 the Apollonian and Dionysian are 'drives'; TL [P&Tp88: 1873] makes metaphor formation "the fundamental human drive". BGE36 suggests that the only 'reality' we have access to is that of our drives and that "thinking is merely a relating of these drives to one another". The terms 'drive' and 'force' are very common in the notes collected into *The Will to Power;* see especially those gathered under the heading "The Will to Power in Nature". At other times, Nietzsche uses more abstract terms for his basic beings: 'mastering centers' [WP715: 1887–88], 'dynamic quanta' [WP635: 1888]. Other suggestive terms used in this role are 'instinct' [TI/IX/39] and 'affect'. See especially Parkes 1994 on Nietzsche's early and persistent attention to 'drives'.

9. Of course, one must also say that Nietzsche chooses 'will' because he thinks our human will a potentially most-revealing case. Thus WP490 [1885]: "the only *force* there is, is of the same [*gleicher*] kind as the will". But we need to learn to understand this human will better.

1.1.1 Power as growth in activity

I take it to be evident from the expression itself that 'will to power' is a potency for something, a directedness toward some end. So I take it that Nietzsche, despite his repeated attacks on (what he calls) 'teleology', really has such a theory himself: the beings or units in his world are crucially end-directed, and to understand them properly is to grasp how they're directed or aimed.[10] Above all, it's to grasp how they're aimed at power, an end somehow essential to them.

This telic reading is reinforced by Nietzsche's very common treatment of the drive [*Trieb*] or force [*Kraft*] as the typical unit of this will.[11] He adopts these terms from biology and physics and means to build on the sense they have there: "The victorious [physicists'] concept 'force' . . . still needs to be completed: an inner world must be ascribed to it, which I designate as 'will to power'" [WP619: 1885]. Of course, his choice of these as his units also shows that this essential directedness is not (inherently) conscious; he proposes to describe a nonconscious intentionality. Whether this in itself is plausible must eventually be faced.

More immediately useful is something else this choice of cases reveals: just as scientists speak of a variety of drives or forces, so Nietzsche takes the units of will to power to be deeply diverse in their types, differentiated by their distinctive efforts or tendencies.[12] The sex drive, for example, is one pattern of activity aiming at its own network of ends—perhaps these are centered on seduction or coupling or orgasm—whereas the drive to eat aims at a very different network. But now how are these *internal* ends, which distinguish the drives from one another, related to that essential end of power, which they all have in common? Nietzsche thinks of this relation in a very different way than we expect.

10. Nietzsche attacks 'teleology' often and emphatically. This rejection is expressed as early as PTAG19 [1873]; see also, for example, WP666 [1886–87] and WP552 [1887]. But such criticisms seem directed against several specific forms of such a view: against what we might call a 'conscious teleology' (the claim that 'mind' directs the course of things) or a 'steady-state teleology' (the claim that the end aimed at is some stable condition) or a 'holistic teleology' (the claim that the world in general is a unit with its own end). The telic schema I attribute to Nietzsche differs from all of these. So WP675 [1887–88]: "that one takes doing *something*, the 'goal' [*Ziel*], the 'aim' [*Absicht*], the 'end' [*Zweck*], back into the doing, after having artificially removed this from it and thus emptied the doing". Schacht (1983, 242) argues that "'will to power' is not a teleological principle, identifying some state of affairs describable in terms of 'power' as a goal to which all forms of behavior of living creatures are instrumentally related." In denying that power is a concrete condition (such as pleasure might be), I take myself to be in agreement with this.

11. KSA/10/1[3] [1882]: "Everything is force." See n.8 in this chapter.

12. In D119's extended account of our drives, some examples are "our drives of tenderness or humorousness or adventurousness" and "of annoyance or combativeness [*Kampflust*] or reflection or benevolence".

Power is not, first and most clearly, merely one among the ends that individuate drives. By contrast, political power is such an internal end, the object of one type of drive in particular, one pattern of effortful pursuit. Nietzschean power must somehow motivate all these pursuits, so it has to be an end of a different sort. What could it be such that a striving for it could 'enter (essentially) into' all of these other drives, instead of being an alternative to them?[13]

I think we have a natural response: we expect that power is a 'highest end', for whose sake all those internal ends are adopted as means. Achieving the latter is either a partial achieving of power itself or a step toward it. Thus the drive's overall strategy is to maximally accomplish its internal end, because it's in that very act—in each state or event of its satisfaction—that it achieves power. This natural way of thinking of the relation between lower and higher ends is displayed in the most familiar version of psychological hedonism: all our other goals are valuable to us, because in achieving or having them, we experience pleasure. So our particular projects are really just routes converging toward a single condition—different doors chosen by each but through which each hopes to arrive at the same place.

Nietzsche says some things that suggest this view. It seems clearest in his occasional attempts to explain the content of the diverse drives as having evolved, in the distant past, out of an undifferentiated will to power; that bare and primitive form of this will originally selected the main types of internal ends as means to its satisfaction. For example, WP651 [1887–88] speaks of hunger as a specialized form of will to power, which once arose from it through a division of labor; presumably, the drive coalesced toward the end of eating, because that act is a specific way of taking power over something else, of 'incorporating' it. Nietzsche also thinks that drives continue even now to draw strength from such ways their ends involve 'taking power'. So the sex drive impels us, as an effort to appropriate or possess another person.[14]

Despite such supports, I think that natural conception of power, as an end achieved by means of these lesser ends, misses the major novelties in Nietzsche's notion in two ways: (1) by overstating how far drives' distinctive ends are chosen as means to power, it misses how the goal of power crucially presupposes such internal ends as given; (2) by locating achievement of power in the maximal achievement of those

13. So I take it that Nietzsche expresses himself less aptly when he speaks of will to power as a *particular* drive; in GM/III/18 it is "the strongest, most life-affirming drive"; in TI/X/3 it is the Greeks' "strongest instinct".

14. This 'cosmogony' looks similar to Anaximander's, which places the origin of things in the *apeiron*. BGE36 and WP658 [1885] suggest such a view. KSA/10/7[77] [1883]: "*And one and the same amount of force-feeling can discharge itself in a thousand ways:* this is 'freedom of the will'—the feeling, that in relation to the necessary explosion a hundred actions serve equally well." See GS14 on the sex drive. And note how GS360 also points this way.

internal ends, it misses how power involves growth of the drive itself, and hence improvement in those ends.

1. Those cosmogonic stories about the origins of the main drive types stand at odds with Nietzsche's much more common deployment of his notion of will to power: to explain not why (e.g.) the sex drive wants sex but how. He has in view drives or forces already having distinctive characters of their own, *about* which they will power. So it's not that the sex drive (at some metaphysical core) possesses a sense of power in the abstract, for whose sake it chooses sexuality as a means to an end; rather, it's already polarized into valuing only specifically sexual power. Nor is the person such an undifferentiated will, choosing by turns those internal ends; instead, we're composites of many preformed drives, rising by turns to expression and prominence.

Power can't play that role of highest end, because it's essentially enhancement in an activity already given. A drive finds itself already pursuing given ends through a given project; that it wills power explains not why it has this project but how it now tries to improve what it has: it tries to raise to a higher level the activity it finds distinctive of it. To be a will to power, it must already want something other than power. Thus each drive is a specific way of pursuing power in a project whose overall lines were drawn beforehand. So Nietzsche thinks of drives as belonging to largely stable types, not able to redirect themselves onto radically different routes toward power; the sex drive doesn't transform itself into an urge to eat. Instead, he strikingly thinks, drives change through 'sublimation' or 'spiritualization' of their distinctive pursuits—by their amendment not their replacement. Thus the sex drive becomes 'the love of all mankind' but remains inherently sexual.[15]

This means that power has a different logic from ends like pleasure or political power. It can't be a highest end in the same way they are, because it's not a concrete or 'first-order' end like them. It's not definitionally separable from some (or other) 'drive', some preexisting pattern of effort, with its own internal ends; power isn't an independent state, that could be described without supposing some such effort as given. Pleasure, by contrast, is usually considered a concrete state, one that many activities can produce—as sex or eating does—but itself an experience distinct from these causes or means.[16] Nietzschean power can't have this independence, because it is (roughly) improvement in whatever a drive's activity already is; it's growth or development *in* that pattern of effort and therefore amounts to a different 'concrete condition'

15. BGE189 and TI/V/1, 3. In § 3.4.1, I describe this movement of spiritualization, showing just how it's always a development of a preestablished project.

16. Some, however, have viewed pleasure more in the way I go on to treat power, making pleasure a 'function on' some activity—always the pleasuring *of* that particular activity. There are suggestions of such a view in Aristotle (*NE* X/5), for example.

for each different drive.[17] Thus power, as something willed by every
drive, 'lacks content', requiring a contingent filling out from some given
case. So by this new telic logic, the routes to power don't converge on a
common target. Willing their own development leads drives in diverging
directions. This point is the main metaphysical root for Nietzsche's individualism in values: "The deepest laws of preservation and growth command . . . that everyone invent for himself *his* virtue, *his* categorical
imperative" [A11].[18]

To put the point another way, the will to power doesn't and can't
steer the drive 'from the ground up'. In commending it to us, Nietzsche
doesn't propose it should be an ultimate directing aim, remaking us
entirely by its own standards; he takes himself to diverge here from
philosophers' usual way of promoting their 'ideals of reason'. However,
we still need to specify how this will to power bears on those given
projects, that is, what its second-order guidance of them is.

2. Again our usual telic conception suggests an answer: these drives
'will power' inasmuch as they will the 'full achievement' of their internal
ends, at the expense, if need be, of all competing drives' efforts. So the
will to power is just the will to maximally satisfy the given internal end;
it's the drive's aim to achieve that end as quickly and lastingly as it can.
This might seem to render the point trivial. Yet, it's precisely this usual
conception that Nietzsche means his notion of power to deny. Here his
target is another part of our telic logic: we expect that a drive (or directedness) aims at ends by (above all or exclusively) aiming to *accomplish* them—a state or event in which it achieves satisfaction and rests
content, its effort either ceasing or shifting into merely maintaining that
state. We presume a type of end we might call a 'steady state', its ideal
achievement the unbroken continuance of a condition or repeating
of an event. But Nietzsche's promotion of power as a second-order end
is a denial that drives do or should pursue their internal ends in this
manner.

To begin with, power is a movement of growth or enhancement
rather than a persisting state (or repeated event). As will to power, a
drive's essential end is movement beyond what it now is or does. And
this doesn't just mean that it wants to be more than it is; a drive's
essential aim isn't even to arrive at some better state. If we think of the
ends distinguishing drives as states of achievement, then will to power's
object will be the passage toward and into these states and not their
occupation. This shifts importance from those ends to their pursuit, to

17. This is perhaps a point intended by Heidegger 1979–87, 1:42; and Deleuze
1983, 85. Clark's account (1990) is partly similar: "It amounts to thinking of the will
to power as a second-order desire for the ability to satisfy one's other, or first-order,
desires (cf. Frankfurt)" (211; see then 227ff.). I diverge from this in point 2 following.
See also Schacht 1983, 222f.
    18. I develop this point in § 3.1.3.

the effortful and not-yet-satisfied approach toward them. So BGE175: "In the end one loves one's desire and not what is desired."[19]

On the one hand, we can think of the passage toward those internal ends as itself such a movement of growth, and so a case of power itself. At least among the most familiar drives, this passage takes an episodic and cyclical form: the end is achieved at intervals, with the drive waning in vitality just after that, its interest in the end only gradually reviving and then growing in intensity (and power to absorb us) as it reapproaches that end. Within each periodic cycle, the drive retraces the same ascending arc, asserting itself ever more vehemently and effectively; so it finds a first form of power, in each episodic rush toward its end.

But Nietzsche considers such 'intra-episodic' growth to be much less important than another sort: growth from cycle to cycle, in the pattern or structure of the project itself. A drive that merely repeats itself—the habit—misses a fuller or truer power: instead of trying just to eat or seduce again and again, it should try to raise its whole pattern of effort 'to a higher level'. Nietzsche calls this truer, 'inter-episodic' growth 'sublimation' [*Sublimierung*].[20] We humans are preeminent as wills to power, because of our capacity for it—for the pace at which our drives are able to break habitual patterns and evolve new forms.

19. WP125 [1885]: "For so sounds the teaching preached by life itself to all that lives: the morality of development. To have and to will to have more—growth, in a word—that is life itself." In fact there are two general strategies, or two choices of terminology, available to us for accommodating this point about power within a telic schema. We can present it as a point either about the ('internal') character of the ends that drives pursue, or about the ('external') way they pursue those ends. Thus on the one hand, we might reinterpret the distinguishing ends of our drives, redescribing them such that their 'maximal achievement' would be this perpetual heightening in a characteristic activity. This would treat 'power' as a component in drives' ends; the will to power thesis would then demand that we change our common conception of the ends they pursue (though not of the way they pursue them). So the goal of the sexual drive would be not intercourse or orgasm but the continual heightening of its sexual activity (broadly understood). Or on the other hand, we might say that drives 'will power' by ultimately aiming not at maximal achievement of their goals but at the enhancement of their activity of pursuing them. Here that aim would be a 'higher end' not in the sense that all others are adopted for its sake, but in the sense that it regulates the manner of their pursuit. This is the terminology I adopt for stating Nietzsche's point. It involves a drastic revision in the type of telic structure most natural to us, but this aptly reflects the drastic nature of Nietzsche's claim.

20. Kaufmann (1974, 218ff.) helpfully surveys Nietzsche's uses of 'sublimation' but misses the important point at hand. He takes sublimation to occur when the undifferentiated will to power, displaced from its (for example) sexual expression, directs itself toward quite different, nonsexual ends; all that remains constant is will to power itself. But would it then be apt to call this 'sublimation of the sex drive'? In the examples Nietzsche gives, we find a greater continuity: ends are modified, not replaced. So WP312 [1887]: "[One] has refined cruelty to tragic pity, so that it may

This makes the connection between power and a drive's internal end even less direct than we expected: not only does power not lie in this end's achievement, it doesn't even mainly lie in progress toward it but in improving this progress. Moreover, the criteria for this 'improvement' aren't set by the end—it's not just an improvement in the route's efficiency for achieving the end. Rather, as we'll gradually see, it lies in an enrichment or elaboration of the drive's activity pattern. For this reason, it will often involve deferring or postponing achievement of the end— hence a loss in efficiency. Indeed, it can involve a revision of the internal end itself: its 'location' may shift, as in the shift in focus from swallowing to tasting. Although will to power indeed supposes a defining allegiance to its given end, it also tries to work changes in it. (We'll see that this is its form of allegiance to it—to help it 'become what it is'.)

So a drive wills power by trying to develop its activity pattern. And its effort is properly here, because (for Nietzsche) this activity is just what the drive is. We mustn't imagine it as an agent or source of that activity, as what causes or engages in it. Nietzsche insists that the 'doer behind the doing' is a fiction; really there are no such abiding things, only processes.[21] (I examine this claim in the account of the 'theory of becoming' in chapter 2.) So the world consists of behavior patterns, each striving to enhance itself, to extend its own scope of activity. Thus the sex drive is strictly the activity of trying to seduce (etc.), which, as will to power, is also trying to improve itself in a certain way. Processes themselves are willful, in this twofold directedness. They aim at ends, but not so as to dissolve or release their own tensed effort by a full and lasting accomplishment of these ends; nor do they aim just to continue themselves. Rather, each such activity pattern wills its own 'self-overcoming' [Selbstüberwindung]: it wills to rise toward a new and higher level of effort—perhaps indeed a level at which its internal ends are also overcome and replaced by descendents—one that will then have to be overcome in turn.[22]

In a way, this makes drives 'selfish': each essentially aims at its own development or growth. But it also begins to open up a sense in which this is not so. Nietzsche calls this crucial growth a 'self-overcoming' to make a further point, to be increasingly important as we proceed. With

---

be *disavowed* as [cruelty]. In the same way sexual love [has been refined] to *amour-passion;* the slavish disposition as Christian obedience". I take 'spiritualization' to be an especially effective form or means of sublimation, for Nietzsche.

21. GM/I/13: "there is no 'being' behind doing, effecting, becoming; 'the doer' is merely a fiction added to the doing—the doing is everything." WP631 [1885–86], like many other passages, associates this fiction with the structure of our language. See also WP550 [1885–86], WP551 [1888], WP625 [1888].

22. So TSZ/II/12 (entitled "On Self-Overcoming"): "And life itself told this secret to me: 'See,' it said, 'I am that, *which must always overcome itself* '''. See also GM/III/27.

that favorite expression, he means that a drive presses or tends beyond the borders to its 'identity'; its will is to pass beyond itself, by evolving into some stronger 'descendent' drive or pursuit. And if the activity doesn't itself persist in this future it wills, its intent is less clearly selfish.[23] We'll see that the ambiguous boundaries around a drive, and the ambiguous nature of its interest in what lies beyond them, have a crucial bearing on Nietzsche's own values.

An important qualm must be addressed, however: doesn't it seem that some drives just do want to satisfy their (internal) ends, just do aim at those episodic end states themselves, again and again in the same way? This may suggest that we've gone too far in attempting to specify a content for the end of power; perhaps we've already strayed over the boundary between the power ontology and the perspectivism it generates. Perhaps there's just no one way that drives will power; perhaps here it already 'depends on the individual' (drive), on its own interpretation of power. So perhaps I've forced on Nietzsche a greater specificity in the notion of power than he would accept.

This danger—of assigning too determinate a content to the 'power' he says all things will—must make us cautious as we proceed. I address the issue more fully in § 1.1.2. There, as here, the problem will be complicated by a further factor.

Nietzsche is well aware that some wills—some persons—do aim at steady-state ends and want only to rest in them; this is indeed a common charge in his critical diagnoses. But he can still see them as 'essentially' wills to power, because he understands this essence in a way we might not expect: a thing can 'fall away from' its essence or achieve it in only a 'deficient' way. His ontology treats a sort of being that comes in degrees.[24] Thus drives that will ends of that stable sort are failing to will appropriately to their own essence; to understand them is to see them as misdirected this way. This and other ways that wills aim askew—with a distorted sense of power—Nietzsche stigmatizes as 'reactive'; only the active achieve essence, by willing power itself.

We'll have to face some obvious questions this odd use of 'essence'

23. WP488 [1887]: "No 'substance', rather something that in itself strives after strengthening, and that wants to 'preserve' itself only indirectly (it wants to *surpass itself*—)." KSA/10/1[73] [1882]: "The *highest love of self* [*Ich*], when it expresses itself as heroism, is close to pleasure in self-destruction [*Untergange*], so to cruelty, self-assault."

24. GM/II/12 equates the role of will to power as the essence of life with "the principal priority . . . that the spontaneous, attacking, encroaching, newly-interpreting, newly-directing, and form-giving forces have", whereas adaptation "follows only after this", as "an activity of the second rank, a mere reactivity". See A6 (quoted in § 1.3) and WP485 [1887]. But note, too, the skepticism in WP583 [1888]: "That a correlation stands between *degrees of value* and *degrees of reality* . . . is a metaphysical postulate proceeding from the assumption that we *know* the rank-order of values".

raises—for example about the testability of claims concerning it. The power ontology may seem too slippery if it shifts between the claim that everything *does* will power and the claim that everything *should*.

In any case, Nietzsche says many times that will to power aims at growth and not mere stability; for example: "the only reality is the *willing to become stronger of every center of force*—not self-maintenance, but appropriation, willing to become master, to become more, to become stronger" [WP689: 1888].[25] We'll see that several others of his key ideas are rooted in this point. So it seems safe to take at least this much to belong to power itself, secure above the level of perspectival differences: power is growth, in level of activity or in 'strength'.[26]

1.1.2   Power as over others

We must try to develop this account of will to power a step further, by giving this 'growth' or 'enhancement' a more definite sense. In willing power, a drive strives to become stronger, to grow in its distinctive activity. But this is still quite vague. What is the criterion or measure for growth? What makes it the case that a drive's strength is expanding or increasing rather than diminishing? Again, we must try to press beyond our everyday use of these terms, which measures growth in such an unsorted variety of ways. Unless we can do so, 'power' won't have a sense definite enough to support an ontology with much content. Moreover, it won't support the valuative claims Nietzsche roots in it, because (as we'll see) these amount to a 'power consequentialism' and so depend on 'power' being given a definite enough measure to serve as a useful deliberative and evaluative criterion.

It's clear from the bulk of Nietzsche's remarks that growth has to do with a drive's relation to other drives: one drive typically enhances its strength relative to, or even at the expense of, others. Usually, at least, power is power 'over others'. This may indeed be taken as a second main

25. BGE73 reads: "Whoever reaches his ideal even thereby comes out above it." See also WP696–97 [1887–88] and WP688 [1888]. More generally, WP708 [1887–88]: "becoming has *no goal-state*, does not flow into 'being'." In D108: "Development does not will happiness, but development and nothing further." And WP649 [1886–87]: "the *feeling-more*, the feeling of *becoming stronger*, wholly apart from any uses in the [Darwinian] struggle, seems to me the genuine *progress*". This is most of the force of his attack on Darwin, whose theory is in other ways importantly similar. Nietzsche takes Darwin to say that living things pursue their own preservation; this seems to him too static (and even cowardly) a goal. See BGE13, for example.

26. So understood, strength and power are distinct: whereas the former occurs as a state—as a level or amount (of strength)—the latter occurs as a passage between two such states. Thus Nietzsche just spoke of 'willing to become stronger' [*Starker-werden-wollen*], and in WP488 [1887] he speaks of striving toward 'strengthening' [*Verstärkung*]. To keep his point clear, we might try not to follow him in his frequent looser uses of 'power' for a level of strength. WP663 [1885–86]: "All that happens out of aims is reducible to the *aim of increasing power*." See also WP633 [1888].

aspect of power, alongside its aspect as growth—a more disturbing aspect, for obvious reasons. Here we must try to avoid the temptation that presses on sympathetic interpreters to diminish this aspect and thus 'tame' Nietzsche's power notion. And with this aspect, too, we have to press for more specificity. Not only are there many everyday ways to hear this 'power-over-others' but Nietzsche's own remarks seem to describe it diversely. Because some of these sorts of power over others are themselves more socially acceptable or attractive than others—so that Nietzsche is more palatable if these are what he thinks essential to us—this choice is a focal point for disagreement among his interpreters. We may catalog the possibilities in this way:

1. A drive's strength level is measured by the perspectives on it of other drives (and its perspective on them), in particular perhaps by whether they 'look up to it' or not, by whether they think it better or worse than themselves. So drives grow by improving the views others take of them (and maybe by deflating their own views of others). As concrete cases of this motivational structure, the strivings for fame and for love come to mind. WP677 [1886–87] seems to speak so: "What is *common* [to the artistic, scientific, religious, and moral views of the world]: the mastering drives will to be viewed also as *the highest courts of value in general*, indeed as *productive* and *ruling authorities* [*Gewalten*]." This first option brings the perspectivism close to the heart of the power ontology; it leaves little independent content for that ontology. By contrast, the next several readings make power something more 'objective'.

2. A drive's strength level is measured not in relation to other drives but by some independent or absolute standard; yet it is (usually) only possible to improve this level at the expense of others—as it were, by expanding into territory that was theirs. So the diminishing of others is a means—even a practically necessary means—to self-improvement but does not constitute it. Begging some questions, we might take pursuit of wealth as a project typically adopted from this sort of motivation: one wants wealth (taking this to include the fine things money buys) for its own sake and asks oneself whether the best means to it requires depriving others. Does pursuing power require struggling against others only as such a best or usual means? Nietzsche might think of power this way in WP728 [1888]: "It belongs to the concept of the living that it must grow—that it must extend its power and consequently [*folglich*] take into itself foreign forces."[27]

27. Danto (1965, 220) suggests this account: "Each force occupies a territory (an area of space) and is pretty much what it is as the result of counter-forces meeting and opposing its territorial expansion."

3. A drive's strength level is measured relative to others, by their comparative performances in independent pursuits: Does it do these things better or worse than they? These shared pursuits are thus crucially *contests;* their point is to set up tasks, with scales for success, against which the competing wills test themselves and are compared. So, unlike in (2), power is relational: a drive's essential aim is to improve with respect to others. Simplifying again, we might take an athlete's will to be first to belong to this type; his winning requires that others lose, as something more than a mere means. Nietzsche's great stress on 'rank order' [*Rangordnung*] might express this sense, as also his admiration for the Greek *agon*.[28]

4. A drive's strength level is measured by whether it is able to rule or master others in some way (which then needs to be specified). So its current level consists roughly in its ruling *abc* and its being ruled by *xyz*, whereas growth or decline lies in ruling more or fewer (or ruling these more or less fully). Like (1) and (3), this would make power essentially 'over others'—indeed, in a blunter way than by merely impressing or surpassing them. It suggests a cruder sort of *agon*, in which the competing wills work more directly on one another, instead of at independent tasks: the goal is to subdue, and not just outperform, the other—as in wrestling, for example, by contrast with racing. BGE259 speaks for this sense: "life itself is *essentially* appropriation, injury, subjugation of what is foreign and weaker".[29]

Of these possible readings, each supportable by things Nietzsche says, the last has the harshest effect. It places aggression nearest the core of the beings he claims we are. Struggle against others is here not just a means to an end (2); a means would have alternatives (at least logically possible ones), but (4) makes struggle essential to us, and indeed to all beings. Moreover, it suggests a more desperate sort of struggle than those for fame (1) or victory (3): it requires forces to grow, it seems, not just by impressing or outperforming others but by oppressing and subjugating them. If power is also Nietzsche's ultimate value, (4) would mean he commends an ideal that is much harder to accept.[30] This surely is some

28. See the draft "Homer's Contest" [1872] in PortN. Kaufmann seems to have this reading in mind—see n.31 in this chapter.

29. Schacht (1983, 220) presents will to power as "the basic tendency of *all* forces . . . to extend their influence and dominate others". See, too, Stern 1979, 117ff.

30. Stern 1979, 120: "If there is anything in the recent 'Nietzschean' era that comes close to an embodiment of 'the will to power', it is Hitler's life and political career".

of the attraction the other three readings have had for many interpreters.[31]

Of course, the goals named by these different senses are, in a way, not mutually exclusive; they can 'nest within' each other, one being pursued as a means to another. Thus fame could be wanted as a means to wealth or vice versa—and so perhaps with each other pair. This might explain why Nietzsche sometimes singles out each. Or, we might suspect that he hasn't really pried them apart. But even if he hasn't explicitly separated these alternatives, deliberately chosen from among them, and persistently held that choice in mind, one sort of power over others might still be most operative in his thinking and best connected with his other main thoughts. So does any of the four have such priority, so that the others are best grasped as means or approximations to it (and not vice versa)?

Here again, we may feel a reluctance noted earlier in our hunt for will to power. Perhaps we should respond to this question by rejecting its demand for a choice. Perhaps Nietzsche thinks that which way power over others is pursued just depends on which drive is doing the pursuing. He'd then be allowing that diversity of types quite deliberately. The measure for growth would vary with the drive, so that it wouldn't be possible to specify any further content for the 'power' aimed at by all drives alike. We might all the more expect this given that we've already seen drives vary in the activities they will to enhance: maybe these different activities pursue quite different types of 'power over others', so that ingestion and seduction (e.g.) have nothing concrete in common. Have we come as far as Nietzsche is willing to go, in specifying an essential content for drives as will to power?[32]

This reason not to choose from those options might also be counted as a choice of (1)—or rather of a near cousin to it. It lets the content to power over others be determined perspectivally: not (principally) by the direct comparisons drives make of one another, as in (1), but by their differing conceptions of what 'power over others' involves. It makes all the ways perspectives interpret this (ranging, e.g., from killing to persuading the other) count equally well as cases of it: all further specific

31. Kaufmann (1974, 201), in the course of his influential effort to render Nietzsche more palatable, emphasizes how will to power is a *self*-overcoming and suggests that it's only in this that competition with others occurs: "In Nietzsche's vision the world becomes a Greek gymnasium where all nations vie with each other, each trying to overcome itself and thus to excel all others." Schutte (1984, 76ff.) helpfully surveys some of the interpretations of will to power and argues that to be viable the notion must be purged of the suggestion of domination, which she takes Nietzsche to have included in it.

32. GS13: "it is a matter of taste whether one prefers the slow or the sudden, the assured or the dangerous and audacious increase of power—one seeks this or that spice depending on one's temperament." See also BGE194.

content to power would arise only *for* a viewpoint and would vary by viewpoint. (One version might so allow perspectives to determine power 'conceptually' but then make it a factual matter whether the concept thus specified is satisfied (e.g., whether the other *is* killed); a more thorough perspectivism would put even this satisfaction 'in the eye of' the perspectives.)

I return to this perspectival problem in § 1.2, but won't come to final grips with it until chapter 4. Here my answer can be little more than to reaffirm my guiding approach. But we can at least notice certain raw evidence that Nietzsche rejects a 'subjectivist' notion of power. First, it seems he can't think a will's power is 'in the eye of' the will itself, because he holds that wills can be wrong as to whether they grow. Growing doesn't just lie in my thinking I do; that can often be 'wishful thinking', a mistake about my real status.[33] Second, it seems he can't think a will's power depends on other wills' views of it, because he so clearly denies that power is a matter of reputation or recognition. Instead, will to power aims at a real condition, specified independently of any perspectives *about* power.[34] This point is reinforced by what we've seen of Nietzsche's odd use of 'essence': most drives might misconceive their essential end. This insistence on the prevalence of error about power makes Nietzsche far more a realist than an idealist about it: a drive's enhancing its activity or strength is a real change in its activity or in its real relation to other drives.

Moreover, I think the great weight of evidence suggests that, among the ways power might thus be 'real', Nietzsche thinks mainly of (4). He most often and most emphatically identifies growth as increased 'mastery' [*Herrschaft*] of others; the second is not just a means to the first. So he says, "every single one of [the basic drives of human beings] would like only too well to represent just *itself* as . . . the legitimate *master* [*Herr*] of all the rest of the drives. For every drive seeks to be master [*ist herrschsuchtig*]" [BGE6].[35] We might have found the other lines more

33. WP917 [1887–88] speaks of *"artificial* strengthening: whether it is by stimulating chemicals or by stimulating errors", and gives several examples of the latter. WP48 [1888] says that "the experience of *intoxication*" has sometimes misled, because it *"increases* the feeling of power in the highest degree . . . therefore, naively judged, *power"*. HH/I/545 says that vanity seeks to seem to itself to rule.

34. A more 'realist' account of power is implied by passages saying that the interaction between two drives proceeds according to their preexisting degrees of strength. WP633 [1888]: "It is a matter of a struggle between two elements of unequal power: a new arrangement of forces is reached according to the measure of power of each of them." See also WP855 [1887–88], WP634 [1888].

35. TSZ/II/12 presents will to power as "the will to be master". BGE259: "'Exploitation' . . . belongs to the *essence* of the living, as an organic basic function". GM/I/13 says that strength expresses itself as "a willing to subjugate, a willing to throw down, a willing to become master, a thirst for enemies and resistances and triumphs". GM/II/11: "life functions *essentially*, that is in its basic functions, by injur-

attractive, as giving Nietzsche's valuation of power an easier chance to be acceptable to us. But most of what he says really requires this more aggressive vision, which calls up immediate sentiments against itself, and must say so much more in its own defense to seem plausible or attractive.

Once again, Nietzsche's willingness to give this further specificity to the will to power as the essence of all things is still compatible with his recognizing that some drives don't, in fact, will such mastery but rather the ends specified in (1), (2), or (3) above. He thinks these drives have 'fallen away from' their own essence as will to power, an essence that in some sense is still theirs. They have, as it were, misidentified the end they essentially will and have misguidedly shunted their efforts onto a diverging track.

Incorporating this result into our previous findings, we say that drives are 'will to power' in that they essentially pursue the continual enhancement of their distinctive activities, enhancement that consists in increasing their mastery of others. So the level of a drive's activity, its strength, is measured by 'how much' it rules over others.

Yet this can't satisfy us either. We must press to see whether this notion of mastery can itself be given a more concrete content. And we must make it concrete, if we can, in a way that reveals some principle of unity in this dual account of will to power. Why might increased domination also be an enhancement of that distinctive activity?

My suggestion is this: drive A rules B insofar as it has turned B toward A's own end, so that B now participates in A's distinctive activity. Mastery is bringing another will into a subordinate role within one's own effort, thereby 'incorporating' the other as a sort of organ or tool. As his important term 'incorporation' [*Einverleibung*] suggests, Nietzsche very often thinks of this process by analogy with physical ingestion.[36] But he thinks it not physically and spatially, but 'psychically'—or, better: in applying it to wills, he thinks it telically. Drive

---

ing, assaulting, exploiting, destroying, and simply cannot be thought of without this character." WP490 [1885]: "the only *force* that there is, is of the same [*gleicher*] kind as that of the will: a commanding [*Commandiren*] of other subjects, which thereupon alter." WP369 [1885–86]: "There is no egoism that remains by itself and does not encroach. . . . 'One furthers one's I always at the expense of others'; 'life lives always at the expense of other life'. — Whoever does not grasp this, has still not taken the first step toward honesty with himself." UM/II/1 already speaks of a force that "masters and directs". D113: "The striving for distinction is the striving for subjugation of the nearest". See also BGE19, BGE230, and WP481 [1886–87].

36. BGE230 speaks of a will's "appropriating force, its 'digestive force', to speak in a picture—and really 'the spirit' is most similar [*gleicht*] to a stomach." GM/II/1 entertains the similar 'inpsychation' [*Einverseelung*]. GS14: "Our pleasure in ourselves so wills to preserve itself, that it again and again changes something new *into ourselves;* that is what possession means." See also HH/I/224, WP769 [1883], WP656 [1887].

B's activity comes to be telically contained within A's, and this is the crux to the mastery involved in Nietzschean power.[37]

This makes B's serving A a matter of the former's willful intentions, but not in such a way that ruling is 'in the eye of the ruled'. It lies not in B's viewing itself as serving A but in its setting its sights by reference to A's own project, which it may or may not notice that it does. Thus there's a fact to the matter how far A rules B, a fact that both A and B can (and usually do) mistake, a fact not 'transparent' to either, even though it lies in the intentions (the willing) of B. Indeed, Nietzsche mainly describes the many subtler ways of being ruled and subsumed than by intending to serve: all the other ways of fixing one's course out of fascination with another will, even (or especially) in rejecting reaction *against* it. In all such cases, one has been induced to adjust one's own aim into some reference to the other; the other thus 'shows up' in one's activity, whether in positive or negative image.

This account finds important support in its ability to explain why growth should necessarily involve or include rule over other drives. We can understand better the dimension in which the will 'grows stronger' by developing this mastery as incorporation. As we've seen, each will is a pattern of behavior—a habit, as it were—but one that aims not merely to continue itself but to grow. Each such activity is bounded or disrupted by the different efforts of other wills, by other such self-asserting patterns. Such resistance shows the behavior limits of its scope—how much is 'not-it'—but also how to overcome these limits: by compelling or inducing the collaboration of those independent forces, by bringing their practices into service of its own.

On the one hand, so aligning different wills to its own effort gives the behavior a new facility or smoothness: served by those wills, it can more easily and more often secure its internal ends. But as we saw in § 1.1.1, Nietzschean power lies chiefly not in those intra-episodic satisfactions but in developing the first-order project itself: it lies in enriching the effort at those ends, and so also those ends themselves. For this, incorporation must work a different way than by marshaling 'efficient servants'—transparent functionaries to its ends. To help to the more important sort of power or growth, the forces subjected must keep their own characters and not be utterly made over into mere facilitating tools; they must add their own telic patterns and viewpoints to its fabric. It's only by coming to rule persistently different forces that a will expands not just quantitatively, reproducing its own pattern in others, but qualitatively: to include those still-foreign behaviors as phases or elements in its own thus fuller effort. I think this is a key point in Nietzsche's distinctive notion of power: it knits together power's main aspects as growth

---

37. WP552 [1887]: "domination [*Übermacht*] over a lesser power is achieved, and the latter works as function of the greater".

and domination, by specifying the best ('truest') way of growing by ruling. We'll notice many important recurrences of this point as we proceed.

This completes our first sketch of Nietzsche's 'will to power'. The metaphysical notion now has content enough for us to go on to see how it's situated in his thought as a whole, and especially how it supports his perspectivism. Of course, many puzzles about this notion remain; let's finish this section by marking one major issue we must return to.

We still need to settle whether (and how) mastery can be reciprocal. If A grows stronger by ruling B in the way described, does it follow that B cannot at the same time be growing by ruling A? Is B necessarily diverted from its own ends, and thus diminished, when A employs it in this way? Or can drives simultaneously rule and encompass one another? And does A rule B any the less if B also rules A? These issues are important for Nietzsche's values: if the will's egoism, which these values seem to aid and abet, necessarily pursues the destruction or diminishing of others, those values will be the more troubling to us. In the following, and especially in chapter 3, I develop and weigh the main Nietzschean resources for reaching a less brutal lesson than this: (what I call) the *agon* and spirit points.

1.2 Wills to power as perspectives

We've anticipated that Nietzsche takes his power ontology to generate a 'perspectivism' and indeed that the relation between these will be the key topic of this book. We're now able to take a first look at the way this perspectivism arises. This Nietzschean 'doctrine' has been often discussed.[38] But it's important to keep clear, as is not often done, how the 'perspectives' this teaching speaks of are those of drives or wills to power. His power ontology, with its distinctive conceptions of wills and of power, stands prior to this perspectivism as (something like) its objective precondition, and thereby gives to that teaching some unexpected features. Or at least, this is the relation between ontology and perspectivism that Nietzsche usually suggests and whose tenability we're exploring now (by that two-level strategy announced in the Introduction).

We've seen that, as will to power, a drive aims at ongoing growth in its distinctive activity. Nietzsche's perspectivism begins in the thought that this *telic* directedness goes together with an *intentional* one, with being a perspective, 'at' or 'on' some intentional content. Just by virtue of striving in the way it does, every drive involves, is partly, a particular 'view': a view of its purpose or end and of the surroundings as helps or hindrances to that end. In thinking this an aspect of all will to power,

38. The account by Danto (1965, 68ff.) has been especially influential. See also Schacht 1983, 61ff.; Nehamas 1985, 49ff.; and Leiter 1994 for other statements of this teaching.

Nietzsche attributes views to far more than just human beings; he calls perspective "the basic condition of all life" [BGE/P]. And (still more generally) he speaks of "this necessary perspectivism according to which every center of force—and not only the human being—construes the whole rest of the world from itself, i.e., measures, touches, forms, according to its own force" [WP636: 1888].[39]

We must try to see how a drive's telic thrust can, in itself, already involve a distinctive perspective on the world. In willing its own power or growth, the drive acts and reacts toward other things in accordance with this aim, by whether they help or hinder its pursuit. It senses, and differentially responds to, different things in its environment. And (Nietzsche thinks) these patterns of effort and avoidance in themselves constitute an 'interpretation', of things in their relevance to its aim. They constitute this viewpoint whether or not they occur consciously. Each drive's end-directed activity already 'polarizes' the world toward it, giving everything a significance relative to it. So, for example, the sex drive views the world as inspiring or requiring a sexual response; the world appears with erotic potential as its meaning or sense.

I think there are three important points here that distinguish Nietzsche's perspectivism from those more 'cognitivist' cousins we usually find in idealism. First, he denies that these perspectives are necessarily conscious, though he applies to them many of the intentional or cognitive terms we might normally restrict to consciousness. "Our most sacred convictions, the unchangeable in regard to our supreme values, are *judgments of our muscles*" [WP314: 1887–88]. Second, this perspective is not something prior to the activity or even something separate that accompanies it, as we take plans or pictures (even unconscious ones) to be. Nietzsche stresses its unity with the doing itself, with the way it tends in a certain direction, adjusts to other behaviors, and in general differentially acts on, and is affected by, the world. This perspective is an aspect or ingredient in this. Third, this essential or original perspective—this way things appear to the striving will—is deeply valuative. Values are not a secondary estimation of beings previously met and picked out in some neutral or objective way. To this primary viewpoint, things already appear as potentials or opportunities: they appear *as* they bear on the will's own end.

In order to follow Nietzsche into this vision of the perspectives essential to beings, we have to struggle on each of these points, because the opposite positions are so natural and tempting to us: we find it hard not

39. WP643 [1885–86]: "The will to power *interprets*: . . . it demarcates, determines degrees, differences of power. Mere differences of power could not perceive themselves as such: there must be something there that wills to grow and interprets the value of every other thing that wills to grow." WP567 [1888]: "every center of force adopts a *perspective* toward the whole *remainder*, i.e. its wholly determinate *valuation*, mode of action, and mode of resistance." See also WP481 [1886–87].

to think of viewpoints as (1) conscious, (2) separate from 'doing', and (3) chiefly theoretical (in aiming at 'facts'). To reinforce Nietzsche's revisions, let's go back through these points in different order.

Beginning with (3), we mustn't think that these perspectives aim basically at truth, at mirroring the world. It's not that the drive takes a theorizing view aimed to see how the world truly is, as a step before applying that neutral information back to its practical ends. It views the world from its interests: "It is our needs *that interpret the world*; our drives and their For and Against" [WP481: 1886–87]. And so Nietzsche stresses that even perception isn't neutral: "There is no doubt that all sense perceptions are wholly permeated with *value-judgments* (useful, harmful—consequently, agreeable or disagreeable)" [WP505: 1885–86]. How far it's possible to overcome this willful interest and to aim at truth itself is a major issue in chapter 4. But if a neutral view of things can somehow be achieved, it would have to remain dependent on this more basic perspectivity.

This way that perspectives are rooted in interest shows the deep place Nietzsche finds (in his power ontology) for 'value' [*Wert*]. This lies in what each will 'sees' as conducing to its own development: the conditions that help or allow it to grow. "But willing = willing a goal. Goal includes an evaluation" [WP260: 1883–84].[40] Value lies in the way the world is 'polarized' for each will and not in any theories or beliefs about value. It lies in how things 'matter' to the will and so depends on that deep receptiveness of will that Nietzsche calls 'affect' [*Affekt*] or 'feeling' [*Gefühl*]. A perspective on the world always involves an 'experiencing' of it, as it bears on the drive's pursuit of power.[41] This conjunction of willing, viewing, valuing, and feeling is already evident in HH/I/32: "A drive towards something or away from something, without a feeling that one is willing the beneficial or avoiding the harmful, a drive without some kind of knowing appraisal of the value of its goal, does not exist in human beings." The main polarity in feeling is that between pleasure and pain which Nietzsche (metaphysically) defines as the will's experience either of growth or of frustration and decline.[42]

But this talk of feeling and experience, of pleasure and pain, mustn't tempt us back to another mistake (1)—not only are perspectives not detached, they're also not (originally) conscious. We'll eventually see [§ 3.5.1 and § 4.3.1] how Nietzsche explains the rise of consciousness

40. WP715 [1887–88]: "'Value' is essentially the viewpoint for the increase or decrease of these mastering centers".

41. BGE19 analyzes 'willing' to involve "a plurality of feelings, namely the feeling of the state *away* from which, the feeling of the state *towards* which"; it goes on to say that the will "is above all an *affect*, and specifically the affect of the command [*Commando*]". WP688 [1888] says that "will to power is the primitive form of affect".

42. WP688 [1888]: "pleasure is only a symptom of the feeling of power achieved, a consciousness of a difference". See also WP693 [1888], WP699 [1888].

out of drives, as an unusual and secondary event. Drives or forces proceed mainly 'beneath the level of consciousness' even in persons—not to mention in the animals, plants, and nonliving things in which or as which Nietzsche also finds them. So when he says that a drive 'aims' at certain ends, 'views' the world in a consequent way, and 'experiences' certain values within it, none of this is supposed to entail that the drive is conscious. "For we could think, feel, will, and remember, and we could also 'act' in every sense of that word, and yet none of all this would have to 'enter our consciousness'" [GS354].

If it's hard for us to think so, it's even harder to see all of these as (2) not self-sufficient events, separate in particular from the physical behavior they accompany. So even as we try to render them 'nonconscious', we tend just to displace these views and feelings into a 'sub- or unconscious' stream of cognition, still proceeding apart from bodily actions, still observing and guiding them from outside. But for Nietzsche these intentional events are just aspects of the will, as the directed activity of some body. The power ontology, as a monism, means to fuse the physical and the intentional, as aspects of a single being; neither is a thing in its own right, but each is a structural feature of will to power. Nietzsche's attacks on materialism and idealism are guided by this aim to find a middle ground between them.

Thus his notion of perspectives is both richer and poorer than we first expect. They each involve a valuing and feeling we mightn't expect in them, but they're also stripped of the consciousness, and the independence from bodily acts, that we do expect viewpoints to have. Nietzsche takes away the latter, in part to allow perspectives to be posited as universally as the power ontology implies. But of course it still seems highly dubious to extend viewing/valuing/feeling beyond people to animals, plants, and even inorganic forces.[43]

This analysis of Nietzsche's notion of perspectives is not itself enough to specify that 'perspectivism' that we're so particularly interested in. The latter doctrine involves some inference from that notion, against 'realism' or 'objectivity'—as, for example, in the familiar note: "no, facts is precisely what there is not, only interpretations" [WP481: 1886–87].[44] Not until chapter 4 will we fully face this problem of specifying—and disarming—Nietzsche's perspectivism. But our two-level strategy requires a provisional account of it, of how it could not conflict with (and undermine) the power ontology.

So the (tentative) point must be that Nietzsche's vision of a world of perspectives presumes that each of these has the essential structure of

43. I can't answer this difficulty directly but will try to reduce the implausibility gradually, by developing the peculiar way Nietzsche's ontology means 'being' or 'reality'.

44. WP556 [1885–86]: "There is no 'fact-in-itself' [Thatbestand an sich], but a sense must always first be laid in, so that there can be a fact". See also WP567 [1888].

will to power, is a certain pattern of activity, aiming at its own growth; this much, this form, is 'objectively' true of them. But what the distinctive content of that activity might be is determined in the viewpoint of each will and can only be grasped 'subjectively', by itself (or by somehow taking its view). What it 'does' is not a merely physical process, open to the public scrutiny of other perspectives; it depends on what it, in its unique way, is *trying* to do. And this requires, perhaps, that we adjust or retune the way we've implicitly been thinking of the drive's activity. We mustn't think this to have a real character or content independent of the drive's intentions; it gets its sense in the directedness of the drive. Each will is self-defining. Thus the sex drive's pattern of activity is 'sexual' only for its own willful perspective; from outside this perspective, there's no particular way that it is, no particular thing that it does. Without taking a drive's distinctive perspective, all that can be said about it is that it's a will to power, albeit with all that (rather elaborate) formal structure we've described. Only this stands 'above' determination by particular viewpoints. So we explain, for the moment, the power ontology's insulation from the perspectivism.

1.3 Will to power's basic forms: active versus reactive

Another key aspect of this power ontology needs to be clarified. I've remarked several times that not all drives pursue mastery in the way this metaphysics describes. Nietzsche supposes that some drives 'fall away from' their essence as will to power, failing to achieve one or another element in the full structure we've just surveyed. But this is puzzling: How is such failure compatible with the claim that all beings are will to power?

We must go on to see how will to power can occur in either of two basic forms, which I call 'active' [*aktiv*] and 'reactive' [*reaktiv*].[45] The contrast is indeed so basic to Nietzsche that he marks it with many other pairs of terms: the most important are 'health' [*Gesundheit*] and 'sickness' [*Krankheit*], 'ascent' [*Aufgang*] and 'decline' [*Niedergang*], 'overfullness' [*Überfülle*] and 'poverty' [*Verarmung*]. And he claims special insight into this difference: "I have a subtler sense of smell for the signs of ascent and decline than any human being before me; I am the teacher *par excellence* for this" [EH/I/1]. The distinction rests on the notion of will to power: the active drive wills power itself, whereas the reactive has somehow turned aside from its essential end. So the contrast marks the dimension of Nietzsche's metaphysical values, those embedded in the power ontology itself.

45. I've been influenced by Deleuze here; indeed, these terms 'active'/'reactive' are more his than Nietzsche's, who shifts freely among many different contrast pairs ('healthy'/'sick' etc.). But I think Deleuze is right that 'active'/'reactive' best states the gist of the others as well. (I'm less sure how similar to his my analysis of this contrast

Two important issues arise here. First, we must weigh how this contrast helps with the problem just noted: If the reactive drive does not will power, why call it a will to power? Nietzsche seems to shift between saying that will to power is what everything is, and saying it's what everything should be; surely we must be suspicious here. Second, our leading problem also comes up: How could Nietzsche offer any such values, consistently with his perspectivism? If, as we saw in § 1.2, values mark the bias or bent of particular willful perspectives, won't this hold, too, for these judgments about 'sickness' and 'decline'? How can they aspire to that metaphysical status? To weigh these problems, we must first make more vivid to ourselves the dimension of this active/reactive contrast.

This contrast is closely connected with that between master and slave, but we shouldn't conflate them. Whereas the latter are types of persons, 'active' and 'reactive' apply to wills more generally, including to each of the multiple drives in persons. Nietzsche has stories to tell about how persons are formed out of these drives and then how those types are developed by psychological and social-historical processes; I discuss these accounts in § 1.4 and § 1.5. It will emerge that the master *is* active and the slave reactive but that they're so in richly specific ways; before developing these, we need the more abstract distinction.

So what might Nietzsche mean by active and reactive? Perhaps we think first of the traditional contrast between having the causes of one's behavior within or without. Does a drive originate its own activities—is it 'free', as the 'cause of itself'—or is its behavior determined by external forces? This certainly approximates to Nietzsche's intent but can't be quite right, because it ignores his emphatic attacks on both causation and freedom as incompatible with the world's essence as will to power. Or, as he also puts it, that essence shows how our notions of causation and freedom need to be (not given up but) revised.[46] So we must stop thinking of causation as a merely external relation between purposeless things and reinterpret it as the struggle among purposive wills. And we must replace that notion of the *causa sui* with the type of freedom wills *can* have; this will be Nietzsche's rewriting of the Kantian autonomy.

On the one side, 'reacting' doesn't mean being caused to act by an external force, where this force is conceived as delivering an impetus

---

has grown to be.) The terms are most prominently used in GM/II/11, which distinguishes at length between the active and reactive affects; see also GM/II/12. GM/I/10 says of resentment: "its action is fundamentally reaction". Sometimes the contrast term for 'active' is 'passive'. WP657 [1886–87]: "What is 'passive'? — To be *hindered* in the forward-grasping movement: thus an act of resistance and reaction. What is 'active'? — grasping out for power." KSA/12/7[48] [1886–87]: "What do *active* and *passive* mean? is it not becoming-*master* and becoming *subjugated*".

46. WP658 [1885], WP633 [1888]. I treat this topic in § 3.5.2.

that compels such action. Not only must we avoid thinking of this causation mechanically (e.g., with the familiar billiard balls), we mustn't frame it on the model of one will obeying a stronger other, under duress. Reacting is indeed a matter of 'obeying' but in a stronger sense, in which one will obeys another only by adopting, 'internalizing', the latter's views and values, and indeed by adopting them in preference to its own. It obeys not especially in what it does but in what it views as worth being done. A reactive will is one with a tendency—a habit or an instinct—to obey in this special sense.

So a drive obeys (in this sense) not when some constraining force temporarily displaces it from pursuing its own goals, while it keeps these goals for itself and regrets being so diverted from them. It obeys by being persuaded into willing and valuing foreign goals as superior to its (original) own, by being colonized by the other will and induced to adopt the latter's perspective in preference to its own. So reacting is more a consequence of temptation than constraint. Thus a weak drive need not be reactive; the power ontology deploys these terms differently.[47] A weak drive may be forced to obey in the ordinary sense, but without doing so in our stronger one: unable to enact its distinctive behavior, it may still keep its allegiance to it, waiting for its opportunity. Yet we can also see how being forced to obey in the former sense can promote obedience in the latter: a drive that finds itself always compelled by some force stronger than itself is easily tempted toward and into that other's viewpoint, as able to constrain, perhaps by virtue of some strength intrinsic to the viewpoint itself.[48]

There's a second way we need to reinterpret obeying if we're to use it to explain reactivity. A drive 'obeys' foreign forces even in reacting against them; it obeys by taking over their values, whether positively *or negatively*. When a drive takes its task as the struggle against what some other is, it still sets its sights by reference to that other and is still diverted from its own development. It gives that other drive further presence in the world by installing it within itself as a guiding mark, if only as what it negates. It therefore obeys (in our sense) even when it obsessively denies. Thus, if one is sick, "[o]ne does not know how to get loose of anything, to become finished with anything, to repel anything— everything injures. Human being and thing obtrude too closely; experiences strike one too deeply; memory is a festering wound" [EH/I/6].

47. So, perhaps, Deleuze 1983, 53: "Forces are said to be dominant or dominated depending on their difference in quantity. Forces are said to be active or reactive depending on their quality."

48. GS347: "the less one knows how to command, the more urgently one desires someone who commands, who commands strictly—a god, prince, class, physician, father confessor, dogma, or party conscience." Nietzsche goes on to speak of this as a *"disease of the will"*. BGE199 suggests that a "herd instinct of obedience" is inherited. See WP721 [1887], WP738 [1887].

Now in fact, Nietzsche most often uses 'reactive' (and its relatives) for wills of just this sort: for those obsessively, resentfully struggling against others; his analysis of 'resentment' is a highly characteristic teaching. He distinguishes (we might say) two main species of reactivity: the herd animal and the person of resentment, the former obeying by following, the latter obeying by reacting against. Although Nietzsche pays much attention to the herd instinct, he takes far more interest in resentment: it's both harder to notice than simple conformity (being more devious), and also more important to understand (being indeed more distinctively human and the source of most of our values).[49] I pursue these subtypes further, when I look at Nietzsche's analysis of the 'slave' type of person, in § 1.5.2.

Turning now to the positive notion, the active is Nietzsche's rewriting of freedom: it's a will that is not so tempted away away from its own distinguishing activities and values. This is why, contra Kant, "'autonomous' and 'ethical' [sittlich] exclude one another" [GM/II/2]. 'Ethics' [Sittlichkeit] is both a custom [Sitte] one conforms to and a custom that expresses resentment; it fuses both species of reactivity, both types of diversion from self.[50] By contrast, the active will keeps allegiance to itself and to the values favoring its own activity. It has an eye, indeed, for what's distinctive to itself, and a confidence in the worth of what it finds there.[51] As such, it 'commands', though once again not in the usual sense. A drive may command (compel) in that usual way, even out of a resentful animosity toward the other; the strength to rule others so no more implies activeness than (we saw) weakness ensures a reactive obeying. Instead, the active will commands others 'internally', by interpreting them and their values from the viewpoint of its own, thus granting them only a subordinate role in a world still revolving about itself. Once again, Nietzsche's further refinements on this valuative notion will concern us as we proceed. We'll see how his own ideal (often named 'overman') is an elaborate specification of a form of activeness.

49. Perhaps Nietzsche's emphasis shifts, early to late, from the herd type to resentment. Will that straightforwardly obeys or copies is a major theme of *Daybreak*, for example at D104. His later accounts of the herd instinct stress how this hates exceptions, so that he now finds resentment even in conformity; see the other notes on the herd type grouped as WP274–87. Resentment is already noted in HH/I/60: "but to think revenge without possessing the force and courage to carry it out, means to carry about a chronic suffering, a poisoning of body and soul".

50. Or perhaps Nietzsche chiefly finds the herd conformity in *Sittlichkeit* (with its link to *Sitten*), whereas the element of resentment bulks larger in *Moral*. (This is another reason not to translate them both as 'morality'.)

51. UM/II/10p122: "The Greeks gradually learned *to organize the chaos* by following the Delphic teaching and reflecting upon themselves, that is, back upon their real [achten] needs, and letting their seeming-needs die out. Thus they again took possession of themselves". WP918 [1888]: "For what does one have to atone worst? For one's modesty; for having given no hearing to one's ownmost needs; for mistaking oneself; . . . for losing a fine ear for one's instincts".

Now let's recall the first problem: If reactive drives don't will power itself, how can they still be wills to power? How can Nietzsche justify attributing this essence to them? Or does he just mean that this is what those drives 'should' will, and if so, how could he justify this? But he so often makes both the factual and valuative claims, as if they were a single point, that we really must try to see how to combine them. Notice how they're fused, for example, in A6: "Life itself counts for me as the instinct for growth, for duration, for an accumulation of forces, for *power*: where the will to power is lacking there is decline."

As already suggested, I think Nietzsche so combines these points because he operates with a sense of 'essence' that is clear in the tradition, yet still surprising and odd to us. With his power ontology, he means an essence that is 'differentially realized', achieved to different degrees, in different cases.[52] But we need to be cautious here: the active will doesn't 'realize' its will to power essence in the sense that it 'becomes conscious' of it. It's not that all drives 'deep down' will power, and only the active ones do so deliberately, in self-awareness. In fact, Nietzsche thinks that conscious wills tend to be *re*active, whereas simpler, nonhuman wills are more easily and usually active. So we need some other way to parse the distinction than with consciousness.

Nietzsche's claim of essence is in part the claim of a certain logical priority of the active, a teleological priority: the reactive will's way of aiming presupposes the active.[53] It does so not in the sense that there can only be reactive wills because others are active, but because the reactive is intrinsically a *failing* to be active. It belongs to its motivational structure that it gets meaning from others because it can supply none itself; it belongs to the way it wills that it adopts its course as second best. By contrast, the active will 'realizes' its essence not consciously, and not cognitively, but telically, in aiming at what it, as a will to power, wants first and foremost. (This shows how Nietzsche's claim of a will to power essence can depend on his psychology, on his diagnosis of the reactive type.)

On the other hand, the claim about essence is also, ineliminably, a claim of the valuative priority of the active; we can't suppose the logical point can fully generate and justify the preference that Nietzsche's power ontology expresses.[54] Indeed, since this preference gives priority to the 'highest forms', the essential is for him less what (logically) must come

52. By better 'realizing' its will to power essence, a will achieves a higher degree of being or reality. In § 2.1.2, I compare this with Plato's teaching. See also Nozick (1989, 128ff.), whose criteria for 'being more real' are partly like those I attribute to Nietzsche.

53. Recall GM/II/12 on "the principal priority . . . that the spontaneous, attacking . . . forces have; 'adaptation' follows only after their working".

54. Compare GM/I/5's account of the Greek masters' word for themselves: "*esthlos* means, in its root, the one who *is*, who has reality [*Realität*], who is real [*wirklich*], who is true".

first but more what's achieved at the end of long effort and development. We find the essence of things when we find the highest and best they can become.

What of our second problem: How are these values embedded in the power ontology, compatible with the perspectival analysis of values, given just now in § 1.2? Values were explained there as expressing the distinctive interests of behaviors bent on their own development. So how can Nietzsche's values of power and activeness not be idiosyncratically *his*—accounts of what *his* growth or progress would be?

For now, I'll merely reiterate how the two-level account (generally and tentatively) answers this: the perspectival thesis applies only to values lying at a level 'below' that of power itself. It applies to that idiosyncratic activity content, that power is (in each case) growth *in;* any such content has value only for those particular viewpoints that presuppose it. But the value of power lies in a 'form' of allegiance or commitment to that content which is essential to every will and doesn't vary by perspective. Thus power's essential value is not inconsistent with, but indeed a presupposition for, the perspectival values of particular wills.

1.4   Persons and societies as synthetic wills

I've now sketched the deep structure of the power ontology to some detail and length. But there's still another way this choice of starting point might seem distorting: most of Nietzsche's thoughts are at a much less abstract level and seem to have little to do with any such metaphysical claims. So I must go on to show how this ontology infuses and structures his other main thoughts—and that we understand them crucially better by grasping them so.[55] In the rest of this chapter, then, I survey, much more quickly, the rest of the Nietzschean system, seeing how it builds on the abstract positions just sketched.

In order to pass from these abstract wills to power to Nietzsche's more usual topics, we must take a certain structural step: we must see how simple wills to power combine into more complex, *synthetic* wills; we must look, as it were, at Nietzsche's 'chemistry'. Although we've artificially focused so far on single drives or forces, his interest is mainly in persons and societies, complexes synthesized out of countless such simple parts. Indeed, it's in application to these complexes that Nietzsche's thoughts about will to power find their main plausibility and interest. This study of combination is all the more important because with it a new valuative standard emerges: internal complexity or 'richness' is a Nietzschean value at least partly independent of activeness, and even in some tension with it.

55. As I noted in the introduction, and will examine in § 4.5, the ontology 'supports' these other views not by serving as an a priori foundation for deduced conclusions, but by conceptually structuring those views—a structuring whose worth we're to judge empirically.

This combining of wills occurs at a hierarchy of levels, beginning with that of atomic forces.[56] But let's focus on the most important and least implausible stages, of synthesis into persons and societies. A crucial point in both analyses is that the (person's or society's) parts both do and do not combine to constitute a real being, a higher-order will in its own right. Nietzsche finds a great ambiguity here and is often inclined to deny that any such synthetic being, any person or society, really exists. But while holding this reservation in view, we must ask how are persons made up out of drives, and societies out of persons? What new form does will to power take in these, as beings of this new complexity?

A person, then, isn't a simple will for Nietzsche but an organized complex of numerous drives of various strengths.[57] Of course, we must understand these drives in our Nietzschean way: not as 'doers behind the doing' but as activity patterns or behaviors themselves. Each habit or practice enacted in a person's life tries to extend and enrich itself, by crowding out competing practices or making them serve it. So these drives struggle to dominate one another, but this struggle is not just a chaos of forces successively overpowering one another. They reach (shifting) balances of power by arriving at relatively stable relations of command and obedience toward one another. A person is just such a balance among simpler wills, an interweaving of those behaviors, allowing each to express itself proportionately to its strength. For the most part, Nietzsche thinks of this compromise as a being in its own right, as a 'synthesis' of those parts. He treats it as a new will with some independence from those that compose it. It shows this in sometimes restraining them—even the strongest drive is now somewhat moderated in its expression. This synthetic will thus restrains these parts, because it now wills power itself—tries to develop itself, as this synthesis. Thus a person's identity lies in the system of his drives, but this system isn't simply their sum but the power relations, the 'order of rank', among them. And so Nietzsche analyzes the expression 'who he is' with "in what rank order the innermost drives of his nature are set toward one another" [BGE6].[58]

56. Nietzsche's freedom in applying his concept of will to power to 'wills' of so many different types might arouse a certain suspicion. He might seem to be proceeding more from an unreflective enthusiasm for the notion—leading him to apply it indiscriminately wherever his attention falls—than from any worked-out schema for the levels at which it occurs. Or he might seem to suppose it is a sort of cosmic force that 'enters into' or 'possesses' beings already otherwise constituted in their different levels or types. Interpreters seem often to hear him this way. And yet I think attention and effort can discover an intriguing account of the way these 'higher-order' wills are formed from simpler ones.

57. Compare the accounts of this drive constitution in Parkes 1994 and Thiele 1990, 51ff.

58. See BGE36 again. BGE12 commends the phrase "soul as social structure of the drives and affects", and BGE19 says "our body is only a social structure of many souls". GM/II/1 says "our organism is arranged oligarchically". KSA/10/7[94]

Indeed, this is the structure of every living thing: "A multiplicity of forces, connected by a common mode of nutrition, we call 'life'" [WP641: 1883–84]. Thus Nietzsche's analysis makes persons the same in type as animals, more continuous with them than if some quite new component, such as mind or reason, were introduced. Human beings are distinguished simply by bearing more such drives, and drives that are more opposed to one another.[59] Not only is there no detached theoretical subject standing above this struggle among our drives, there is also no preexisting 'overwill', no simple second-order will whose function it is to control them. So at BGE117: "The will to overcome an affect is ultimately only the will of another, or of several other, affects." Thus when Nietzsche attacks 'the will'—for example, when he says, "There is no 'will': it is only a simplifying conception of the understanding" [WP671: 1883–84]—he is usually not expressing doubts that bear against his own proposed will to power; he's rejecting his predecessors' faith in such a simple self or faculty.[60]

We still need to examine more closely the logic of this combining of wills, what I've just called their 'synthesis'. Consider first the relation between a pair of drives, the one dominating and using the other for its ends, the latter pursuing goals imposed on it by the first. Then the complex composed of this pair can't be understood by attempting to 'sum together' the two forces, as if these were vectors pressing off in

---

[1883]: "The most general picture of our essence is *an association of drives*, with constant rivalry and particular alliances with one another." WP492 [1885] states that the 'subjects' we suppose ourselves to be are really "regents at the head of a communality"; it speaks further of "rank order and division of labor as the conditions that make possible the individual [*Einzelnen*] and the whole." And WP524 [1887–88] describes "a kind of leading committee where the different *chief desires* make their voices and power count." See also WP490 [1885] and WP647 [1886–87]. Nietzsche already thinks with this model at UM/IV/9p242; he speaks (with sympathetic reference to Wagner's drama) of calculating "the grand course of a total passion out of a multiplicity of passions running off in different directions". And D119 speaks of "the totality of *drives* which constitute [a person's] essence", D422 of "one's fifty particular [*eignen*] drives".

59. Nietzsche stresses this continuity as early as "Homer's Contest" [1872], which begins: "When one speaks of *humanity* [*Humanität*], the idea is basic that this is something that *separates* and distinguishes human beings from nature. In reality, however, there is no such separation". A14: "We no longer derive the human being from the 'spirit' or the 'deity'; we have placed him back among the animals." WP966 [1884]: "As opposed to the animals, the human being has bred large an abundance of *opposing* drives and impulses [*Impulse*] within himself: thanks to this synthesis, he is master of the earth." See also BGE291, GM/III/13, WP259 [1884].

60. D109: "While 'we' believe we are complaining about the vehemence of a drive, at bottom it is one drive *that is complaining about another*". A14: "today we have taken from [the human being] even the will, in the sense that no faculty [*Vermögen*] may any longer be understood by it." Also TI/III/5, TI/VI/3, WP692 [1888].

different directions. The weaker drive joins in the project commanded by the stronger and thereby enhances it; but as always struggling to assert itself within this relation, it also modifies that project with something of its own. Unlike vectoral forces, these projects adjust to one another, proportionately to their relative power; each thereby finds some expression within the other. As before, we should stress how all of this occurs in the concrete behaviors of these drives—now, in the ways their respective activities are intertwined in the daily life of the person. For the most part, the weaker practice is taken as a stage within the stronger and must shift direction to better serve this role. Yet the dominant project, even by thus absorbing the other as an epicycle within it, takes on new character itself.

In such a case, in which one drive quite rules the other, we identify the resulting complex with the dominant drive: this is still its activity, now enriched by that other, which it has absorbed or made (mostly) like itself. But if we think of a case in which the drives are more evenly balanced, with one perhaps dominant in some respects or contexts but the other dominant in other respects, we won't still attribute the activity of the resulting whole to either of its members. They now form a unit with a distinctive activity of its own, not to be identified with either of the others, nor even with their (vectoral) sum. Think, for example, of eating with other persons: our interests in food and in social interaction here intertwine, and not merely in the sense of being pursued simultaneously. Two practices now express themselves within one another and so join to form a new and more complex practice. Nietzsche thinks this practice has, as it were, a life of its own: 'social eating' will tend to repeat and develop itself. Thus there arises a second-order power unit, one that can itself be entangled with other such pursuits and so enter into still higher syntheses.[61]

We should imagine the person, then, as such a unit, though one vastly more complex, because it is a synthesis of many parts, which are themselves syntheses of simpler parts; the different organs of the body, or rather their functionings, are such lower-order complexes. Thus a person is formed of a vast network of power balances, struck at a hierarchy of levels. What differences between persons become important— turn out to reflect our deep structure—given this analysis? I catalog some of the main dimensions along which such systems of drives might vary:

61. WP642 [1885]: "To what extent a striving-against lies even in obeying; its own power is by no means given up. In the same way, there is in commanding an admission that the absolute power of the opponent has not been vanquished, incorporated, disintegrated." WP488 [1887] says that a subject "can transform a weaker subject into its functionary without destroying it, and to a certain degree form a new unity with it." WP636 [1888] speaks of each body as striving to extend its force but meeting other bodies whose similar efforts oppose it; it therefore "ends by coming to an arrangement ('union') with those of them that are sufficiently akin to it: thus *they then conspire together for power*. And the process goes on—".

1. How many different drives does a person bear? Nietzsche does not suppose there's a standard set intrinsic to all human beings; some will be far more complex in this way than others. His overstress on 'breeding'—his notion of these drives as mainly inherited ('in the blood')—is misleading here: we must bear in mind his Lamarckism. My drives are the product of the lives my parents led; rather than some common human endowment, they're those particular practices I've been (we will say) trained up into. So they include not just eating, for example, but even quite specific meal rituals and tastes.[62]

2. How compatible with one another are a person's drives? Of course all drives are by their nature as will to power at odds with one another; it's their essence to try to rule one another. But (pairs of) drives will vary in how opposed and irreconcilable their distinguishing activities are. Because each drive seeks dominance by impressing others *to* its activity, how far it will thereby try to turn those others *from* their own natures will vary. So a person is made up of drives that are more or less 'tolerant' of one another, more or less capable of 'harmonious' relation.[63]

3. What are the relative strengths of a person's drives? Are one or two much stronger than the others, or are all on roughly equal footing? If the latter, it may be harder for stable power relations to form, especially if the many equal rivals are incompatible with one another in the way just described. Such a person might more nearly approach the condition of that chaos of succeeding impulses mentioned before.[64]

4. How thoroughly have a person's drives been synthesized with one another? Nietzsche thinks the unity of a person is never complete—this is why he sometimes denies any persons exist—but a matter of varying degree.[65] This most important difference among persons depends on some of the other differences in ways we've seen; it deserves special attention.

Let's think a bit further about the privative case. Here the constitutive drives haven't found any balance with one another, or only a very unstable one. There isn't, that is, any overall pattern of behavior, any

---

62. See BGE200, 224 on the great internal diversity of moderns. BGE264: "One cannot wipe from the soul of a human being, what his ancestors have done most gladly and continually."

63. See again BGE200.

64. WP778 [1888]: "the against-one-another of the passions; two, three, a multiplicity of 'souls in one breast': very unhealthy, inner ruin, disintegrating, betraying and increasing an inner conflict and anarchism". See also TI/IX/41.

65. WP488 [1887]: "*No* subject 'atoms'. The sphere of a subject continually *growing* or *decreasing*, the midpoint of the system continually *shifting*". See also WP635 [1888].

comprehensive practice in which they all find their expression, but instead just a sequence of their separate, private doings. Instead of being channeled to contribute to some such overall effort, each drive squirms to break loose in a spasm of pure self-assertion, followed by its total suppression by some equally unrestrained drive. Such a person will lack 'self-control', which is now shown by Nietzsche to be a different condition than we usually think. What's missing isn't strength of 'the will', as a part or tool of 'the self', but the capacity of this set of drives to combine in the way described.[66] And they may lack this capacity merely because of such 'chemical' incompatibilities as we've noted.

We'll see that the extent of unification achieved by a person's drives is a major valuative standard by which Nietzsche ranks him. This value can be understood as a new form of the activeness we've already seen his ontology values. When we rise to the level of complex wills, the active/reactive distinction can be drawn not just by whether the will commands others 'outside' itself but by whether it commands the simpler wills that it comprises.[67] Indeed, Nietzsche supposes that such self-mastery is a crucial precondition (or at least aid) for mastering others. Is the synthesis able to hold its constitutive forces to their contributing roles and prevent them from asserting themselves disruptively against it? A person can either 'command' or 'obey' his parts, whereas the simple drive can do neither—neither restrain nor give way to itself. Thus the poorly synthesized person exhibits a new form of reactivity; he obeys away from himself, by obeying too small a part of himself. Nietzsche thinks this brand of reactivity is typical of persons: just because we're distinguished from other living things by our greater complexity of parts, it is harder for us to achieve synthesis. This is why man is 'the sick animal', 'all too human'.[68]

Thus the standard of unity, by which Nietzsche often rates persons, might be counted a special application of the value of activeness (already placed in his system). But Nietzsche will also rate persons by another standard, somewhat in tension with this one: by their degree of complexity, by their multiplicity of parts. How does this other value emerge? Activeness was valued, recall, as a well-directed pursuit of one's own power. But power amounted to growth by incorporation: having one's activity come to encompass the behaviors of others. So growth involves

66. WP46 [1888]: "Weakness of the will: that is a simile that can mislead. For there is no will, and consequently neither a strong nor a weak will. The multiplicity and disgregation of the impulses, the lack of system among them results in a 'weak will'; their coordination under the dominance [*Vorherrschaft*] of a single one results in a 'strong will'". See Nehamas 1985, 170ff., on the task of unifying the self.

67. So is the whole active only at the expense of the parts, by forcing them into a reactive obedience? We'll see that Nietzsche thinks personal unity ('self-control') can be secured by a 'taming' or 'suppression' of the drives, but need not be.

68. GM/III/13, A14. KSA/9/12[163] [1881] identifies 'the human individual' as "the highest and *most imperfect* being [*Wesen*]".

an advance in internal complexity; a will that is now complex, is so because of successful power willing in the past, by itself or others. However, such achieved complexity makes it ever more difficult to continue to will power healthily. The greater the richness of parts at hand, the harder it is to marshal them together. We can see, then, how the values most deeply rooted in the power ontology—those of power and activeness—support an oxymoronic standard for rating persons: the extent to which they show a 'complex unity'.

We mustn't stop, however, at the level of the person in exploring the synthetic forms of will. Nietzsche's discussions of societies and their practices show that these should be treated in parallel to persons: they, too, are made up from simpler parts—from drives or persons or simpler complexes of these. They, too, become synthetic units of will to power in their own right, able to pursue their own development and to command their members to serve that end.

Nietzsche often speaks of peoples or races as having or being wills to power. Yet it's tempting not to take such applications of the concept quite strictly. We might suspect that they're merely shorthand ways of referring to the behavior of the persons who make up those groups, to the sum of the ways they themselves will power. This seems confirmed when we notice that he even applies that concept to such amorphous beings as religions: sometimes, he says, "they themselves will to be ultimate goals and not means among other means" [BGE62]. It's hard to see how he could mean this literally; is it a case of that loose or metaphorical expression we so expect from him?

There's indeed less evidence that Nietzsche has fully thought out a definite sense for such talk, that he pays as much attention to the task of analyzing societies in his power terms as he does with persons. We'll later find other important differences between his treatments of these two, which suggest he indeed has more qualms against treating societies as real beings than we've seen he has against persons. Still, there are many indications of another tendency, which gives them just the analysis we expect, given the power ontology.[69]

We can extract this line from the striking discussion of punishment in the second essay of *On the Genealogy of Morals*. Nietzsche argues that we mustn't conflate the origin and the purpose of this social custom or

---

69. From early on, Nietzsche tends to view societies as living beings. UM/II/1p67 gives as examples of living things *"a human being or a people or a culture"*; UM/II/4p80 says, "a people to whom one attributes a culture has to be in all reality a living unity [*Eines*]", and offers the analogy of many threads wound into a knot; UM/II/10p122 says, "Hellenic culture was no mere aggregate. . . . The Greeks gradually learned *to organize the chaos*". HH/I/99 says that morality arises "when a greater individual or a collective-individual, for example the society, the state, subjugates all other single ones . . . and orders them into a unit [*Verband*]." See also GM/II/11 (a legal order is "a means of creating *greater* units of power"), GM/II/20 ("the conclusive rank order of all the people's elements, in every great racial synthesis"). See also BGE259 and WP728 [1888].

practice; they're different because, in general, everything that comes into being "is again and again interpreted to new views, confiscated, remodeled, and redirected to a new use by some power superior to it" [GM/II/12]. He illustrates this with the case of an organ in a living body: as the organism as a whole grows, it assigns ('commands') that part to ever new roles. The institution of punishment, he thinks, has a similar place within an encompassing being; this practice, as "a certain strict sequence of procedures" [GM/II/13], is directed to a series of uses by the society as a whole, or by other forces within it. Punishing thus takes on a series of 'meanings', which Nietzsche catalogs at some length.

So his picture seems to be this. Such a custom is a particular system of interactions among persons, but one that has taken on a life of its own, as a synthetic will to power. It thus tends to continue and extend itself and in doing so shows independent power over its parts: it draws persons into performing it. This system of behavior persists in a fairly constant form from one generation to the next. But it's also always changing, because it is always being jostled by other such practices competing with it. Together, these compose a still larger power unit: the society as a whole, the system of these systems of behavior, their organization into a network of power relations. This higher-order unit acts back on its parts in just the same way, commanding them into the roles in which they most contribute to its overall effort—or at least, the healthy, active society will command in this way.

This parallel analysis shows that societies will crucially vary in the same ways we saw persons do; we shall ask the same questions of them:

1. How many different types of persons and customs enter into this society? Nietzsche uses the standard of complexity at this level as well: he'll rank societies by the richness or diversity of their parts.
2. How compatible with one another are the society's parts? Along with their diversity, the contentiousness of these parts helps to determine how far they can be synthesized into a stable whole.[70]
3. Are a few of these persons or practices dominant over the rest, or are there many, roughly equal in strength? The distinction between aristocratic and democratic societies of course falls here. We'll explore Nietzsche's preference here and how it's related to his ranking of the parallel types of persons.
4. How thoroughly synthesized are these parts? Once again, the most important question about any society is how fully formed it is as a will in its own right. The more tightly knit its parts are into a whole, the more power it has over them and the less free they are to upset the balance in a solitary self-assertion.[71]

70. D272 speaks of "crossed races, in which, together with a disharmony of bodily forms . . . there must always go a disharmony of habits and value-concepts."
71. See again D272.

This raises a certain problem: activeness of the society looks incompatible with activeness of the person. The former involves a subordination of society's members to its comprehensive project: it limits them to roles it requires. So in the fully formed and active society, it seems persons would be least allowed to develop themselves in idiosyncratic directions, which we've seen their power requires.[72] Thus we can expect that Nietzsche's judgments on the value of 'freedom' will be most important, because they'll reflect his judgment on the relative values of a person and a society. To anticipate: it's a striking feature of his thought that although he values persons as greater quanta of power formed as syntheses of lesser drives, he doesn't follow the parallel by valuing societies as still greater quanta formed from those persons themselves; this is a clue to the differences in the ways these two synthetic power units are formed. I reconfront these issues in chapters 2 and 3, as I dig more deeply into Nietzsche's social views.

1.5   The typology of persons

Having seen how the notion of will to power is used to analyze what drives, persons, and societies 'are', we've finally acquired the conceptual tools to lay out Nietzsche's division of the basic types of persons. These are certain basic variations on the ontological structure he assigns persons, in how they are composed of drives and are components of societies. Along with his views about the ways these basic types typically evolve and interact, this typology makes up a Nietzschean psychology, though again we mustn't suppose them to be types of minds. They are types of directed behavior: basic different ways the complex practices making up a person's life can be organized and enacted.

Of course, Nietzsche's psychology is extremely rich: on these topics, too, he expresses a tremendous scattering of opinions. He achieves richly separate insights, many unconnected or opposed to the schema I sketch. Yet here, too, we find a most common core whose overall lines are surprisingly stable through his twenty years of thought. Nietzsche recurrently discovers, or thinks in terms of, a few general such types, though he approaches them in many different contexts and often under different labels. I suggest that these strike him so often as the 'natural kinds' of persons, by reason of their roots in the power ontology: each is a basic variant of the human power will. I use the terms 'master', 'slave', and 'overman' for these schematic types, which Nietzsche has much more often in mind than his own use of these three words suggests.[73]

72. WP719 [1887]: "A *division of labor* among the *affects* within society: so that individuals [*Einzelnen*] and classes cultivate an *incomplete*, but for that reason *more useful* kind of soul." D9 develops the incompatibility between the 'ethics of custom' and individuality.

73. Compare White 1994, 63: "the terms 'master' and 'slave' refer to basic modalities of individual existence, and in this respect they are 'types' which still concern us all".

Indeed, these types of persons are only part of Nietzsche's story here. He applies a similar analysis to persons' parts and to the wholes persons form. So, on the one hand, he makes a parallel tripartition of (temporary) attitudes: of how one wills in passing situations or moods, even if not overall. One can will, value, and feel 'slavishly' (e.g.) in given cases without being of that personal type. Nietzsche's analyses also sort these situational behaviors, which gives them a microapplication to the details of even our own lives. On the other hand, he also thinks that each of those personal types is most likely in a certain type of society, and he tends to think of these encouraging societies as *isomorphic* with the personal types they produce. This gives these analyses a macroapplication to the societal types he thinks cultures tend to pass through. Nietzsche tells a familiar historical story here, locating master, slave, and overman as phases in Western culture's long development; this story offers us easiest access to his broader point.

1.5.1 The master

When we try to give a firm sense to the familiar Nietzschean 'master' [*Herr*], using the ontological terms sketched above, it's tempting at first to define him simply as a powerful person, or as an active person. Such a straightforward link to the metaphysical schema is suggested by the way *Herr* reflects *Herrschaft*, which, as our 'mastery', played so crucial a role in that schema. But it doesn't collect enough of the content to Nietzsche's picture of the type. The master is active but in a particular way, which we'll need to distinguish from another (that Nietzsche rates above it). Moreover, Nietzsche usually thinks of the master as inhabiting a particular social-historical place—as not just a certain synthesis of drives but a member of a certain type of society, in a certain historical phase. He takes the master type to occur prototypically—in fullest and most pronounced form—in a rather specific societal context. Moreover, he has in mind some favorite examples of this master-making context: above all (what he thought were) the peak phases of Greek and Roman culture. He takes these as ideal cases of a certain societal health and also as founding phases of our broad Western culture, whose history has been (in this respect, and with some exceptions) a decline from those peaks.[74]

This prototypical context can be quickly stated, in a picture easily drawn from the first essay of GM. In his purest and most perspicuous form, the master is the product of a young society—a fairly brief phase, because it tends by a natural route to evolve (or deteriorate) toward, and into, other types. But the master type stands in clearest relief in this early

74. PTAG [1873] takes the Greek 'tragic age' as an ideally healthy culture. GM/I/16: "For the Romans were the strong and the noble, and nobody stronger and nobler has yet existed on earth or even been dreamed of".

case: when a warlike people or tribe subjugates a weaker one and forces it into a hierarchic or aristocratic society, sharply divided between the ruling and ruled castes.[75] The achievements and situation of the ruling group encourage its members to value in a certain way: in their happiness and confidence in themselves and their success, the masters count themselves 'good', while with mild contempt they look down on the others as 'bad'. This way that they rank persons or lives is of course their 'master morality' [*Herren-Moral*].

But we need to improve on this simple story. Nietzsche doesn't just call this ruling group 'stronger' than those it commands; he has an explanation of why or how it is so. It's not accidental that this group finds itself ruling, the other ruled. Nietzsche describes the internal structure of this master tribe—the sort of synthesis it is—and the parallel structure of the persons that compose it; he thinks this constitution explains the strength both group and members possess. Thus "their predominance did not lie mainly in physical force but in that of the soul—they were *more whole* human beings" [BGE257]. And the master's "mastery over himself also necessarily gives him mastery over circumstances, over nature, and over all more short-willed and unreliable creatures" [GM/II/2].[76] This 'wholeness' and 'self-mastery' are the characteristic activeness of the master. How are we to understand it?

Above all, these synthetic wills—the tribe and its members—are simple in structure: they're composed of relatively few and relatively cohesive parts. (So the master type is deficient in that second Nietzschean virtue: richness.) The caste consists of persons closely compatible with one another, just as these persons consist of a few complementary drives. But again it's not just good fortune that has made them so. Nietzsche thinks such simplicity is (usually) achieved through a history in which a people has had to struggle against external forces threatening its very survival. It's only through a struggle in which defeat is most fearsome that this process of self-creation occurs. In this struggle, the group finds which qualities allow it to overcome those obstacles, and "these properties they call virtues, these virtues alone they breed large"[BGE262], while they ruthlessly excise whatever doesn't help in this way.

In this Nietzschean story, it's the society, as a higher-order unit of will to power, that accomplishes this self-creation. It strengthens itself by

75. See also BGE257, GM/II/17. Note that in GM/I/6–7 Nietzsche distinguishes between the original 'knightly' form of aristocracy and a 'priestly' form that evolves from it; here, of course, I speak only of the former.

76. HH/I/45 (an earlier sketch of the distinction between master and slave moralities): "The good are a caste, the bad a mass like dust." GM/II/17 speaks of "a conquerer- and master-race which, organized for war and with the force to organize, unhesitatingly lays its terrible claws upon a populace perhaps tremendously superior in numbers but still formless and wandering." TI/X/2: "Thucydides has *himself* in control, consequently he also holds things in control".

pruning its parts and organizing them into more effective combinations. The result of this self-surgery is a potent structure of practices, as well as a pool of just those types of persons needed to perform them. In this mobilized society, parts at these several levels are organized from above into stable relations of command and obedience; parts are constrained to contribute to the growth of the whole. They create "a mastery-structure that *lives*, in which parts and functions are delimited and coordinated, in which nothing whatever finds a place that has not first been assigned a 'sense' in regard to the whole" [GM/II/17].[77] And this active mastery of its parts enables this people to be active as well toward forces without: it's more capable of commanding them because of this history in which it has learned to command itself, to bring its parts into complementary effort. By trimming itself into a more cohesive and hence potent structure of drives, it masters groups whose drives are dispersed and at odds.

In this process of self-creation, such a society 'breeds' the type Nietzsche calls 'master'. By their birth and upbringing—he tends to overstress the former—into such a focused society, persons are formed from (relatively) few drives.[78] These drives are well synthesized: they're channeled to serve a broader personal project, which in turn plays a needed role in the still broader social practice: "Here good, sound custom strengthens, here the subordination of the individual is learned and firmness given to character, as a gift at birth and by training afterwards" [HH/I/224].[79] Of course other types of persons are also shaped within such a society: an underclass to play other, supporting roles. The masters are those this society shapes as the persons in whom it culminates.[80] Indeed, in our purest case of the conquering tribe, those others are slaves, hence not quite members of society at all, more its tools or beasts of burden. Both the master's preeminent place in such a graded society and his constitution—the simplicity and harmony of his drives—make it most unlikely he will be either forced or tempted away from his personal project by foreign wills or drives. Because his society is active, he will be, too.

This explains the familiar features of the master morality. As simple in structure, and as not subjected or tempted by foreign wills, the master judges by a univocal system of values. They express the synthesis of drives, the person, that he is and not either isolated internal drives disruptively rising against it, or foreign wills dictating to it. It's in this

---

77. BGE262: "the type [Art] needs itself as type, as something that, by virtue of its hardness, uniformity, and simplicity of form, can prevail and make itself durable".

78. And they are formed from drives that have been relatively little 'spiritualized' (cf. § 3.4.1, so that these prototypical masters exhibit a "powerful physicality" [GM/I/7].

79. WP942 [1885]: "There is only aristocracy of birth, only aristocracy of blood." See also HH/I/96. This counts against MacIntyre's claim (1981, 121–22) that Nietzsche mythologizes the Homeric heroes by presenting them as self-creating.

80. BGE258.

(weak) sense that a single master 'creates his own values'—a sense compatible with his group's creating *him* as one to whom these values are native.[81] He holds to the viewpoint of his overall project, consistently seeing the world as being for the sake of just such a life as his. So BGE287 offers as a key of nobility: *"The noble soul has reverence for itself."* Indeed, this wholeness or single-mindedness makes it hard for the master even to understand or empathize with other drives. He can't enter into other perspectives, bearing so little of their drives in himself. He has little sense of others' values as serious alternatives to his own and is little inclined to take a relativist distancing from his view.[82]

This way that his values reflect his own synthetic unity means that he sees himself, and the others homogeneous with him, as 'good': "The noble human being honors himself as one who is powerful, also as one who has power over himself" [BGE260]. And because, in his success, the world as a whole seems fitted to his own activity, he (in a favorite expression for Nietzsche) *"says Yes"* not just to himself but to all of life.[83] Only secondarily does the contrasting shade of 'bad' appear; he seldom notes, and little cares about, the persons his values rank low. But insofar as he can, with an effort, not just view those he masters as his own tools—their lives just parts of his own—but grasp them as wills or persons in their own right, striving for power of their own, he takes for granted that they want to be like himself but simply fall short. He feels neither envy nor ill will toward them but only a contempt mixed with (a type of) pity—the 'pathos of distance' [*Pathos der Distanz*] Nietzsche speaks of so often.[84]

This is, then, the master type in his archetypal social setting and role.

81. TI/VI/2: "a human being who has turned out well, a 'happy one', *must* do certain actions and shrinks instinctively from other actions; he carries the order, which he represents physiologically, into his relationships to human beings and things." BGE260: "The noble type of human being feels *itself* as value-determining; . . . it is *value-creating*. Everything it knows of itself it honors; such a morality is self-glorification [*Selbstbeherrlichung*]."

82. HH/I/228: "Narrowness [*Gebundenheit*] of views, through habit become instinct, leads to what is called strength of character. . . . Those of strong character lack knowledge of the many possibilities and directions of action". See also HH/I/270 and GS18. BGE224 speaks of the "very determinate Yes and No of their palate, . . . their hesitant reserve toward everything foreign, their horror of the poor taste even of a lively curiosity, and in general the bad will of every noble and self-sufficient culture to own a new covetousness, a dissatisfaction with its own, an admiration for the foreign".

83. A57 (speaking of the highest caste in a healthy society structured by 'the law of Manu'): *"'The world is perfect'*—thus says the instinct of the most spiritual, the Yes-saying instinct; 'imperfection, the *under*-us of every kind, . . . even the chandala still belongs to this perfection.'"

84. HH/I/45: "It is not he who does us harm but he who is contemptible who counts as bad." BGE173: "One does not hate so long as one still esteems little, but only when one esteems equal or higher." GM/I/10: "The 'well-born' *felt* themselves to be the 'happy'; they did not have to establish their happiness artificially by a look at their enemies". GM/I/11 says that the noble man "conceives the basic concept 'good'

But Nietzsche thinks societies inevitably fall away from this phase of simple health. Their tensed effort loosens and unfolds into ever more channels, and the persons they breed are ever less clear cases of the master type. I follow this decline ('decadence') in 1.5.2. However, Nietzsche still finds cases of this type—this structured attitude—in these inhospitable settings, where it has closer relevance to us.

Some persons have the crux of it, even in very different social contexts. This crux is simple activeness: being formed from a few cooperating drives and holding an unshaken confidence in the value of the synthetic practice they project. We can find such persons around us now and can ask to what extent *we* are like them. To be sure, that 'masterly' confidence is harder to keep up outside its archetypal context: a society like our own offers so rich an array of alternative behaviors, all tempting away from valuing one's own, that a masterlike simplicity threatens to depend on a certain dullness or unawareness. In such 'democratic' diversity, persons will never be as purely or constantly of the master type; it occurs now only as an element in persons (the character of some of their drives and behaviors).[85]

So this master type can also be ascribed to temporary behaviors and attitudes: one can will and act 'masterly' in given situations, even if one doesn't overall. And this brings the type into still closer connection with our experience; it prompts the question, in any moment, whether we are doing/viewing in this active way right now. Nietzsche will invite us to sort our various habits and behaviors (our 'drives') between this and the 'slavish' type. But to understand this choice, we must now look at this alternative.

1.5.2   The slave

Again, let's begin with Nietzsche's historical story. In the primary case, the 'slave' [*Sklave*] appears in that same societal setting, as a member of the caste dominated by those masters. But whereas the master's simplicity let us tell a simple story about him—looking only at this single setting in which he briefly flourishes—with the slave we meet a more complex and evolving type. With the slave, human beings first become 'interesting',[86] because they now become 'historical': whereas the mas-

---

in advance and spontaneously out of himself and only then creates for himself a representation of 'bad'". See also BGE260. On the 'pathos of distance', see BGE257, GM/I/2.

85. GS18: "We lack the ancient coloring of nobility because our feelings lack the ancient slave."

86. GM/I/6: "it was on the soil of this *essentially dangerous* form of human existence, the priestly form, that the human being first became *an interesting animal*". GM/I/7: "Human history would be altogether too stupid a thing without the spirit that the impotent have brought into it". See also HH/I/136, GM/II/16, WP864 [1888].

ter was a culmination, the slave takes a path from his start. This development largely explains, Nietzsche thinks, the movement of society as a whole out of that primitive phase and the end of those purest masters.[87] So our story about the slave type must sketch its progress through a natural series of phases or forms. I focus on three of these: subjection, resentment, and nihilism.

1.5.2.1 Subjection

The first is perhaps more a cause or precondition than the phenomenon itself. It is, so to speak, the 'physical' state of enslavement, the brute fact that one's will is constrained by forces without. Nietzsche thinks, as we'll see, of the slave (in his stricter sense) as enslaved more 'inwardly' than this—as reactive, which a merely thwarted will need not be. But he also thinks of that 'outer' subjection as the natural route to the inner. So in particular, in his archetypal story, the slaves are of course those conquered and ruled by the warlike masters—he names the type after them. They are members of a "weaker, more civilized, more peaceful" society [BGE257], now subjugated by the simpler, aggressive tribe and forced into a new order as its lowest caste.

Why do they lose? Nietzsche tends to think of their weakness, like the master's strength, as not just 'physical'—not a matter of smaller numbers or muscles or weapons—but 'psychic', a matter of their poorer organization as a synthetic will to power. In his favorite case, it lies in their 'decadence' [he uses the French *décadence*]: in their decline from active ancestors (who were like the tribe that now subjects them). These ancestors have left them with a strength or preeminence they now want only to enjoy, in peace and security. In this ease, society unfolds into a richness of persons and practices aiming in diverse ways, hard to marshal together. And again, this group structure is mirrored in (most of) its members: each is himself more complex and loosely knit, a less-formed system of drives. Persons are not born and trained by society for any definite life; each is instead composed of concerns and practices haphazardly falling to it from a general pool—hard to bring into stable arrangement, and often not. So Nietzsche speaks of the inability of the decadent,

---

87. See HH/I/224, including: "Degenerate [*abartenden*] natures are of the highest significance wherever progress is to ensue. . . . The strongest natures *hold* the type *firm*, the weaker help it to *evolve* [*fortbilden*]." Of course, Nietzsche doesn't think that human history runs all in unison through any so simple a sequence; this aggregate history is the upshot of countless groups, practices, and individuals, all at different stages in these lines of development, these 'ways up and down'. WP339 [1887–88]: "It is no whole, this humanity: it is an inextricable multiplicity of rising and falling life-processes—it does not have a youth and then a maturity and finally an old age. The strata lie through and over one another".

of members of exhausted races, to resist their own impulses.[88] It's this lack of self-control (self-synthesis)—which we've seen is a form of reactivity—that chiefly explains their subjection.

But Nietzsche doesn't intend this as a metaphysical justification for slavery. His attacks on 'responsibility'—I pursue these in § 3.5.2—show that he doesn't (mainly) mean to blame these 'decadents' for their fate. Moreover, he sees that theirs is not the only route to slavery. Although active self-synthesis may indeed render one more potent in struggle, it's certainly no guarantee of success. Even the healthiest can be enslaved, even those weaker only in the 'physical' ways just mentioned.

Reached by whatever route, the 'subjection' that slavery first and most concretely involves has the character of an external constraint. One's drives, whether organized or not, are hemmed in and prevented from acting; one is barred from one's natural and preferred behaviors. Moreover, this constraint is imposed by a will (or wills) that uses the slave for ends of its own. Inevitably, one suffers from this chronic frustration of one's own impulses and aims; the slave type begins in a type of suffering the master has no experience of.

But, as I mentioned, none of this is yet enough to constitute one as a 'slave' in Nietzsche's fuller sense, because none of it requires that one be reactive. As we saw in § 1.3, the latter involves a certain 'internalizing' of the subjugation; it requires that one 'obey within', by taking on the other's viewpoint and values, whether positively or negatively. Healthy wills can long resist this corrupting step. But we can see how relentless external constraint—and by a force that profits from it—will tend both to pull and to push them into it. They'll find it hard to avoid a certain obsessive stance toward that force (the master); this fixation makes them not just worse off, but worse.

On the one hand, the master 'attracts' the subject into reaction. The privileged life the master leads gives the slave constant and deeply persuasive grounds for thinking him better and for wishing to live that life instead of his own. He quite naturally wants to be a master, and at first, at the simplest level that yet persists beneath all his more developed views, this simply means being just as the master is. It's a further subtlety to distinguish the master's social-political place from the particular practices he pursues there. So the slave wants to do those very same things; they might even be the secret to the master's success. This immediate attraction to that other form of life derails the slave from the task of

---

88. WP734 [1888]: "The trouble is that a certain inability to 'master' [*beherrschen*] oneself (—*not* to react to stimuli, even to very slight sexual stimuli) belongs to the most regular consequences of general exhaustion." TI/II/9 describes the degenerating Athens Socrates found himself in: "no one was any longer master over himself, the instincts turned *against* one another." And TI/II/11: "To *have* to fight the instincts—that is the formula for decadence: as long as life is *rising*, happiness equals instinct." See also BGE200, BGE208, WP45 [1888], WP334 [1888], WP737 [1888].

developing his own activity; it distracts him from the regard he needs for what's distinctively his.[89]

At the same time, the master 'repels' the subject into a different type of reaction, partly at odds with the first. Combined with this embrace of the master is a certain denial of him, also continually prompted and reinforced in daily experience. The master stands over the slave as a constraint on his will and as one who has what the slave wants himself. So while still half under the sway of the master's values and practices, the slave also singles him out as his archenemy. The slave's envy for the master thus typically becomes only an ingredient in his hatred of him.[90] Nietzsche thinks these attitudes combine into a special obsessive fixation on this other person or group. It's this odd yet likely mixture—which he calls 'resentment' [he uses the French *ressentiment*]—that makes up the second main stage or form of the slave.

1.5.2.2   Resentment

Resentment is the form of sickness and reactivity that Nietzsche has most interest in; his analyses of this psychic type are pervasive in his writings and quite distinctive of them. This is the slave type whose development first makes the human being interesting and gives him a history. Resentment plays such major roles because of the way it spurs and focuses the slave's will. Its mixture of a fascinated attraction to the master with a vengeful opposition to him has a remarkable capacity to intensify one's willing of power, though also misdirecting it.[91] Indeed, many wills need this spur to make themselves care. So at GM/I/10: "in order to arise, slave morality always first needs a hostile outer world; it needs, physiologically speaking, outer stimuli in order to act at all—its action is at basis reaction." As with the master, we should bear in mind that Nietzsche thinks this a human type that can occur in quite different social-historical settings; indeed, it is even a type of attitude we can observe episodically at work in ourselves. But here I'll stress his historical story.

We saw how the masters' self-control was achieved through a struggle against fearsome obstacles; the effect of subjection on the slave is similar. By acquiring the focal project of overcoming the master, he (or his group) wills with new unity and effectiveness. Struggle against the master now polarizes the world more simply and decisively; by viewing all things in the light of this project, the slave forms a cohesive system of

---

89. The master's viewpoint and values are all the more compelling when it's he that names, when he imposes his language (and especially his words for virtues and goods) on the other. See GM/I/2.

90. See GM/I/7 on how the 'impotence' [*Ohnmacht*] of the priests makes them great haters.

91. GM/III/15 calls resentment "that most dangerous explosive".

values. Indeed, it's only here that he arrives at a 'slave morality', as Nietzsche chiefly means this. The decadent was too dispersed among his separate interests, whereas the (straightforwardly) obedient slave simply took on the values of his master. With resentment, reactivity first creates values.[92]

However, this creative act is little more than the negation of the content of the master values, and not a positive synthesis of the slave's own drives and practices. He still sets his sights in relation to the master: "While every noble morality grows out of a triumphant saying-Yes to itself, slave morality from the outset says No to an 'outside', to an 'other', to a 'not-itself'; and *this* No is its productive deed" [GM/I/10]. His values don't express what he or his people have done and are. He has no eye for what's really himself, and so no experience of mastering others to himself—of drawing them into the scope of his proper activity. Thus he has no sense of the genuine 'affect of command' or of power itself. The resentful slave pursues a deviant and nonessential type of mastery or power.

His deep admiration and envy of the masters—his tendency to 'obey' in the strong sense of ingesting their values—inclines him to take these others as the standard even for the mastery he wills over them. So, first, he tries less to raise himself than to lower those masters; he wants to destroy these enemies, by contrast (as we'll see) with the ideally healthy will, which wants its enemies stronger. Second, the slave takes as his criterion for power the masters' viewing him as powerful: they must come to concede, preferably in pain, his superiority to them. He tries mainly to raise himself in the eyes of these others.[93] By contrast, we saw how little the master cares about the slave's view of him; the slave is there for use, and the master seeks no self-validation through him. The slave's preoccupations with hurting and impressing the master show how he wills power only under a guise: not power itself but a distorted or imperfect form of it.

How will the slave set about changing the masters' view? How can he induce them to value him, to envy (and even hate) him as much as he does them? First choice would have been to win at the masters' game, because the slave so deeply regards that privileged life. But this is seldom possible: he hasn't been bred and raised into these practices, with the drives that make for success in them; indeed, this incapacity is just what his enslavement involved.

So the slave who progresses and develops his type is the one who takes a different tack: he tries to change the game both he and the masters play. He works to convince both himself and those others to

92. GM/I/10: "The slave revolt in morality begins when *resentment* itself becomes productive and gives birth to values".

93. BGE261: "the ordinary human being still always first *waits* for an opinion about himself and then instinctively submits to that".

replace the accepted standards with new ones, ones by which he ranks very high and they very low. Masters will only admire him if they can be thus tempted away from the values of the practice they excel at. Thus the slave becomes a 'moralist', and his values become a 'morality' in a stronger sense than the masters' ever were. He now fashions and offers his values—to himself as well as to others—inspired by a deep-seated preference for the master's life and by hatred of the master. This gives to his statements of value the note of devious preaching we (and Nietzsche) can sometimes hear and mean in the term 'morality'. Such values are chiefly developed as a hidden weapon against the other they're offered to—as "an act of the *most spiritual revenge*" [GM/I/7], [94] and (Nietzsche thinks) this explains much of their content.

A crucial difference between master and slave is that the former can act out his drives, the latter not. The slave suffers the frustration of his desires; when he notices them, it's mostly as painful. This is all the more so when he's of that half-formed type Nietzsche attributes to decadence: then he experiences the drives as a chaos of disruptive demands. All of this prompts the slave to reject the master's game and values on just this point: to disvalue these drives and those practices in which they're (straightforwardly) acted out. His values 'say No' to these simple and original drives and to that life of the master in which they're expressed; all these are 'evil'. Instead of developing a practice that expresses his own special mix of drives, as an active will does, the slave wills restraint or negation of drives in general: "The same means in the struggle with a desire—castration, rooting-out—will be instinctively chosen by those who are too weak-willed, too degenerate [*degenerirt*], to be able to impose a measure on themselves" [TI/V/2]. [95] Resentment gives birth to the 'ascetic ideal'.

So the slave aims at a passive sort of happiness. [96] Thus he esteems, in himself and others, such negative qualities as peacefulness and un-selfishness; in these he calls himself 'good', "just as if the weakness of the weak—that is to say, their *essence*, their working, their whole un-avoidable, irremovable reality—were a voluntary achievement, some-thing willed, chosen, a *deed*, a *merit*" [GM/I/13]. Yet, once again, the slave posits these goods only in afterthought, and hypocritically. He

94. BGE219: "Moral judgments and condemnations are the favorite revenge of the spiritually limited against those less so". WP345 [1885–86]: *"The basic tendency of the weak and mediocre of all times is . . . to weaken and pull down the stronger: chief means, the moral judgment."* See also GM/III/14, WP204 [1887] (on *"moral castra-tionism"*), and WP252 [1887–88].

95. BGE200: "his most basic desire, is that the war he *is*, should have an end". See also WP385 [1887], WP778 [1888], WP383 [1888].

96. GM/I/10 says that to the impotent and oppressed, happiness appears "essen-tially as narcotic, numbness, rest, peace, 'sabbath', slackening of feeling [*Gemüths*] and stretching of limbs, in short *passively*".

deeply thinks the master better, and his praise of himself is a ploy in his project to convince all parties (including himself) to want something else than they do. Because the slave finds unity only by pressing his drives to an end defined in reaction or negation of something foreign, he fails to take up the bent of his own drives. In the master these are at least allowed to express themselves within roles—under control; the slave, however, tries either to erase or to ignore them and to live by an independent ideal that has no such roots in his own constitution.

This denial of drives finds many concrete expressions; one will be of special importance later. It produces what Nietzsche calls 'the will to truth': the theorist's life in pursuit of knowledge or objectivity. This is valued and developed as an increasingly complex practice in the society, as a part of the slave's resentful project. Confronted with that chaos of unactable drives, he hopes for relief in a viewpoint with several main features. First, he wants to maintain himself in a single perspective, gripping enough to fend off the temptations of all his drives' interests. Second, he wants a viewpoint that is 'cooler' than theirs, one less intensely and painfully interested in its ends. Third, he wants a view that values those types of activities that the constraints on his behavior will still permit him. The will to truth fits each of these bills; Nietzsche claims it takes its character precisely in order to play these roles. This is why the theorist expects to find, in a practice of thinking which even enslavement can't keep him from, a perspective privileged above all others by the way it escapes precisely their interestedness, their subjectivity.[97] In chapter 4 I examine this account and evaluation of truth and the theoretical life a lot more fully; it plays a main part in Nietzsche's perspectivist attack on objectivity.

Not only is the project of truth adopted from this motive, but the specific truths the theorist then goes on to find are typically prompted by it. This shows that he doesn't ascend to a disinterested point of view after all: his views reflect his interest in the project of resentment. This is most clearly so in his theories of value, but also in his metaphysics. We saw how the denial of the master becomes a denial of drives in general; the slave tends to see all the world as incurably infected by evil forces. And the theorist reflects this denial in his metaphysics. This world of struggle and strife is less real than another he posits: a world of being rather than becoming, a world from which will to power is purged. "The concept 'beyond', 'true world' invented in order to devalue the *only* world there is—in order to retain no goal, no reason, no task for our earthly reality!"

97. TI/II/9–11 describe Socrates' promotion of reason, in response to the anarchic instincts in a decadent age: "The drives will to play the tyrant; one must invent a *counter-tyrant* who is stronger". GM/III/23ff. present science as allied to the ascetic ideal. WP457 [1888]: "But it is revenge above all that has become useful to science—the revenge of the oppressed, those who were pushed aside and oppressed by the *ruling* [*herrschenden*] truths".

[EH/IV/8]. The main case is of course Plato's realm of Forms, which I pursue in chapter 2.

We still have to ask whether the slave will succeed in his project of resentment. In tempting the masters with his new values, he aims to make them reactive like himself; he needs to unseat their native standards, which rate him so low. Yet why should the masters succumb to this temptation, when we saw that they notice or care little about the slave, and indeed find it hard to enter into any foreign views? Isn't their activeness, as we've analyzed it, just what would make them immune to the slave's attempts? But the slave finds help in a tendency already at work among them. Leaving behind the period of struggle in which they first overcame the other tribe, and settling into a stable rule over it, these masters are no longer challenged by dangers demanding the cohesion and strength of purpose they achieved. We saw how this secured domination isn't the principal form of power but a sort of afterimage of it; true mastery is a progressive overcoming of obstacles. So in this absence of hurdles, even the master comes to lose sight of power itself. He grows content with having overcome and no longer strains at further growth. And this affects his stance toward himself: he no longer works to prune and shape his drives or behaviors, and neglect lets these grow diverse and diluted. He becomes less limited to a single personal perspective and more sympathetic to other views, because of this new diversity he bears. Gradually he even becomes able to enter the slave's point of view, to empathize with and (in a new way) pity him. All of this makes him ripe for the slave's seduction.[98]

Thus the 'logic of wills' at work in both master and slave leads to a degeneration of society's original aristocratic phase. The slave morality gradually diffuses itself into the society, replacing or engulfing the active values. Nietzsche calls this event 'the slave revolt'.[99] We're not to think chiefly of violent insurrections or political upheavals. These certainly occur in the course of that long event but as mere consequences of a very gradual process that lies mostly concealed. This is the slow weaving into the social fabric of more and more views and behaviors expressing resentment against any elite, any privilege. More and more, the many concrete practices of the society are adopted, reinterpreted, and revised from the viewpoint of a resentful sufferer: they're infused with that spirit, hence altered, as is (e.g.) the practice of punishment, when the

98. See especially BGE262: "But finally someday a happy condition arises, the tremendous tension is relaxed; perhaps there are no more enemies among the neighbors. . . . Variation . . . is suddenly on the stage in the greatest abundance and splendor". BGE258 describes corruption as "the expression of a threatening anarchy within the instincts". See also GM/III/14 and WP712 [1887].

99. See BGE195 and GM/I/7 on the 'slave revolt' [Sklaven-Aufstand]. Of course, this development is not uninterrupted; GM/I/16 describes the Renaissance and Napoleon as temporary reversals in it.

motive of revenge grows stronger in it. The ascendance of that psychic stance—envious hatred of the stronger—produces a gradual 'leveling' of society. This 'equalizing' applies not just to persons but to those viewpoints and practices: these, too, come to be viewed as 'democratically' equal, all just as good as one another. It becomes more and more accepted by all, as a basic background truth, that no way of living or thinking is better than any other and that an aspiration to distinction is the root of evil.

1.5.2.3 Nihilism

This brings us (rather quickly; I tell this part of Nietzsche's story more fully in § 3.3) to the third and last phase of the slave, nihilism. As the master's rule brought about his degeneration, so there's a logic to the dominance of the slave morality, which leads to its own dissolution. Nietzsche famously proclaims that we now live in this culminating stage, in which this system of values undermines itself and society lapses into a certain blankness or valuelessness. Let's take a first look at this point.

What will happen when the slave values quite suffuse the society, and it has been so thoroughly 'leveled' that there's no longer a class of active masters whose values degrade the slave and incite him to struggle against them? When the slave fully accomplishes his will in this way, we can expect a degeneration in this willing, analogous to what we found in the master. Indeed, we've seen that the slave's willing is especially dependent on the obstacle it strives against. When this opponent disappears from the scene and the world is made safely democratic, the resentment that has focused and driven the slave must lose its impetus. The only uniting goal the slave's system of values has had is removed, and the values begin to lose their strength, their ability to give direction to people and meaning to their world. The reactive practices, having gradually overpowered the active ones by corrupting them, lose that focusing purpose of opposition, and so also their cohesion and sense. (This is a 'decadence of the slave society', analogous to that of the masters.)[100]

This finds a most telling expression in that special practice evolved by the slave: the theorist's pursuit of objective truth. In society's nihilistic phase, this will to truth now turns against the values from which it emerged. It discovers that the metaphysical world, drawn up to confirm those values, is a fiction. And it sees that those values themselves express just one more 'subjective' perspective—that they, too, represent special interests.[101] The theorist reaches, that is, some of the very conclusions

100. BGE201: "Supposing that one could altogether abolish danger, the basis of fear, so one would abolish this morality, too: it would no longer be needed".

101. WP5 [1886–87]: "But among the forces that morality bred large, was *truthfulness: this* eventually turned against morality, discovered its *teleology*, its *interested* view".

Nietzsche just has. He's able or even impelled to reach them because of this nihilistic context: through the withering away, in himself and his society, of resentment against master and world. As this fades, it no longer spurs or directs the will to truth, as it did when the great philosophers uniformly offered their separate 'objective' proofs for God and for Christian values. Thus the will to truth finds itself free of the force that inspired and constrained it; we'll have to see whether Nietzsche thinks it can now sustain and direct itself.

But where has society arrived, on the whole? The long dominance of the slave morality has spun out many new practices, of a more complex and 'spiritual' sort than those of the younger society; theoretical efforts at truth are among these. This richness grows even more as resentment ebbs: the relaxing of the slave's values brings ever more tolerance of diverse types: of exotic religions, personalities, ways of life. No way of life is agreed to be better, more moral than any other; all lie on an equal footing, juxtaposed in person and society. So TI/IX/41: "the *modern* [is] physiological self-contradiction".[102] This great pool of possibilities is no longer pressed to any single end, not even the merely negative end of resentment. Thus they lie available, as raw materials that can be taken up actively and into a richer and subtler synthesis than was ever possible before.

1.5.3   The overman

A person synthesized in the right way, in this specific cultural context, will be (Nietzsche thinks) sufficiently unlike both master and slave that he will amount to a new basic type: an 'overman' [*Übermensch*]. Or, rather, he will be a clearer and higher instance of a type we can then retroactively discern, already present as rare individual exceptions back in that 'slavish' history. Nietzsche fluctuates between a narrower and a broader conception of a personal type that is (I argue later) his ideal: one that he commends to the best of us and aspires to achieve himself. In its narrowest form, this ideal is the specific 'revaluer of values', at this crucial historical point, that Nietzsche wills to become. Indeed, we'll see that this ideal even acquires a religious aura for him, by virtue of its world-historical role: he aspires to be a prophet (Zarathustra), verging into a deity (Dionysus).[103] I appropriate the term 'overman'—at some odds with Nietzsche's own use—as a label for this multifaceted ideal,

102. TSZ/II/14 (addressing "those of the present"): "Motley, all ages and peoples look out of your veils; motley, all customs and faiths speak out of your gestures." Also BGE200, 215, 224, 242.
103. EH/TSZ/6: "My concept 'Dionysian' here became a *highest act*; measured against it, all the rest of human doings seem poor and secondary [*bedingt*]. That a

whose structure I progressively analyze. Here we begin with its aspect as a new character type in Nietzsche's historical tale.[104]

Because these overmen become most feasible in a society that has passed through nihilism, this last phase of the slave morality's rule constitutes a great opportunity—thus Nietzsche looks mostly favorably on it. It bears the potential that persons of an unprecedented complexity, yet also with a higher health, might form within it. But he also worries that they might not appear; such persons are now only more possible, not inevitable. The difficulty of such a synthesis, of achieving that oxymoronic 'complex unity' out of this overrich mix, could mean that no one *can* accomplish it. All those who (on purpose or not) do bear this diversity, might fall apart into it, remaining unstructured mixes of drives or viewpoints. Indeed, even the aspiration to completeness and unity might be lost; people might learn not even to will them. Nihilism might produce only these ambitionless 'last humans'; so it's also the great danger.[105]

Nietzsche sometimes thinks of these possible outcomes as distinct types of societies our nihilistic age could come to. The one that breeds only last humans amounts to a kind of institutionalized nihilism, in which will- and valuelessness become common practice. Or instead, we're to hope, another society might emerge 'on the other side' of nihilism, one that Nietzsche associates with the overman. We'll see that he makes this link in two main ways: (a) it is the overman who founds this new society, and/or (b) this society is characterized by its effort to bring about overmen (by its adopting the overman ideal). In either case, it will be this new society that serves us as our best candidate for a Nietzschean 'utopia'. Yet we'll also see grounds for doubting whether Nietzsche has any ideal for societies at all, any societal twin to his ideal for persons, the

---

Goethe, a Shakespeare, would not know how to breathe for one moment in this tremendous passion and height, that Dante, compared to Zarathustra, is merely a believer and not one who first *creates* truth, a *world-ruling* spirit, a destiny". In taking Nietzsche's aspirations to mount toward self-deification, I find in him more self-confidence than Simmel 1991, 142: "This is the same passion which fills Spinoza and Nietzsche: they cannot bear it not to be God." Note how WP712 [1887] and WP639 [1887] bring the standards for divinity into nearer reach.

104. Contrast White's account (1994) of Nietzsche as anticipating "the return of the master". Also contrast Magnus's argument (1983, 1986) that the *Übermensch* is not an ideal type, but stands for a certain attitude toward life (and especially toward the thought of its eternal return)—an attitude that implies no specifiable character traits; I agree that the overman has this attitude, but I argue that he can have it only because of a certain structuring of his drives—so that Nietzsche does have in mind a type of person.

105. On decadence and nihilism as making possible a higher type of person, see BGE200, BGE242, GM/II/24, WP109 [1885], WP111 [1887]. On the danger that this type won't appear, see BGE203, GM/I/12.

overman. He often focuses his interest on the individual against, and rather than, society. For now, I postpone these complications, by confining my attention to the overman himself; later (in § 2.5.3 and chapter 3), I weigh what an overman-produced or -producing society might be like and whether this is Nietzsche's political ideal.

It's when the slave values, developed in reaction to the master's, undermine themselves that overmen become most feasible. So Nietzsche's historical story suggests a sort of dialectical progression from master to slave to overman. Indeed, his overman turns out to be a synthesis, in important ways, of the first two types. Although this ideal person may be more akin to the masters, he's distinguished from them by certain crucial features he shares with the slaves. So a common first impression of Nietzsche—as thoroughly on the side of the masters and against the slaves—needs to be improved. As a structuring of drives, the overman differently resembles each of his predecessors.

We can see this by pursuing the way Nietzsche himself calls his ideal person 'synthetic': "Most [persons] display pieces and details of human beings: one has to add them together for a [whole] human being to come forth. . . . [T]he only issue is the occurrence of the synthetic human being" [WP881: 1887].[106] The parts of this synthesis are just those elements we found in the power ontology: drives or practices. We saw that any person is already essentially a synthesis of these, but one that is usually poorly or partially achieved. So in Nietzsche's ideal, as we'd expect, this essential synthesis is now at last adequately realized.

In what ways can persons fall short? From what we've seen, master and slave are both incomplete or fragmentary, but in opposite ways. The master bears only a very limited variety of drives within; because these are (relatively) few as well as alike or compatible, they're more easily joined in an overall personal project, yet this project remains rather simple. The slave has the opposite deficiency: his drives are many and conflicting but (or therefore) not well synthesized into a cohesive whole; he's thus more complex and encompassing than the master, but only as a collection of parts, not as an integrated person.

The overman combines the assets of master and slave: he has the latter's richness of drives but the former's ability to organize them toward an active overall practice. As we might put it, he represents the

---

106. We find this already in UM/III/6p163: "the human beings with whom we live resemble [gleichen] a field of ruins of the most precious sculptural models, where everything calls to us: come, help, complete, bring together what belongs together, we have an immeasurable longing to become whole." TSZ/III/12/3 seems to say that producing the overman means "to compose and carry together into one what among human beings is fragment and riddle and dreadful accident." BGE256 says *"Europe wills to become one.* In all of the deepest and most comprehensive human beings of this century, the genuine overall direction in the mysterious working of their soul was to prepare the way for that new *synthesis"*. WP866 [1887] speaks of "a *synthetic, summarizing, justifying* human being". See also BGE219 and WP883 [1887].

reachievement of activeness in this far richer, spiritualized social context accomplished by the slaves; this new context makes his activeness rather unlike the master's. Nietzsche may be marking this other way that his ideal is a synthesis, in his famous phrase "the Roman Caesar with Christ's soul" [WP983: 1884].[107] The complex or spiritual person becomes able at last to organize his multiple drives or views with the proper economy. He learns true control of his inclinations, passing beyond the slave's standard responses of either giving way to whichever is currently strongest or working to ignore or destroy them. The overman is that very rare person who can form a wealth of conflicting parts into a system in which they all find expression, yet also are phases in an encompassing project: "The highest human being would have the greatest multiplicity of drives, and in the relatively greatest strength that can be endured. Indeed, where the plant human being shows itself strong, one finds instincts that drive powerfully *against* one another (e.g. Shakespeare), but are restrained" [WP966: 1884].[108] The result is an unusually complex and distinctive whole: a new higher-order power unit that is formed out of, and disposes of, diverse and divergent parts.

In these terms, the overman is distinguished from the master by his greater complexity. Of course, by itself this catches little of the overman's special type. But the other important differences follow from this one; activeness in this context takes a different character than in the master's. We saw that the latter's wholeness is due to the prior simplicity and cohesion of his tribe: a person born and raised into this group is fitted with drives or concerns that naturally settle into a whole. It's the group, not the member, that is really responsible for constituting this whole, as is reflected by the masters' similarity to one another; they form a society of like-minded members. Thus, as we also saw, the master 'creates his own values' only in the sense that these follow from this whole that he is and not from extrinsic drives that would tempt him away from himself.

107. WP899 [1885] speaks of the "union of spiritual superiority with well-being and an excess of force". WP1051 [1885], more ambiguously, speaks of an imperative "to *overcome* everything Christian through something over-Christian, and not merely to put it aside".

108. TSZ/III/16/4: "If ever I drank full drafts from that foaming spice- and mixing-mug in which all things are well mixed; . . . if I am myself a grain of that redeeming salt which makes all things mix well in the mixing-mug". WP1051 [1885]: "an overflowing richness of the most manifold forces, and the most agile power of a 'free willing' and masterly disposing dwell amicably beside one another in one human being". WP684 [1888]: "the higher type represents an incomparably greater complexity—a greater sum of coordinated elements"; this note suggests that the expression 'higher type' "means no more than" the "richest and most complex forms". WP928 [1887–88] stresses not diversity but strength in one's drives: "Greatness of character does not consist in not possessing these affects—on the contrary, one has them to the most terrible degree—but in leading them by the reins." See also WP933 [1887].

Although he can sustain this identity against such pressures, he does not create it.

By contrast, the overman creates himself and his values in a much stronger sense; he must do so, since his divergent drives are not prefigured for any easy synthesis. His inclinations or practices still come to him from his social-historical context—but separately, not as a set. The overman neither inherits his type nor is formed to it by his society. So WP684 [1888] says, "The short duration of beauty, of genius, of Caesar, is *sui generis:* such things are not inherited. The *type* is inherited; a type is nothing extreme, no 'lucky case'." This means that the overman begins by facing a threat the master doesn't: he experiences conflicts within, to which the naturally harmonious master isn't subject. He suffers in a way the other doesn't—another similarity to the slave. But unlike the latter, the overman wins through this suffering a higher health, by accomplishing that self-synthesis.[109]

In shaping himself as an idiosyncratic individual this way, the overman at the same time is forming a new system of values. These values differ from the master's in some basic ways; those differences in structure and history lead to a different overall view of the world. We've seen how the master 'says Yes' to life, because he principally experiences things as obeying his will, as collaborating in his efforts. The world is the beautiful setting for his life. But this affirmation isn't based on any insight into other things' own character—quite the contrary. The master affirms them not as willing what they do for themselves but only as aids to his own ends. He's very little capable of understanding other types of persons, because he bears so little trace of them in himself. His structural purity limits his ability to empathize with other wills and so to comprehend the way they will.

The overman's perspective also includes a universal affirmation, but one that more nearly affirms things as they inherently are. His greater 'completeness' means that he bears a greater share of the many different forces that constitute life. He experiences more of its diversity 'from within'. He experiences how these distinctive wills do not just serve but give some of their own character to the unity they obey; thus he feels "a depth of happiness in which what is most painful and gloomy works not as opposite, but rather as conditioned, provoked, a *necessary* color within such an overflow of light" [EH/TSZ/3]. Whereas the master affirms other wills as means appropriated to his own end, the overman more nearly

109. I develop this notion of a 'great health' in § 2.5.3. It's important to keep in mind a point the language tends to obscure: in this self-creation, the overman isn't a being apart from the synthesis he achieves. It's not that a separate 'will' or 'ego' acts on the drives; instead, they organize themselves, progressively settling into fuller and tighter systems. A first power unit, tenuously constituted out of some share of these concerns, struggles to bring more and more into its union as contributing parts, thus making itself more complex and distinctive.

affirms them in themselves, as contributing to an overall process made not just more efficient but richer for their distinctive presence. So the overman accomplishes that truer sort of 'growing by ruling', analyzed near the end of § 1.1.2. And so EH/BT/2: "This last, most joyous, most wantonly exuberant Yes to life is not only the highest insight but also the *deepest*". In chapter 4 I develop how this amounts to a special type of knowledge, one the overman is preeminent in.[110]

This brings us to a last major point, in this opening exposition of Nietzsche's views. The overman's universal affirmation involves his willing the 'eternal return' [*ewige Wiederkehr*]. Since this notion clearly has a strong temporal content, a fuller account should wait until chapter 2, where we'll see the subtler temporal point of many of the ideas just surveyed. But here I must at least show where this last basic Nietzschean teaching might rest in the system I've sketched. Familiarly, this teaching stresses the role of eternal return *as a thought*: Nietzsche usually offers it as an especially revealing test or sign of a person's character or rank. We learn how strong (and even how wise) a person is by whether he can think this thought—or, rather, by whether he can will that everything eternally recur. The overman is especially able to do so, because he brings such diverse parts into such a whole.

By contrast, first, this thought will be disturbing or oppressive to the other types of persons. The slave is at war with his drives, with the purpose of not assimilating but obliterating them. He wills that such forces, in himself and elsewhere, cease to exist, that the world be cleansed of them and brought into an ideal and eternal end state. The possibility that these forces will always break out again, and in particular that he himself will repeatedly endure their oppression, is intolerable to him; a world in which everything recurs would be evil.[111]

The master, by contrast, of course isn't hostile to will itself in this way. But he's prevented by the homogeneity of his parts, by the simplicity or narrowness of his practice, from truly sympathizing with other forces and views, and this keeps him from embracing the eternal return, as the overman does. The thought that not only he himself, and others like him, will recur, but also the vast preponderance of other types may seem wasteful or ugly: not all of these are needed for his flourishing; a world in which everything recurs would be bad. In his confident preference for just such a life as his own, he, too, tends to will that the world should arrive at an end: a utopia fully engineered for the living of lives

110. Anticipating, note WP259 [1884]: "The wisest human being would be *the richest in contradictions*, who has, as it were, antennae for all kinds of human beings—and in the midst of this his great moments of *grand harmony*".

111. WP351 [1888]: "it thinks up a state in which all that is evil is annulled and in which in truth only good beings [*Wesen*] are left." See also WP881 [1887], WP386 [1887].

such as his. He welcomes the occurrence of other drives or practices only as external aids to his own, and not in and for themselves.

To welcome the recurrence of the world just as it is and has been, and to welcome it because this world is good not just on balance, but in all its parts, is the overman's special mark. It requires a person synthesized out of an exceptional share of the drives present in that world, because this enables him to enter the range of these other viewpoints and to understand them for themselves. It requires that this person be synthesized in such a way that all of these parts contribute to his life as a whole, because this enables him to 'say Yes' to such a range of the world's diversity. He sees, in particular, how even the reactive or slavish or ugly plays a needed and positive role in himself, and he transfers this lesson to the world as a whole. His different structure from the master thus fits him for a wider and more insightful embrace of the world just as it is, and for the thought that it might over and over again be just this way. So can he be "the most high-spirited [*übermüthigsten*], most lively, and most world-affirming human being, who has not just learned to bear and be reconciled with what was and is, but wills to have it again, *just as it was and is,* throughout all eternity" [BGE56].

2

BECOMING

There are several main grounds for resistance to the view I'm developing: assigning a metaphysics or ontology to Nietzsche. The objection I'm
chiefly concerned with is the one that cites his perspectivism; in chapter
1, I gave the beginnings of a reply to it, by showing how the power
ontology might generate, and then exempt itself from, this perspectivism. But there's a second main objection, one that at least seems quite
distinct from the first. This arises from Nietzsche's apparent effort to
replace, within his basic vocabulary for describing the world, 'being'
[*Sein*] with 'becoming' [*Werden*]. This seems to involve a disavowal of
any ontology as a 'theory of being'. My question in this chapter is
whether the will to power metaphysics can also explain, and show itself
consistent with, the priority Nietzsche thus gives to 'becoming'. This
requires that I unfold the 'temporal' implications of his ideas.[1]

Retracing the sequence of topics in the previous chapter, we'll see
that many of Nietzsche's concepts and claims make (what are in effect)
points about time. In particular, his account of the will to power essence
of things and his distinction among master, slave, and overman crucially

---

1. This attention to the temporal aspects of Nietzsche's thought is one main way
this reading may seem 'Heideggerian'. But if it is, it's not by restating Heidegger's own
views about Nietzsche, but by applying to Nietzsche certain abstract lessons taken
from *Being and Time*. I argue that some important Nietzschean claims are explicitly
temporal and that many of his other ideas are implicitly so. It may be that a certain
conception of the temporal structure of human life is common to Kierkegaard,
Nietzsche, and Heidegger and is a key reason for grouping them together as 'existen-
tialists'. But I won't complicate my discussion by pursuing these further comparisons.

refer to ways this will and these persons are 'in time'. These temporal points that are implicit in the power ontology and in the fuller philosophical system it generates only occasionally find expression by him. But when they do, it's in points of vital importance to him. Besides that preference for 'becoming', the most significant is the teaching of the eternal return. Nietzsche takes these temporal points to be major ways he breaks from philosophers before him,[2] which gives us further reason to suspect that his insistence on becoming may reflect a disavowal of metaphysics.

This point is stressed by interpreters who emphasize Nietzsche's perspectivist side. Derrida puts obvious emphasis there, when (following Heidegger) he presents the rejected tradition as defined by its 'ontology of Presence'—of present being instead of temporal becoming. I argue, however, that although Nietzsche's claims for becoming clearly do attack ways in which his predecessors give priority to presence, they still allow and indeed involve an account of the being (essence) of beings (what is). The theory of becoming is a theory about reality. I suggest that Nietzsche himself denies this largely because he intends (or just tends) to hear the term 'being' in the Parmenidean-Platonic sense—in such a way that (roughly) only what never changes in any respect can 'be'. Because he thinks that change of a special sort is basic to the world, he places himself at the opposite extreme from these and chooses to reflect this by inverting their own contrast between being and becoming. But in fact his insistence on becoming has the sense of specifying an unusual ontology, or metaphysics, and not of renouncing any such theory. It has the character not strictly of replacing 'being' but of better characterizing it: it says that 'being is becoming', in a sense we must clarify at length. As we do, we recover some of the radical story told by Derrida, by retelling it in systematic, ontological terms.

There's a third main objection to my opening hypothesis, which also needs to be confronted. Quite apart from Nietzsche's refusal to allow 'being' in accounts of the world, the great number and vehemence of his attacks on the content of prior ontologies also seem at odds with the reading I've sketched. In our first experience of Nietzsche, these emphatic attacks, from a self-claimed position of great isolation, simply overwhelm any thought of important continuities. His extreme sense of distance from thinkers before him suggests that his own views and goals must be different across the board from theirs. Even if it could be argued, on abstract or structural grounds, that he does have a theory of being, it

2. WP570 [1887–88]: "If one is a philosopher as one always was a philosopher, one has no eye for what was and will be [wird]—one sees only what is. But since nothing is, all that was left to the philosopher as his 'world' was the imaginary." Yet Nietzsche also credits prior German philosophers (Hegel in particular) with the discovery of becoming; see GS357, BGE244 (which however seems to mock them for it), WP1058 [1883–84].

seems we would have to allow that he ascribes to this being a radically different character from all the tradition before him. If the description is so thoroughly new, we might still prefer to conclude that it's about a different topic than theirs ('being'), whatever those abstract grounds suggest. A very thorough difference in the details of the theory I attribute to Nietzsche might in fact count against viewing it as an ontology after all. So I must also weigh how novel this Nietzschean description is.

To consider better the extent of his break from earlier views, we really need to pick out some representative predecessors and explore in more detail the structure of Nietzsche's relation to them. Such concrete comparisons will also improve our grasp of his ideas themselves, including those on time; we can place or specify these better by using others as points of contrast. For this purpose it's natural to turn to the Greeks, whom Nietzsche himself had so often in view.[3] Indeed, the very contrast between being and becoming recalls the debate passed down to the classical period by the pre-Socratics. As is already clear in his early draft on those first philosophers, *Philosophy in the Tragic Age of the Greeks* [1873], Nietzsche intends to align himself in this debate, especially on the side of Heraclitus. Equally early, *The Birth of Tragedy* announces his fascination for Socrates and his divided but mainly negative judgment of him. In his later works, Nietzsche retains both his interest in these two figures and his respective assessments of them.

Interpreters have often discussed these relations to Heraclitus and Socrates, and on certain points I shall do so as well. But it may well be doubted whether either of these philosophers has a metaphysical system of the sort we're principally asking after in Nietzsche. For this reason, Plato will be more continuously rewarding as a point of comparison: he more obviously belongs to the tradition with which we're weighing Nietzsche's connections. Indeed, by Nietzsche's own account Plato is the chief inventor of the metaphysical tradition from which we need to break;[4] thus his thought seems intended as much against Plato's, as he more obviously announces himself to be 'anti' Christ. We must ask, how should we understand this reversal? Is everything turned on its head? Is philosophy to turn aside from everything Plato attempted and to deny

3. WP419 [1885]: "A few centuries hence, perhaps, one will judge that all German philosophy derives its genuine dignity from being a gradual reclamation of the soil of antiquity, and that all claim to 'originality' must sound petty and ludicrous in relation to that higher claim of the Germans to have joined anew the bond that seemed to be broken, the bond with the Greeks, the hitherto highest type 'human being'."

4. BGE/P credits Plato with inventing "the worst, most protracted, and most dangerous of all errors so far"; BGE191 allows him "the greatest force any philosopher so far has had at his disposal", and says that since Plato "all theologians and philosophers are on the same track". PTAG2p34 [1873]: "from Plato on there is something essentially amiss with philosophers".

every one of his main or distinctive claims? Or is there an underlying affinity that even permits the inversions Nietzsche does demand?

I try to support my conservative reading by arguing that Nietzsche is akin to that seeming epitome of the philosophical tradition, not only in having an ontology but also in basing on it a parallel structure of further claims. Nietzsche's disagreements with Plato thus appear not as radical overturnings of the deep structure of that tradition-founding thought, but as internal, and incomplete, revisions of content. Specifically, he preserves those seven structural features of 'metaphysics' that were distinguished in the Introduction. Like Plato, he claims (1–3) a systematic truth about essence, an essence or being that is (4) temporally specified and (5) differentially realized, generating (6) values that ground an ethics, in which (7) the metaphysical project is rated our highest activity.

2.1 The temporal aspects of the power ontology

Once again we begin at the most abstract level, with the basic notion of will to power, whose structural content was analyzed at the start of chapter 1. We saw there how Nietzsche uses this notion to propose a new telic schema as essential to all things, though he oddly allows that some 'fall away from' a full realization of this primary pattern. To what extent are his claims about time consistent with this grounding ontology? I try to show that many are even expressions of it. Thus the basic point about end-directedness involves one about time: it suggests that things are in time in a different way than we usually suppose. Moreover, this temporal schema will be 'essential' in that same surprising way, which allows that many or most things fail to realize this essence fully. Thus we find a temporal application of the standard or value we've seen is built into Nietzsche's thought at the most abstract level: his ontology will favor a particular way of 'being in time'.

We also see that this network of abstract claims has strong precedents in the tradition. Plato in particular also roots his values in this way, because he, too, has them reflect his account of fullest being, which he, too, specifies in temporal terms. To be sure, just how he then determines being with respect to time calls Nietzsche into clear opposition: a key dispute between the two lies in just how their 'most real' beings are in time. And yet, as we examine this conflict more closely, we find crucial points of agreement even here.

Just what lessons about time does Nietzsche's telic ontology imply? As we might first and roughly put it, if the essence of all beings—as wills to power—is a striving to grow or develop, but this growth never culminates in any stable end, then these *beings are essentially changing*. WP1064 [1885] might be taken to draw just this lesson: "In a determinate moment of force, the absolute conditionedness of a new distribution of all its forces is given: it cannot stand still. 'Alteration' belongs to the essence, therefore also temporality".[5] Because only such forces, or wills to power, 'are' for Nietzsche, such change would be essential to all beings. On this obvious line, which it's clear Nietzsche often takes, the claim about change would be a part of his theory of being in a straightforward way: by describing (at least part of) the essence of beings. To be sure, this stands in conflict with his (occasional) explicit denials of any *beings* in a world of becoming. But because he does sometimes think the point in that natural way, and because it's our own best intuitive route to his more considered sense of becoming, we should begin here. Thus in its opening version, our question is: What type of change does Nietzsche claim is essential to beings?

The great importance of this claim to Nietzsche is reflected in the weight it bears for him—in the major further conclusions he takes it to imply. This claim, which I call his theory of flux [*Fluss*] or becoming, is a main support he gives for several other of his most distinctive ideas. In particular, it supports certain hypercritical—skeptical and nihilist— lessons. First, he takes it to show that most of our commonsense views, as well as the theories of scientists and philosophers, badly distort reality—they are all false.[6] Second, he believes not just that we don't have knowledge of this world of becoming but that we can't—those views and theories can't even be improved to secure the truth they seek.[7] Third, he thinks this ineliminable distortion partly and importantly lies in our everyday acceptance of things and in philosophers' positing of substances—there are none.[8] And fourth, he sometimes radicalizes this attack in the way just touched on: we go wrong not only in accepting things or substances but even 'beings'—there are none of these either.[9] Thus we hear two versions each—weaker and stronger forms—of the negative positions in epistemology and ontology.

5. But bear in mind how this note ends: "with this, however, the necessity of alteration has only been posited once more conceptually." The point is also suggested in the Heraclitean line "Everything flows", cited, e.g., at TSZ/III/12/8.

6. See again WP570 [1887–88]. Clark (1990, 107) suggests Nietzsche denies only the philosopher's conception of substance, not the ordinary or scientific notions of things. But HH/I/18, though she cites it, runs against her: "belief in unconditioned substances and in equal things is likewise a more original and ancient error committed by everything organic", one of "the basic human errors". The philosophical elaboration and defense is of a mistake already made pretheoretically. In science, it occurs especially, but not only, as the belief in atoms (ultimate particles), a belief Nietzsche often attacks. See also the GS110 quote in n.8.

7. WP517 [1887]: "The character of the world of becoming as *unformulatable*, as 'false', as 'self-contradictory'. *Knowledge* and *becoming* exclude one another." See also WP520 [1885], WP617 [1886–87], WP715 [1887–88].

8. WP634 [1888]: "there are no things (that is our fiction)". GS110: "Such erroneous doctrines, which were always handed on and finally became almost the basic endowment of the human type, are for example these: that there are enduring things, that there are equal things, that there are things, stuffs, bodies".

9. So TI/III/2: "being is an empty fiction" (for context, see n.10).

I'll develop these claimed implications of becoming more fully as we go. But they make it all the more vital that we press beyond the dim and intuitive sense of the point—that 'change is essential'—with which we begin. Stated so inexactly, it could hardly justify the stress Nietzsche gives it, much less those major results. As we work to interpret the claim, we can use these implications as a test for our reading: we must specify a type of change that can show why Nietzsche might have believed them to follow; we'll naturally allow that he might have been wrong, but should try to attribute to him at least a plausible point.

We immediately associate the theory of flux with Heraclitus, and because Nietzsche, too, takes his point as 'Heraclitean', we can be helped to understand its details by considering that earlier expression of it. This point seems to be Nietzsche's strongest link with the predecessor who seems closest of all to him. From the time he first announces this filiation—in PTAG [1873]—he presents it as the preference for becoming over being.[10] So it will help, in developing what Nietzsche might mean by 'becoming', to take into view how Heraclitus and his interpreters have treated these matters. When we do, we find some of our own issues anticipated in those thoughts and analyses. For example, interpreters sometimes dispute whether Heraclitus does have a theory of flux or becoming,[11] though most take this to be one of his core views. Among the latter, some again take this theory of becoming to have anti-ontological implications: in particular, that Heraclitus isn't a 'material monist' like Anaximenes, only teaching fire instead of air, because he hasn't a 'theory of being' at all.[12] We can profit by glancing often at this largely parallel case.

Moreover, because Nietzsche does feel so close to Heraclitus, we can, with some caution, use his readings of the latter as statements of his own conception of becoming. He announces disagreements as well, and we'll have to learn to carve these away. But consider his strong statement of affinity in EH/BT/3, explaining why only Heraclitus might challenge Nietzsche's own claim to be the first 'tragic philosopher': "I re-

10. He there opens his treatment of Heraclitus by suggesting that the latter made vital progress on the 'problem of being' posed earlier by Anaximander. He has Heraclitus first say, "'Becoming is what I contemplate,' he exclaims, 'and no one has watched so attentively this eternal wavebeat and rhythm of things'" [PTAG5p50: 1873]. He never really shifts from this view. So in TI/III/2, he proclaims "the highest respect" for Heraclitus, later adding (paradoxically): "But Heraclitus will remain eternally right, that being is an empty fiction."

11. Wiggins allows that he has a 'doctrine of universal flux', but says (1982, 26): "the rubbish that philosophers have sometimes talked about rivers or men not being but only becoming seems to be entirely of Plato's and other post-Parmenidean philosophers' confection." (In part, I concur in this and will argue a related point about Nietzsche: he mistakes his own theory as not an ontology, because he takes over the Platonic contrast between 'being' and 'becoming'. But fuller justice must also be done to the strength of argument that prompts this denial of being.) See also Heidegger 1979–87, 1:22; Kirk 1951; Barnes 1982, 69.

12. Kahn 1979, 20.

tained some doubt in the case of *Heraclitus*, in whose proximity I feel altogether warmer and better than anywhere else. The affirmation of passing-away *and destroying*, which is the decisive feature of a Dionysian philosophy; saying Yes to opposition and war; *becoming*, along with a radical repudiation of the very concept of 'being'—I must acknowledge this, in any case, the closest kin to me that has so far been thought." Nietzsche may not always judge this closeness quite rightly, but there really is a deep affinity here, due to both having 'seen the same thing'. We must try to lay out the structure of this view about becoming.

We need more precision in two ways here: What sort of change does Nietzsche have in mind, and just how does he think it essential? It's clear that we need to treat the latter issue as well, because we've already seen that his notion of essence is peculiar: he allows (and even stresses) 'drift from essence'. This suggests we must be prepared for the possibility that beings can rest, even if it's their essence to change; such rest would then be a deficient exception, negatively valued by Nietzsche, rather than denied to exist. But then again, it might also be that he does deny rest (any) existence, being less lenient here in his use of 'essence'. Does he hold, as it sometimes seems, that all apparent rest is just 'relative rest', slow change, and not a genuine exception to change?[13]

The more pressing issue, also still obscure, concerns the notion of change itself. What condition is it, from which there are either no exceptions or only deficient ones? As mentioned, we begin, in § 2.1.1, with the natural assumption that change is 'of beings', that Nietzsche's theory of flux says it's essential to them; this is how he and we ordinarily hear that theory. But it turns out to be hard to state this ordinary version in a strong but plausible way; the ways it seems reasonable to believe that everything changes don't seem to justify those strong hypercritical results Nietzsche draws from his claim. This may explain why others tend not, in that same brief glance at the theory of flux, to take it very seriously and as worth working through. With the help, in § 2.1.2, of a look back at Plato, we'll see, in § 2.1.3, that the power ontology has further, more powerful implications about time and ways for change to be essential, which don't come as easily to mind, and which Nietzsche himself states less often and less directly.

2.1.1 A world 'essentially changing'

Our immediate sense of change, still sometimes shared by Nietzsche as well, is strongly suggested by this way Heraclitus speaks of it: "Cold warms up, warm cools off, moist parches, dry dampens" [DK126]. We

13. WP552 [1887] says that what we call subject and object "are complexes of happening apparently durable in comparison with other complexes—e.g., through the difference in tempo of the happening". WP560 [1887] : "perhaps that which changes slowly [*Langsam-Wechselnde*] presents itself to us as 'objectively' enduring, being, 'in-itself' ".

naturally suppose that this saying intends some quite general point—and general in the sense of applying to everything that is or exists. This point seems to be about change 'of' cold and warm, moist and dry—to be 'of' these beings. Its claim seems to be that every such being passes out of existence, and by 'becoming'—by turning into or being replaced by—a different being. Something like this may well be our first association with change or becoming. Because it's at least sometimes Nietzsche's point, too, we must try to give it more precision.

We might take as another such case the way the green of the apple doesn't last but changes to red. Of course we must also include the way the apple itself is destroyed when it changes (e.g.) into its digested products. Thus change seems to be *being replacement* (so involving both destruction of one and beginning of another), and the claim that such change is essential seems to be the claim that everything has a limited (at both ends) duration or temporal extent. (So note that in this sense, the apple doesn't change simply by virtue of altering in color unless it is thereby destroyed and replaced by something else.) In denying any being opposed to such becoming, Nietzsche would then be claiming that nothing is that has not replaced something else or will not later be replaced itself.

Let's recall two of those hypercritical conclusions Nietzsche draws from becoming: it renders false our everyday and philosophical conceptions of the world—in particular, by ruling out the things or substances they presume. So becoming bears against apples (at least as ordinarily or as traditionally philosophically conceived) in a way that it doesn't against cold or green. The apple needs to be unchanging in a way those others don't—but in a way no being can *not* change. Nietzsche links his theory of becoming so closely with this denial of things that the points sometimes seem to coincide; so in WP538 [1888]: "The teaching of *being*, of the thing, of all sorts of firm unities is *a hundred times easier* than the *teaching* of *becoming*, of development."[14] Since his stress is so often against these things or substances, we might hear him as allowing cold and green in his world of becoming, no longer as qualities of things, but as 'features' of the world, freed from any bearers.

Surprisingly, though, it's disputed whether Heraclitus also infers this denial of things from his theory of flux; some have argued that he doesn't. The latter reading usually goes along with the claim that Plato distorts Heraclitus's view in his famous version of the river image: "Heraclitus somewhere says that everything changes and nothing stays, and likening beings to the flow of a river he says that you could not step twice into the same river" (*Crat.* 402a). It's argued that, despite Plato's testimony here, Heraclitus doesn't take the flow to imply that 'the river'

14. KSA/9/6[433] [1880]: "We speak as if there were *beingful things* [*es seiende Dinge gebe*], and our science speaks only of such things. . . . A becoming, a motion in itself is for us completely inconceivable."

doesn't persist.[15] But if Heraclitus does allow things, this would be an important place at which Nietzsche parts company with him—although unknowingly, because he finds his own view there and accepts that saying from Plato.[16] Thus it would be, oddly, Plato's renderings of Heraclitus (or even of contemporary followers), making him more radical than he is, with which Nietzsche is identifying.

As Nietzsche's theory of flux has been stated so far, however—as the point that every being begins and ends in replacement—it's far from strong enough to support even this narrower attack on things. Such replacement seems true of everyday things and quite consistent with their really existing: the apple is easily seen as replacing whatever it's formed from and as being replaced in turn by its decayed or digested descendents. This shows that Nietzsche, if not Heraclitus, must mean something more than (or some stronger form of) this point about replacement. Why should the fact that every being undergoes change as replacement show that none can be a thing, instead of merely that as a thing it, too, must change (begin and end)? Why should it bear so against both our common sense and our theory, as Nietzsche supposes?

Our immediate sense of the theory suggests that it takes these things or substances to require a special degree of stability—greater than their qualities do—and that it takes the world, as becoming, to change 'too much' to allow such persistence. But along what dimension might this change be too extreme —for things but not for qualities? The answer seems obvious: speed, the world changes 'too quickly' to allow things, which need—perhaps from their defining role as persisting supports of those qualities as they replace one another—to last longer than anything can. A vision of the world as racing along is surely bound up in our first sense of the theory of flux, and presumably in Nietzsche's own. So let's try to say something about how fast this change as replacement is supposed to occur.

At one logical extreme is the point above: every being has at some point come into existence and will eventually pass out—none is eternal. Each being begins and ends in a process of becoming, but the temporal interval between its beginning and end can be specified (in advance)

---

15. Here 'beings' translates *ta onta;* the central contrast is *panta chorei kai ouden menei.* Wiggins argues (1982, 10n.) that if Heraclitus did say this, it was "a hyperbolical restatement of what is said soberly and correctly in B12". See also Kirk 1951; Guthrie 1962, 436–37, 452; Hussey 1972, 55; Kahn 1979, 169, 223. Of course, even Plato's version allows that something identified as a river exists, if only momentarily. So perhaps for Heraclitus to allow 'things', if not 'substances', it's only necessary that his position not be the more extreme version supposedly adopted by Cratylus, who, according to Aristotle, "criticized Heraclitus for saying that it is impossible to step twice into the same river; for *he* thought one cannot do it even once" (*Met.* 1010a13).

16. At PTAG5p52 [1873] he has Heraclitus say, "You use names for things as though they had a fixed duration; yet even the stream into which you step a second time is not the one you stepped into before." See also HH/II/223.

only as finite. Nietzsche does indeed make this claim about beings, and often enough to show that it is important to him; for example in HH/I/2: "But everything has become: there are *no eternal facts*, just as there are no absolute truths."[17] This claim might well seem plausible enough, but we've already seen that it cannot capture the full force of Nietzsche's becoming, because then that theory would hardly support the denial of things, which he so emphatically roots in it. Clearly, whatever philosophers may have supposed about their 'substances', *we* don't suppose that the apple is eternal, and the fact that it's not doesn't render false our everyday belief that it exists (indeed, its existence at *this* time even seems eternally true). To rule this out, the theory of becoming must make some stronger point.

Might this point be, at the other extreme, that every being changes into another 'in every instant'? The theory of becoming would then claim not merely that beings aren't eternal but that they're literally momentary, that each passes away in the 'next' moment after it comes to be. This would explain Nietzsche's inference against things or substances: if nothing lasts more than a moment, nothing lasts longer than anything else; so there can be no persisting supports for changing qualities. However, at least at first sight, this claim of 'change in every instant' suffers the disadvantage of being wildly at odds with our experience. Are we really to imagine the cold changing to warm, or back again, in every moment? The green of the apple lasts more than a moment before it becomes red; the apple surely seems to last, too. Most beings appear not to be merely momentary.

It might seem, then, that we must look for a way to specify change as replacement at some rate slower than constant—somewhere between the extremes of immediate and eventual destruction, thereby in play between the absurd and the unsurprising. But the very notion of such an intermediate rate is puzzling. By what means could Nietzsche think to have discovered such a specific 'speed' of the world? To imagine him attempting to measure the period of time a being persists before being replaced—using his clock for example—is to verge on parody. Nor is it clear how a less empirical method could locate a rate in that middle ground. Indeed, how could there be one rate at which every being is replaced?

Perhaps Nietzsche does 'fix' this speed between those extremes,

17. Notice how often PTAG [1873], e.g., at 4p46 and 5p54, associates being with eternity and permanence. Schacht (1983, 31) stresses this denial of eternity. Kirk (1951) attributes the point to Heraclitus. Perhaps this point is more damaging to our ordinary views about types than to our views about things; so HH/I/2 applies it to "the human being". It may also have more force against how we view values; so TSZ/III/12/8: "'How?' say the blockheads. 'Everything is in flux? Planks and railings are *over* the flux! Everything *over* the flux is firm, all the values of things, the bridges, concepts, all 'good' and 'evil'—all that is *firm!*'"

though only in a looser sense: by saying that in all or most cases it's closer to one side than we tend to suppose or admit. Perhaps he states the length of persistence of beings only in relation to our ordinary and commonest views about it, finding a distorting bias there. Indeed, he stresses that we usually exaggerate the stability of the world and its contents, underestimating how widespread and constant change is and in how many places and at how many levels it occurs.[18] Perhaps he just means to offer a rough corrective to that common tendency, by harping on it so: we must always strive against our innate inclination to understate change. Then it would turn out that we've been expecting too precise and too 'objective' a specification of the rate of becoming; he would mean to fix it only roughly and 'subjectively', by reference to our own ordinary views. The point would be more about us than about the world.

This point might be reinforced by another with a similar effect, another way Nietzsche's claim about constant change might be a looser one. We've already anticipated that he might mean that change is essential only in the weaker sense discovered already in the power ontology. Then even though 'constant replacement' is essential, deficient exceptions—unchanging beings—might still occur. So Nietzsche's attack on stability would have the force of assigning it a lower degree of being, inevitably accompanied by a lesser value. His claim would be that changing beings are 'most real' and that although stable ones exist, it's only in a secondary, inferior way, which renders them less worth our valuing. So perhaps GS357: "We Germans are Hegelians . . . insofar as we (as opposed to all Latins) instinctively attribute a deeper sense and richer value to becoming and development than to what 'is'".

Either of these readings would make Nietzsche's claim about change more plausible. But the same problems arise for both. The less absolute denial that Nietzsche would then be making against stability seems at odds with those hypercritical conclusions he draws from the world's becoming. His denial of things and substances seems absolute: it's not just that they exist more rarely or briefly, or more derivatively, than we usually think; they are quite ruled out. How could those looser denials of rest support such an absolute exclusion? They would also make it puzzling why knowledge should be impossible. Couldn't we compensate for our tendency to underestimate change? Moreover, even if Nietzsche's denial of stability does say merely that it occurs more rarely or secondarily than we usually think, we still need to see how he would justify even this weaker claim. He must still have some argument to show that

18. He often suggests that our senses are first to blame for this; they already present the world as more constant than it is. Pragmatic motives reinforce this overestimation of stability. A certain cowardice makes it even stronger in some: "[Metaphysicians] have feared *change, transitoriness:* this expressed a straitened soul, full of mistrust and bad experience" [WP576: 1888].

they pass 'quickly', even if his point is only that they pass 'more quickly' than we usually suppose. And he still needs some argument for privileging this quickness as essential, even if he allows that it's not universal.

Thus we still need to find some way in which 'constant change' might look plausible. There are two main further points here that separately and together encourage Nietzsche to hold this view.

The first main point has two stages; it lies in a counteranalysis of the apple (a) as a whole with parts, and (b) as having parts of a certain kind.

a. This general part-whole analysis, compared with that of a thing or substance with qualities, tends to highlight change and to promote doubts against constancy. To be sure, there may be ways to combine these analyses: perhaps the apple could be both whole *and* substance. But a stress on the former model can so magnify change as to undermine confidence that there's anything persisting enough to satisfy the latter model. If the apple is crucially a whole with parts, and of parts so small as to lie beneath our senses' discrimination, then surely some of them will be changing. And the whole is not insulated from this change, as the thing is from change in its qualities. Change in parts is change in the very composition of the whole, whereas change in qualities is change in mere accessories to the substance. Thus we find that these opposite extremes are at least thinkable: any change in parts must change the whole, but even a change in all qualities might not change the substance. Because of this difference, the part-whole model can be used to coopt the other model and erode its insulation, by explaining change in qualities as due to changes in parts, hence symptoms of changes within the subject itself. (Or it may encourage thinking of those features as themselves parts.) Nietzsche employs this first strategy principally when he argues against any ego substance by stressing the multiplicity of drives that compose us.[19]

Heraclitus states this part-whole analysis in DK10, which has the air of an ontological crux (we'll return to it in 2.1.3): "Takings-together: wholes and not wholes, converging diverging, singing-together singing-apart, from all one and from one all." He famously employs this model to argue for flux in DK12, the other and better-accepted statement of his compelling river image: "As they step into the same rivers, other and still other waters flow upon them." Although this statement seems to allow that a river does persist—so that some take it as evidence that Heraclitus allows enduring things—its suggestion of a part-whole model and its stress on change in the parts are at least designed to shake and refigure our trust in any such continuing. So the river image mainly serves that first strategy.[20]

19. WP490 [1885] proposes "the subject as multiplicity". Nietzsche thinks our mistaken faith in the ego is the original source of that substance model; so WP635 [1888]: "If we did not hold ourselves to be unities, we would never have formed the concept 'thing'." See also WP485 [1887].
20. See n.15.

b. In addition to this, Heraclitus offers a specific account of those parts that reinforces their liability to change; this is a second stage to that counteranalysis. Again, he offers the point in an image: "They do not comprehend how it agrees while differing with itself; it is an attunement turning back on itself, like that of the bow and the lyre" (DK51). So his wholes' parts are opposing-yet-agreeing forces, and (we find elsewhere) forces thus 'directed' at one another in an intentional sense: they strive for and against one another. These Heraclitean opposites seem simpler cousins to Nietzsche's wills to power.[21]

We've already seen how Nietzsche's power ontology not only uses that part-whole, compositional model but also analyzes those parts as forces—telic units struggling intentionally, for themselves and against one another. These constituting forces, wills to power, serve him as an ever-running engine for change insofar as they inherently tend or try to change, to overcome their present. As we and he might well suppose, if a force will change unless it is in balance against an equal opposing force, and if quite equal balances are likely to be rare and fleeting, then change may well be the usual condition of things.[22]

However, this first line of argument can't really clinch the conclusion of a constant change that rules out things. We can see this from Heraclitus's case: he does, or we can see that he consistently could, allow the bow to persist despite being formed of opposing forces, and the river to persist despite its change in parts. As we saw in first introducing this strategy, it gives no real reason why the whole with its parts couldn't also be a thing with qualities. There's an obvious way to reconcile these models: take the thing's identity to lie in a structure or organization—in its form, not its matter. Heraclitus's key term *logos* can be heard to express this point. Wholes can persist, by maintaining rough balances between their constituting forces (the bow) or between their efflux and influx of parts (the river).[23] So when Nietzsche insists that there are no things and takes changes in even the smallest parts to imply changes in the wholes, he must have some further ground for his more radical lesson.[24]

We can approach Nietzsche's second main point once again through Heraclitus. In a fragment quoted previously, he speaks of cold warming, and we interpreted this to mean the cold becoming warm. But perhaps this misled us, by inducing us to think of change as across an interval or

21. On intentionality in Heraclitus, see n.70.

22. KSA/9/11[281] [1881]: "In absolute becoming force can never rest, *never* be unforce". WP715 [1887–88], explaining becoming: "*there is no will:* there are treaty drafts of will that are continually increasing or losing their power".

23. This route is more clearly taken, and more elaborately charted, by Aristotle. Compositional (material) change is overriden by functional (formal) continuity. Whereas Heraclitus presents the formal, organizing power—his *logos*—as a generalized cosmic principle, Aristotle catalogs it in a host of species forms.

24. This disagreement about things is part of Nietzsche's main complaint against Heraclitus—over his insistence on *logos* and law; cf. WP412 [1886–87].

as between separate 'ranges', such as warm and cold seem to be. We can't believe in an oscillation between these 'in every moment'. Yet there's still a way we can find constant change in these cases: any water might always be growing either colder or warmer, always varying, if minutely, in its 'temperature', where this is now identified not just as a range, such as the range of 'cold' or 'warm', but as (or to) a quite precise degree. If the real beings are (individuated as) *points* along this and other continua, along continuous processes, we could better believe that they constantly replace one another.

It may be doubted that Heraclitus intended his image to convey so much content. Although the river image, captured by his successors in the phrase 'all beings flow', is well suited to bring out this constant gradualness of change, it's debatable whether Heraclitus himself meant this to be an analysis of all beings (and even whether he concludes that the river doesn't persist). The notion of infinite divisibility, which so reinforces this thought (suggesting, for example, how even stones might 'flow'), seems absent from Heraclitus, though familiar to those successors.[25]

The argument about continuous processes might first occur to us in epistemological form: our senses aren't fine-tuned enough to discern the gradual changes in beings. But as such, it stands open to a natural reply: these imperceptible processes could still 'keep within' the broad boundaries we draw with our concepts, for example, within that range of temperature points we call 'warm'; in this case, won't the thing's temperature continue to be warm? So the argument must take an ontological turn if it is to deny the reality of these broadly bounded beings.

The argument tries to erase these conceptual boundaries—to show them arbitrary, not marking any real divisions—by citing the continuum. For any boundary points we might mark, there are points 'outside' that are only infinitesimally different from them that we have no good reason to exclude. So GS112 says that with our concepts of cause and effect, "we have merely perfected the image of becoming without reaching above the image or behind it . . . there is probably never such a duality [as cause and effect]; in truth a continuum stands before us, out of which we isolate a couple of pieces". The only nonarbitrary way to mark boundaries along a continuum is at every point. So those 'ranges' like cold or green, within which constant process might (for a time) be contained, are not real beings. This argument can be extended to (for example) the apple, which at first seems not to lie along any such continuum; we can find one by reconceiving the arc of its origin, applehood, and decay as a continuous process not aptly divisible into any such ranges. This being needs to be individuated down to those quite particu-

25. See Kirk 1951 against, and Guthrie 1962 for, taking Heraclitus to teach constant change. Aristotle (*Phy.* VIII/3) rebuts the argument from infinite divisibility to constant change.

lar versions of applehood that this process traverses. The only real beings, then, are momentary ones. The argument leads to an insistence on
precise degree.[26]

This gives us a full first reading of Nietzsche's theory of becoming,
taken as a theory that beings are constantly changing. He thinks this
because, first, this world consists of forces in struggle against one
another, so that all those 'things' we're chiefly concerned with are really
just tenuous balances of multiple forces, and, second, this world is continuous in such a way that there's no nonarbitrary way to draw borders
around beings except at every 'point'. The first claim reinforces the second: given that beings are precisely individuated, the analysis of things
as wholes with parts allows any change in a part to change the whole;
moreover, the account of the parts as forces is meant to suggest an
infinite divisibility, in contrast with an atomist matter. But the second
claim bears the greater weight. Without it, those forces could well generate constant process—yet this process could often keep within the broad
boundaries of beings, and so not be identity depriving (not change as
replacement). The green could stay green, the apple an apple—and not
have to stay that precise shade of green or that precise specimen of apple.

The importance of that second argument raises an interesting problem, however: now the central feature of the theory of flux won't be an
especially temporal point after all. This continuum argument is applica-
ble in other ways than along a temporal dimension (to processes). The
world is gradual in other respects, and these will serve just as well to rule
out things and knowledge as that temporal point will. Thus the argument is as easily applied across space as through time: to rule out any
nonarbitrary borders between beings adjacent in space, instead of between those succeeding one another in time. The argument concludes
that spatial beings are points, saying nothing about how long these last;
this spatial constriction of beings would also rule out 'things'.[27] More
basically, the argument applies (neither spatially nor temporally but) to

26. P&Tp43 [1872–73]: "Nature's *infinity*: it has no boundaries anywhere.
Only for us is anything finite. Time itself is *infinitely* divisible." KSA/9/11[156] [1881]
speaks of "the secret, that there is no individual, that in the smallest moment it is
something other than in the next". KSA/9/11[281] [1881]: "A continuum of force is
without after-one-another and *without next-to-one-another* (the human intellect presupposes this, and gaps between things)." WP520 [1885]: "Constant transitions
forbid us to speak of 'individuals', etc.; the 'number' of beings [*Wesen*] is itself in
flux." See also HH/III/11. KSA/9/11[293] [1881] adds the epistemological point:
"The tree is in every moment something *new*: the *form* is maintained by us, because
we cannot perceive the finest absolute movement". See also KSA/9/11[149] [1881].

27. Nietzsche's replacement of atoms with forces is (partly) meant to convey
that there are no smallest particles; thus not even atoms can be things. BGE12 credits
Boscovich with doing away with the atom. WP715 [1887–88]: "there are no durable
ultimate unities, no atoms, no monads: here too 'beings' are only *introduced* by us
(from practical, useful, perspectival grounds)."

'types': because no two beings are exactly similar, none can properly be classed together under our concepts; each being is a kind only to itself. So Nietzsche stresses the specificity and uniqueness of all beings: all likenings are false, because even infinitesimal differences differentiate.[28] We find here a strong version of the familiar slogan 'Everything is what it is, and not another thing'. This attack on types undermines our use of concepts and threatens the possibility of knowledge, even apart from any point about change. But note again the oddity of this: the most decisive argument in Nietzsche's theory of becoming won't be about time after all.

That argument has a more serious disadvantage: in all these applications it just fails to convince us. The standards by which it judges our ways of bounding beings or types seem unreasonably high; we feel that it works by an artificial inflation here, by an overpreciseness. Consider how the argument applies to the types 'bud' and 'flower': even if there's no one best point to mark off the first from the second, we take these to reflect a real difference in the world, which it's knowledge to note and ignorance to deny. We're inclined to concede the continuum between them but to allow both, as types with imprecise borders yet many clear cases, into our accounts of the world. So this argument doesn't convince us that the things of our everyday views don't exist and endure. We may grant one by one all these points about change yet take their lesson to be only that we need to revise our conception of these things, not disown them altogether. Don't our references to apples only need to be spoken and heard in a different sense, to be reinterpreted? Hasn't Nietzsche really just shown that they're complex composites rather than simple substances, and with imprecise boundaries in many respects, including at their temporal beginnings and ends?

There's another problem with rooting the theory of becoming too much in the continuum argument, a problem that has from the start threatened our reading of becoming as constant change. In this temporal application of the argument—and in this whole temporal assault on things—the ultimate object of Nietzsche's attack isn't touched. Not only does this argument seem to allow beings, as what constant change occurs between, but it even seems to multiply them infinitely: every precise, momentary condition is now a being in its own right, though none lasts for more than a moment. Yet becoming was supposed to rule out beings.

28. TL [P&Tp83: 1873]: "Every concept arises through the setting equal of the unequal. Just as it is certain that one leaf is never wholly equal to another, so it is certain that the concept leaf is formed by arbitrarily discarding these individual differences and by forgetting the distinguishing [aspects]". WP521 [1887]: "the form has merely been invented by us; and however often 'the same form is attained', it does not mean that it *is the same* form—*what appears is always something new*". See also HH/I/11,19.

Thus the theory of becoming, in this version we've detailed, seems neither sufficiently convincing nor sufficiently strong to support all the claims Nietzsche bases on it. Can we find any further sense for it? Perhaps we've by now exhausted Heraclitus's usefulness for us and need to turn for help to some other thinker who addresses these issues less oracularly and more systematically. Plato treats in more detail the topics before us, and we may hope for refreshment and progress by turning aside to see how. We'll learn important lessons from him, to bring back to our project of clarifying Nietzsche in § 2.1.3.

2.1.2   Plato's attack on becoming

As we judge Nietzsche's break from metaphysics, the comparison with Plato has special importance.[29] We have a certain natural model for their relationship: it's Plato's reaction against Heraclitus's vision of a world of becoming that launches—and best represents—the metaphysical tradition Nietzsche means to reject. Although Plato agrees that the world about us merely becomes and never is, he posits another world whose unchangingness gives it the highest ontological status: it alone fully or really is. Nietzsche then denounces this timeless world as a fabrication, one that has infected, in various forms, all of Plato's successors as well. Against this whole metaphysical tradition, it seems, he reaffirms Heraclitus's original vision of a real becoming. Let's consider this simple and familiar model for Nietzsche's break from Plato. Surely it must be roughly right, but how should we state its specifics?

On this model, Nietzsche's reversal of Plato takes place on the ground of two crucial agreements with him, and here at least that model seems well supported by texts. First, Plato shares with Nietzsche a certain 'meta-ontology'; the deep structures of their positions are partly parallel. Each has a theory of reality crucially characterized in temporal terms, whether as being (Plato) or as becoming (Nietzsche). Each thinks of his reality as gradational, as capable of different degrees of realization. And for each, these grades of reality are also grades of value. So the most real is the best and is picked out as such by its distinctive temporal character.[30] Second, they also share a specific temporal account of the sensible

29. In these notes, I try to 'place' my reading of Plato by discussing especially its relations to those of G. E. L. Owen and Gregory Vlastos. Some might prefer to skip the involved discussion of Plato that follows and to resume with Nietzsche in § 2.1.3.

30. Owen argues (1953) that in the *Republic* Plato denies that change 'is' because of "muddles about existence" that he later sees through; but Fine (1988, 377f.) shows how Owen himself later sees (1970) that in denying being, Plato is not denying existence. Vlastos (1965, 1966) argues that Plato thinks of 'being' as gradational, because he means by it not existence but (what Vlastos plausibly calls) 'reality'—fully existing things' genuineness as the kinds of things they seem to be. He offers (1966, 11–12) two points in analysis of this 'reality': a real *F* is a cognitively reliable *F* and a

world, as one of becoming or flux; moreover, they agree in inferring from this that the world can have no beings, nor any things, and also can't be known. Plato concurs in drawing those same skeptical and nihilist lessons about a world of becoming that we attributed to Nietzsche in § 2.1.1.[31]

Nietzsche himself sees his relation to Plato this way. He takes Plato to have recognized and experienced the world's hard reality as becoming, but to have then been too weak for this insight, expressing a weakness and misdirection typical (Nietzsche thinks) of his society's declining phase. TI/X/2: "Plato is a coward before reality, *consequently* he flees into the ideal".[32] He retreats from properly facing this unsettling feature of reality, distracting and consoling himself by imagining another world that above all does not change or become. Nietzsche, standing before the same questions, claims for himself the courage and honesty to give them opposite answers.

All of this makes it natural for him to take over Plato's terms for framing these issues, in particular 'being' and 'becoming' themselves. Yet, from what we've already seen of that meta-ontological structure he shares with Plato, his consequent statement of his point as a denial of any being can't mean as much as we might have supposed. Nietzsche's very replacement of 'being' with 'becoming' occurs within a theory of reality, of the world's true nature; in a broader sense of 'being', it still belongs to a theory of such. It was presumably Parmenides who first appropriated 'being' (and associated forms of the verb 'to be') for that narrower use, that partisan restriction to the stable, laying this over its broader reference to the world's real or true character (whatever temporal form this might have). Plato trades on both senses in effecting his elevation of the unchanging Forms to highest ontological status. And, it

---

reliably valuable *F*; we've seen and will see that Nietzsche shares these meta-ontological criteria. In a note, Vlastos mentions a third "part of the meaning, expressed by Plato's phrase 'being in itself' in contrast to 'being in another'"; I try to develop this sense in this section.

31. *Tim.* 27d–8a: "That which is apprehended by intelligence and reason is always in the same state, but that which is conceived by opinion with the help of sensation and without reason is always in a process of becoming and perishing and never really is." *Phil.* 59a says that the scientist falls short of the clear, precise, and true, because he "takes on a project concerning what becomes and will become and has become, and not concerning what always is." See also *Rep.* 479a–e; *Crat.* 440a–b. We'll see that Plato varies in how strongly he states these hypercritical lessons and in how strictly he takes being and becoming to exclude one another.

32. WP572 [1886–87]: "Plato, as the artist he was, basically *preferred appearance* to being: hence lie and invention to truth, the unreal to the present-at-hand—but he was so convinced of the value of appearance that he gave it the attributes 'being', 'causality', and 'goodness', truth". See WP435 [1888] and WP427 [1888] on Plato's decadence. But also note the admission in WP374 [1887] that "Plato . . . becomes a caricature with me."

now seems, this misleads Nietzsche into supposing his theory of becoming to be not an ontology at all.

Let's look more closely: Do they really mean the same thing by 'becoming'? It's here that we've hoped to grasp Nietzsche better by a look at Plato. But turning to the latter, we at first find little new to help us. Like Nietzsche, Plato often refers the point to Heraclitus, so much so that he often rather presumes a sense for 'becoming', instead of explaining or analyzing it.[33] He casually develops the point as being about change or motion, which he presents with some of the structure we analyzed in § 2.1.1. Thus in the *Symposium* 207d–e, things change because they are vast composites of constantly changing parts: "[A person], while never having the same [features? parts?] in itself [*ta auta echon en hauto*], is called the same. But he always becomes new, perishing in those: in his hair and flesh and bones and blood and all of his body. And not only in his body, but his soul." Although Plato (in his character Diotima) doesn't make clear how often this replacement of the person occurs, we easily hear him (in his 'always', perhaps) to mean constantly, in every moment; thus we sense the continuum argument here: since change is along continua and the slightest change in the slightest part changes the whole, no being lasts more than a moment.[34]

However, we've already pressed this whole line—about beings as constantly changing—as far as we could see how to do. We suspected in § 2.1.1 that the argument really serves to multiply beings (though infinitesimal and inexperienceable ones) rather than to rule them out. We were unconvinced by its conclusions against ordinary (macroscopic) things and against knowledge; these latter hypercritical results seemed

33. Aristotle stresses the importance of this reaction against Heraclitus; he begins the *Metaphysics*'s account of Plato: "having in his youth first become familiar with Cratylus and with the Heraclitean doctrines (that all sensible things are ever in a state of flux and there is no knowledge about them), these views he held even in later years" (987a31). See also his *Met.* 1078b12. Plato might suggest at *Tht.* 179e–80d, how indefinite a conception he can find in the Heracliteans.

34. *Tht.* 166b raises (on Protagoras's behalf) the doubt whether "a person who is made unlike, is the same as he was before, or rather, that he is a person, and not persons, becoming indeed indefinitely many, as the making-unlike becomes". *Phil.* 43a: "it's necessary that one of these [pleasure and pain] is always happening in us, as the wise say, since all beings are always flowing up and down." See also *Crat.* 439e. And note how *Tht.* 159b employs that model of wholes to magnify change: "*Tht.* / You mean, is the ill Socrates taken as a whole like Socrates in health taken as a whole? *Soc.* / . . . that is just what I mean. *Tht.* / . . . he is unlike. *Soc.* / And consequently, inasmuch as he is unlike, a different being? *Tht.* / Necessarily." *Phd.* 78c shows how closely Plato associates destructibility with being a synthesis of parts. Cf. Owen's spatial analogue to an argument about time that he finds in Aristotle: "there is no reason to stop at any of these arbitrary and dwindling frontiers in trying to determine what really answers to 'here'" (1976, 13); Owen takes Aristotle to think such an argument would fragment time into momentary nows—except for a further argument given in n.47.

to be achieved only by an insistence on overpreciseness.[35] Is there anything else?

Another reason for looking further for Plato's notion of becoming is that he seems in certain later works to conclude (if he ever did hold otherwise) that the sensible world is not subject to such constant change after all. Although he still thinks this world unknowable, and still because it becomes rather than (fully) is, he now often puts these hypercritical claims in less extreme ways: sensibles *are*, but to a lesser degree, and we can at least have true belief about them.[36]

The *Theaetetus* and the *Cratylus* make the negative case. The first attacks a radical flux theory of constant (in every moment) change in every respect. It shows that this view contradicts the earlier-claimed equation of knowing and perceiving (which it was introduced to support); moreover, it undermines not just that claim but any claim one might try to ground in it. It undermines the very activity of claiming, all truth-seeking discourse: "if all beings change [*panta kineitai*], any answer one might give about anything is equally correct" (*Tht.* 183a). But (arguably) this attack is only against an extreme form of flux, associated less with Heraclitus and more with some wilder followers.[37] Similarly, the *Cratylus* argues against the view "that all things pass over [*metapiptei panta chremata*] and none remains". This view entails not just that there can be no knowledge but that indeed there is "no one to know and nothing to be known" (440a–b). But again the attack may be against an extreme Heracliteanism, for which Cratylus himself was of course noted.[38]

Both attacks argue the incomprehensibility and even incoherence of an utterly temporally atomized world, none of whose features (even very general ones) lasts more than a moment and which no predicates

35. Compare how Owen (1953, 86) takes Plato to argue that process is analyzable into states; he cites *Parm.* 152b–d and *Tht.*'s 'atomizing' of perception into a succession of *aistheta* and *aistheseis*. He makes this part of his evidence that (late) Plato rejects "the disjunction of *genesis* and *ousia* in the form propounded by the *Timaeus*''. I try to show that Plato instead means to revise his notion of becoming, precisely by binding those moments together into 'processes'.

36. Famously, Owen (1953) takes Plato to renounce flux in the late critical dialogues, and he explains the *Timaeus*'s acceptance of it by redating that dialogue into the middle period. It seems better to distinguish senses of flux; cf. Fine 1988, 79.

37. Because flux is specified in this extreme way only in the course of the final attack, some of the *Tht.*'s earlier account of flux could survive that attack, in particular, whatever does not render all speech false. So I take parts of that account as positive evidence below. See how Burnyeat (1990, 45ff.) surveys this way of reading the dialogue, in contrast to another (which Burnyeat prefers) that denies that Plato accepts Heraclitus's account of the world. Contrast (with the following) Bostock's account (1988, 108–9) of the 'more moderate thesis' he thinks Plato might assent to in Heraclitus.

38. Indeed, the *Crat.* might attack only the view that flux is universal, and so rules out Forms; it might allow that it applies to the sensible world.

can continue to describe. But the very extremity of this view may make us doubtful Plato ever believed it himself. Its hypercritical conclusion is easily separable from most of his accounts of becoming, including those in the *Theaetetus* itself. So these attacks instead belong (I think) to Plato's effort to work out a more plausible and fruitful sense for 'becoming' than its loudest advocates had. In particular, he means to give becoming a type of regularity, and a type of persistence or being, that will better fit our experience of it.

The *Timaeus* supplies some of the positive story, of a less extreme becoming. It tells how an original chaos, perhaps that radical flux, is ordered by the Demiurge into *our* world. This creation includes standardizing (as atomlike geometrical shapes) basic units for the world, setting up a 'clock' in the divinely moving heavens (thus standardizing also basic units for time), and infusing the world with soul. Because of this ordering, we can at least have true belief about the world, though still not knowledge. So the world is still one of becoming but no longer ineffably, inexpressibly so; that constant change in every respect is no longer the case.[39] Before we can understand what these specific orderings accomplish, however, we need to reapproach Plato's general notion of becoming; it has aspects not yet accounted for, in that story about constant change.

We get a clue to these further aspects when we reflect on the temporal status he attributes to the Forms, understood as what doesn't become. The Forms don't merely persist unchangingly through time, as that constant-change account would suggest. Sometimes, indeed, Plato presents the contrast that way—for example, in *Symposium* 208a–b: "In this way every mortal being preserves itself: not by being always in every way the same, like the divine, but by the departing and aged being leaving behind a different being such as it itself was." (From the context, quoted above, this applies not just to parents and children but to those successive selves through which even 'one' life passes.) Here, what we want is to continue, through all time, the same. However, this isn't quite the condition of the Forms themselves; it's not just that they don't change in time but that they're not 'in' time at all. So the *Timaeus* (37e–38a) explicitly presents 'eternity' [*aion*] as without temporal parts or properties. The intervals marked by regular heavenly motions "are all parts of time, and the was and the will be are forms of time that become, which we forgetfully apply to the eternal being [*aidion ousian*], incorrectly. For we say that it was, is, and will be, but only the is belongs to it, by the true account."[40] Because eternity is most strictly not permanence

---

39. Plato hints, with his claim that not just *kosmos* but *chronos* comes only as a later construction on or out of that radical flux, that the extreme Heracliteanism isn't really about time after all; there could be no time in the world it imagines.

40. Owen (1966) diagnoses Plato as here importing a mistake from Parmenides: the attempt to magnify unchangingness beyond mere permanence, by

but this more radical removal from time, we ought to suspect that becoming might not be merely impermanence or changeableness, either. If being is not not changing, becoming must not be (just) changing.

Many of Plato's treatments of becoming speak often of 'same' (*autos*) and 'different' (*heteros*), which can serve as a further clue: might Plato have in mind some more general point about these?[41] Perhaps 'being' means being in 'all' ways the same, with persistence through time merely one type of sameness. And perhaps 'becoming' applies to many other ways of 'differing', besides changing through time. That Plato gives these concepts 'same' and 'different' an extremely basic status, is evident in the *Sophist* and the *Timaeus*. In the first, they're the 'vowels'—along with being itself—by means of which all beings (including these three themselves) stand in their relations to one another. In the latter, they're the 'stuff'—again, along with being—from which souls are formed.[42] But exactly what might Plato mean by 'same' and 'different'? Other than by changing, how can things be 'not the same'? I think there are three most important points, further senses for 'becoming' than the change we've so far considered.

We can approach the first point through a related one developed by Irwin: Plato often links the Heraclitean flux not with this change as replacement, but with 'aspect change' or 'compresence of opposites'. He raises cases in which something 'differs with itself' not by changing through time but by having at the same time aspects in conflict. Indeed, Irwin argues, whereas Heraclitus made both points about the world, Plato means only the second; his 'becoming'—at least insofar as this precludes knowledge—isn't (what we call) change after all.[43] So (now leaving Irwin) things that become, are things that are F but also not-F, having but also not having (all of) their features. We think to call a thing F, but can always find it to be in an another way not-F: the tree seems tall, until we think to compare it to the mountain. Everything turns out

---

counting even time's passage as a sort of change; Owen thinks this reduces that concept to a mere 'logical torso' (335), its insufficiency reflected in Plato's continual slide back into speaking of it as permanence. But just as Owen's complaint against denying being to change rests on a misreading of being as existence, so his complaint against denying 'in-timeness' to the Forms, might rest on a misconception of what *sort* of subjection to time Plato has in mind. See n.46. See also Sorabji's review (1983, 108–12) of Plato's waverings between the atemporal and omnitemporal points.

41. Compare the role played by 'same' in the arguments at *Phd.* 78–79. The weight and the sense I give to the notion of 'difference' owe an obvious debt to Derrida.

42. See *Soph.* 254e and following, and *Tim.* 35a–b.

43. Irwin 1977a; 1977b, 148ff. The point is originally due to Owen (1957, 108), who develops compresence as a consequence (for Plato) of the incompleteness of some predicates. Note that both Owen and Irwin take Plato to apply compresence only to a restricted range of predicates, so as to generate Forms only for these.

to be less-F than it could be, thus not a real or full F after all. And so for any other way we might try to say what it is; sensible things are never anything with the thoroughness Plato thus means by 'same'.

It's puzzling that Plato should refer to this compresence as 'becoming'. The crux seems not about change or time at all but about what we might call the 'relativity' of features: we can't assign F-ness to x unequivocally, because it's F toward y but not toward z, or F by comparison with y but not with z. Change and time seem to enter in only secondarily, as we imagine turning from one way of seeing the thing to the other. Only thus do these aspects 'change': features that are themselves cotemporal succeed one another as objects of our view. But, we take it, the point is really about those conflicting features themselves not our discoverings of them: things bear these differences simultaneously, whether or not we manage to see them that way. So why should time be especially stressed?

Moreover, if this is Plato's point, it seems much too weak for the work it must do: to rule out the (full) reality and knowability of the sensible world. Surely it only shows that a thing's features must be stated more specifically, as particular relations; we mustn't think of the tree as simply tall but as taller than *these* other things. Is it not, quite unequivocally, each of these? Can't we securely know it as such? It seems our theories of things only need to be thus specified, to match this more detailed structure of their relationships. We can easily know them as having these conflicting aspects. So does Plato's complaint against the sensible world rest on a rather simple mistake?

Behind this point about compresent relative features lies a more radical one, a first main idea Plato may mean by 'difference' and 'becoming'. I call it *relationalism* or *contextuality*. Perhaps his thinking is aimed a bit differently here, his point not just that these relations conflict but that any sensible thing is constituted by such relations, so that its very identity is diffused outside itself, into its context of others. So (e.g.) there's no height to the tree apart from those countless comparisons with other things; all the facts about the tree (including its treeness) lie in these patterns of similarity and difference; there's no way it is in or by itself. Then Plato would mean by the contrasting 'sameness' of the Forms their being something 'in their own right', and not just relationally, in their 'differences'. So it's not just that the Forms stand in the same relations to every other but that their relations aren't constitutive or 'internal' to them. It's in this sense that a Form is, but a sensible being is not, *auto kath hauto* (itself by itself).[44]

44. The rendering of *auto kath hauto* with 'itself by itself' unfortunately hides the link with 'sameness'. Other uses of the phrase to characterize the Forms are *Sym.* 211a–b and *Rep.* 516b. Sameness and difference do double duty for Plato. On the one hand, they point respectively to the in-itselfness of being and the contextuality of becoming. But they also serve as the main relations that constitute contextuality: a sensible thing's identity lies not just in its differences from others but in its similarities

This account of becoming makes the point look strong enough to do the work Plato assigns it: if this is what he means, we can better see why he denies that what becomes either is or is knowable. If we can't think a (sensible) being is some way in itself, how are we to go on to think of it as related to others? What is it, to be related to them—and what are they, to be related to it? The task of knowing such an interdefined world is daunting; we seem barred from finding any first grip on it. This account of becoming can also help explain the puzzling way the *Theaetetus* connects the Heraclitean flux with a Protagorean relativism, as well as why it introduces the former as "the theory that nothing is one, itself by itself" (152d). This point is elaborated in the perception theory, which stresses the relationality of *aistheseis* and *aistheta*. It's suggested elsewhere, too.[45]

This account might also explain why the Forms' eternity should be not just unchangingness but timelessness: to be 'in' time, means to have (all) one's features 'relative to' the times at which one has them, even if one were to have them unceasingly. So the Forms are 'outside' time, in the sense that they escape this specifically temporal contextualization.[46]

(above all to the Forms). This 'sameness within difference' is not that metaphysical sameness but 'similarity' (even if exact). Plato's concern for contextuality would explain his interest in the 'incomplete predicates' Owen stresses (1957, 107ff.). Cf. Nehamas 1975, 116: "what distinguishes sensible particulars from Forms is the fact that particulars possess their properties only in an incomplete manner, only in relation to other particulars, while the Forms possess them completely, in themselves". (Note that Nehamas, like Owen and Irwin, limits the point to *some* properties.) This suggests that Fine's (1988, 387ff.) shifting of weight from incompleteness to compresence (of opposites) carries us away from Plato's crux.

45. *Tht.* 157a–b: "there is nothing, as we said at the outset, which is one, itself by itself; but everything always becomes [in relation] to something. So 'being' must everywhere be removed." But see McDowell's (1973, 123ff.) denial that the relational point should be heard in 'becoming'. They indeed seem distinguished in *Tht.* 160b: "Hence, whether you apply the term 'being' to something or the term 'becoming', you must always say 'for somebody' or 'of something' or 'towards something'. You must not speak of anything as in itself [*auto eph hauto*] either being or becoming." *Soph.* 247d–e: "I say that what possesses any sort of power—whether its nature is to make something different or to be affected even slightly by something minor, and even if only once—that every such thing really is [*ontos einai*]." It might be clearer that Plato at least thought sensible things to be 'relational' in having their features through relations to the Forms. And *Tim.* 52a might ascribe nonrelationality to Forms: "never receiving anything into itself from without, nor itself going out to any other".

46. So the Forms still can, as we might put it, exist 'alongside' time, and be described as permanent with respect to it, so long as all such datings of them are realized to be quite 'external' to their identity (in contrast with the case of sensible things). (They still stand, we might say, in relations to time, but only in relations that terminate on them not ones that diffuse their identity outside them.) This can help explain and excuse Plato's waverings between timelessness and permanence; perhaps it can also help against Owen's criticisms (1966), which attack a different type of removal from time than Plato might mean.

But now once we've noticed this temporal application of the context point, we can easily see reason to give it special importance: it can help explain why Plato so often expresses the context point as one about time and change (and why he also sometimes distinguishes them), if it's this application of the point that comes first to his mind. We might even count it as another sense for becoming, in its own right.

A second main idea Plato might mean by 'difference' and 'becoming' is that a sensible being is defined by the context of its own past and future states: it is, but only in its relations to what it was and will be. So we shouldn't posit moments as if these were self-sufficient or complete in themselves. There's no way that these beings are in the moment, but they're this as having been that and as going to be still something else; their identities lie in their emerging from this and becoming that. What really is, in this world, are processes: 'becomings'. Instead of claiming that (sensible) beings change—even that they change in every moment—the theory of becoming says that these beings *are changes*. It denies not just unchanging beings but even momentary ones; reality consists in structure through time.[47]

Like the more general context claim, this process claim makes a radical change in our view of the world; thus again we can see why we (and Plato) might conclude that such a world's parts can't be said to *be* or to be known. If we can't pin down how any moment is, how can we even begin to understand its relations to moments before and after? There is evidence of this point, too, in Plato. Even his uses of *gignesthai* suggest it; the term is well suited to state the reality of process. We can also hear it in *Theaetetus* 156a: "the principle on which all that we have just been saying also depends, namely, that everything is really change, and there is nothing else besides this". Indeed, when the perception theory that follows interprets those interrelated *aistheseis* and *aistheta* as motions, we can hear it as fusing the context and process points.[48]

Although these processes may not be knowable, because they can't be analyzed into their parts, they can still be more accessible to us than those splintered moments, in the (radical Heraclitean) story of constant change. A process lasts and can be described; it binds those moments together into a continuing 'being'. It's precisely this, the continuing 'white flow', that the radical flux view denies (*Tht.* 182d), a denial that lands it in absurdity or incoherence. By deciding differently here himself, Plato can rescue another, more fruitful sense for becoming. However, this raises a new puzzle: How are these moments thus connected so that

47. Compare the argument Owen (1976, 20) attributes to Aristotle, in answer to the paradox of time as splintered into moments: "there cannot be temporal points—'nows'—without periods that terminate in such points"; cf. n.34.

48. *Tht.* 157a: "all beings, or all kinds, become through intercourse with one another, as the result of change." *Tim.* 38a: "'was' and 'will be' are only to be spoken of becoming in time, for they are changes".

reality no longer falls apart into them? What explains these processes' persistence?

I think the answer lies in a third main idea we can hear in Plato's treatments of becoming, one that reinforces the first two but also reconceives them. We reach it by reconsidering our recent reduction of aspect change to compresence: perhaps the way that aspect change *is* change—in the shift of our view from one aspect to another—is more revealing of Plato's intent than we thought. When he thinks of flux, he thinks first of the flux of perspectives: of the way one can never hold a steady view on worldly things. So *Tht.* 152d continues: "nothing is one, itself by itself, and you can't correctly call it anything, or any sort of thing, but if you say big, it also appears small, and if heavy, light."[49] We supposed that these shifts were dictated by the nature of the objects in view, and we looked there for a type of becoming we might (now retrospectively) call 'objective'. But what if Plato's notion of becoming is mainly 'subjective', so that he finds it principally in a flux of views, as a feature of intentionality? What if the 'motion' of becoming lies in the 'directedness' of viewpoints? This might then explain why becoming is structured into both contexts and processes.

Consider first the *Timaeus*'s creation story, and the role it gives soul: by infusing the world with this, the Demiurge makes it a living being, composed of many other living beings. 'Before' he does so, the raw 'stuff' possesses only protofeatures and a protomotion: it is the Pythagorean (and Anaximandrian) *apeiron* (unlimited), a connection made clear in the *Philebus* (from 23c).[50] Structure and motion, a fullfledged reality of becoming, arise only through that infusion of soul into the chaos and indefiniteness of mere material space. So the world's souls are responsible for all the large-scale facts about it, which we can have truth about, though still not knowledge. Through these souls, becoming 'comes into being', into fuller reality, *as* their intentionally structured motions.[51]

Plato's view of motion as (in the chief case at least) intentional emerges in other ways and places too. The *Sophist* (249a–b) argues that change must be admitted into being, because it belongs to soul, life, and mind. The *Phaedrus* (245c–e) presents soul as the source of all motion, a

49. Note also the importance *Gorg.* (e.g., 527d) places on "holding to the same views about the same questions"'. *Tim.* 40b says that the heavenly souls "ever continue to think consistently the same thoughts about the same things, in the same respect". Plato's distaste for flux in views can be heard in Theodorus's account of Heracliteans at *Tht.* 179e–180a. It was apparently a flux in valuings that originally disturbed and inspired Socrates.

50. See *Tim.* 50d on the formlessness of the receptive space. *Sta.* 273b–d associates 'the bodily' with a primal *"apeiron* of unlikeness".

51. Cornford 1937, 41: "Plato looks upon the whole visible universe as an animate being whose parts are also animate beings." See also *Sta.* 269c.

claim elaborated by the *Laws*, which argues (896a) for "the sameness of soul with the primal becoming and change of all that is, has been, and will be, and of all their contraries [i.e., all the contraries in becoming]". This implies (896c–d) that "the characters of soul must be older than those of body", so that "moods, customs, purposes, calculations, and true beliefs, practices, and memories, will all be prior to lengths, breadths, and depths of bodies".

Surely it seems even here, however, that Plato allows nonintentional, 'material' facts about the world; he just makes them *effects* of a structuring by soul. He speaks of a separate, if secondary, motion generated in bodies, 'set loose' by the self-motion of souls.[52] So although this material motion may indeed be structured by an intentionality, it seems not to be 'in' an intention or viewpoint. Or is it? At issue here is whether Plato is an idealist with respect to becoming, treating bodily process as itself just an intentional content. From what we've already seen, he will not be so in our usual sense, in which idealism holds that only intentionalities (and their contents) exist. The 'being' that becoming comes into, by getting structured out of chaotic indefiniteness, is not (our) existence but a gradationally achievable condition of honor. That chaos, perhaps the infinitely splintered continuum of § 2.1.1, might indeed fully *exist*, but it lacks the structural definiteness required in order to *be*. So we must ask: To what extent does Plato think bodily facts and motions acquire such a structure in their own right (and not just in how they're viewed)? How far does he move toward a dualism for becoming, toward recognizing both intentional and material species of it?

On the one hand, it might be doubted whether he does at all. Perhaps that material motion rises to the definiteness of 'being' only *as* it is viewed by souls. In favor of this reading, the *Theaetetus*'s perception theory can be read as intending a phenomenalist analysis of becoming: what makes the sensible world 'real' is the coupled occurrence of *aistheseis* and *aistheta*. The active motions of the former generate the latter as structurings not present before, structurings that occur only in the act of perception.[53]

Although this might indeed be the force of the *Theaetetus* perception theory, I think this is a part of the theory that Plato means to jettison, in his subsequent refutation of the extreme Protagorean-Heracliteanism. The parts of those doctrines he must oppose are those that support the opening equation of perception and knowledge: the claim that all and only perception grasps truth. The phenomenalism gives major support for this: deployed on the background presumption that all cognition—

52. See *Laws* 897a.

53. See Bostock's argument (1988, 65–70) in defense of 'the usual interpretation', that Plato analyzes the 'slow changes'—eye and stone—as series of 'fast changes'—seeings and seens. McDowell (1973, 143–45) notes differences between the 'perceiveds' and sense data.

intentional directedness at things—is a kind of perception, it ties each perceiving to its own perceived, as all that it can mean and what it must be true of. Against this, Plato makes room for both truth and error about becoming, first by siting these in a different type of directedness than perceiving, in belief (*doxa*), which he then (in the *Tht.* and later in the *Sophist*) must pry enough apart from its object to let it be sometimes false (contra Parmenides); and second by allowing there to be real material motions 'behind' what is perceived, as in the *Timaeus*'s different version of the perception theory.

Although these material motions are thus not mere 'contents' of intentions, they're not as fully separated as caused results, either. They need to be understood *as* structured by soul, and, because 'like understands like', they *can* be understood only because they are such. Thus accounts of material motion remain deficient until tied into accounts of psychic motion; the former must be grasped as 'conditionally necessary' for the achievement of some soul's purposes. This dependence of the material story on the psychic is especially clear in the *Timaeus*, which stresses throughout how matter must be understood as made by soul (the Demiurge) and for soul (so as to be comprehensible by us).[54]

Given this dependence of material on psychic motion, what is the nature of the latter? The *Symposium* passage gives content to the soul's directedness, in its account of *eros*, the telic thrust toward immortality or persistence. As suggested previously, such persistence is itself just an approximation to being, as the metaphysical 'sameness' of the Forms. The soul finds this atemporal and absolute self-identity unachievable, at least in this world, and must lower its sights in two ways: first, by aiming not at eternity (full sameness) but at persistence (sameness through time), and, second, by aiming not at its own straightforward persistence but at survival in the person of descendents or disciples, or in (other) created works. It adopts these lesser aims as second-bests, to that ultimate good of being. This is reinforced by the *Philebus* 54c: "all becoming becomes for the sake of all being [*sumpasan de genesin ousias heneka gignesthai sumpases*]".[55] Together, these passages show Plato thinking of becoming as life's intentional directedness toward being, a directedness that is precisely the way it falls short of being. As essentially striving, as

54. So the Demiurge forms all matter into geometrical atoms, as a 'condition of the possibility' of our experiencing it. This is why the elements are generated: there must be fire to make the world's body visible and earth to make it tactile. Thus although these atoms and elements constitute a structure really in bodies themselves (and not just in how they're viewed), these structural units can't themselves be understood simply in bodily terms.

55. Perhaps also *Phd.* 75a–b's account of "sensible equals [as] striving after absolute equality but falling short of it." *Phil.* 53d: "There are two sorts: that which is itself by itself, and that which is always aiming at an other." So Nietzsche says that Plato wanted "to prove to himself that reason and instinct of themselves tend toward one goal, the good, 'God'" [BGE191].

stretched toward this end, we (and all of the soul's motions) are something incomplete in this present, something merely *toward*. This supports the process point: moments lack self-sufficiency because of this intentional directedness.

All of this describes only the pure form of soul however. Familiarly, Plato thinks soul can degenerate and its direction can shift: instead of striving at being, becoming can take satisfaction in itself. He blames this degeneration on the state of embodiment, and so on the stuff of things. There are hints that he even attributes to this stuff (that *apeiron*) an antimotion of its own, opposing soul's aim at being or sameness with a drift toward difference.[56] In any case, the lesser types of souls, and lesser parts of the human soul, aim aside from being. This shows up above all in our appetites' pursuit of pleasure, whose character as becoming Plato so stresses: pleasure, as joy in becoming, is "the greatest bait to evil" (*Tim.* 69d).[57] This is becoming's self-perpetuating aspect: the aim to rise along topless scales, rather than toward determinate goals.

A lot more would be needed to evaluate Plato's attachment or commitment to these views. For our purposes, these hints are enough, and we can turn back to Nietzsche with what we've learned. Can we find in him, too, any of these further senses for 'becoming'?

2.1.3 Nietzsche's theory of becoming

We've found three ways that Plato's concept of becoming goes beyond our earlier account of it as constant change. (1) It denies the self-sufficiency of the moment: the basic unit of becoming is not states, whether momentary or not, but processes. (2) More broadly, it denies the self-sufficiency of any simple parts: this reality is distributed contextually, so that these processes themselves take their identities only in relations to others. And (3) this concept takes becoming so, because it views this reality as intentional: becoming is (in a certain way) directed, and this is why it consists in those contextually identified processes. (Of these three, the first is the crux insofar as the point is literally about becoming; the next is a generalization of one aspect of process, and the third is a ground for accepting the other two.) Of course Plato takes becoming, as so characterized, to be of a deficient or degraded being and goodness; he sets over against it a realm of being itself, valued precisely

56. The *Timaeus* attributes the protomotion—before the Demiurge's ordering—to 'powers', suggesting it may have a directedness of its own; we might then read the dialogue's 'necessity' as resisting *in intention* the divine ordering. Plato wavers between explaining evil as due to an eternal bad soul (*Laws* 896c) and as due to a soulless tendency that corrupts (some) souls (*Sta.* 269e–270a, 273b–d).

57. *Tim.* 90c–92c explains lower souls as resulting from the degeneration of man's soul. *Phil.* 53ff. develops pleasure as a becoming, rather than a state or condition in its own right.

as free from those three features. But (it can be no surprise) I claim that it's in just this complex sense that Nietzsche posits and promotes becoming as indeed all of being and reality.

He hears becoming this way, rather than as the continuous change of beings, the concept developed (as a complex of arguments) in § 2.1.1. Or rather, this new point emerges in a certain way from the old: it shares some of the same presuppositions but then goes on to draw a further, partly reversing lesson. Because these points thus overlap, they can be confused—by us, and Nietzsche, too. So some of the arguments that were taken in § 2.1.1 as supporting constant change can be reinterpreted as supporting the three more radical lessons here.

Recall the overall point in § 2.1.1: things are wholes of forces whose struggle produces constant process, which implies, by the continuum argument's insistence on precise degrees, the constant change as replacement of all real beings. But we must hear those forces as intentional, indeed as wills to power. So the becoming that is of or by them lies in their directedness, not in the 'objective' changes supposed in § 2.1.1. And we must hear those forces as gathered (by their struggle) into wholes, in a different meta-ontological manner than we presumed in § 2.1.1: these forces aren't complete in themselves; their very identity lies in their role in these contentious wholes. This twist reverses (in one way) the lesson of the continuum argument: instead of driving being down into the smallest parts, it disperses it out to ever-larger wholes. Thus, temporally, it reverses the splintering of processes into infinite momentary states and lets states be, only as stages in (relation to) processes. So the continuity of becoming, as perhaps we should have guessed, serves not to divide it maximally, but to weave it together out of manifold processes. Combined, these points explain better the great weight Nietzsche puts on becoming, a weight the continuum argument wouldn't bear.

2.1.3.1   Process

I begin with the process point, because this speaks best to our strong sense that the theory of becoming is mainly about time. This point may first occur to us in its epistemological form: we can never understand a being or thing 'in the moment'; it must always be grasped in a temporal context, as having been this and as about to be that. But beneath this lies the ontological crux: real beings are essentially extended in time, so that there 'is' no real being in any moment. What there is are becomings, transitions, or processes. The 'identity' of beings, their 'meaning', 'what they are', involves reference to their earlier and later stages.

This suggests we've been mistaking the relevance of change for Nietzsche's theory of becoming, in presuming it a condition that beings are subject to. We were wrong in § 2.1.1 to stress the warm becoming cold and to think that his aim was to shrink these termini to temperature points, by making change replace them continuously. Instead, he means to shift stress away from those 'beings that change', to make them dependent on the change, rather than having the change be just something that happens (if constantly) *to* them. He means to deny that those beings are complete in themselves: they're not fully 'present' for the question then to arise of whether they change or not. Losing their self-sufficiency, these beings are appropriated into the changes themselves, as stages or episodes of them.

Thus the continuum really serves not to splinter reality into moments but to clot it all the more thoroughly together. Reality stretches out as processes; these, and not states (not even momentary ones), are its 'units', which all adequate descriptions must speak of. Being occurs only as a temporal spread.[58] Nietzsche sometimes says this fairly directly.[59] And, I try to show, hearing him this way explains much better the particular implications he takes becoming to have.

On the one hand, this shows that the theory of becoming does not infinitely multiply beings, as it seemed when we heard it as constant change. It doesn't posit every momentary and simple feature as a being

58. The old continuum argument fragments all apparent persistence into momentary parts, in order to sweep away those 'states' that common sense takes as real. But this is only a preliminary to gathering those parts together into a more cohesive type of time stretch, a process. Compare Chappell's distinction (1962) among three responses to Zeno's Arrow: as requiring time atoms, time points, or time continua. Bergson (1946, 147) draws the third lesson, arguing that the points traversed by change aren't actual but potential, derivable out of the change but not constituting it: "If you imagine a change as being really composed of states, you at once cause insoluble metaphysical problems to arise." Popper (1966, 12) attributes the process point to Heraclitus: "He visualized the world not as an edifice, but as one colossal process; not as the sum-total of all *things*, but rather as the totality of all events, or changes, or *facts.*" But he says little to clarify what 'being a process' might involve.

59. GS112, after what was quoted in § 2.1.1, claims that although we experience 'effects' as sudden, "[t]here is an infinite number of occurrences in this sudden second that elude us. An intellect that could see cause and effect as a continuum, as a flux of happening, and not in our way, as an arbitrary division and dismemberment, would repudiate the concept of cause and effect and deny all conditionality." In UM/II/1p61 this temporal point is limited to persons: "struggle, suffering and disgust" remind the human being "what his existence basically is—an imperfect [tense] that can never be completed." WP655 [1885] speaks of "[p]rocesses as 'essence'", WP552 [1887] of "complexes of happening". WP672 [1886–87]: "The nearest prehistory of an action relates to this action: but *further back* lies a prehistory which points *out further:* the single action is at the same time a segment of a much more comprehensive, *later* fact. The *briefer* and the *longer* processes are not separated". Also relevant are Nietzsche's many denials of any 'doer behind the doing'; see n.21 to chapter 1. Consider also his inclination to treat time as real; KSA/10/1[3] [1882]: "Space is like matter a subjective form. *Not* time."

in its own right. Yet apparently it doesn't, if this way of stating it is correct, perform the opposite and promised task either: ruling out beings, and with them the project of ontology. In the terminology I've adopted (but not explained), its point is only to *redescribe* beings, by insisting that temporal stretch is essential to them: they're processes. And so this new reading seems just about as unfaithful as the old one was to Nietzsche's intent to replace beings with becomings.

Should we renounce that terminology and not call becomings (processes) Nietzsche's 'beings'? Perhaps, although that way of putting it was useful in a first approximation to his temporal point, it must be replaced once we've grasped it. That point strikes so deeply at our everyday view that it could well seem more than just a different account of the same subject matter. It strikes at part of what we mean by that verb 'to be': what is, is complete in the moment it is, so that an adequate account would only need to refer to its state at that moment. If there's no such self-sufficiency to any present, past, or future, then all our uses of these tenses of 'to be' might rest on a misconception of reality's temporal logic. And perhaps when we speak of 'beings' we similarly suppose that they last, if they do, only by being fully present at every moment. By speaking instead of 'becomings', of how a future is now being approached from a past, we can hope to avoid resettling into that misconception. All of this suggests, that for Nietzsche a theory of reality must be not an ontology but a *genealogy,* taking that term to imply not merely an interest in something's kind and origin (*genea*), but in it as a becoming (*genomenon*).[60]

This shows that the process point does better explain Nietzsche's insistence that a world of becoming has no room for beings. It also makes this point pose a greater challenge to my claim of a Nietzschean ontology. My answer is implicit in the last paragraph. If Nietzsche's replacement of beings with becomings is still part of a theory of reality, isn't it still part of a theory of 'being', too, once we've purged that term of its usual presumption of self-sufficient moments? To be sure, this purging reaches deeper into the notion than our earlier ejection of the Parmenidean-Platonic accretions to being: unchangingness and eternity. But I think there remains an evident core, which justifies treating Nietzsche's project of description as still generically the same as the traditional one, still a theory of 'what's there', an ontology. And by this, I hope to have it both ways: it's reasonable for Nietzsche to treat becoming as excluding being, but we needn't follow him in this choice of terms. We can aptly say that his 'beings are becomings'.

60. This is why Nietzsche thinks genealogy is required to grasp even the 'current' significance of beings. The attempt to interpret an activity without regard to this past rests on a mistake about the way it's 'in time'. The discussion in GM/II/13 is again relevant; see § 2.4, especially n.109.

2.1.3.2   *Contextuality*

As we saw in discussing Plato, the point about process is merely one application of the contextual or relational point, of the claim that worldly things are metaphysically 'different', constituted by their relations to others. We find this more abstract point in Nietzsche as well.[61]

Its presence is hinted at by how often he denies that things are 'the same'. Here he mainly means 'with one another': things (as we've seen that he argues) are too unlike to be classed together by our concepts. So his denial of equality is stated as a claim about a specific relation in which beings *don't* stand to one another. But I think it signals the more radical claim that these beings are constituted by the relations, the differences, in which they *do* stand. Behind the denial of sameness with respect to others is the denial of self-sameness: worldly things lack self-identity, the character of being unequivocally 'this' in and by themselves. Thus Nietzsche not only claims there are no 'temporal simples' (self-sufficient nows) but no 'spatial' ones either: a thing is what it is in its relation to other cotemporal things. So WP557 [1885–86]: "The properties of a thing are [its] effects on other 'things': if one thinks away other 'things', then a thing has no properties, i.e., *there is no thing without other things*, i.e., there is no 'thing-in-itself'."[62] We should note that Nietzsche's denial of the thing-in-itself is part of a positive account of reality—of the world's real structure—and not a confinement of our attention to 'mere phenomena'.

Because this context claim is a key point of contact between Nietzsche and Heraclitus, we can further explore it by returning to that connection.[63] We then see how to reinterpret the significance of the part-whole analysis we attributed to Heraclitus in § 2.1.1. Rather than driving reality down into the parts, as if these were self-sufficient,

61. WP635 [1888]: "no things remain but only dynamic quanta, in a relation of tension to all other dynamic quanta: their essence lies in their relation to all other quanta, in their 'effect' upon the same." WP568 [1888]: "the world . . . does *not* exist as a world 'in-itself'; it is essentially a world of relations [*Relations-Welt*]". WP625 [1888]: "there is no 'essence-in-itself', relations first constitute essence". Nehamas 1985, 82: "Nietzsche in effect claimed that nothing in the world has any intrinsic features of its own and that each thing is constituted solely through its interrelations with, and differences from, everything else."

62. WP584 [1888] speaks of "the real world, where absolutely everything is linked and conditioned". Nor is this dependence or 'conditioning' merely a causal and external relation; part of Nietzsche's complaint against our notion of causality is that it interprets the relation as external, as not contributing to the identities of the relata.

63. Nietzsche attributes this point to Heraclitus at PTAG5p53 [1873]: "so too everything that is in both [space] and time has but a relative existence, and is only through and for another of the same kind [*Gleichartiges*]".

this analysis stresses that they *are* parts, and so diffuses their identity out to their contexts or wholes. Thus the river is both a composite of water and a part in the overall system of water cycling up and down. By reapplying this contextual point up through hierarchies of wholes, Heraclitus arrives at the conclusion that all things are such contextualized parts—except for the whole that includes all. So only this is a being 'in itself'.[64]

On this context view, then, it will be the fuller wholes that have primacy, that are to a higher degree, because they're less incomplete. Yet Heraclitus stresses that even these wholes both 'are and are not'. So DK10: "Takings-together: wholes and not wholes, converging diverging, singing-together singing-apart, from all one and from one all." Among his most basic views is this bivalent answer to the question whether these wholes exist or are merely brought together in our views of them; this clear statement makes it seem quite unapt to insist, within that earlier debate, either that Heraclitus does or that he doesn't allow that things like rivers exist. We see that his point is precisely the ambiguity to the matter.[65]

But why does Heraclitus hold that these wholes are also not wholes? He may have in mind partly their status as parts of some larger whole, their incompleteness. This is the reiteration of the contextual point which leads up to the fullest whole. But because he thinks that even this sum of all things isn't unambiguously whole, he must have some other, more crucial criterion, which even this sum fails to meet. And one is mentioned in the saying just quoted: the 'disharmony' among the whole's parts, the way they don't fully 'cooperate' in a unified project. Thus whereas the parts lack self-sufficiency or 'in-itselfness', the whole lacks the unity we demand of a single thing. Its parts pull in opposite directions; the one is also a many. That the discovery about wholes concerns this internal opposition is strongly suggested by DK51's image of the bow, as quoted.

We find Nietzsche thinking along these same lines, and here we come to the deeper structure of his attack on beings. This attack is based on the ambiguities generated by the contextual ontology he shares with Heraclitus. Nietzsche assumes two criteria for 'being a being' that are also found in our everyday view: first, being complete, an 'in-itself'; second, being unified, a 'one'. On that contextual view of parts in wholes, however, nothing satisfies both conditions; the parts are ruled

---

64. DK50: "Listening not to me but to the *logos*, it is wise to agree that all beings are one." The holistic conclusion is also generated by the continuum argument, turned to opposite effect by the context point: the absence of definite boundaries, instead of driving being down to parts as points, makes it ramify out to the most complete whole.

65. So (the disputed) DK91: "at the same time it [the river, any mortal being] joins and separates".

out by the first, the wholes by the second criterion.[66] And so Nietzsche dominantly concludes that no beings are and that his vision of a world of becoming is not an ontology.

Once again we must ask whether he's right to use these criteria for 'being'. Why not alter these two standards to make them better match reality's contextual character? When we reach the crux in this way, we can see how finely balanced this main issue is. Indeed, Nietzsche himself sometimes draws that opposite lesson. So WP584 [1888]: "This is the greatest error that has ever been committed . . .: one believed one possessed a criterion of reality in the forms of reason. . . . And behold: now the world became false, and precisely on account of the properties *that constitute its reality:* change, becoming, multiplicity, opposition, contradiction, war".[67]

Heraclitus, with the same contextual vision, more consistently takes this route. Although he also stresses that neither of those everyday standards is met in our world, he doesn't conclude that no beings are. And this tolerance fits with a crucial way he implicitly accepts those parts and wholes: he thinks it all-important to speak of them, because his wisdom is precisely a grasp of their relations and internal structure.

Nietzsche, too, never tries to give up speaking of his composites, of persons, for example. His insights are chiefly about these, and above all about their ambiguous status as parts and wholes. His denials of them thus jar with his practice. To be sure, what he says gives them a character deeply at odds with our usual notions, not only of them but of what *can* be; they're not as complete or unified (or stable) as we expect the 'real' beings in our world to be. In his vision of a world of becoming, what is most real is the whole-with-parts, the context of interdependent elements. Reality or being is portioned out in a peculiar way: not to single beings individually, but to half-unified systems, so that we're never fully right to use either singular or plural. Our accounts will be accurate to the extent that they do justice to the diffuseness, multiplicity, and temporal stretch of things; these are the correct criteria for real beings. Thus although the contextual sense for Nietzsche's theory of flux helps further

66. For Nietzsche's denials of any simple yet self-sufficient parts, see n.61. He denies there is any 'all' or 'totality' in WP331 [1886–87] and WP711 [1887–88]. WP561 [1885–86] says that the only 'unity' there is, is not what we suppose (but rather what the power ontology projects): "All unity is unity *only* as *organization and cooperation* [*Zusammenspiel*]: just as a human community is a unity: thus the *opposite* of an atomistic *anarchy;* consequently a *mastery-structure* that *means* a one but *is* not a one." TI/VI/8 seems to make both points, against both simples and wholes: "One [*man*] is necessary, one is a piece of fatefulness [*Verhängniss*], one belongs to the whole, one *is* in the whole". And soon after: "the world is a unity neither as a sensorium nor as 'spirit'".

67. TI/III/6: "The grounds on which 'this' world has been described as apparent, establish instead [*vielmehr*] its reality—any *other* kind of reality is absolutely unprovable."

to explain why he denies beings, we again have the option not to follow this choice. We only need to hear differently the decisive terms 'being' and 'is' so that they require and not exclude relationality.

A question has been evaded throughout, however: On what grounds does Nietzsche make these context and process claims? Why should we accept his assertion that being or reality is 'diffused' in these ways?

2.1.3.3   Intentionality

Unsurprisingly, I think the 'ground'—shaky footing for us?—is his central ontological thought about will to power. Reality consists in these wills, these intentional forces. Only by and in them does the chaos and indeterminacy of mere existence rise to 'being', to a real becoming. Only with and in their structures and meanings does the world get structure and meaning; they give it its 'joints' and so 'units', temporally and otherwise. (Perhaps only in this way do extended realities crystallize out of that continuum of § 2.1.1.) "All happening, all movement, all becoming, as an establishing [*Feststellen*] of relations of degree and force, as a *struggle*" [WP552: 1887].[68] The context and process claims are then inferred from the nature of these wills and above all from their intentionality: reality must be dispersed in these ways, because intending or meaning is so. Since these willful views get their content not individually and in isolation but only by their inter-interpretations, becoming must be contextual. And because these wills are arcs towards ends, becoming must involve stretch through time, must be process.

This third point adds further content to both of the others. So first, Nietzsche not only thinks reality is process, but process with a certain structure: that type of stretch through time that belongs to will to power. Will's telic structure lays out the temporal structure of processes: these aren't just valueless fluctuations in properties but becomings-stronger or -weaker; to understand any given change one must grasp it as one or the other (or both). So Nietzsche says that becoming involves not just change but 'development'.[69] Second, he thinks the relational point in these terms: the context that determines identity is a context of wills, opposing and like-minded, in intricate ways. The aim of one depends on the like and different aims of others, with and against it, on how their perspectives bear on it. Things are connected not by mutually affecting one another in the manner of mechanical causes but by giving meaning to one another, as voices in a conversational web.

---

68. Compare Bergson's claim (1946, 155) that "we almost never know [about changes outside us] whether we are dealing with a single change or one composed of several movements interspersed with stops. . . . We would have to be inside beings and things as we are inside ourselves before we could express our opinion on this point."

69. WP778 [1888] and WP538 [1888].

We saw evidence of this intentional point in Plato, too, as his reason for thinking that the sensible world is subject to both Heraclitus's flux and Protagoras's relativism. Indeed, the point seems already present in Heraclitus: these forces that do and don't make his wholes, oppose and agree with one another *intentionally*.[70] But the point is still clearer in Nietzsche: it's because the world is perspectival that it's one of flux and context. "[T]he will to power not a being, not a becoming, but a *pathos* is the most elemental fact from which a becoming and effecting first emerge" [WP635: 1888].[71] Indeed, he explains (away) *movement*, as just the way one intentionality is perceived by another.[72]

All of this shows that Nietzsche's becoming point is not fully separate from his perspectivism after all. Because the latter doctrine will require much fuller treatment (see chapter 4), I won't pursue it here. We must be content to have analyzed the independent part of the sense to the becoming point and to have seen just where it grows from the perspectivism. With this much content and structure for Nietzsche's metaphysical notion of becoming, we're equipped to go on.

2.2   The temporality of the active and reactive

Having eased our worry that Nietzsche's views about becoming might preclude his having an ontology, we go on to see how this temporal metaphysics reverberates up through the other layers of his thought; we'll pass more quickly through the rest of the sequence of chapter 1. And as we go, we'll note the comparable echoes of a temporal metaphysics in Plato's secondary views; again, we find a striking similarity in their overall structures of claims.

Begin by recalling how the power ontology involves *values:* the claim that will to power is the essence of beings doubles as a claim about how they should be. Like Plato (and others) before, Nietzsche means an essence that is *differentially achieved*. In particular, the active/reactive distinction serves as his criterion for whether a being 'realizes' or 'falls away from' its essence as will to power; this runs as the deepest and

70. So DK10 depicts the world's parts as singing together and apart. DK51 makes these parts "say the same" (*homologeei*). Kahn (1979, 165) notes that DK126 ("Cold warms up . . .") "describes qualitative change between physical opposites in the language of felt experience rather than scientific observation."

71. This is reflected in TSZ/III/12/2: "Where all becoming seemed to me the dance of gods . . .—as an eternal fleeing and seeking each other again of many gods, as the blessed contradicting of each other, listening to each other again, belonging to each other again of many gods". WP556 [1885–86]: "One may not ask: '*who* then interprets?' for the interpretation itself is a form of the will to power, has existence (but not as a 'being' but as a *process*, a *becoming*) as an affect." See also HH/II/19 and WP616 [1885–86].

72. WP492 [1885]: "wherever we see or guess movement in a body, we learn to conclude that there is a subjective, invisible life belonging to it. Movement is a symbolism for the eye; it indicates that something has been felt, willed, thought." See also WP634 [1888].

strongest current in his judgings and rankings. Do these metaphysical values also have a temporal aspect or sense? Are active and reactive different ways a will can be 'in time', the former more adequate to power's temporal essence? It will take a while to see that and how this is so.

We're immediately struck by one simple and likely-looking way to find temporal sense in those opposites. 'Reactive' readily suggests a fixation in the past: present activity or plans for the future are guided by reference to something past, to which one now responds. This temporal stance might be found at the root of that 'habit of obedience' we identified with reactivity; perhaps it's out of a preoccupation with the past, a tendency to dwell on it or to set one's sights by it, that one 'obeys' some other will than one's own. Perhaps listening to the past is listening away from oneself. This seems supported by Nietzsche's explicit remarks that reactive forces are unable to forget or to digest their experiences adequately; resentment seems a brooding on the past.[73] Conversely, we can see how a drive might be active, precisely by a tendency to turn its back on its past, to ignore it—not for the sake of the present, however, for of course Nietzsche thinks we also mustn't rest content with this. Instead, activeness seems a forward-directedness, an intentness on the future, the dimension to which he indeed so often gives priority. His interest typically seems all focused ahead: his readers are in the future, as are the hoped-for overman, his ideal.[74]

These reflections suggest how Nietzsche's temporal views might count in a further, unexpected way against my claim that he has an ontological system. If those views imply a negative evaluation of the past, or of attention to it, we naturally expect that he himself must evaluate in just this way his own philosophical past: the tradition, and

73. WP233 [1888]: "Not to become finished with an experience is already a sign of decadence." See also GM/I/10, GM/III/16.

74. GM/II/1: "Forgetfulness is no mere *vis inertiae* as the superficial believe; it is rather an active and in the strictest sense positive capacity of restraint". GS/JCR/4: "For he is healthy, who has forgotten." See also BGE217, BGE244, GM/I/11, GM/III/16. Nietzsche's rejection of the present is even expressed in one of his titles: the *Untimely Meditations* often remind their reader that they're not measured to the tastes and views of the present age. (And one of the chapters of TI has the title "Skirmishes of an Untimely One".) In TSZ/II/20 Zarathustra says: "The now and the formerly on earth—alas! my friends—that is what I find most unendurable; and I should not know how to live if I were not also a seer of that which must come. A seer, a willer, a creator, a future himself and a bridge to the future". TSZ/III/12/12: "O my brothers, your nobility [*Adel*] should not look backward but *outward!* Exiles should you be from all father- and forefather-lands! Your *children's land* should you love". BGE212: "More and more it seems to me that the philosopher, being *of necessity* a human being of tomorrow and the day after tomorrow, has always found himself, and *had* to find himself, in contradiction to his today: his enemy was ever the ideal of today." See also UM/II/F. Note also Nehamas's reading (1988, 58) of BGE's phrase "philosophers of the future".

even his own prior thoughts. If his view recommends (as active) abandoning tradition, then we'd expect the break he intends in his thought to be all the more drastic. And how could it be right to attribute to him some overall system if he constantly abandons even his own old ideas? Nietzsche gives many signs that he deeply opposes allegiance to the past, including to his own past views.[75] Philosophical activeness thus seems to be turning one's back on what has been thought and thinking afresh for oneself. Early readers in particular commonly find this lesson in Nietzsche; there it encourages dismissal of any such approach as this book's.

There's something apt in this line, but it needs amending. We expect this from the temporal metaphysics just sketched. The process point preaches the relevance of past and future to the present; we expect the active will to 'realize' this temporal breadth, along with the other aspects of its power essence—to realize it (we saw in § 1.3) not consciously but 'telically', in the way it aims. But to ignore the past—to leave it out of account in one's aiming—seems to be to deny this breadth. How could attention to the past be attending away from oneself when one 'is' one's stretch from a past toward a future? Why would Nietzsche narrow on the future in his values when his key or pervading view about time is that reality is more dispersed through it than we normally think? In fact, as we look more closely, we find that he does require a reference or attention to the past, clearly not that one just ignore it. This is reflected, indeed, in his own great attention to origins: to see what some practice is, we must see how it was first shaped up from active and reactive forces. And he suggests that what most distinguishes persons from simpler wills is their ability to take this backward view, or more generally the way they reach out through time.[76] So the active can't be to forget the past.[77]

However, by itself this doesn't require a drastic revision of that simple lesson, it may just mean that the past is to be denied a different way. It shows that one shouldn't, in pursuing one's project, ignore the past— that it is, and is oneself. It leaves open that the ideal view on the past could be negative; the proper attention to it could be merely to the purpose of attacking and replacing it. Perhaps a will's essential or proper

75. See BGE41 on the necessity "not to remain stuck". UM/II attacks the modern age as 'historical', claiming that this backward turn inhibits its drive to the future; this is said [II/8pp101–2] to reflect a Christian denial of the future. See Small (1989) on Nietzsche's links with Emerson here.

76. See n.96.

77. I take Nietzsche to be thinking along lines taken by Bergson (1946, 157): "Thanks to philosophy, all things acquire depth—more than depth, something like a fourth dimension which permits anterior perceptions to remain bound up with present perceptions, and the immediate future itself to become partly outlined in the present. Reality no longer appears then in the static state, in its manner of being; it affirms itself dynamically, in the continuity and variability of its tendency."

relation to its past lies precisely in struggling to destroy it and put in its place a quite different future. Perhaps an active will attends to the past just in order to uncover the hidden ways that past affects it, the better to escape its self-perpetuating sway. At once this seems a more plausible account of Nietzsche's own attitude to the past: he clearly neither ignores it nor denies its importance, but his attention seems often intended to 'put it out of play'. His genealogies would then be a means to this end, designed to loosen the grip of past practices on us. His important term 'overcoming' can easily be heard with this sense.[78]

All of this seems reinforced by another way we might state this point. The active is now, we might say, a preference for change (or becoming), the reactive a preference for stability (or being). If change is replacement of what was, attacking the past seems very much the same as pursuing change. This seems to fit well with that temporal metaphysics: from the claim that the world is change, it's a quick and easy step, in a valuative ontology, to a preference for change and for effort at change. If change is the essence of beings, but an essence differentially realized, we expect that beings will be better or worse according to how hard they press toward change.[79] This is, indeed, roughly the way we took Nietzsche in § 2.1: as valuing effort at change or 'difference', in opposition to Plato's basic value of being or 'sameness'.

Yet I think this still attributes to Nietzsche too simple a point; it misses a love for the past that he also insists on. We can see this by considering a key passage in which he explicitly demotes the effort at change to a secondary value. In GS370 (whose importance is attested by its reuse in *Nietzsche contra Wagner*), he distinguishes two criteria to be used in judging artists and their works. He states the first: "has hunger or overflow become productive here?" The second asks "whether the demand for making-fixed, for perpetuating, for *being* is the cause of creation, or rather the demand for destruction, for change, for the new, for the future, for *becoming*''. He argues that these two dimensions of difference lie askew, so that either need or abundance can prompt either temporal aim, for constancy or change. But he also claims that the former scheme is 'preferable', as a basic classification and standard for appraisal, so that effort from abundance for stability is finer than effort from need for change.[80]

78. TSZ/II/12: "And life itself told this secret to me: 'See,' it said, 'I am that, *which must always overcome itself.* . . . Rather would I perish that renounce this; and truly, where there is perishing and a falling of leaves, see, there life sacrifices itself— for power!'"

79. WP585 [1887]: "*Overcoming of philosophers*, through the destruction of the world of being . . . before the force is there, to reverse values and to deify becoming and the apparent world as the *only* world, and to call them good."

80. To be sure, the passage applies these distinctions only to artists' creatings and to the 'aesthetic values' these express. But when Nietzsche takes the artist as the "most easily *transparent*'' phenomenon [WP797: 1885–86], he means it as the clearest, emblematic case of will to power itself; see Heidegger's development (1979–87,

Nietzsche reports here a shift in his basic values, one that reverses his esteem for Schopenhauer and Wagner because he finds them to lack this abundance. What matters most is for a will to have it; it's a secondary matter whether this overfull will then aims at stability or at change. The latter contrast, we'll progressively see, is another facet of the difference between master and overman and of the parallel contrast between Apollonian and Dionysian art. But the precondition for both is that abundance. So what is abundance, and what is its temporal character?

At first, it seems 'overfullness' must mean something cumulative and quantitative: possessing an actual richness of parts. It appears to be that value of internal complexity or richness that we met back in § 1.4. But I think inspection of this and other places Nietzsche speaks of this condition shows that he has in mind less the quantity of resources on which a will draws and more the quality or direction of its willing: the abundant will 'overflows', in that it puts itself forth, loving and delighting in its own activity, in enacting its distinctive drives, whether these are many or few. By contrast, the 'needy' will might bear all the internal richness and complexity of a Schopenhauer or Wagner, yet never find this enough to love to do and be. It lacks confidence or gladness in what's its own and can only find impetus to act by affirming or negating others. It can only get itself to *care* by focusing (in the main case) on some blow or imposition from without.

So this abundance, I think, is really that activeness or health we've had in view all along, but now in a new aspect that improves our temporal grasp of it.[81] It shows how the active will must love what it was and is. It must find in its past and present its singular and defining web of inclinations and attitudes; it must will power *in* these distinctive practices. So it needs a deep allegiance to them. What it already is it reveres and continues, though trying always to enrich this received activity by 'playing this game' better than before (the Apollonian) or by revising it into a better game (the Dionysian). The active will's love of, and allegiance to, the past show how this crucial Nietzschean value runs quite against our expectations, which too singlemindedly stressed change and the future. For Nietzsche, it's only reactive need that hates what was or is; this is the stance of the slave—and of the tyrant and the romantic.[82]

1:69ff.) of this point. Moreover, he elsewhere suggests all values should be aesthetic ones. For such reasons, I think we can properly extend these two criteria to judge wills quite generally.

81. In his reading of WP846 (a note ancestral to GS370), Heidegger identifies (1979–87, 1:132) the abundance/need and active/reactive distinctions. WP1009 [1887] and WP935 [1888] also suggest this connection. Nietzsche very often stresses the question of whether a phenomenon arises from 'overfullness' or from 'weariness and decline'; see, for example, BT/ASC, TI/IX/9.

82. BGE260: "when . . . [those] of 'modern ideas' believe almost instinctively in 'progress' and 'the future' and more and more lack respect for age, this in itself would sufficiently betray the ignoble descent of these 'ideas'." Relevant also is TI/I/10:

Nietzsche analyzes this reactive grudge against the past most abstractly in another important section, TSZ/II/20 ("On Redemption"). Here the will experiences time itself as an imposition, because its relentless passing carries more and more into the past and (apparently) out of the will's field of action. Reactivity's deep root is frustration with this limiting circumstance, that it can't 'will backward': "This, indeed this alone, is what *revenge* is: the will's ill will [*Widerwille*] against time and its 'It was'." So reactivity hates even that there is a past (not only some specific past facts or events).[83] And yet, Nietzsche thinks, the past doesn't lie beyond (every) will's scope after all. The active will overcomes this revulsion and embraces its past, by learning how to will it 'retroactively': "All 'It was' is a fragment, a riddle, a dreadful accident— until the creative will says to it: 'but thus I willed it!'—Until the creative will says to it: 'But thus I will it! Thus I shall will it!'"

What can this mysterious backward willing be? It's clearly something stronger than just 'accepting' the past. Yet it's not the type of effort for the sake of the past that we think of first: it's not attempting to continue or repeat or revive this past.[84] We've seen that will to power is a will to enrichment. So it also sees the past as what it can and must improve on, specifically in the senses mentioned earlier: it sees this past as founding a form of life worthy of being lived better and better (the Apollonian) or as worthy of being refashioned (the Dionysian). In either case it continues that past; it wants a future that's different yet also the same. Indeed, it wants the new as a sort of favor to the old, as a gift out of its love for the past. So its revisings accomplish a 'redemption' of the past: giving it a higher value and a richer identity and making a finer future from it. This brings us to a new and fuller expression of Nietzsche's active: out of love of the past and present, the active will forces

---

"That one commits no cowardice against one's actions! That one does not leave them in the lurch afterward! The bite of conscience is indecent." See also BT/ASC/7 and EH/II/1. So when GM/II/1 speaks of forgetting as "an active and . . . positive capacity of restraint", it means the forgetting of what has been inflicted on one, the hurts or influences reactivity would dwell on; it's a forgetting of what's other than oneself and one's distinctive doings.

83. Alderman (1977, 91) reads this interestingly: revulsion against the past is against one's inability to make a radical new beginning; what one really wants is to shuck off the past and create oneself out of nothing.

84. Though UM/II/F concludes: "I do not know what sense classical philology could have in our time if it were not untimely—that is to say, working against the time and thereby upon the time and, let us hope, in favor of a time to come." Here it does seem a noble (distant) past is to be used as a model for improving the present. MacIntyre (1981, 122) takes Nietzsche's overall view to be such, and after arguing that he has misunderstood the past he favors, concludes that the "contemporary Nietzschean . . . is condemned to an existence which aspires to transcend all relationship to the past."

them (and itself as it was and is) to pass over into a finer future that yet continues them.[85]

This lets us see at last the limit to Nietzsche's attacks on the past. A drive is reactive not because it dwells on its past or even because it shows allegiance to it, but because it does these unaptly, not seeing that true allegiance is making this past turn out to bear something finer than itself. Nietzsche's attacks bear only against misguided loves of the past, misguided because they're deeply not loves at all but needy resentments of what is, of the lives these wills find themselves living. To love the past from abundance is to will that it become a future that elevates it retroactively, by continuing it in different form.[86] It's to will that this past be 'digested' or 'incorporated' into a future that thus honors it. So we should hear in Nietzsche's frequent use of *über-* compounds (e.g., 'overman') that the prior has been 'taken up' into the new, not just replaced by it.[87] Thus, already in UM/II/1p62: "The stronger the roots of a human being's innermost nature, the more he will also appropriate or compel from the past; and . . . the most powerful and tremendous nature . . . would draw toward and into itself all the past, its own and the most foreign, and as it were transform it into blood." The overman will be such a nature, and his highest status will lie in this way that he takes up so much of the past in his ongoing will and view.

Just how does this temporal stance of the active will 'realize' its essence as becoming, that temporal contextuality developed (as the 'process point') in § 2.1? Again, it does so not by becoming conscious of that point—of the metaphysical interinvolvement of past, present, and future—but by enacting that interinvolvement telically, in the way it wills. The active will brings past and present into relation with the future when it takes them as motivating effort at the future. Moreover, it takes them to motivate effort in a quite specific way: they're to be honored by destroying/improving on them. Nietzsche claims that this way of acting from past and present has 'telic priority' to all others, because others are recognizably failures at it: it's wills that can't will so, because of weakness, misperception, or other incapacity, that will otherwise. Thus Nietzsche's claim that only the active will realizes essence rests (as we saw in § 1.3) on his psychological diagnoses of the reactive.

---

85. This view is prefigured at UM/II/1p62: "I mean [by plastic force] the force to grow out of oneself in one's own way, to transform and incorporate what is past and foreign, to heal wounds, to replace what has been lost, to re-form broken forms."

86. This seems at odds with Nietzsche's denials that different temporal phases can be justified by one another; see WP708 [1887–88]: "the present must absolutely not be justified by reference to a future, nor the past for the sake of the present." But I take his point here to be that an original love for past and present is indispensable. See § 3.5.2 on this aspiration to 'redeem' the past.

87. Recall WP1051 [1885]: "to *overcome* everything Christian through something over-Christian, and not merely to put it aside".

This analysis of Nietzsche's 'temporal values' throws better light on his main valuative difference from Plato. It shows that his basic 'angle of attack' against Plato is not quite, or simply, what we supposed in § 2.1. There we thought this attack to be focused against Plato's claim that the best, most real is being or sameness, rather than becoming or difference. We noted how Nietzsche disputes this 'psychologistically': diagnosing it as due to a sickness and unaptness for becoming and conflict. But now we've seen that the first distinction (willing being, willing becoming) doesn't entail the latter (being sick, being healthy), because Goethe and others are eternalizers out of 'abundance'. So we see that the diagnosis must rest on some finer judgment: there must be something in the manner in which Plato wills being that marks his view as the product of sickness or poverty.[88] What might this be?

Indeed, the subtlety of this judgment is reflected in Nietzsche's own ambivalence and shifts on the topic: he stresses Plato's "hiddenness and sphinx-nature" [BGE28], and sometimes he rather judges him noble and strong. So GS372: "all philosophical idealism so far was something like sickness, where it was not, as in Plato's case, the foresight of an overrich and dangerous health".[89] He sometimes explains this ambivalence by distinguishing a Socratic element in Plato, as a plebeian intrusion into an otherwise noble host.[90]

On the whole, though, Nietzsche attributes a great valuative mistake—a misdirectedness, a sickness—to Plato's thought, if only as infected by Socrates.[91] This lies not in his willing being but in his willing it out of poverty, a kind of poverty consistent with his great multiplicity and great strength. In the temporal terms this section has developed, this indicting poverty is Plato's lack of a basic allegiance to what was and is: the allegiance presupposed in the active effort to 'become what one *is*', that 'growth in a pregiven content', which we saw is power itself.[92] It's this inability to love past and present that makes Plato ultimately pin all his hopes on a future discontinuous with them. It's this temporal misdirection that makes him render being as *another world* than this one; it grounds his 'idealism', his flight toward the ideal. So it lies at the root of the several basic ways Nietzsche thinks Plato 'denies this life'—and which he holds most against him.

---

88. Nietzsche stresses the need for subtle discriminating faculties in these judgments, e.g., in GS370: "and my look [*Blick*] sharpened itself more and more for that most difficult and entangling form of *inference* [*Rückschlusses*], in which the most mistakes come to be made—the inference from the work to the author, from the deed to the doer, from the ideal to those who *have need* of it, from every way of thinking and valuing, to the commanding *need* behind it." See also EH/I/1.

89. BGE14 calls the Platonic "a *noble* way of thinking".

90. BGE190, 191.

91. See BGE/P on Socrates as perhaps to blame for Plato's decisive error. On Plato's sickness, see also D168.

92. His mistake lies at the 'hinge' of his effort *from* past and present *at* the future.

By contrast, he thinks healthy eternalizers like Homer and Goethe find or make their being precisely *in* this life. They are, indeed, eternalizers *of becoming* [TI/X/4], of what happened or happens. They show this 'Apollonian' love by typically placing their perfected moments in the past, a heroic or an idyllic past. Nietzsche himself showed a strain of this temporal attitude early on, in his glorying in Greece. But in him this nostalgia is increasingly ruled by a Dionysian urge to show his love for past and present by destroying and remaking them, thereby 'redeeming' them. This 'Dionysian' aspect is thus also Nietzsche's messianic and revolutionary strain; it explains his great stress on the future.

By contrast, he thinks that Plato's way of stressing the future is a symptom of poverty or sickness, because Plato launches his hopes at a future quite detached from his past, thus expressing a basic disallegiance to this life.[93] However, even at this crux, Plato keeps his mystery nature, for Nietzsche and for us. He sometimes rather takes that Apollonian stance: polishing the image of becoming, placing his ideal there, dreaming of a perfection *in* it. Indeed, he sometimes displays the temporal attitude typical of this stance: idealizing some past. So he shows tendencies that, if we judged them dominant, would reverse the main Nietzschean verdict against him.[94]

2.3 Persons' complex time

This web of ideas is further enriched, as we next reconsider Nietzsche's analysis of the person. We saw (in § 1.4) that he views each of us as a synthetic power unit, formed by the tension among many different drives, and that activeness takes a special form in such synthetic wills. We also saw how this notion of synthesis introduces another dimension to which Nietzsche gives valuative force: he ranks more complex, encompassing wills more highly. Thus we found a second basic standard besides that of activeness or health: richness of parts. These standards together are most of the crux of Nietzsche's estimations of persons; his

93. He sometimes attributes this basic denial to Plato's overly-strong senses: D448, GS372.

94. Vlastos 1957 can be read as a defense of Plato against this diagnosis of a Platonic 'pessimism'. He argues that "Plato's cosmological pattern is systematically ambiguous", because its designation of the world as a 'copy' can lead to opposite conclusions: either "It is *only* a copy", or "But it is an excellent copy, such as only supreme intelligence joined with perfect goodness could produce" (232). He points out Plato's lasting interest—both theoretical and practical—in the (sensible) world; the *Laws* shows Plato still "earnest about reforming it", even after the collapse of his hope for a philosopher-king (237–38). Sometimes Nietzsche, too, judges that Plato finds 'being' here in this life. So TI/IV associates Plato with a first stage of the error of a 'true world', in which it is "attainable for the wise, the pious, the virtuous [one]—he lives in it, *he is it.* (Oldest form of the idea, relatively sensible [*klug*], simple, convincing, a rewriting of the sentence 'I, Plato, *am* the truth'.)" See also D550.

ideal is, roughly, a will that's especially complex but also active. So much we've seen; now our temporal approach casts better light on this deep structure of values.

First let's note the temporal content already implied in the analysis of the person as a synthetic will. This analysis allowed that a person, as a sum of interacting drives, can be more or less well unified. At one extreme, these drives might remain a mere chaos of warring forces; then it's unclear whether there's really a synthetic being, a person, here after all. At the other extreme, these struggling forces can settle into some stable system of power relations, with a clear identity beyond that of its parts. Recalling this contrast, we see that it has some obvious temporal aspects: persons at these extremes will have radically different ways of 'living through time'.

Where drives are poorly integrated, we expect frequent shifts in relations of dominance, and so in the direction of pursuit and concern. One drive temporarily masters the others and guides the whole's bearing for a while, before being displaced by some other and pressed to a subordinate role in its quite different project. (These shifts in command are encouraged, we know, by the spasmodic and cyclical tempo of drives individually: on reaching their internal goals, they lose force, as the sex drive familiarly does.) Such a person's disunity has a temporal expression: his activity is a choppy succession of episodes little related to one another and not well gathered within projects of broader scope. He views and cares about things now within the perspective of one drive, temporarily dominant, and now within that of another; he can't sustain interest or effort across any longer spans.[95]

Nietzsche thinks this was the typical condition of persons at an early historical stage and that one of the longest and most crucial tasks of society has been to shape its members into units with greater temporal scope: "How can one make a memory for the human animal? How can one impress something upon this partly obtuse, partly silly understanding-of-the-moment [*Augenblicks-Verstande*], this incarnate forgetfulness, in such a way that it remains present?" [GM/II/3]. The cruelest punishments of early societies were imposed to expand their members' memory. But it's not just reaching back to the past that was at stake; such memory was itself pursued for the sake of the 'long chain of will' that promising requires: to be able to intend distant actions, one must have the capacity to remember long-prior intentions. And this longer reach into the future, this ability to will at great distance, is a distinctive achievement of human beings: "To breed an animal that *is allowed to promise*—is this not the paradoxical task that nature has set itself in

95. BT11 says that after the Greeks gave up their belief in an ideal past and an ideal future, they had only "the cheerfulness of the slave who has nothing difficult to be responsible for, nothing great to strive for, and who does not know how to esteem anything past or future higher than the present."

regard to human beings? is it not the genuine problem *about* human beings?" [GM/II/1].[96]

At the opposite extreme from the primitive chaos of drives, the person organized as a more thorough synthesis will show this greater unity or stretch through time. Because his synthetic project attracts, and draws on the strength of, these many particular drives, it's able to keep each within bounds in a way not possible in the original struggle of all against all. Each drive finds its own project partly achieved in the whole, and if it seeks more than this, it finds itself opposed by an organized array of the other drives. Thus that primitive succession of briefly dominating forces is replaced by a will able to command with much greater consistency. Such a person's activities, what he really amounts to, stretch out through time in a way the ill-synthesized person's don't; he 'holds together' periods of activity otherwise disjointed, binding them up in an ongoing effort. By contrast, a single drive expresses itself episodically: when the sex drive hasn't been incorporated into a larger 'personal' project, it acts and is absent by turns.[97]

We saw (in § 1.4) that this self-synthesis and self-control is one condition for activeness in persons. An active will must have a practice of its own that it works to enrich; yet that radically akratic person has no overall project, only the disjointed pursuits of his diverging drives. Also reactive would be a milder case, in which the chaos isn't complete and there *is* a comprehensive project, but one often abandoned and sacrificed to urges or whims of the moment: such a half-synthesized will can't command even its own parts. By contrast, the active person unites his drives, and toward a definite project: enrichment of this synthetic whole itself. So he shows that temporal reach of the unified, better-synthesized will.

In the best case, the active person accomplishes this synthesis over a richness of drives, and so instantiates both of Nietzsche's main values. Again, this combination has a temporal sense: not only does the person, in his unity, stretch out through time, but he does so with a richly

---

96. This view is anticipated in UM/II/1p61, though in a stronger form that denies any temporal scope to the nonhuman, and with that early pessimistic flavor: "Then the human being says 'I remember' and envies the animal, which at once forgets and for whom every moment really dies. . . . Thus the animal lives *unhistorically:* for it goes into the present like a number without any odd fraction left over". HH/I/94: "It is the first sign that animal has become human being when his actions are no longer directed to momentary well-being but to the enduring". See also HH/I/12.

97. Of course, Nietzsche also thinks that the taming of drives to a synthetic end can go too far. They must keep their competitive energy and should only be induced to channel it into a certain type of 'contest' with other drives, analogous to that we'll see he commends among persons. So he's not breaking here with the Heraclitean vision—against Pythagorean 'cooperation'—of forces opposing one another, yet balanced in this opposition.

complex 'rhythm', laid down by his wealth of interlocking projects. Each of his drives is itself a simple telic effort, with its stages toward its ends; so each drive lays down a simple rhythm in the structure of steps in its project. So does, for example, the sex drive, in the stages of (mutual) seduction or indeed of the sex act itself. The activities of such a drive show a distinctive structure of movement through time. And the person, in whom this drive is interwoven with many others pursuing ends of their own, has a far richer telic structure, hence a far richer rhythm: he lives through projects that succeed, overlap, intertwine—their rhythms intersecting intricately. Nietzsche often shows that he values not just the stretch of persons but this rich rhythm held together within that stretch.[98]

Of these two values, we've already seen (in § 2.2) how activeness 'realizes' essence as becoming (the process point), by connecting past and present with future telically, in the way it wills. Now let's note how richness or complexity enhances this achievement, by taking up another aspect of becoming: not process, but context (or 'difference'). The latter point implies, recall, that a drive's identity lies not just in how it strives and interprets, but in how it's interpreted and experienced by other wills. A drive by itself, or a simple will, is fixed in its own viewpoint, and encompasses none of this inter-interpretation. But persons, with their general richness of drives, and more complex persons especially, enact within themselves this interweaving of perspectives. They encompass and embody the diversity and conflict of viewpoints, which is the real 'unit' of reality, because the identity and status of individual drives are determined only in it. They thus 'realize' the contextuality of Nietzsche's becoming point—again, not (necessarily) in consciousness, but in aiming.

Persons accomplish this only when the richness of drives is harnessed actively, only when these drives are induced to collaborate (in a certain way) in a common project. By contrast, the rogue (autonomous) sex drive wills only its own pure activity; its intentional horizons are confined to its own project—everything else is only a help or hindrance to it. Such a will's failure of insight into other willful perspectives is a failure to grasp itself in its context, to see how other forces, with their own views on it, contribute to its own identity. But where instead this drive is 'sublimated' and made to express itself by weaving itself as an ongoing thread in a larger project, its relational being 'appears' to it, is even (in a sense) 'explicit' to it inasmuch as its effort now takes account of the bearing on its behavior of other views.

Of course, the person's grasp of this contextual identity is only very partial; there are many more viewpoints that bear on what he does and

98. BGE252: "But what offends even in the most humane Englishman is his lack of music, to speak in simile [Gleichniss] (and without simile): in the movements of his soul and body he has no beat and dance".

wants than he could hope to encompass. Still, the more drives a person includes and the more divergent these are (for 'richness' must mean this, too), the more he'll embody of the world's range of views and the better his synthetic viewpoint will approach the truth of not just his drives' but his own identity. In chapter 4 I return to examine the epistemological implications of this.

For our purposes now, it is enough to say that power is realizing becoming or difference and involves both richness and activeness, complexity and unity. The becoming point supports a valuing of complex wholes, the 'stretching' and the complicating of beings, both through time and across different (types of) wills.[99] This basic value again links Nietzsche with Heraclitus, just as they shared the metaphysical point that supports it. They both hold that the human being, as an especially rich such whole, has the privileged possibility of 'mirroring' the structure of the world as a whole. This is how we best understand the 'fire' Heraclitus attributes to us, and through which he says we achieve true insight: it's the copresence of many contrary parts in a balance of tension.

This whole Nietzschean account of the person, with these temporal and valuative aspects, is again very intricately both like and unlike Plato's treatment of the same matters.[100] This comes out clearly in the *Republic*'s familiar analysis of the soul, as a complex of intentional parts: mind, will, and the appetites. Like Nietzsche, Plato classes and ranks persons by how well these parts are organized in them, and organized, indeed, by their 'power relations', by which part rules and how. Plato, too, takes as a basic standard in his rankings how well this 'balance of power' in a soul brings unity to it, gives it a single project. The descent he describes from the best aristocratic type to the worst tyrannic one involves a progressive deterioration in the soul's (or society's) organization. And like Nietzsche, Plato stresses how this unity involves temporal stretch, continuity through time.[101]

I explore these comparisons in more detail in § 2.5. But let's antici-

99. BGE212 says that today a philosopher "would be compelled to posit the greatness of the human being, the concept 'greatness', precisely in his comprehensiveness and manifoldness, in his wholeness in many"; but note how this judgment is presented as historically local.

100. See especially Parkes 1994. Nehamas (1985, 182–83) also touches on these relations, in the course of a useful account of how Nietzsche values 'unity of the self'.

101. For Plato, the least satisfactory types of souls—the tyrannic and democratic—are characterized by the inconsistency or choppiness of their lives. *Rep.* 561cd says that the democratic man lives his life "day by day indulging the appetite of the day. . . . And if military men excite his emulation, thither he rushes, and if moneyed men, to that he turns, and there is no order or compulsion in his existence". Only in the aristocratic person is a genuine stability—an approximation to sameness—achieved, under the rule of reason.

pate one result: Plato's principal difference from Nietzsche lies in his different commitment to that continuity; he values it not as a precondition for a rich and extended becoming but as a next-best to eternal sameness or being. Whereas Nietzsche's ideal person enacts the contextual process of his metaphysics, Plato's ideal is the one who best approaches the self-sameness of the Forms. This would not be possible were we formed only of appetites, because these aim at pleasure, and so favor an ever-renewed becoming; they're irredeemably episodic. So Plato posits will and (especially) mind as separate parts of the person, not constructs from the drives, as Nietzsche has them.[102] Mind's supraphysical presence lets into persons a different sort of temporality: mind can, and in itself would, think the same about the same, always.[103]

2.4   History as societies' time

Inevitably, the question next arises as to why Nietzsche doesn't extend this metaphysically grounded preference for synthetic wholes up to the next higher level: to value societies even more than persons. From the arguments just considered, we'd expect him to do so, because these favor generally any more encompassing synthesis, any whole uniting a greater richness of parts. Yet we've already found that he weights his values toward persons, making individual overmen his highest ideal, while (in his later years) rarely considering what a best society might be.[104] In § 1.4 I explained this as due to his doubts that societies really are beings (i.e., well-synthesized wholes) in their own right. Can our fuller picture now improve this account?

Indeed, we really need to replace that account, because it seems annulled by what we've meanwhile learned about wholes. We've seen that Nietzsche casts general doubt on how far *any* multiple wills are gathered or synthesized as wholes, as units: the ambiguous way in which different wills combine rules out altogether the type or degree of

102. WP387 [1887–88]: "The misunderstanding of passion and *reason*, as if the latter were a being [*Wesen*] for itself and not rather a system of relations between various passions and cravings".

103. A fuller look would examine the differences between Platonic appetite and Nietzschean drive. One way that these aren't the same is that drives, as will to power, involve feeling, willing, and thinking (i.e., interpreting) together. Thus we might rather say that Nietzsche admits the three parts of Plato's soul but not as (separable) parts, only as aspects. Plato carves off as independent 'things' what are really just sides of a single phenomenon: the willful perspective. This is how WP492 [1885] attacks Plato's tripartite division; in speaking of the ruling and subordinate drives in the person: "But the most important thing is: that we understand the ruler [*Beherrscher*] and his subjects as *of the same* [*gleicher*] *kind;* all feeling, willing, thinking". Of course it's not 'thinking' as *Plato* means it that Nietzsche admits as such an aspect; it lacks, for example, the affinity with eternity that Plato gives it.

104. KSA/10/7[98] [1883]: "All states and communities are something *lower* than the individual, but *necessary* kinds for his *higher development* [*Hoherbildung*]."

unity we ordinarily presume things to have. But Nietzsche applies this argument as much (or more) to persons as he does to societies, so it can't be a reason for focusing attention on the former rather than the latter. Both lack the type of singleness we've tended to demand of real beings, but neither is thereby rendered any the less important to describe and explain, and neither is thereby dismissed by the power ontology, which demands no such (utter) unity. Thus Nietzsche allows that synthesis is always a matter of degree; he takes the interesting question to be not whether a person or society is a being but to what degree (or how adequately) it is such.

Thus he pays frequent attention to how societies, too, can be better or worse unified, can be more or less fully constituted as beings in their own right. As at the level of persons, here, too, he's struck by the temporal aspect of this variation. If a society's parts (whether persons or factions or practices) are less fully drawn into synthesis—if they periodically command the whole to their ends—that society's history will show the same choppy, fragmented character we've seen some lives have. Here, again, Nietzsche gives this failure a valuative force: the akratic society, like its personal twin, is reactive; it fails to will through time in a way that properly 'realizes' its will to power essence. When he thinks this way, he also imagines societies at the other extreme, with that very type of unification that constitutes synthetic wills as beings themselves; he then shows his attraction to the societal ideal projected by this part of his system. He imagines a society that's an active synthesis: one that best constitutes itself as a most-real whole above all its parts and does so precisely by directing these parts into proper interaction, whereby they join together in a distinctive overall practice.[105]

This better-formed society has the same temporal character as the active person: it stretches out across a real history, through progressively higher versions of a project it takes from its past. Nietzsche stresses this historical stretch; it's (part of) the true goal of societal syntheses. Thus he refers, as a mark of distinction, to how the Roman Empire willed so distant a future. He says that a people, like a person, can and should will its self-overcoming.[106] Again, this doesn't mean dismissing its past; the

105. PTAG1p33 [1873] says that genuine culture is characterized by unity of style. UM/I/1p5 develops this: "Culture is, above all, unity of artistic style in all the expressions of life of a people." Its opposite, barbarism, is "the lack of style, or the chaotic jumble of all styles".

106. WP730 [1885–86]: "So that something should last longer than an individual, . . . every possible kind of limitation, one-sidedness, etc. must be imposed upon the individual." Nietzsche soon says that morality is a means to this end. HH/II/89: "The origin of custom goes back to two thoughts: 'the community is more valuable than the individual [Einzelne]' and 'an enduring advantage is to be preferred to a fleeting one'; from which the conclusion follows that the enduring advantage of the community is to take unconditional precedence over the advantage of the individual". A58 describes the Roman Empire as "the most magnificent form of organiza-

active society honors the past by embracing its inherited practice, though embracing it as something to be enriched. The society, like the person, must act out of faith in the worth of its distinctive form of life. Nietzsche thus values 'tradition' much more than we likely expect; his attacks are against an unhealthy, repeating adulation, which indeed he finds much more common among us than we ever suspect or admit.[107]

It's important to distinguish this stretch of Nietzsche's ideal society from what we ordinarily expect of utopias. These are usually thought of as permanent or extremely stable (the millennium); indeed, this is one common reason for caring more about societies than persons: persons all die, but a society might not. Nietzsche attacks any such hope for a perfect, permanent society, one that brings history to an end. His ideal social group is instead a stage in a history, inevitably overturned. (This renders this ideal consistent with eternal return, at least in its cosmological sense.)[108] Indeed, it's precisely this place in a history—the way this society best holds together its past and future—that marks it as a best becoming and establishes it as ideal. And yet Nietzsche's theory of becoming doesn't altogether cast off that ordinary hope for permanence; his ideal society has that stretch through a history, given by its cultural project. This society makes a history; it causes broad stretches of time to come into existence as parts with organization.

Not only is Nietzsche attracted to the image of such an ideal society, he sometimes seems to weight it above any ideal persons. This tendency seems strongest earlier on, when he's also more optimistic as to what (his) society could be. But even later, he's still occasionally inclined to value societies above the persons they comprise. In this frame of mind, the health of societies becomes of overriding importance to him; thus he even offers a sort of moral duty binding on persons, to make our societies such and such. I examine this in chapter 3.

---

tion under difficult conditions, that has yet been achieved'', as ''the ground for a great culture *that has time*'', and as ''designed to *prove* itself with thousands of years''. See also HH/I/224 on the duration of societies. HH/II/323: ''Whenever a people goes forward and grows it always bursts the girdle that until then gave it its *national* appearance. . . . So if a people has very much that is firm, this is a proof that it wills to become petrified''.

107. UM/II/3p73 warns against the condition of ''a people . . . that has lost loyalty to its antiquity''. Consider also GM/II/19, which tells a more complicated story: the strongest tribes feel most indebted to their ancestors; in primitive cases this is due to fear (and so seems not active or healthy), but in an 'intermediate' period of 'noble tribes' it's due to a 'piety' that Nietzsche treats more favorably. He proposes that the reverence of such a society for its ancestors is the origin of belief in gods.

108. Plato's ideal society is not eternal, either: the aristocratic inevitably declines. Perhaps this flaw, contrasting with the permanence souls can achieve (in the realm of Forms), shows that societies are not fully analogous to souls for Plato, after all. The soul of the well-formed person can escape these cycles of becoming, into that realm of being, but surely societies cannot; they're nothing outside those becomings.

Nietzsche's tendency to shift his attention up to this level is reinforced by his contextual point. He naturally thinks this applies not just to
drives but to persons: these are not (full) beings in themselves but are
their relations to other persons, or to their social context: "The single
one, the 'individual', as hitherto understood by people and philosopher,
is indeed an error: he is nothing by himself, no atom, no 'link in the
chain', nothing merely inherited from former times—he is the whole
single line of humanity up to himself" [TI/IX/33].[109] Thus, to anticipate,
we have to be understood in our context: as members of a society
coming to the end of a long reactive phase. Perhaps even our standing on
the active-reactive scale isn't a fact about us in ourselves but in this
cultural situation; so BGE215 makes "our actions shine alternately in
different colors" because of the different moralities of our modern age. If
a person's status in this crucial dimension is true of him only by virtue of
his society's status, we must lay more stress on the latter. Insofar as being
is diffused to this broader level, so, too, will the theorist's interest tend
to be.

To grasp this context point more concretely, and especially in its
temporal form, let's return to the important discussion of punishment in
the second essay of *On the Genealogy of Morals*. We saw (§ 1.4) how
Nietzsche claims that a custom or practice, for example, punishment, is
progressively reinterpreted to new purposes or roles in a society, and
that these successive meanings are still 'present' in the institution today.
So "the concept 'punishment' in fact no longer sets forth one sense but a
whole synthesis of 'senses': the previous history of punishment in general, the history of its employment for the most different goals, finally
crystallizes into a kind of unity that is . . . totally *indefinable*''; thus we
find "concepts in which a whole process is semiotically combined" [GM/
II/13]. These historical meanings are embedded in the practices passed
down to us, and we punish with those meanings whenever we enter
those practices. What we do gets its identity from its role in the overall
pattern of doings that is its encompassing social practice. This overall
practice in turn gets its identity from its place between a past and a future
practice; it's a becoming from one to the other. This helps explain
Nietzsche's frequent emphasis on the historical study of moralities; we
have to return from this study of temporal and social wholes if we're to
grasp the character of an individual now.

Although we thus find Nietzsche shifting his interest up to this
broader level, and sketching his odd utopia there, we also find him with

109. WP785 [1887]: "every single creature [*Einzelwesen*] is just the *whole process* in a straight line (not merely as 'inherited', but [the process] itself—)". WP682
[1887]: "The ego is a hundred times more than merely a unit in the chain of members; it is this *chain* itself, entirely". The point is made often; see WP659 [1885],
WP678 [1886–87], WP687 [1887], WP379 [1887], WP373 [1888]. And compare
the earlier version of the point in HH/I/272.

dominant qualms against this shift, against giving this ideal highest place in his values. He mainly chooses not to stress societies above persons, as we've seen he does stress persons above drives. So WP766 [1886–87]: *"Basic mistake:* to place the goal in the herd and *not* in single individuals! The herd is a means, no more! But now one is attempting to understand *the herd as an individual* and to ascribe to it a higher rank than to the single one—deepest misunderstanding!!!" The solitary flash of the overman outweighs all else; nor is it even the 'healthiest' or best-synthesized society that best produces such persons. With this, Nietzsche takes a position on a guiding question of the age, a position at odds with how he's often read.[110]

Of course we can find many types of reasons or motives for this turn from society and this focus at the level of persons. But our interest here is in seeing how this choice might reflect a metaphysical point. And it can. Nietzsche thinks societies fall short of a still stricter standard than activeness, one that some persons can meet. We best see why this is by returning to Nietzsche's account of the overman, in his contrast with the other basic human types, the master and the slave.

2.5   The basic temporal types of persons

We can observe some of the more concrete ramifications of Nietzsche's temporal views by reconsidering his typology of persons. Here we're helped again by the comparison with Plato, who of course offers a famous typology of his own: the *Republic's* familiar division of souls (and of cities in parallel) into five types: aristocratic, timocratic, oligarchic, democratic, and tyrannic.[111] As we try to map against this our Nietzschean division of the master, slave, and overman types, we further illuminate the very intricate structure of agreements and disagreements Nietzsche has with Plato. Here, too, he concurs with much more than he usually suggests, and his principal difference is again that point about difference and becoming.

Many of Nietzsche's agreements are once again in the 'form' of his account. We've already seen how he, like Plato, offers parallel typologies for persons and societies. They do so for similar reasons. First, they both analyze persons and societies as structurings of intentional parts: for Nietzsche, the (numberless) drives and persons (or social practices); for

110. Stern (1979, xviii) discusses these issues well, though his conclusion is overstated: "His most serious concern is with the single solitary man; 'the community' and 'the people' (exalted at the expense of 'the masses') are hardly more than concessions to human sociability." This point shows, in the end, how Nietzsche turns from the fascist ideal that later tempts Heidegger.

111. Here I focus on the *Republic's* position and set aside questions of Plato's development, especially his later treatments of the topic in the *Statesman* and *Laws.* I've been much helped by the discussion in Parkes 1994.

Plato, the three psychic faculties and three social classes (and civic functions). Second, they both treat the parts as isomorphic: Nietzschean drives and persons are both wills to power; Platonic faculties and classes both fall into rational, willful, and appetitive types. Third, they both identify the main types of persons and societies as the basic ways these parts can rule and obey one another; this focus on power structures is especially worth noting in Plato. Fourth, they tend to connect these two typologies 'causally', by supposing that each personal type occurs most commonly and purely in the isomorphic society (the society in which that type is indeed dominant).[112]

More relevant to our temporal theme is a further agreement. Like Plato, Nietzsche presents his parallel typologies in the course of interlocking stories—one psychological, the other historical—telling how these types evolve into one another. He presents these types as stages in a certain common or natural development, by which (to begin with) master tends to decline into slave (whether in one life or intergenerationally), in the midst of a larger, and isomorphic, social process.[113] Nietzsche's stress on the 'genealogy' of these types fits of course with his theory of becoming, but we should note that Plato is similarly insistent on placing his types in process. Indeed, even the overall plot or direction of his story—how the aristocratic type degenerates down through all the others—resembles Nietzsche's account of decadence from a masterly health.

Of course there are disagreements, too. First, Nietzsche's types themselves are importantly different from Plato's and don't map easily against them; for example, his master is not quite Plato's aristocrat. Second, this is partly due to different accounts of what the parts of persons and societies are. Third, even where their types do coincide sufficiently for us to take them to have the same 'objects' in view, we find Nietzsche valuing and ranking these types differently than Plato does. Fourth, befitting this reranking, Nietzsche's story takes in the end a different turn: the decline from that healthy beginning is only a phase, not the constant logic of all (earthly) psychic and social development. His story has, he hopes, a 'happy ending' in the overman who recaptures the master's health, but in a higher form made possible by the experience of the slave. Fifth, at this different ending, Nietzsche disrupts (as

112. On the first point, see how *Rep.* 437–41 establishes the three parts to the soul by showing how they oppose one another. On the second point, *Rep.* 435e: "[W]e are surely compelled to agree that each of us has within himself the same parts and characteristics as the city? Where else would they come from?" On the third point, *Rep.* 444d: "to produce justice is to establish the parts of the soul as compelling [*kratein*] and compelled by one another according to nature, while injustice is that they are leading [*archein*] and led one by another contrary to nature." On the fourth point, *Rep.* 544d–e: "governments are born . . . from the characters of the citizens, which tip the scales and drag other things after them".

113. WP712 [1887] gives an abstract account of these basic movements.

Plato nowhere does) the isomorphism between personal and social types. He doubts whether a society could be structured as the overman is, could 'realize' will to power to the extent the overman does. These doubts might be his ultimate ground for valuing persons above societies. Once again, we'll find all these points to have strong temporal aspects.

2.5.1   The master's active effort to preserve

The starting points to Plato's and Nietzsche's stories are surprisingly similar.[114] Both begin by describing an original healthy society, with an aristocratic power structure. Both stress how this structure gives the society a degree of unity and self-control that is then progressively lost. And both take this societal unity to be mirrored in the personal unity of each of its members. So in Plato's ideal city, each citizen "must be directed to the one task he has by nature [*pephuken*], so that he should pursue his own one task and himself become not many but one, and the whole city should grow [*phuetai*] one and not many" (*Rep.* 434d).[115] We've seen (in § 1.5.1) that Nietzsche thinks of the early master society in just this way. Moreover, he credits this society with originating those traditional virtues Plato famously restricts to his ideal republic; so he stresses that truthfulness and justice are 'masterly' virtues.[116]

Of course, Nietzsche's original society shows a major difference from Plato's: it lacks the philosopher-kings. It is rather ruled, we might say, by the spirited or timocratic type, but as he's described in the ideal, aristo-cratic city and not as Plato thinks he would be if really in command, in a timocracy.[117] This is the Platonic type on which we best map Nietzsche's master, as is confirmed by the similar roles they assign these types. So Plato stresses how this type *preserves;* he defines the courage of the spirited (their special virtue in the ideal city) as "preservation of the belief which has been instilled by the law through education as to what things . . . are to be feared" (*Rep.* 429c). Nietzsche attributes to the masters much the same function, but with one large difference: his masters take this law (which they then preserve) not from philosophers, the reason-ruled type, but from their own instincts and tradition. He claims these can guide them healthily, as reason and Platonic philoso-phers in fact could not (being themselves symptoms of decline).

---

114. These similarities are partly due to the way both Plato and Nietzsche partly model this type after (their notions of) an archaic phase of Greek society.

115. See also *Rep.* 462a–b on disunity as the greatest evil for a city.

116. On truth, see GM/I/5 and BGE260. On justice, GM/II/11: "Wherever jus-tice is practiced and maintained one sees a stronger power seeking a means of putting an end to the senseless raging of resentment among the weaker ones . . . that stand under it".

117. On the character of the spirited type in the ideal city, see *Rep.* 429a–30c. On this type when it rules, see 547c–50b. (This critique of the type when loose from

So Nietzsche redescribes Plato's aristocracy, by expelling reason from it or (differently put) by infusing this reason back into the instincts (the 'bodies') of the spirited, willful ones. At the same time, he reappraises this type; its very unity or cohesiveness, its ability to preserve itself, are indeed the grounds for its strength and health, yet also its limitations. Nietzsche's ideal person, and perhaps his ideal society, will be less fully unified than Plato's and less purely healthy.

Leaving Plato for now, let's examine more closely this ambivalence Nietzsche shows toward his master type, noting especially its temporal side.[118] In our earlier look at the master and his society (§ 1.5.1), we saw that the latter has priority in a certain way: the master is chiefly the product of his society. He is as he is, because so he was born and raised; his virtues are his group's, the activities he excels in precisely those they customarily practice. He shares not just in these concrete practices but in a certain form or structure, one with a strong temporal aspect.

His group holds (political) mastery, because its energies are committed to a simple and well-organized system of practices. This commitment amounts to a temporal stance: the master group views its current practice as given to it by ancestors it reveres and as deserving to be preserved and carried forward through its descendents.[119] The group transmits this same structure to its members; it creates them in its image. So each master is raised to be a simple and stable structure of drives himself, also willing growth in an activity with which he identifies—his role. Command is delegated downward, and each part of society rules its own parts: the master holds his drives to a more abiding project in which they find joint expression. Thus, like his group, he stretches through time: committed to an overall project, he has memory and conscience, hence the 'right to make promises'.[120]

Both the dependence of the master on his group and this 'conservative' temporal stance, however, make him fall short of Nietzsche's high-

---

the control of reason might be developed as a Platonic 'counterdiagnosis' of Nietzsche's ideal, to be set against the Nietzschean diagnosis of Plato's philosopher-king, which follows.)

118. Nietzsche is less critical of this master society in his earlier writings: this is the 'healthy society' that appears as so prominent a good in PTAG [1873] and UM.

119. TI/IX/39: "In order for there to be institutions, there must be . . . the will to tradition, to authority, to responsibility for centuries to come, to the *solidarity* of chains of generations, forward and backward *ad infinitum*. When this will is there, something like the *imperium Romanum* is founded".

120. So Nietzsche speaks of the noble tempo as *lento* [BGE256] and says that the master morality includes the "capacity for, and the duty of, long gratitude and long revenge" [BGE260]. The importance he places on this extended temporal scope is also clear from BGE72: "Not the strength but the duration of high perception makes high human beings." See also WP47 [1888] and WP45 [1888], which speak of the ability of the strong 'to postpone reaction', i.e., not to be shifted away from their course by internal or external forces.

est ideal. As preformed into a synthesis by the natural bias of his simple drives, the master identifies with, and strives to enhance, an activity that was settled before him and is little open to revision now. He values only variations on this activity itself; it's something necessary for him, embedded as he is in habits or customs. He does indeed will power actively—'from abundance', loving his past and striving to improve it—but this self-improvement is 'better playing the game' and not refashioning current practices into new ones. His effort is mainly at continuing just such a life as his own; what's foreign is not worth doing, and he keeps it away or makes it simply serve his existing practice.

This means that the master has no experience of creating, which is the fullest type of growth or power. His straightforward health stands in his way. His preset simplicity of drives leaves him little acquaintance with that flux of perspectives—that worrying oscillation between opposing viewpoints, that upsetting of any attitude temporarily uppermost—which most spurs effort at change. He stands, as it were, before the revenge-inspiring complaint against "time and its 'It was'". Self-contentment belongs to his Apollonian health. So he's unable to benefit from that "discipline [*Zucht*] of suffering, of *great* suffering, . . . [that] has created all enhancements of humanity so far" [BGE225].[121] And so those inflating myths the masters tell about their ancestors—how "it is only through the sacrifices and accomplishments of the ancestors that the tribe [*Geschlecht*] *continues*" [GM/II/19]—must have a germ of truth for Nietzsche: as preservers, they do rank lower than originators.

As we might put it, the master's temporal stretch isn't broad enough. His hard-won self-memory, which stretches him out through past and future, doesn't reach over the borders of his practice itself, to grasp it in its own becoming, in its coming to be and passing away. He misses the practice's temporal contingency, misses it not in his theories or stories but in the way he himself wills. He doesn't stretch beyond his way of life, to accept how it came to be and to pursue its proper death (its self-overcoming). Rather than living in his practice as at the tipping balance between different practices past and future, he rests comfortably within it. Thus he fails to reflect, in this deep attitude toward his own activities, their external context, the way they indeed 'are a becoming'.

Consider in particular the master's reach to the past. To borrow the

---

121. TI/IX/47: "The beauty of a race or family . . . is the end result of the accumulated work of generations. . . . The good things are immeasurably costly; and the law always holds that one who *has* them is someone other than one who *acquires* them. Everything good is inherited; whatever is not inherited is imperfect, is a beginning." Nietzsche describes this past training—with emphasis on the brutality it involved—in GM/II/1ff.; see also BGE188 and WP969 [1887]. Yet the masters attribute their creation to gods or godlike ancestors. Consider also HH/II/90: "The good conscience has the bad conscience as a preliminary stage, not as opposite: for everything good was once new, consequently unfamiliar, contrary to custom, *unethical*, and gnawed at the heart of its happy inventor like a worm."

terms in *Untimely Meditations*, he's at once both 'antiquarian' and 'un-historical' toward his past. On the one hand, he's reverent toward the past that's his own: "The history of his city becomes for him the history of himself; he understands its walls, its towered gate, its council-decrees, its holidays, like an illuminated diary of his youth" [UM/II/3].[122] At the same time, he forgets whatever is other than himself; his confidence in his own way of life is so thorough that he scarcely notices other types of lives as rivals or sources for it. So he shrugs off assaults and temptations from other wills. He forgets how his project arose from others. It seems to him something complete and timeless, it exhausts his horizons.[123] The overman's temporal reach will be longer than this. But the route to the overman lies through the slave.

2.5.2   The slave's revenge against time

Let's approach this Nietzschean type by returning to our comparison with Plato. The two agree, as we've seen, in a certain general story about an inevitable decline or degeneration from the original healthy aristocracy. Both present this as a relaxing of the society's unifying discipline, expressed above all in its 'breeding' and 'education', which no longer shape new generations into a single-minded commitment to traditional roles.[124] Both think this indiscipline results in a gradual multiplying and diversifying of the types of persons (or lives) the society holds, an enrichment at the expense of its unity. And both think this enrichment accompanies a breaking down of the hierarchic divisions among types, a 'leveling' that misguidedly tries to render all persons equal.

This overlap between the two stories emerges most clearly in Plato's description and critique of his 'democratic' type, which looks, in all these ways, much like Nietzsche's. So *Rep.* 561e stresses the type's internal richness: "this man is manifold and full of the greatest number of char-

---

122. As the passage continues, it makes some of the temporal points above: "Here one could live, he says to himself, for here one can live; and here one shall live, for we are tough and not to be ruined overnight. Thus with this 'we' he looks beyond his transitory, odd single life and feels himself to be the spirit of his house, his race, and his city." BGE260: "The deep reverence for age and tradition—the whole law stands on this double reverence—the belief and prejudice in favor of ancestors and disfavor of those to come are typical of the morality of the powerful".

123. GM/I/10: "To be incapable of taking one's enemies, one's accidents, even one's *misdeeds* seriously for long—that is the sign of strong, full natures".

124. I've mentioned how Nietzsche seems (to our ears) to overstress the role of nature (as opposed to nurture) here; again, he follows Plato, who (with a share of irony hard to estimate, in words he attributes to the Muses) blames the beginning of decline on mathematical errors that lead the rulers to "join brides and grooms at the wrong time [*para kairon*]" (*Rep.* 546d). (The passage speaks next of the neglect of education.)

acters [*ethon*], just like that city". And *Rep.* 562–63 develops 'freedom' [*eleutheria*] as democracy's own good, a freedom that breaks down all the society's hierarchies (subject-ruler, father-son, teacher-learner, master-slave, man-woman, human-animal), in each case 'likening' high and low to one another. Plato's clear distaste for this anticipates Nietzsche's. Indeed, Plato even mocks similarly the democratic pity for the low: "All these things together make the soul of the citizens so sensitive [*hapalen*] that if anyone brings up a word about slavery, they become angry and cannot endure it" (*Rep.*563d).

Like Nietzsche, Plato offers a parallel account of how this 'equalizing' occurs in the 'politics of the soul', within each democrat: "he puts pleasures on an equal footing and so spends his life, always giving over the leadership of himself to one, as if chosen by lot, until he is sated and then to another, not disvaluing any but nourishing them all equally" (*Rep.* 561b). "And he lives on, yielding day by day to the desire at hand" (*Rep.* 561c).

Of course, there are also major differences between these stories of degeneration—above all, I think, that Plato's gives no role to resentment, which is so crucial to Nietzsche's. Whereas Plato indeed makes envy a factor in his story—the envy of those who have less[125]—he shows no inkling of that obsessive, reactive envy and hatred for any fortunate ones, nor of the deviousness, often subconscious, with which it shapes new values. (This fits with Plato's innate nobility, as Nietzsche saw it.) So Plato thinks of that 'degeneration' as chiefly a consequence of the top class's own decline, not crediting the underclasses with the will or wit to tempt and subvert them. By contrast, we saw (in § 1.5.2) how Nietzsche makes such resentment the main author of the 'slave morality', which is itself the key weapon in the 'slave revolt'; resentment is thus a major ingredient in his notion of the slave type itself.

Let's compare more closely Nietzsche's and Plato's notions of the slave. Both abstract this from the economic condition of enslavement, making it a psychic condition and a type for persons. So Plato's slave is anyone who lacks (is deficient in) the rational part and hence needs other persons to play this role. This sense extends the term's reference to nearly everyone, perhaps to all but the philosopher.[126] Such persons, where they rule themselves, act from irrational appetite (and spirit); they act, indeed, like animals. Most metaphysically, they express the corrupting tendency inherent in matter itself: becoming's love for itself, instead of being. Other than by obedient service to the rational ones, they are good for nothing, for Plato.

---

125. See, e.g., *Rep.* 556c–d.

126. Vlastos 1941, 291: "The fully enlightened aristocrats are a small minority. . . . All the rest are in some degree *douloi* in Plato's sense of the word". Vlastos goes on to argue that the master/slave relation is fundamental not just to

By contrast, the Nietzschean slave is at once uglier—sicker and more malevolent—but also more fruitful and promising. Indeed, far from embodying the animal in man, it's in this type that humanity becomes 'sicker and more interesting' than the animals, hence more itself. The slave type is largely responsible for the 'spiritualizing' of society and species. Hence, whereas for Plato the degeneration of persons and societies toward this type is an unalloyed evil, Nietzsche thinks of this movement 'dialectically', as a retreat that could allow a great advance, as this sickness is taken up into a 'higher health'.

Of course, Nietzsche's redescription of the slave is meant to make the term apply to Plato, or at least to that aspect of him touched by Socrates; it implies a diagnosis and critique of that thrust in Plato's thought that expresses (Nietzsche thinks) Socrates' resentment.[127] Plato redirects this resentment metaphysically, against all the sensible, passionate world; he hates it as mere becoming and invents a world of being to put it to shame. This attitude is shared, of course, by his 'philosopher', his ideal human type and ruler in his ideal society. Nietzsche's diagnosis finds this type secretly akin to that degenerate 'democrat' he and Plato are agreed in rejecting. And yet, with this diagnosis Nietzsche isn't dismissing Plato as Plato does his own slave type. First, the diagnosis applies only to that aspect of Plato and his philosopher (in § 2.5.3 we'll see how another aspect fits with Nietzsche's own ideal). Second, the diagnosis recognizes even that resentful element as productive and as a necessary phase in a fuller view.

Again, let's put Plato aside to look more closely at the temporal aspect to Nietzsche's views here, returning first from his slave to his decadent. As the masterly discipline is relaxed, and persons and society cultivate ever-richer drives and practices, they take on that inconsistency through time, that 'choppiness' in activity and experience, that mark the poorly synthesized will and stand in clearest contrast to a masterly continuity. The decadent is jostled constantly from one view of how to live to another, taking them all as democratically equal. In this flux of the drives

---

Plato's politics but to his psychology and cosmology, which rest on the conception of material necessity (and the body in particular) as slavelike and as properly ruled by the soul (and especially *nous*). Vlastos (1941, 303) links this "hierarchic pattern" with Plato's "dualist epistemology" (his separation of Forms from sensibles) and contrasts it with "another world-view that is [its] antithesis"—that of the Ionian physicists (along with the Sophists). But Nietzsche straddles the fence: he rejects that dualism, replacing it with a quasi-Protagorean 'perspectivism', yet still keeps Plato's insistence on hierarchy. (In chapter 4 we'll see how this position rests on a way of 'ranking' perspectives epistemologically.)

127. BGE190: "There is something in the morality of Plato that does not genuinely belong to Plato but is merely met in his philosophy—one might say, in spite of Plato: namely the Socratism for which he was genuinely too noble." See also BGE191.

and perspectives, he experiences becoming more vividly than the master does. He suffers from this flux, and this is even the overwhelming feature of all his experience: shift in perspective occasioned by the uncontrolled play of his drives.

Resentment changes this. When one who suffers, whether from decadence or simple subjection, finds someone or something to blame for his pain, he can acquire a new focus. The new personal project of revenge against what makes him suffer can help him impose a new order on his chaos of drives. And yet this is a flawed unification, toward a reactive project. It confers only a defective continuity. So the resenter, the slave type proper, is 'antiquarian' and 'unhistorical' in opposite ways from the master: toward what's other and what's himself, respectively. So he 'dwells in the past' unhealthily: he's fixed on things done to him and reacts resentfully to them. But he fails to find in his own past anything positive in which to grow; he lacks memory for what's really his. So he wars against the past and works for a future that altogether cancels or denies it.

This negative project also distorts his temporal rhythm. It fails to include and express his richness of drives and to take a natural rhythm from these. So he lives through time in a wooden way, without tempo or spontaneity, trying always to hold in view that artificial ideal and to allow none of the shifting play of his drives to break in on that constant effort; as it were, he continually plays the same note. This contrasts with the master's temporal texture, laid down by the interplay among his channeled drives. Thus the two types of sickness miss having such texture in opposite ways: the decadent by living with no ordered rhythm at all, the resenter by marching to an artificially measured one.[128]

An especially revealing case of this detexturing occurs in the slave's pursuit of objective truth. We saw (§1.5.2) how the struggle against the chaos of drives can prompt this goal: objectivity is attractive as a viewpoint above all those warring forces. This attractiveness has a temporal side: one wants a truth to 'possess' unceasingly, in a steady state of belief and understanding. One wants 'to think always the same about the same'. Indeed, the goal of objective truth is shaped by the desire for a 'pure present', for an experience complete in itself, not taking its sense or value contextually, from its past or future. I pursue this further in chapter 4.

The evolution of the slave type has a final stage, however—a decadence of its own, in the slide toward nihilism. By leveling society, these values based in resentment tend to undercut themselves at their source; that focusing resentment fades. So the slave or slave society tends to lose its will and coherence just as the master did. Drives and persons are freed

128. This may be why Nietzsche says at BGE216 that "the music in our conscience, the dance in our spirit" opposes (slave) morality. See GS76 on the metronomic tempo of virtuous conformity.

again from constraint; practice and experience are splintered again. In fact, the sway of those reactive values has multiplied the stock of drives or activities of which persons are composed; it has made them more complex and spiritual. So an even greater diversity now unfolds.

This has its temporal expression, too: it repeats, in more intense form, the temporal features of that masterly decadence. So BGE224: "The past of every form and way of life, of cultures that formerly lay right next to one another, upon one another, now streams into us 'modern souls', thanks to this mixing; our instincts now run back everywhere; we ourselves are a kind of chaos".[129] This sense for the past doesn't imply the sort of long-reaching will the master has. In fact it reflects a great temporal fragmentation. So TI/IX/39: "One lives for today, one lives very fast". Nietzsche hopes, of course, to organize this richest chaos.

2.5.3   The overman's embrace of becoming

Let's start by quickly placing this type, Nietzsche's ideal,[130] against Plato. We saw how Plato's own ideal, his philosopher, king in the ideal aristocracy, is diagnosed by Nietzsche as infected by a slavish resentment, which makes this ideal turn its back on becoming, to aim at an imaginary being. However, this diagnosis undermines only a part of Plato's conception of the type. There are other aspects of his philosopher-king that Nietzsche appropriates into his own ideal, which is indeed largely a rewriting of Plato's.[131] So the overman is a different type of philosopher, one who rules a different society in a different way. I largely postpone treating these aspects of Nietzsche's ideal—what type of society he rules and why he still is a 'wisdom-lover'—until chapters 3 and 4, respectively. Here let's focus on how this new ideal overcomes resentment by turning back from being to becoming. It will emerge that even here Nietzsche tries to save some of Plato's point, tries to win that 'being' after all, in the thought of eternal return.

We've seen how the overman is one among many who bear, microcosmically, this nihilistic age's exceptional richness of conflicting drives.

129. So the fragmenting of its will is expressed in a like democratization in the way it looks back: all pasts, of the too many forces it's able to sympathize with, are accorded equal weight. In UM/II the unhealthy 'historical' view holds that all pasts are relevant, because none is really its own.

130. As noted in § 1.5.3, I adopt the term 'overman' for a Nietzschean ideal he more often speaks of in other terms. For example, he describes it (I claim) in speaking of the 'new philosophers' of BGE, and indeed of that one new philosopher who accomplishes the 'revaluation of values' that leads us out of nihilism. (This suggests how the ideal narrows from a type to that one 'world-historical' individual Nietzsche aspired to become.)

131. These affinities emerge most strongly in Nietzsche's discussions of the 'laws of Manu' in A57 and elsewhere. In chapter 3, I weigh his commitment to the very Platonic social structure he attributes to Manu. Is this his ideal society?

He's the very rare one of these able to accomplish a healthy synthesis of them; most such inclusive persons collapse under the stress of this task. In succeeding, the overman imposes a masterlike activeness on a slavelike diversity. He unifies the opposite forces he bears, ordering the flux that the slave, too, suffers but can't overcome. Thus he meets a challenge unknown to the master, whose drives (concerns and practices) are a simple fit with one another. In the person of Zarathustra, "all opposites are bound to a new unity" [EH/TSZ/6]; he frames a richest synthetic whole.[132]

This has some first, obvious temporal implications. Such an overman has an especially rich and expansive rhythm through time. He has "an instinct for rhythmic relations, that arches over wide spaces of forms—length, the need for a *wide-arching* rhythm" [EH/TSZ/3]; in him "all things have their streaming and counterstreaming and ebb and flood" [TSZ/III/12/19]. This ordering into an overall project gives the overman temporal stretch, gives it even to an exceptional degree.[133] But this ordering is not imposed on the drives from without, like the slave's mechanical and rational rhythm; instead, it expresses 'organically' the drives themselves, mixing their idiosyncratic tempos into a broader pattern. These intertangled expressions of his drives make a most elaborate yet still ordered music: "the *dance* is not the same as a feeble reeling back and forth between different impulses. High culture will look like an audacious dance" [HH/I/278].

We've seen how such points explain the overman's capacity for the thought of eternal return. The slave wants all to culminate in an end state that is perfect because it is beyond all becoming, whereas the master wants to preserve just his own practices. Neither can accept that all things eternally have and will become in the opposing ways they now do; for the slave, this leaves too much that's evil (potent) in the world, for the master, too much that's bad (sick). Because the overman takes up in himself these oppositions, he can accept, feelingly, that same diversity in the world in general. He can delight in the play of forces around him and can want more of them all, more of the same.[134] So he gives widest

132. TI/IX/49 says of Goethe: "What he willed was *totality;* he fought the apartness [*Auseinander*] of reason, senses, feeling, and will . . .; he disciplined himself to wholeness, he *created* himself".

133. WP962 [1885]: "[The great human being] has in his gathered doings a long logic, hard to survey because of its length, and consequently misleading; he has a capacity to stretch out his will over great expanses of his life".

134. WP967 [1885]: "The essential point is: the greatest perhaps also have great virtues, but in that case also their opposites. I believe that it is precisely through the presence of opposites, and their feelings, that the great human being, *the bow with the great tension*, arises". TI/IX/49: "Such a spirit *who has become free* stands with a joyous and trusting fatalism in the midst of all, in the *belief* that only the single is loathsome [*verwerflich*], and that all is redeemed and affirmed in the whole—*he does not negate any more*".

scope to that active way of willing the past, which we analyzed back in § 2.2. We saw there (interpreting TSZ/II/20) how the inability to will the past—a will's impotence toward it—is the metaphysical motive for revenge. Now we see that it's the overman who overcomes this deep root to resentment most broadly or thoroughly: he sees all the world's past as him or his and wants it all again.

Of course no person could include, literally or strictly, all the detailed diversity of the world's forces. What counts is that one bear certain types—certain pairs of opposed types of forces—and indeed one pair above all. The overman must accept, as a welcomed part of himself, sickness as well as health; in doing so, he wills the interinvolvement of opposites, 'difference', even in the essential valuative dimension of the active-reactive, the most testing place to do so. It might seem he *can't* will so. Mustn't the ideal person be most purely healthy?[135] But although the overman's values do favor health—and indeed pick sides in all the other oppositions he bears—he sees in each case the worth of the other. Above all, he sees the value of sickness in health: how the highest activeness isn't purely so but has taken reactivity up into itself.

The overman acts on this lesson: he finds and even cultivates sickness in himself as a necessary stage in his self-creation. So GM/III/9 describes the self-experimentation of modern thinkers: "Afterward we heal ourselves: being-sick is instructive".[136] The overman loves his own past sickness and wills that it recur, because he sees its role in a higher health that incorporates it. This is his Dionysian health, unlike the master's Apollonian in not being uniform, not a health that wills only health. Nietzsche also calls it *"the great health*—that one does not merely

135. This is an instance of a problem that arises for other philosophical (or, more often, religious) positions that also recommend a 'universal affirmation', while continuing to express valuative preferences for some things within the whole. It arises in Heraclitus, most obviously if we accept the disputed DK102: "For god all things are fair and good and just, but men have taken some things as unjust, others as just." This raises a puzzle about the many preferential judgments Heraclitus himself elsewhere makes.

136. WP1014 [1885–86]: "It is only a matter of force: to have all the sickly tendencies of the century, but to balance [*ausgleichen*] them in an overrich, plastic restorative force." WP1013 [1885–86]: "Health and sickliness: one should be careful! The standard remains the efflorescence of the body, the agility [*Sprungkraft*], courage, and cheerfulness of the spirit—but also, of course, *how much of the sickly it can take upon itself and overcome*—how much it can *make* healthy." WP864 [1888]: "And all human beings, especially the most healthy, are *sick* at certain times of their lives". Compare TI/IX/45: "Almost every genius knows, as one of his developments . . . , a feeling of hatred, revenge, and revolt against all that already *is*, that no longer *becomes*". Many other passages stress the necessity of (not quite sickness but) suffering in the highest lives; e.g., BGE225, BGE270, WP382 [1887]. We might think here of Wittgenstein, who so regrets (or does he?) his ever-recurring fall back into confusion, which then needs to be cured by philosophy again.

have, but also continually still acquires and must acquire, because one always again gives it up and must give it up" [GS382; quoted EH/TSZ/2]. He gives it up by becoming reactive again and again, and then struggling to create a still more comprehensive health beyond that illness. This shows a still stronger sense in which the overman is, as we saw before, a synthesis of both master and slave. It gives us a new way of hearing GM/ I/16 (speaking of master and slave values): "today there is perhaps no more decisive mark of a *'higher nature'*, a more spiritual nature, than being divided in this sense and still really a battleground for these opposites".[137]

Nietzsche stresses in many ways the importance of this rise to a higher health—and its difficulty. It's reflected in our age's special task, overcoming nihilism; Nietzsche thinks he has struggled through this himself.[138] It's the great challenge faced by Zarathustra throughout TSZ/ III: the overcoming of nausea, the masterlike distress he feels at the thought that even the sickest and weakest will recur.[139] So (in 2/2) just after he first thinks the thought of eternal return, Zarathustra has a vision: "A young shepherd I saw, writhing, gagging, in spasms, his face distorted, and a heavy black snake hung out of his mouth." This is what still prevents him from embracing eternal return; when (in 13/2) he overcomes this distress, he identifies the snake (and the shepherd): "The great disgust [*Überdruss*] with human beings—*this* choked me and had crawled into my throat." "And the eternal recurrence even of the smallest!—That was my disgust with all existence!" He succeeds in affirming eternal return when he bites off the head of the snake and spits it out, when he spits out his nausea and can will that even the worst will recur. But it's important to see that the snake is not just nausea over the sickness of others but also Zarathustra's own sickness; he was sick with this nausea. So, in this image, he also finds sickness lodged within and spits it out, in the act he now learns to love most: becoming healthy. He thus makes himself overman, out of what's masterly and slavish in himself. But he doesn't expect to remain snake-free; he wants to repeat again and again this becoming sick for the sake of creating a still higher health.[140]

137. See HH/I/P/3–6's account of how the "free spirit" must slowly win a "great health" out of sickness; also HH/II/P/6, GS/P/3, NCW/E/1.

138. WP/P/3 [1887–88]: "[He that speaks here] has already lived nihilism to the end in himself—has left it behind, beneath, outside himself". Also WP273 [1886– 87], WP25 [1887], WP1031 [1887], WP1041 [1888]. WP/P/4 [1887–88] speaks of "a movement that in some future will replace this perfect nihilism—but *presupposes* it, logically and psychologically, and surely can come only *after* and *out of it*".

139. Zarathustra indeed must feel this nausea more intensely and personally than the master, because he bears this sickness himself. For him the issue arises over himself, whereas the master finds weakness and sickness only in others, and so can view it in more detachment—as a useful tool, an external means.

140. Note how this nausea is only a last and most severe among many ways Zarathustra 'becomes ill'. At the very opening, he explains (to the sun) his decision to

This shows how the special achievement of the overman—what we've so far called his 'acceptance' or 'embrace' of opposites and eternal return—isn't (as those terms might suggest) just a thought, not a state or possession or momentary event, but a way of willing, of moving through time. It lies not in anything the overman says or thinks but in the structure of his stretch toward the future, in his pursuit of the project of bringing sickness to health. It's in the style or point of his effort, that he 'realizes' being as becoming and wills eternal return. Let's see just how this works.

Like the slave, the overman experiences the world's flux quite directly: his drives tend to fly apart, and he suffers from their struggle. This flux within is his sickness. But he doesn't respond to this pain as the slave does, by blaming and attacking the drives that produce this flux and by trying to freeze himself into an objective or moral perspective (and activity) quite foreign to them. Nor indeed does he proceed as the master type has, by pruning his drives into a simpler and univalent set, able to maintain itself stably. He overcomes that painful disunity by creating a coherent practice that bears those opposites in a newfound but tentative balance. He creates this new self not to endure but in the expectation that it will be dissolved or disrupted by still-new forces and pressed into a still-higher synthesis with them.

Of course, the overman identifies with this practice he creates; he prides himself in the distinctive life he is making. But he loves it also for its roots and its fruits, for the different behaviors it's coming from and going toward. Thus he identifies across the borders of his own activity, thereby 'realizing' its true contextual identity. He acts in the view that his practice has come from and will go back into ways of life ambiguously other than this one that defines him. He makes his new self *as* out of something other and *as* on the way to becoming something other again. He shapes an organized viewpoint (and practice) out of the disparate forces he finds at hand, giving these parts a richer expression and sense. But he shapes this viewpoint not as an end or culmination but as one to be given a richer sense in turn, by being itself destroyed and replaced.

This shows how he grasps his behavior as a becoming: from one other, toward another other. He experiences not just the 'internal' temporal rhythm to his way of life but the 'external' temporal flow by which it's generated and destroyed. He's not, like the master, quite 'habituated to' or 'immersed within' his current activity. He wills destruction, death,

---

teach as a "climb into the depths" of (ordinary) human beings: "I must, like [*gleich*] you, *go under*—as the human beings call it, to whom I will [to go] down." See also the accounts of his being bitten by an adder [I/19] and a tarantula [II/7]. And in III/16/6: "this is my alpha and omega, that all that is heavy should become light". Perhaps Nietzsche has this in mind in BGE70: "If one has character, one has also one's typical experience, that always recurs."

and going under as the master doesn't: he strives to create a self, but one he intends to dissolve into suffering conflict again, for the sake of one still further.[141] This makes his own temporal structure transparent to him: he acknowledges the relevance to what he is of a differing past and future, acknowledges this not consciously but in how he wills.

By reaching this way across the borders of his self, the overman's will has great temporal stretch. But it has it another way, too: the overman is also defined by his special social role, by how he shapes his society's overall course. He does for it just what he does for himself: he creates for it, too, a great health, out of the nihilism he finds it in. This is why he's "a *world-ruling* spirit, a destiny" [EH/TSZ/6].[142] His being the overman, and the highest type, lies not just in what he is or how he wills 'in himself' but in this role he plays, in his place in a context, which is what we expect, of course, from that contextual ontology we've already found in Nietzsche. The overman 'is' (partly) what he brings his society from and then toward.

So he has in fact two roles: he's the announcer of nihilism or the death of God, the destroyer of resentment's values, and he's the creator of new and healthier values. He's the one who tips a nihilistic society over into a new health. He thereby lives at a pivotal moment—"on a high ridge between two seas, . . . between past and future" [TSZ/III/16/1]—his *life* is a pivotal moment, the 'great noon': "My task, to prepare a moment of the highest self-reflection for humanity, a *great noon* when it looks back and looks outward, when it emerges from the mastery of accidents and priests and for the first time poses, *as a whole*, the question of Why? and For What?" [EH/D/2].[143] Just as the overman's ecstatic vision of eternal return is a 'special moment' that embodies and illuminates the temporal logic of his life as a whole, so his life, in turn, encapsulates and occasions his society's transformation. With his revaluation of values, he redeems not only his own past but also that of his society: he gives new meaning to that history of reactive values by making it issue in this higher health.

Thus Nietzsche anticipates a newly active society achieved by the overman on the far side of nihilism; this is the closest we find to a

141. TI/X/5: "*to be oneself* the eternal pleasure of becoming, beyond terror and pity, that pleasure which included even *pleasure in destroying*". We now see this must mean even pleasure in destroying one's self.

142. WP999 [1884]: "*Rank order:* he who *determines* values and guides the will of millennia by guiding the highest natures, is *the highest human being.*" So Nietzsche says at WP976 [1884] and WP979 [1885] that the philosopher must be a legislator.

143. KSA/13/25[5] [1888]: "I have the *destiny* of *humanity* in the hand—: I break it invisibly apart into two pieces, before me, after me". (Cf. EH/IV/8.) WP639 [1887] suggests that such a person might be called 'God': "God as a *maximal state*, as an *epoch*—a point in the development of the *will to power* by means of which further development just as much as the previous, the up-to-him, could be explained". See also WP712 [1887]. I touch on Nietzsche's divine aspirations again in § 3.5.2.

Nietzschean utopia. And yet this society isn't fully isomorphic with the overman and is not as highly valued as he, for a reason we can now at last see. Society has needed the overman to bring it to this health, to create its new values; it couldn't have done so itself. And this has always been so: "It was creators who created peoples and hung a faith and a love over them: thus they served life" [TSZ/I/11]. Any society must be held together by values it can't see beyond. So none can be that open-ended synthesis, always pressing to overcome itself, which is the type of the Dionysian overman. This will even hold true of the new society the overman makes possible: it, too, will live stably with institutions, even within a morality, the values the overman himself has created and imposed. In the end, what prevents societies from being highest beings for Nietzsche is not that they are less complete or unified than (some) persons but that they are too much so, too structured by conventions that aim only at preserving or continuing.

In chapter 3, I turn to examine Nietzsche's ideal, both for persons and societies, more methodically.

3

VALUE

We've been seeing how Nietzsche's thought can be read as a power ontology and how, as such, its structure is very (and its details partly) similar to Plato's traditional system. We've seen how this reading is consistent with Nietzsche's genuinely radical views about change and time, with his theory of becoming. There's still another very prominent aspect and topic of his thought, which we've so far left on the side: his values and what he says about value. Both the vehemence with which he values and the importance his theory attributes to value show that any adequate reading must treat this topic in a more focused way. And as with the claim for becoming, my conservative reading is especially required to do so, because here again Nietzsche proclaims himself in polar opposition to the history of thought before him, a self-appraisal often accepted by his interpreters.[1] Yet as we explore, we again find a more complex relation than mere negation.

Indeed, we've so far seen quite the opposite. By my opening plan, I've unfolded how (it might be the case that) Nietzsche posits values in very much the traditional way, hence quite centrally or basically in his ontology. I've argued that he means his 'theory of being' with a deeply valuative point or intent. This being that he says that all share in is still shared unevenly among this all: there are higher and lower degrees of being, as degrees of realization of the will to power essence. We saw (§ 1.3) how the active/reactive contrast marks this deep valuative scale;

---

1. MacIntyre (1981, 238) says that Nietzsche's project was "to raze to the ground the structures of inherited moral belief and argument".

it ranks wills by how 'well' (how healthily) they pursue that essential end of power. We eventually found (§ 2.2), a quasi-temporal expression for this standard: Nietzsche grades beings, in effect, by how closely they approach a metaphysical 'difference', understood in contrast with Plato's ideal, the self-identity of sameness. Thus even if Nietzsche's deepest value might be an opposite to Plato's, it seems to play the same basic role in his ontology—in this, seeming quite traditional.

Moreover, from this metaphysical root, I've traced implications out into Nietzsche's more concrete topics; that deep value finds a more complex expression when applied to particular types of beings, such as he analyzes persons to be. We saw how persons' structural complexity, the way they're constructed from drives and into societies, generates a more elaborate classing and ranking of them. The typology of master/slave/overman (and the further distinctions we traced within each main type) lays out the system of ways in which health and sickness are had by such diversely synthetic wills, diversely synthesized into their groups. And the very way that all these implications unfold from that metaphysical core also looked rather traditional: they remind of the *Republic*'s classification and rating of souls, again in their structural place or role, if not always in their content.

In all this account I've given of Nietzsche's values, however, I've been running against (and mostly ignoring) certain other things he says. In our closer look, we must face this countervailing evidence. Indeed, we should try to take more systematic account of all the evidence relevant here. So let's pause with a procedural point: What basic types of textual evidence, ways Nietzsche's words imply certain values, are there? What is it that an adequate theory of his values must answer to? A certain distinction is natural and helpful here: our two main types of evidence for Nietzsche's values must be what he says about values and how (and what) he actually values.

The first sort of evidence has obvious importance. Here Nietzsche expresses his 'theory of value', his 'metaethics', by explaining and appraising the act or practice of valuing. We'll especially look at this evidence in trying to answer two crucial questions: Does he think values can be true, the chief priority that past philosophers have imputed to their own? And does he claim any other priority for his own values, even if not that they're true?

The second set of evidence, how Nietzsche values, can itself be divided into the content he values and the force with which he values it. As we might put it, we must ask—of Nietzsche's so varied judgments (all his praisings and belittlings and rankings)—not only what they dominantly posit as 'the good' but also in what sense they mean it as 'good'. For example, is it good morally or aesthetically? This force is of course much of the subject of those metaethical statements and something we'll partly read back, from Nietzsche's theory of value into his valuings themselves. But we'll also pay attention to the force we find expressed in the latter directly; these evaluations often convey their own force quite vividly. We'll have to ask whether this force so expressed matches the force propounded in his metaethics.

Which type of evidence have I been citing so far, in defense of that traditional reading? It has been chiefly the passages in which Nietzsche values, in which he praises (and raises as an end or good) either activeness or the overman, or elements in their structure. I've used these to suggest a deep valuative commitment in his thinking: to this content as good. I've also implied that this value is meant with a certain force. In presuming that the ontology these values are embedded within is meant as true, I've implied that the values are also. (And how else indeed should we first hear the values—assessments as good—offered by *any* person if not as true?) Thus with sparse metaethical evidence, I've taken his valuings as being meant with this traditional force.

In so proceeding, however, I've neglected (in the first place) many other of Nietzsche's valuings, rankings in which he seems to praise some quite different content, or to condemn the one I've attributed to him. Indeed, he seems remarkably inconsistent for a philosopher, unusually inclined to make contradictory points or to value opposite things. This (non-metaethical) evidence itself suggests he might mean no such value system. How could this chaotic range of views hang together in any such way? How could they issue from any such single source?

And doubt is more strongly raised by what Nietzsche says *about* values: roughly, they're always 'mere perspectives'. A will to power views itself and its world within, from the point of view of, its distinctive project. Its values express this project; they belong to its narrow and interested viewpoint. There's no way, he seems to say, to raise oneself above or out of this interest, out of this particularity and bias and into some purely judging, undistorting view. Because values are always thus 'in the service' of narrowly willful perspectives, they're always 'merely subjective'. Thus, he concludes, the philosopher's project of arriving at absolute or objective values, privileged over those of all other perspectives, is quite misguided. This argument might be the most prominent theme in Nietzsche's 'metaethics'; we could naturally take it to 'tune' his valuings, to show with what force they're meant. Yet if he does mean all of his rankings this way—as 'just his perspective'—surely he can't mean to root them in any ontology he takes to be true. It seems he just can't offer values in that traditional way I've supposed.[2]

Nietzsche makes these very points in developing his differences from all 'morality' [*Moral*], which he thinks pervades all philosophy after

2. Many interpreters of Nietzsche have denied that he has such values; thus Megill (1985, 30) denies that he has a 'natural' morality (because choice must be made on aesthetic grounds). On the other side, Simmel (1991, 161ff.) argues for the objectivity of Nietzsche's values.

Plato. He stresses how radical these differences are, that he attacks not just what these others value but how they do so: the very way they intend that content or offer those values to us. In particular he disputes their claims to objectivity, to have grasped real moral facts. So BGE108: "There are no moral phenomena at all, but only a moral interpretation [*Ausdeutung*] of phenomena". He claims to be the first to have reached this insight *"that there are no moral facts at all"* [TI/VII/1].[3] Thus when Nietzsche calls himself an 'immoralist' or proclaims himself 'beyond good and evil', these expressions intend a radical, preemptive break from the project of offering any such values. But how can all this evidence be reconciled with the metaphysically rooted system of values I've been claiming he has? This is the first and primary challenge this chapter must meet.

A second large problem arises concerning values; it's suggested by another way of taking those self-descriptions. I think we immediately hear them as marking (instead or besides) a difference in the *content* of Nietzsche's values: he prefers something very different than we do, something in fact quite threatening.[4] Even if he doesn't adopt any content as replacement for ours, in rejecting ours he seems to detach himself from what we consider just simple humaneness, which is not something we'd let ourselves be persuaded away from. Further trouble comes from the content he does seem to offer (even if with a different force, as a different type of good) and seems to replace ours with. A value of power or mastery suffuses very many of his judgments; his preference for war over peace, his attack on pity, and his praise for slavery are some of the worrying points in which this value finds expression.[5] My own project holds that he does affirm some valuative content, but if he has just these as his values, his view is much harder to stomach. Once again, it counts against my approach if it gives such weight to some of the least appealing things Nietzsche says.

3. He soon goes on: "Morality is merely an interpretation [*Ausdeutung*] of certain phenomena—more precisely [*bestimmter*], a *mis*interpretation." WP259 [1884]: "Insight: all evaluation is made from a determinate perspective: *preservation* of the individual, a community, a race, a state, a church, a faith, a culture".

4. Foot 1994, 10: "it is quite wrong to see his 'aesthetic' as taking nothing we think precious from the morality he attacks." See also Russell 1945, 767ff.; Mann 1973, 368. Other interpreters respond to this complaint by arguing that his attack on our values is mainly against their force. Nehamas 1985, 203: "Though Nietzsche's attitude toward morality implies that if we accept his views our modes of action will not remain unchanged, his primary concern is not with the specific content of particular actions but with our reasons and motives for acting as we do." D103 lends support: "It goes without saying—assuming that I am no fool—that I do not deny that many actions called unethical are to be avoided and resisted, likewise that many called ethical are to be done and promoted—but I think: the one like the other *for other reasons than hitherto.*'

5. One form these worries can take is that Nietzsche's views might befit the Nazi uses of them, after all. See, e.g., Stern 1979, 120.

This means that my project is challenged on another side. Not only must it fend off the perspectival threat, the dissolving of any 'posited' values into perspectivism, but it must also render these values in a much more favorable light than do our first impressions. This challenge really should be faced across the range of issues on which Nietzsche's values disturb us. One is perhaps most basic: In making my power my highest good, doesn't Nietzsche allow or even recommend injustice toward others? In chasing this good, won't I cross certain proper limits on my behavior toward others? Indeed, isn't my power precisely *over* them, and my gain at their expense? This ethical worry seems confirmed by what Nietzsche sometimes says is my best relation to others, which is not (what *we* mean by) friendship or love, it seems. He argues that it's better to have (in the proper way) *enemies;* this antagonistic relationship is more desirable than those 'positive' ones we esteem. Could we bear to believe what Nietzsche says here?

This basic ethical worry is joined by other concerns, variously related to it. Let's focus on two that have a special significance today. The first concerns a glaring feature of Nietzsche's 'politics': their anti-democratic, antiegalitarian bent. This shows up especially in his preference for a society that is strongly hierarchic, perhaps even practicing slavery. Such a thought seems quite out of bounds for us. Is Nietzsche really committed to it? The second such worry concerns one specific type of inequality he commends, that of men over women. Of course, one might hope to discount his unattractive views about women as peripheral, as expressions of personal idiosyncrasy, not philosophical thought. Yet there's ample ground to suspect a connection with, a rootedness in, his most basic ideas. Put crudely, mightn't the power ontology itself be a male-chauvinist metaphysics?[6]

If these objections can't be met, some of our deepest commitments might speak against Nietzsche's thought, which could thus be ultimately unbelievable for us. And this might not be merely a matter of his thought either suiting or not suiting our personal intuitions. Also in question is whether his ideas are historically viable, whether they haven't been left behind by thought's development since his day, as represented in ongoing social trends toward democracy and feminism. I try to show how Nietzsche's thought might be, in these ways, more attractive and viable, despite that distasteful first impression.[7] There's a danger in such a project. One must not try too hard to 'render him palatable'; it would be an offense to make Nietzsche bland and unthreatening. (His viewpoint must indeed convince us to change some of ours.) Yet his threat can be shown to be at least not the coarse sort of inhumaneness we quickly dismiss.

6. So says Schutte (1984, 176ff.) of what she calls Nietzsche's "domination view of power". See also n.95.
7. Which is not to say that strong worries don't persist here for me as well.

Still a third, seemingly less exciting task faces us concerning Nietzsche's values. We bring to him certain expectations of what any theory of value must (to be a full or adequate theory) include or provide. We expect from him more than just those 'rankings', comparative estimations, we've found him so preoccupied with. For example, we think any such theory should tell us how to answer the practical question What should I do? as this is asked in some concrete life situation. And we think this advice must importantly include guidance for our behavior toward others, something like an 'ethics'. A theory that couldn't help the reflecting agent make such choices, and thereby act better, would fail to play a role we think key for value theories. But (it may well seem that) in our statement of his values so far, Nietzsche gives very little such help: the ideals of activeness and the overman don't easily suggest any usable principles for conduct.

Why haven't his values spoken to this viewpoint? Perhaps only because we've approached them so far in their (abstract) metaphysical role and connections; then we might expect the restatement into such practical principles to go along smoothly. But we should also bear in mind another possibility: that this difference in format is intended by Nietzsche and is ineliminable from his values, that their being a 'ranking' rather than an 'ethics' is part of the special force these values are meant to have.

I begin (in § 3.1) by attempting this restatement into a theory, addressed to 'the anonymous (i.e., any) reflective agent', of how to decide what to do. In so proceeding, we bring into sharper focus the content that Nietzsche values: what he specifies as our good. Although of course he names this as power, several basic questions need to be answered before this tells us much at all. Whose power is my good, and why is it so? Before I can start to pursue it, I need to know better just what it consists in: Can I make this abstract notion concrete enough to guide my behavior? Answering these questions, we arrive at a first, rather straightforward account of Nietzsche's values, at what we might call a 'power egoism'.

This initial statement needs to be clarified or amended in one main way before we can weigh it. Recalling Nietzsche's vehement attack on the ego or subject must give us pause in attributing to him any kind of 'egoism'. We must take account (in § 3.2) of his radical attack on any being, his contextual dissolution of it, developed in chapter 2. As we clarify his values in the light of that contextual point, we see how it actually broadens 'self-interest' out beyond what we naturally expect. 'I', the 'agent', now acquire a positive interest in my descendents, my neighbors, and even my enemies. This might somewhat surprise us in Nietzsche. But it still remains open whether this interest he gives me is of the right sort to satisfy our humane instincts.

So next we confront this worry against the content of Nietzsche's values, and we do so in stages, first at the macrolevel, then at the microlevel. Thus we'll look (in § 3.3) at Nietzsche's social ideal, at his 'politics'. We find here much that immediately repels us, in particular his antiegalitarianism, his preaching of hierarchies and elites. Does closer scrutiny of these views make them any more tolerable to us? Or must we hope to cast them loose from the rest of his thought, to keep that remainder viable? We also find (in § 3.4) much to disturb us in Nietzsche's 'ethics', in his standards for treating individual others. Even taking account of how he broadens my 'self', he seems to commend an aggressive, even predatory stance toward the others about me. This seems to distort or pervert the whole range of our dealings with others: all our different types of relationships, ranging from our distanced interactions with strangers to our closest involvements with friends. It also seems to prompt Nietzsche toward his unappealing views about the relations between the sexes. Are any of these ethical positions even tolerable to us? I try to give them at least their strongest case.

Those doubts that remain against Nietzsche's values would then have to be addressed by a different strategy: by turning instead to the force with which they're offered. Perhaps if we get right the 'tone' with which he speaks these values, we'll worry less about their content. So we naturally turn (in § 3.5) to Nietzsche's metaethical remarks, as telling us directly how he intends his values (or, more commonly, how he does not). Here he often claims such radical intentions that we'll even have to question whether they *merely* amend the force with which a content is offered us. Might they announce an utter renunciation of any effort to propose any valuative content at all? Here we face the radical challenge to all my preceding efforts to assign Nietzsche values—a posited good. Only on settling this worry can we be confident in attributing to him the elaborate system of values I will have sketched. Getting that metaethics straight, we also see just how he does and doesn't address the anonymous reflective agent, after all. We see, that is, that although we need to retune this traditional model for the force of a philosopher's values, it remains apt in Nietzsche's case, too.

3.1 Nietzsche's advice: maximize power

So far I've stated Nietzsche's values in the format he mostly adopts himself: as a rating or 'ranking' of wills and persons. I've sketched two valuative scales: those culminating in activeness and the overman. These lay out dimensions of value, by giving criteria for ranking (respectively) simple wills and certain complex syntheses of them. They thereby address an interest or concern we often have whenever we compare ourselves to others, and others to one another. But suppose we're not interested (just now) in making such rankings. Suppose we have a more immediate concern: we're trying to decide what to do ourselves, among various courses of action. Shouldn't Nietzsche's values be able to address this other (and surely more vital) interested viewpoint we take? We expect any value theory to give us advice for acting, some sort of procedure or principle for deciding what to do. We might even think that such a theory only becomes fully concrete when it gets cashed out in such direct advice.

There's a natural way to make Nietzsche's rankings address this concern. It seems that any valuative scale in effect recommends the following: act so as to increase or maximize value (as measured along this scale). Let's consider how the power ontology might support such a 'practical principle'. Can we make it concrete enough to help us in our situated dilemmas? Let's start with the value of activeness, or with the still more fundamental value of power, on which it depends. Activeness is valued, surely, only as the effective or well-directed pursuit of power, only as a means to this end. And Nietzsche very often names power as the good, most directly in WP674 [1887–88]: "What is the objective measure of *value?* Solely the quantum of *enhanced* and *organized power*".[8] We therefore expect his guide for behavior, his practical principle, to be this: act so as to increase (or maximize) power.

3.1.1   Whose power?

A first big challenge in interpreting this principle is to fix the 'scope' of this power a certain way. Whose power is the reflective agent advised to increase? Two alternatives immediately strike us. Nietzsche might mean for the agent to apply these scales to himself: he should (try to) become more active or powerful himself, and more nearly like the overman. Nietzsche's principle then would be this: act so as to maximize your own power. Or he might mean no such limitation. He might mean for the agent to apply these scales less self-absorbedly, to everything he can affect by his actions. Then Nietzsche's principle would be the following: act so as to maximize power in general. We're familiar with other value theories of each of these types; hedonism and utilitarianism are obvious examples. These types arise out of two different natural ways of applying a value scale to an act: this act can try to raise up in this scale either what acts or else what is acted on. (These things the agent can affect of course include himself, but now with no priority; he's the only doer of his act but is just one of a multitude of beings affectable by it.)

8. WP710 [1888] states a stricter version of the point, first hypothetically but then more assuredly: "The attempt should be made, whether a scientific order of values could be constructed simply on a *numerical* and *mensural scale of force*— All other *'values'* are prejudices, naiveties, misunderstandings— They are everywhere *reducible* to this numerical and mensural scale of force— The *upwards* on this scale means every *growth in value*". A2: "What is good? Everything that heightens in human beings the feeling of power, the will to power, power itself." See also WP858 [1887–88].

We find signs in Nietzsche of both types of value theory, which must make us worry that he may not have settled his views on even so basic a point. Take first the analogue to utilitarianism: act so as to maximize power in general. Nietzsche would then be calling us into a certain extended project, to increase (not the happiness of people, but) the power of wills, as many as our acts can affect. He'd be calling us to sacrifice or subordinate our own interest (and power) to the maximization of power per se. So D146: "We . . . would, through sacrifice—in which we *and our neighbor* are included—strengthen and raise higher the general feeling of human *power*, even supposing we did not achieve more."

If (or to the extent that) this is Nietzsche's point, he means it in a special way; if he does preach the maximization of power in general, it's toward an unusual 'maximum'. For reasons we still need to find, he aims not at the greatest sum of the power of all wills but at the greatest concentrations of power in individual wills; his values are 'maximax'.[9] So, already in UM/III/6p162: "For the question is this: how can your life, the single life, receive the highest value, the deepest meaning? How can it be least squandered? Certainly only by your living for the advantage of the rarest and most valuable exemplars, and not for the advantage of the majority".[10] An agent maximizes power in the world he affects by producing the highest separate peaks rather than the greatest overall mass or sum. He should therefore focus his efforts on that part of the world that is capable of the greatest power—of being an overman. It's in the announcements of the overman that we most find Nietzsche suggesting we value *others'* power.

So Zarathustra calls on his audience to prepare, by their own self-sacrifice, for the overmen of the future.[11] We also hear such a call in the way Nietzsche speaks for a future society favoring overmen, even designed to 'breed' them;[12] here, too, he seems to preach a good quite

9. Cf. Simmel 1991, 154ff.; Rawls 1971, 325.
10. UM/II/9p111: "No, the goal of humanity cannot lie in the end, but only its highest exemplars." See also P&Tpp120–21 [1873–74].
11. Zarathustra tries to rally his first audience to prepare for the overman: "The overman is the sense of the earth. Let your will say: the overman *shall be* the sense of the earth" [TSZ/I/P/3]. And a bit later: "I love those . . . who sacrifice themselves for the earth, that the earth may some day become the overman's" [4]. It should be noted, though, that Zarathustra soon abandons this audience, and this mode of address. Consider also TI/IX/33, which suggests that the worth of a person's selfishness depends on "whether he represents the rising or the falling [*absteigende*] line of life", and that in the latter case "he has small value, and the least fairness wills that he *take away* as little as possible from those who have turned out well." UM/III/5p160 already makes such a point: "It is the basic thought of *culture*, insofar as it knows how to set for each one of us only one task: *to promote the production of the philosopher, the artist and the saint within us and without us and thereby to work at the completion of nature.*"
12. A3: "the problem I pose is . . . what type of human being should be *bred*, should be *willed*, as being higher in value, worthier of life, more certain of a future."

other than the agent's own. Indeed, more broadly or simply, the very stress he lays on the overman, as a highly exceptional extreme of power, suggests that he can't be preaching to us the pursuit of our own power. He opens such a radical gap between that ideal and us, a gap we can little aspire to cross, that it seems it can't be intended as for us to achieve in ourselves. Can't he mean only that we should work so that someday this ideal can be realized in others? Isn't it then another's power we're called on to guide our acts by?

Many other things Nietzsche says, however, suggest instead a more egoistic theory: act so as to maximize your own power. Surely our prevailing impression of the lesson his writings teach is that I'm to work (with clearer or better aim than I had before reading him) to improve my power, to make my future self stronger than I now am. Surely he's strongly suspicious of other-regarding values, of their effort to tempt me away from my genuine interest, to distort or divert my will to power. So TI/IX/35: "An 'altruistic' morality—a morality in which selfishness *atrophies*—remains a bad sign under all circumstances. . . . The best is lacking when selfishness begins to be lacking." Zarathustra pronounces selfishness "blessed, the wholesome, healthy selfishness that wells from a powerful soul" [TSZ/III/10/2].[13] So it seems that Nietzsche's advice to the reflective agent must be how better to pursue his own selfish good and not the interest of any others, whether overmen or not.

Thus we find Nietzsche shifting between these two basic ways of applying his standard of power. How can we resolve this conflict? Does either fit better with the bulk of his other views? And if one does, can it also explain why he sometimes seems to (or does) adopt that other line?

3.1.2   Why power?

We can help ourselves choose between these alternatives by seeing how well each answers a further question: How does Nietzsche *justify* power as the good? Besides expecting a value theory to offer advice to the deliberating agent, we expect it to show him why he should take this advice. Any new principle we're to guide our lives by will have to come well recommended. So what grounds does Nietzsche give us for the value of power, to get us to stop directing our course with the values we already hold and start doing so with his? It seems likely these grounds will clarify how—with what scope—he means for us to apply this stan-

---

Given (what I've claimed to be) Nietzsche's usual view of these persons as self-creating exceptions, I think we must understand this 'breeding' rather loosely, as a setting up of conditions that make these exceptions more likely. This seems supported by WP907 [1884].

13. EH/IV/7 attacks "the unselfing morality [*Entselbstungs-Moral*]" as "the morality of decline par excellence". D105, D148, BGE33.

dard; seeing why we should value power should show us whose power this will be.

My stress on Nietzsche's ontology may suggest an obvious way he might justify power as the good. Surely he simply argues from 'is' to 'ought': from the claim that each being is (essentially) will to power to the claim that power is the objective good, which each being should pursue more effectively or well directedly. Then the ontology would quite straightforwardly support his values. Nietzsche does (sometimes) think this way. So WP55 [1886–87]: "There is nothing in life that has value, except the degree of power—assuming that life itself is the will to power." Interpreters have often read him so.[14]

There's a complication. We've seen (in § 1.3) that these values are not just based on the power ontology but infused throughout it; they're made a part of it, by the very sense of 'being' or 'essence' that ontology intends. Nietzsche posits will to power as an essence whose 'realization' is a matter of degree: his deepest valuative scale is the dimension of these degrees. So (as we might put it) it's not a 'brute fact' that every being does will power; it *is* will to power, because it *ought* so to will. Or (as we also might put it) the power ontology really commends power to us as a good or goal, as our 'essential end' not because we all do strive for it but because we should. Thus 'is' already means 'should be' for Nietzsche, and it makes no strict sense to ask how he 'derives' the latter from the former.

On the other hand, Nietzsche doesn't assign this end to all beings just arbitrarily or willfully, as a value posited a priori, in thorough independence from 'the facts'. He finds grounds within beings, including those who pursue different ends, for attributing this end to them and for judging them by it. He tries to show that those who will different things than power have been thwarted from it and twisted aside toward a distorted image or version of it. Above all, he argues this in his diagnosis of slave morality: those who preach love and altruism do so from motives of power, out of a will that can have only a second- or third-best form of power, and only by disavowing and condemning its primary form. Such psychodiagnoses are therefore the key to Nietzsche's own way of straddling the fact/value distinction; he claims a better right to fuse these (in that metaphysical essence) than his predecessors had, because he claims a keener insight into how we will.

If Nietzsche does indeed claim power to be the 'essential' good, we expect him to commend it to us in a certain way: because all beings will power, power in general is best per se. We expect him to offer it as an 'objective' good, in the sense that Nagel (for example) means this: objective value is what I will when I detach myself from my particular, subjec-

---

14. Schacht (1973, 76; 1983, 349) reads Nietzsche in this way. Wilcox (1982, 198) does so more tentatively, such that this grounding of the value of power, although 'objective' and 'scientific', is nonetheless still 'perspectival'.

tive perspective and interests.[15] Here, 'subjectivity' would lie in my interest's being confined to my own power; to recognize power's objective value would be to generalize the power I take as good. So on this line, Nietzsche would commend to me power in general, rather than my power, because with this value I rise above my subjective bias, into an objective viewpoint.

However, this attributes to Nietzsche a way of justifying his values that he often emphatically rejects, as typifying (slave) 'morality'. That goal of objectivity is just as objectionable as the selflessness it tries to ground. Both of these values ask us to step outside a willful perspective essential to us, in that fusion of factual and valuative senses.

Thus Nietzsche attacks these goals in both fact- and value-based terms: as being impossible fully to achieve but also as being bad to achieve. First, we just can't reach the type of detachment that would let us judge value objectively;[16] we also can't deeply, hence unhypocritically, give up willing our own power. All our detachment and all our concern for others still express a deeper egoism. Second (he simultaneously says), when morality preaches such objectivity and sympathy for others, it asks us to overcome our egoism in a way we could but shouldn't do: it invites us into unhealthy, mistaken ways of willing our power. Hence he attacks that preaching not just as hypocritical (as phony, not really achieved or achievable) but also as corrupting, because these values really can tempt us from our own empowerment.[17]

So the 'power' I'm essentially a will toward, isn't power in general, but *my* power. In calling me to activeness, the power ontology means to call me back from my distracting interest in what's foreign to me: from all my (mostly unwitting) self-sacrifice back to my true self-interest. Thus the very way we've drawn this crucial valuative scale of active/reactive requires that Nietzsche must mean the egoistic point: I'm to choose my acts for the sake of my own growth or empowerment. He commends to me, surely, a *'power egoism'*. (It still remains to explain

15. Nagel 1986, 5: "A view or form of thought is more objective than another if it relies less on the specifics of the individual's makeup and position in the world, or on the character of the particular type of creature he is." For the application to values, see Nagel 1986, 138ff.

16. He often argues that it's impossible to judge the value of life from such an objective stance. So TI/V/5: "One would have to have a position *outside* of life, and on the other hand know it as well as one, as many, as all who have lived it, in order to be allowed even to touch the problem of the *value* of life: reasons enough to comprehend that this problem is for us an unapproachable problem." (See also TI/II/2.) Within Nietzsche's ontology, this argument would apply as well to power as to life; thus it seems he can't mean to claim that power per se has such objective value. (But note that Schacht [1973, 80–81] suggests this only denies that the value of power or life could be measured against anything else, being itself the ultimate criterion.)

17. See, e.g., GM/III/21–23 on the damage done by the ascetic ideal.

those countervailing suggestions of a more general goal; I attempt this in § 3.2.)

So his values are justified to me in a different way than as (in that last sense) 'objective': it's because I already will (my) power that (my) power is best for me. Nietzsche's aim must be to help me to a more effective pursuit of a goal I already have, even if only in distorted form. He clarifies power as my established end and tells me how best to pursue it. This gives his advice to me a much clearer claim to my attention than if he sought to turn me to some new and foreign end and needed to talk me out of those I now have. I'm to abide within my self-interested, 'subjective' perspective; my new values will express this interest more aptly.

On the other hand, there's a type of objectivity that survives even here. Nietzsche still claims a right to criticize the values and goals a person concretely pursues. He claims a right to say, from his own point of view, different from that person's own, what's really of value for him: power, with the structure we've analyzed. (This presumption is expressed in Nietzsche's most typical critiques of persons: his diagnoses of them as sick.) The odd way that power is a person's essential end allows him to 'lose sight of' his own power; what he believes and pursues as his interest might not really be so. The gap that thus opens up between a person's apparent and real ends makes room for a subjective/objective contrast with some of the customary force. It makes external judgments on his explicit values feasible, preventing these from being 'the measure' in the way they would be on the more usual versions of perspectivism or relativism.[18]

Can we make more concrete just what advice Nietzsche gives the reflective agent, to guide him in pursuing his genuine power?

3.1.3   What power is

Back in § 1.1.1, we saw that power is an end with a logic different from that of more familiar goals like pleasure. Whereas pleasure seems the same state for all who achieve it, power is growth in what's distinctively

---

18. There's a further complication here. Because the content of a person's projects isn't an objective fact but lies in his perspective—in what he intends in his action—we can't discover or describe it from an external vantage point. What an agent's activity is lies crucially in how he means it and can't be stated in neutral terms. Hence we can't prescribe to him what his power concretely involves unless we can somehow enter his viewpoint and see 'from within' the point and spirit of what he does. So long as we stand back from his perspective, we can only describe his good as greater power; to go beyond this abstract or formal point, we need to abandon this external, objective view of him. Or better, we need to carry the objective discovery of what power is into a sympathetic occupation of his interested view. The objective point should then help us to see which of his pursuits are properly his and which have been twisted aside in reaction to others.

one's own, so that it takes a quite different content in different cases. This now rules out one type of definiteness we might expect, in the advice Nietzsche's values will give the (anonymous) reflective agent. Because my power is different from yours, these values give each of us different advice. Of course, in a sense this is true of any egoistic values. Hedonism, too, for example, tells me to aim at my pleasure, and others at theirs; as thus indexical, our 'highest ends' already differ and will prompt us to even opposing acts. The hedonist can also allow that because of our differing tastes, each must secure his own pleasure by different (types of) means. But Nietzsche's advice to the agent is self-referential or personalized in a further way: his highest end has an internal reference to the agent's idiosyncracies, because power means enriching one's own pursuits. This peculiar logic to Nietzsche's end helps explain the lack of detail in his accounts of it, about which interpreters have so often complained.[19]

Of course, this logic is hardly unprecedented. We find it as well in 'desire-satisfaction' versions of egoism: here the end we all share isn't some concrete state like pleasure but a second-order satisfaction of whatever desires each has individually. Further features of the power egoism set it apart once again. First, it calls me to develop drives that are 'mine' not in the straightforward sense that I 'have' or 'experience' them but in the sense that they *distinguish* me, by their difference from the drives of others. Growth lies in developing just those pursuits that belong to oneself alone, unshared by others. (It's only in these that one has an 'identity'; only these make one a being distinct from the herd.) Second, although desires are presumably given in conscious intentions, these distinguishing drives are most likely not 'transparent' but indeed very hard to introspect. We require a certain psychological acuity to discount what we've taken reactively from others; the desires we're most aware of probably come to us by this corruptive route. We're conscious of what we have words for, hence of what's as common as our language is.[20] So the power egoism often requires us to see past what we consciously want. And third, the point isn't just to 'satisfy' these drives but to enhance or enrich them. Although desires tend to be taken as given, Nietzsche thinks drives must be worked on: the second-order end is to change (in the right way) that first-order content. Taking these three points together, our task is to discover and develop our distinctiveness.

All of this implies a greater dispersion of personal projects than in the desire-satisfaction model: progress does not converge on some ideal pattern, the same for all; it makes each person's behavior more and more

19. GS120 argues, "there is no health in itself, and all attempts to define a thing so are wretched failures"; it goes on to propose that we "place the distinctive [*eigenthümliche*] virtue of each in the health of his soul: which indeed can look in one like the opposite of the health of another."

20. GS354; I return to this point in § 4.3.1.

idiosyncratic. So the overmen, as ideal extremes of such growth, might even differ most drastically in what they do. This means that the values generated by the power ontology are peculiarly empty or formal. This formal character is another reason for Nietzsche's contrast of these values with what he calls 'morality': "Let us finally consider how naive it is altogether to say: 'Human beings *ought* to be such and such!' Reality shows us a delightful richness of types . . . and some wretched loafer [*Eckensteher*] of a moralist comments: 'No! Human beings ought to be *otherwise*'" [TI/V/6].[21]

Despite these limitations on how much advice the power ontology strictly entails, it still does suggest, Nietzsche thinks, some important general lessons. He has in mind some strategies that are most often useful for enhancing the power of one's drive synthesis. We can take this as his concrete advice, to any reflective agent, on how to pursue his own power. Some of this is familiar already. Using as a crucial diagnostic tool (as a 'tuning fork'[22]) that insight he gives me into the active/reactive contrast, I am to examine and classify my drives or activities. I work to identify the impulses and projects that express my self (are positive), separating these from those that merely obey or merely negate the projects of others. In particular, I'm to locate and overcome the workings in me of resentment, that most potent reactive attitude, which most distracts me from myself. And in looking for my own, I should hope to find (and perhaps can somewhat achieve) a single strongest such distinguishing drive, or a unified synthesis of several strongest. The 'identity' I'm then to go on to construct needs some such core or backbone to it. Besides this, I should wish for a great disparity of other, weaker impulses, available to be mastered by that ruling core. 'My' effort to build an identity is really the effort of this dominating (complex) drive to empower itself, by properly ruling that rich remainder.[23]

Beyond this, Nietzsche makes (I will argue) two further points, which are crucial for us because of the way they seem to 'temper' or 'humanize' his values. We can label these his *spirit* and *agon* arguments.

---

21. TSZ/I/5: "My brother, if you have a virtue and she is your virtue, then you have her in common with nobody." Even naming one's virtue would make her too common; if one must speak of her, it should be: "This is *my* good; this I love; it pleases me wholly; thus alone do I will the good. I do not will it the law of a god; I do not will it as human statute and need".

22. TI/F, explaining how he uses the hammer, when he "philosophizes with a hammer".

23. UM/III/2p130 speaks of two educational maxims: "The one demands that the educator should quickly recognize the distinctive strength of his pupil and then guide all forces and sap and sunshine there, so as to help that one virtue to its right ripeness and fruitfulness. The other maxim, on the contrary, wills that the educator draw forth, nourish, and bring into harmonious relationship to one another all the forces present [in the pupil]." The passage goes on to suggest that these maxims aren't really contrary after all. See also P&Tp119 [1873–74].

Let's take a preliminary look at each; they'll be recurring cruxes when we evaluate his values.

The first gives a certain direction to this dominant drive, or it specifies a condition this impulse must be in. Nietzsche usually assumes that in the best case this drive is a 'spiritual' one. It's a drive, in other words, that has been spiritualized and that now rules other drives in a chiefly spiritual way. We need to grasp this point much more concretely, but we have an immediate sense how it might render Nietzsche's values less threatening to us: if the ideal person is spiritual, he's less a threat to commit the 'material' injustices we worry about most. So defenders of Nietzsche, Kaufmann preeminently, have stressed this point about spirit. We'll have to examine this major defense.

If this first point offers a certain 'domestic policy', advice about how to deal with the drives that constitute me, the second suggests a comportment toward the foreign forces (persons) around me. Nietzsche calls on me to stress and press my differences from these others, and above all from those special others I need to adopt and cultivate as my enemies. This may sound unattractive, not ideal. But he also thinks these aggressions need to be carried out in a certain spirit; they need to be aimed at the right type of 'rule' over foreign forces. The goal is not to suppress the foreignness of the other will but to use its difference to enrich one's own. Negation, as the effort to quite obliterate another will, is a sign or expression of a reactive obsession with that other. To master is not to negate the different but to incorporate it *as* other into oneself.[24] All of this is the logical crux to Nietzsche's sense of the *agon* as enlightened competition. It's easy to anticipate how this point might make Nietzsche's values more humane. Again, however, we need to grasp the point with much more care before we can say how far it can excuse (by softening) his violent, repellent ethical and political views. Moreover, we need to see about both points what justifies them, according to Nietzsche.

3.2   A broader self-interest

There's a glaring problem, however, in attributing any such 'power egoism' to Nietzsche: I've failed to take into account his strong attack on the ego or self. If he denies this even exists, how can he hold or propose values that are 'egoistic' or 'selfish'? He says, "the ego of which one speaks when one censures egoism does not exist at all" [WP370: 1887].[25] This point even threatens to undermine the very role or pur-

---

24. TSZ/I/10: "You must be proud of your enemy: then the successes of your enemy are your successes too." D540: "In an artist [learning] is often opposed by envy, or by that pride which, upon feeling something foreign, at once puts forth its sting, and involuntarily assumes a defensive stance instead of that of a learner." See how he goes on to present Raphael as a 'good learner' (from Michelangelo).

25. See also WP371 [1885–86].

pose we've presumed for a 'philosopher's values': we took these to be those he advises the reflective agent to adopt, but it now seems that Nietzsche doubts there is any such agent and so can't intend to give any such advice. So perhaps he doesn't have any 'values' (in this sense) at all, or (in a broader sense) perhaps he means his values with so different a force, that our opening alternatives (selfish and other-regarding) are simply irrelevant. In § 2.1 we examined the deep (metaphysical) roots to Nietzsche's attack on the self—his denial of 'being' itself—but we've so far largely ignored it in treating his values. Now we have to see whether our first sketch of these values is really consistent with the radical lessons we learned there.

Let's begin with the first way we saw Nietzsche means this attack on being: he denies that anything lasts. Reality is infinitely splintered, reduced (temporally) to fleeting moments. So the self isn't real, in that there *isn't* any being that lasts or continues through all these moments 'we' think we live.[26]

If this is how Nietzsche denies the self, it suggests still a different way of answering the question "Whose power?" than either of the ones we considered in § 3.1.1. Perhaps his values promote the power not of the world in general, and not of the agent (doer) himself, but of each of these momentary doings. Perhaps *this* is the audience they're addressed to: not the reflective agent after all but each passing condition 'of ourselves'. Each moment of acting should act in its own interest, not in that of a fictional lasting self. Each act should strive to grow in power for and in itself, and refuse to embark on any ongoing project of 'self'-improvement. Put another way, Nietzschean selfishness now becomes more extreme, being lodged (below the level of the 'self') in each moment itself, which refuses to identify or concern itself with any future moments. It turns its back not just on other selves but even on its (fictional) own.

This would give Nietzsche's values quite a different temporal force than we surely expect.[27] Both of those other, more familiar ways of

---

26. WP490 [1885] speaks of "the continual transitoriness and fleetingness of the subject".

27. This might seem an odd and unusual way of addressing and applying one's values, yet we're familiar with other theories at least partly of this type. Those that stress either 'virtues' or 'duties' are likely to be so—if these are (most highly) valued in themselves and not just commended as the acts that advance the good of either agent or world. Many theories introduce duties only thus secondarily: utilitarianism (and hedonism) will base on its primary good—happiness in the world (or self)—a secondary value scale for the act itself: it's best if it secures that happiness. But there are other value theories that give an independent and greater value to the act itself; their primary value scale applies directly to the act. Most familiarly, Kant finds highest value in moral worth, which he deliberately denies is just the proper pursuit of good effects from one's acts. Nor is this goodness of acts itself a 'worldly' end, itself a good to be maximized through all the effects of one's acts' on the world. *This* act's moral worth doesn't lie in its making more *other* acts have moral worth.

saying 'whose power' is to be my concern—analogues to hedonism and utilitarianism—try to engage my interest in persisting projects dealing with persisting things (whether my self or a world of selves my acts can affect). Such values are implicitly addressed not to an act but to an ongoing doer of a series of acts. They propose that I undertake an extended commitment and work strategically in ways that can well involve the sacrifice of the present for the future. They tell me to use each act for an overarching good and not to let it seek its own good directly. Against this, the Nietzschean attack on being and the self argues that what's real to this 'me' is just this moment itself, this acting itself. So this real 'I' mustn't be deluded into wasting this moment by using it for the sake of a future in which I no longer am.

This line of development fits with a certain type of 'freedom' we associate with Nietzsche: a refusal of all authority, a refusal to sacrifice life—and life now—for any awaited future. GM/II (entitled "'Guilt', 'Bad Conscience', and the Like") is suggestive here. It explains how the notion of 'responsibility'—allegiance of my present to 'my' past and future, by observing commitments from and to them—was prehistorically inculcated by an 'ethics of custom' [*Sittlichkeit der Sitte*], which imposed certain habits or practices by the cruelest punishments, 'burning' these memories into its members. Harsh authority formed the (extended) self and maintains it through an illusory 'responsibility'. All this self amounts to is a composite of imposed habits. We might well conclude from all this that Nietzsche favors freeing oneself even from one's self.

However, as we've seen again and again, the freedom he favors doesn't overturn all that this criticized, slavish condition involves. The ethics of custom creates an extended self that is sick and unadmirable, yet a type that can then be made healthy—and with a health 'higher' than anything that was never sick in that way. Nietzsche still wants an extended self and *doesn't* preach the atomization we've been imagining. We can see this in his clear admiration for what such a self can then become: "the *sovereign individual*, equal only to himself, liberated again from the ethics of custom, the autonomous and supra-ethical [*übersittliche*] individual . . . , in short, the human being with his own independent, protracted will" [GM/II/2]. So Nietzsche's point clearly is not to return us to that fragmented proto-individuality; as we saw in chapter 2, he preaches not forgetting but a new way of using the memory that custom has fashioned.

We also saw there that Nietzsche's main attack on being isn't this reductive one after all; instead, it's the contextual point, which has for us now quite an opposite effect. To be sure, Nietzsche does indeed use the continuum argument, which so much suggests the atomistic lesson to us. He does indeed dissolve the boundaries we ordinarily draw with such confidence around ourselves, making it indefinite just where my self ends—and never an all-or-nothing matter whether something is part of my self. Yet he draws, in the main, an opposite lesson from this boundary blurring than that atomistic one. Instead of using this argument to contract the self, he takes from it the license to expand or diffuse it, by dissolving the boundaries within which we ordinarily confine it.

We're not those simple and abiding loci of consciousness but shifting patterns of behavior, of aiming/acting. Nietzsche very much stresses the length of these behaviors: how the meaning or identity of any episode lies in its role in very extended developments. Unlike that Cartesian ego, these 'doings' are never fully present in any moment, nor in any of the personal episodes I might suppose to bound them, nor even in my life. They stretch out far beyond my (as I usually think of it) 'self', taking and giving meaning backward and forward, to the ancestral and descendent versions of these practices in other generations.[28]

We're familiar with a related argument in Plato, who gives it great weight: I find a kind of survival in my descendents. Nietzsche often follows Plato in stressing a spiritual analogue to biological pregnancy and giving birth.[29] But whereas for Plato this isn't a true survival—those others aren't really me; our souls are discrete—Nietzsche's power ontology entangles my identity with my descendents, so that I, as my projects, can survive quite literally and 'beingly' in the behavior of (what we count as) 'someone else'. Those descendents aren't simply external effects and reminders of me, as for Plato and others assuming a more 'hard-edged' soul.[30]

This point applies not just through time but 'laterally' through my surrounding society, broadening the scope of my constituting projects in this dimension, too. My own activity isn't itself, by itself—that is, it isn't complete, it lacks determinate identity or meaning, when taken on its own and apart from its place in a societal context. What I do is a function of how my activity is both *like* and *unlike* that of the others about me.

28. Recall how WP785 [1887] says the concept of egoism needs to be revised: "When one has grasped to what extent 'individual' is an error because every single creature [*Einzelwesen*] is just the *whole process* in a straight line (not merely as 'inherited', but [the process] itself—), then the single creature has a *tremendously great meaning.*" WP687 [1887]: "We are more than the individual, we are the whole chain, also with the tasks of all the futures of the *chain*". See also n.109 in chapter 2.

29. D552: "'What is growing here is something greater than we are' is our most secret hope. . . . This is the right *ideal selfishness:* always to care and watch and keep our soul still, so that our fruitfulness *goes beautifully to an end!* Thus, in this indirect way, we care and watch for the *benefit* [*Nutzen*] *of all*". See again Parkes 1994 on Nietzsche's use of the birth and begetting similes.

30. Of course, for Plato I can still really recur as 'someone else' through my soul's reembodiment. For Nietzsche, my interinvolvement with my spiritual descendents explains why I can have a 'selfish' interest in helping others to be overmen. So TSZ/II/2: "But you could well create the overman. Perhaps not you yourselves, my brothers! But you could recreate yourselves into fathers and ancestors of the overman: and let this be your best creating!"

First, to a great degree, my activity is of a type practiced in common with many others; it has its identity in the type. Many others besides me are products of the same training, stamped with the same habits and practices. The meaning in what I do lies not in my individual doing but in that template or pattern from which my life is merely an offprint. An illuminating case of this dependence occurs when I speak: my words have their meaning largely not through me but through an overall practice; what I say can be specified only by referring to that practice. So the real beings here are not my individual behaviors but waves or movements through society in which I merely join and into which my identity is diffused.

I take this to be how Nietzsche means 'common' [*gemein*]: when our experiences are common, they're just type-experiences, without individual identity in us.[31] To the degree that our willing follows such patterns, *we* don't exist (as individuals); the group, the *herd*, is the real being here. Thus his point isn't just that I'm *like* my copracticers (all separate things sharing a quality) but that we're jointly parts of (participants in) the *same* thing. Whereas the former relation need give me no interest in those others,[32] the latter does. It disperses my identity out to a societal (or cultural) movement. Its success reflects on me; it *is* the success of what's real about me. This broadens my positive interest in others 'outside' me: it now takes in not only my descendents (in practice) but my neighbors (copracticers).

Although Nietzsche does think this point, more important to him is a second point, of opposite and yet similar effect: my identity does lie in my relation to my community but, above all, in ways that I'm unlike it. The 'identity' one gets from sameness is deficient, just being a member of this herd; to the extent that I pursue the interests of this (aspect of my) self, I forgo and neglect the project of individuating myself, of creating a more specific self here. The latter depends, Nietzsche thinks, on opposing, on setting oneself apart in difference. By developing idiosyncratic variations on the common practices, by weaving the latter into new syntheses, and especially by shifting that overall practice itself through such efforts, I create a self that *is* as a will to power, in its own right and apart from the wills of the society or herd.

I make this identity not just by struggling against the herd (as an aspect in myself) but by struggling against other individuals, in contests

31. See BGE268 on how the need for quick communication drives society through a "natural, all-too-natural *progressus in simile*, the development of human beings into the similar, ordinary, average, herdlike—into the *common!*" See WP886 [1887] on how few human beings are 'persons'. Compare Heidegger's account of how our self is, for the most part, 'das Man'.

32. But note BGE265, characterizing the egoism of the 'noble soul': "It is one piece of its egoism *more*, this refinement and self-limitation in its interactions with its equals . . . —it honors *itself* in them and in the rights it cedes to them".

with them. In both cases, although this oppositional self is more fully individuated than the herd self, it is so only through and in those oppositions. So my identity is still entangled with that of others; I *am* a being, by being against others. This entanglement emerges best in the case of those contests: my acts aren't narrowly mine but are phases in an interaction, moves in an ongoing competition. What I am doing is held in its logical space by what this other is doing. So what's really present in the place I find my self is a struggle that encompasses that self as one of its sides.

Once again, this diffuses my selfish interest in a certain way. It gives me an interest in the others I struggle against, not so as to dissolve our conflict but to make me value it all the more, in a way that then tempers it. I learn to wish not for obliteration of the forces against me but for their strengthening—for them to be the more challenging (worthy) opponents; I view them in the special competitive spirit Nietzsche names by the *agon*. Thus here we find a deeper ground for that point: before, this tempered aggressiveness seemed a strategy for increasing my personal power; now we see how it expresses an identification beyond that personal level, out to the struggles that encompass and constitute me. It expresses the diffusion of the true self whose interest I pursue. I don't try just to get all that I can (for my self) out of the *agon;* I act in favor of this competitive practice (or system of practices) itself, trying to extend or improve it.

These ways that my self is diffused beyond the borders I usually assume for it diffuse my selfish interest as well. So this interest comes to encompass, in differing ways, my descendents, my neighbors, and even and especially my opponents. This interest makes me care, in these different ways, for their good or welfare. And it makes me care for them differently than just instrumentally, as means to my good (more narrowly conceived). By interweaving my identity with theirs, it makes me, in one complicated sense, care for them 'for their own sake'. All of this clearly does temper the ruthlessness of Nietzsche's egoism.

This shows, schematically, how to reconcile those act-, self-, and other-empowerment views by showing how an interest in the act's own power supports those broader concerns. An act never has its identity in itself but in its part in some encompassing personal project; such projects constitute my self, in which my acts thus have their point and purpose. These personal projects themselves find their identity in how they fit and oppose the projects of my contemporaries, and even those before and after us. This gives my acting self a ramifying interest in the strengthening of others.

It's this diffusion of my identity that explains those passages (cited in § 3.1.1) in which Nietzsche presumes an interest in society or in some overman. He's not preaching altruism here but presuming a proper selfishness, reflective of my self's contextual identity: I am an episode or strand in an enveloping, ongoing *agon*, partly one with others (in my merely common practices), partly distinguishing myself by being against them. I thus have an interest in this *agon* and in the success of the part I play in it. And (Nietzsche thinks) the best such role—the best way of joining *and* opposing society—is to find where it's sick, to be its merciless critic and exposer, and to help heal and renew it. Thus it's to participate in that 'revaluation of values' Nietzsche so promotes, if not as its decisive achiever (the overman), then by preparing for him. In the latter's historical event, I can hope for higher and fuller meaning.

We need to examine this tempering argument. Would such an abstract diffusion of interest generate concrete behavior toward others that we'd count as just? Can it really answer this worry we've had? Before we face this problem with respect to our personal behavior, let's look at a cousin to it. What societal ideal does my aptly diffused self-interest give me? Can this ideal answer the qualms we expressed against Nietzsche's 'politics', in the names of democracy and equality?

3.3 Nietzsche's politics

We've just seen three points. First, a person opposes his society only against a background of obedience and conformity. In these, his identity is diffused out into society; he *is* merely its common practices. Second, although a person should indeed work against this and seek to distinguish himself by opposing his society, this opposition should be tempered 'agonistically', should will its enemy stronger, 'to be the worthier opponent'. Third, the supreme way of opposing society, the highest expression of personal health and strength, is by diagnosing and attacking its sickness or reactivity, thereby reforming and redeeming it.

These, I think, are the three main allegiances Nietzsche gives us to our society—three grounds for wanting its good and health. They rebut, I think, the common suspicion that his egoistic values must make us indifferent to our society or else set us to prey on it. It's because they give us these positive interests that he can then propose to us a certain social ideal and think we have a reason to entertain it. He offers, that is, a conception of how we should want our society to improve and the image of a feasible better society, lying off in this direction. His 'social ideal' is not, then, a perfect society; it's offered as an improvement specific to *our* social-historical site and makes no pretense to rule out still further and higher achievements. Yet Nietzsche also does think it can be the best society so far.[33]

To be sure, this society has value at all for Nietzsche only because of its relation to certain persons in whom he is principally interested. I

---

33. Its main competitor would be Greek society in its 'tragic age', but I think Nietzsche mainly hopes the latter's ideal health can be reachieved on a drastically larger and richer scale.

think here it's important to distinguish two sets of such persons, who stand in quite different relations to this ideal society.

First, more obviously, there are the members of the new elite this society fosters. What makes it ideal is that it can 'breed' a class of individuals in whom our old culture's richness is infused with a renewed health. We're to care for this new society because we value this elite as high points of human power.

Second, and more crucially for Nietzsche, this society is important because of a different relation to a different person: it's the product (not the producer) of the most powerful, valuable one of all, the overman. The latter isn't a type, and so isn't bred by any society; his role is precisely to create a society, by recreating himself—by radically refashioning the pattern his own society bred into him. More specifically, his preeminence lies in his doing the greatest deed: redeeming our culture from nihilism, making possible that newly healthy elite. But although the worth of his achievement makes us rank him so, we then care about that achievement still more because it is his. We're to want the new society not just for its healthy elite but because by working toward it we join in the cause of this redeemer and share in his deed. Here we find the messianic aspect to Nietzsche's values, so prominent in his visions of Zarathustra, Dionysus, and himself, each as the Antichrist who preserves at least this aspect of Christ.

However, in the rest of this section I set aside this interest in the overman and focus on the new society's role as breeding an elite. It's here that Nietzsche expresses the social-political values we find so intolerable. Though he means his basic egoism in a way that gives me a positive interest in my society's good, he also tells me to think of that good in ways I find repugnant. To begin with, the ideal society is radically nonegalitarian: it has strongly distinct classes or castes. These range from a ruling elite to a large lowest class of sickly and suffering persons, perhaps even 'slaves', in some more literal sense than the term has yet had for us. So GS377: "we hold it by no means desirable [*wünschenswerth*], that the realm of justice and concord be founded on earth (because it would be in any case the realm of the deepest mediocritizing and chinesery); . . . we think about the necessity for new orders, also for a new slavery—for every strengthening and elevation of the type 'human being' also involves a new kind of enslavement."[34] In this hoped-for society, all 'weaker' persons are treated, it seems, as mere resources for the benefit of the stronger. How could we ever accept so unjust an ideal? Is it at all defensible? And if not, does it pull down with itself the whole card pile of views I've built for Nietzsche?

34. WP464 [1885] looks for "a noble mode of thought . . . [which] believes in slavery and in many degrees of subjection as the presupposition of every higher culture". WP859 [1886–87] considers "to what extent a sacrifice of freedom, even enslavement itself, gives the basis for the bringing-forth of a *higher type.*'' See also BGE257, WP866 [1887].

3.3.1   Against equality

Let's first consider Nietzsche's antiegalitarianism. Again, this appears at two main points: in his teaching of the overman and in the preference he more generally shows for hierarchic societies. The first is more distinctive of Nietzsche's philosophical thinking, but the second is more deep-rooted there. His writings reveal a preference for hierarchies, long before the thought and teaching of the overman emerge; that eventually domi-nant thought seems merely an intensification of a prior, broader bias in favor of elites. This is already abstractly expressed in PTAG1p30 [1873]: "in all things only the higher steps come into consideration".[35] So this bias toward higher degrees determines, it seems, Nietzsche's social ideal.

This can well seem a matter of bias. Even granting Nietzsche that power is the good to be maximized (in us and in society as we care for it), why should this be in the nonstandard ('maximax') way we've seen: in the highest peaks, rather than the greatest overall sum? Or, as the point could instead be put, why should these peaks be measured as so high that they add quite disproportionately to that sum? Nietzsche works a hyperbolic stretching of the valuative scale, so that one or a few persons can outweigh (in their value and in their claim on our interest) vast numbers of others. Utilitarianism, too, could take this form and so strive to concentrate pleasure in a few lucky hands; but this choice would there seem perverse. Why should naming power rather than pleasure as the good make this route any less odd or unmotivated? Doesn't this thought float free from the power ontology, as a personal idiosyncrasy of Nietzsche the man? And doesn't this show that his social ideal can have no real claim on us?

The concept of power does somewhat prompt and fit with this route. It's not merely that power is intrinsically over others, so that Nietzsche's good consists in differences between persons and not in some feature they might all have equally (like pleasure); this still might counsel a maximization that aims at very many who are strong, rather than at a few who are very strong. It's also that power doesn't diminish at the margin in the way that pleasure seems to do. Indeed quite the opposite, Nietzsche maintains: in the overman, power explodes, as this single person becomes the meaning-giving fulcrum on which his society turns. There's a similar point about elites: they give purpose or identity to their own age; their societies culminate in their lives. Because power can lie in such ontological dominion, it can grow beyond what we might think possible for a person as we usually, narrowly bound him.

This very abstract defense of hierarchy surely won't convince us, however. Even if the power ontology does, in such a way, require in-equality, it could never bear such a weight of argument for us. We'll

35. BGE43: "And how could there be a 'common good [*Gemeingut*]'! The word contradicts itself: what can be common, always has only little value."

never be as sure about it as we are attached to equality and democracy.[36] So how else might Nietzsche convince us?

An important part of his argument for hierarchy lies in his polemical preview of an opposite, thoroughly democratized society, toward which, he warns, we're heading dangerously. If we follow to their end the egalitarian principles that so rebel in us against his ideal, we arrive, he claims, at an alternative, an antiutopia, much less appealing even to us. This is 'nihilism', in its aspect as the culmination of the herd instinct's rise to power.[37] Just as Plato defends his aristocracy in part with critical sketches of certain 'relevant alternatives'—societies rendered ideal by competing principles, or for other types of persons—so Nietzsche argues by sketching a thoroughly equalized and 'leveled' society, made up (in Zarathustra's phrase) of 'last humans'. He suggests that the choice is between this ideal and his own. WP936 [1887–88]: *"Herd-animal ideals*—now culminating as the *highest value standard* of 'society': attempt to give them a cosmic, even a metaphysical value.—Against them I defend *aristocracy.'*[38]

In that opposite ideal, in the society of 'complete nihilism', egalitarian tendencies will have quite prevailed, eliminating classes, and generally leveling social and economic differences between persons. This condition is reached by unstinting application of the principle (to put the point in more recent terms[39]) of benefiting first the worst off. Our society, and even all the world, is progressively organized toward the end that there shall be no worst off. So its resources are turned increasingly to eliminate suffering, and first in its simplest forms: food and housing

36. See Foot's suggestion (1994, 9) that in rejecting equality Nietzsche abandons "the practice of justice".

37. WP215 [1887] tells a fuller story: "In Christianity, *three elements* must be distinguished: a) the oppressed of all kinds, b) the mediocre of all kinds, c) the discontented and sick of all kinds". These fight together against their respective enemies: economic-political rulers, the exceptional, and the healthy. As they succeed and take political power under the banner of democracy, the second element—which is really the herd instinct—"steps into the foreground". WP280 [1887] shows this instinct's defining intent: "Fear ceases in the middle; here one is never alone; . . . here there is equality; here one's own being is not perceived as a reproach but as the *right* being; here contentment rules [*herrscht*]. Mistrust applies to the exceptions". This instinct expresses itself in our liberalism: "The honor-word for *mediocre* is, of course, the word *'liberal'* " [WP864: 1888].

38. TSZ/I/P/5 presents this form of argument as addressed to the pride of its audience: if we can't be attracted to the overman ideal, at least our pride will repel us from 'the last human'. BGE203: "The *over-all degeneration of humanity* down to what today appears to the socialist dolts and flatheads as their 'human being of the future'—as their ideal!—this degeneration and diminution of humanity into perfect herd animals (or, as they say, to human beings of the 'free society'), this animalization of humanity into dwarf animals of equal rights and claims, is *possible*, there is no doubt of it! Anyone who has once thought through this possibility to the end, knows a greater disgust than other human beings—but perhaps also a new *task!* "

39. So Rawls's famous 'difference principle' (1971, 75ff.). See also n.46.

for the poor, medical care for the sick. As the project is more fully implemented, it's not just a matter of so distributing material goods or of regulating members' economic practices. This society restructures its practices quite generally; it (very gradually) revises them to suit this end, to eliminate suffering.

This suffering it fights is really, recall, a will's experience of incapacity, of being resisted and mastered by another will, of losing a struggle against other forces. So society now takes a widening care, to prevent there being any losers. Having, with its ever-higher safety net, obviated struggle to secure those material goods, it campaigns next (with growing directness) against struggle itself. It strikes at the root of interpersonal competition, by throwing into disrepute the very effort to have more or be better than others. By a very gradual progress through partial steps, eliminating 'discrimination' against more and more types of persons, it eventually reveals its ultimate point: that there be no more winners or losers, no better and worse lives.

In this way, the 'last society' relaxes those competitive tensions—between persons, between practices—that had formerly driven it. It no longer bears groups that differ, that compete, in their ways of life and values. Of course there remain different, unlike, practices, but they're no longer mutually hostile and critical.[40] I don't care to impose my practice on others; I don't even think my practice better than others'. I no longer so inhabit my way of life as to view and value everyone else, including those who live differently, from its point of view. I bear in the back of my mind that everyone's equal; to suppose that this (what I'm doing) is better than that (what he does) is to 'discriminate', a notion that thus takes its broadest critical scope. Thus there ceases that struggle between practices whose shifting fortunes once made the society develop; it's 'last', because it's stagnant.

Competition is eased not just between practices, but within each one, among the different persons who perform it. How well I perform in comparison with others matters less and less, a tendency reinforced by that eroding away of material penalties on failure (and rewards for success). I no longer try to do things better than others, only to do them as well as they typically, commonly do. Persons take on, with these practices, the aim to perform them to only an adequate degree, to do them averagely well.[41] The valuative standards once implicit in practices, the challenge to perform them to high or exceptional degrees, are now felt to fail to honor a metaphysical equality. It really doesn't matter what a person does or how well he does it; we're all human beings after all, and so all of equal worth. To disvalue someone as ugly, or unintel-

40. They've been 'harmonized' in a sense we might link with Pythagoras, in contrast with Heraclitus.
41. WP280 [1887]: "The instinct of the herd esteems the *middle* and the *mean* as the highest and most valuable".

ligent, or weak, or even weak-willed, eventually seems as unfair as to do so because of his race or religion.

With this relaxing of tension without and within, all can now alike live comfortable and secure lives. "'We have invented happiness', say the last humans, and they blink" [TSZ/I/P/5]. The common form of happiness they mean is a "happiness of rest" [WP464: 1885], really just "the green-pasture happiness of the herd, common to all, with comfort, the easy life for everyman" [BGE44]. This ideal lies at a merely average level, and if one has trouble even so, society helps one up to it. Thus there's very little gap between the life conceived to be best and the one attained by mere default and inertia: "Everybody wills the same [Gleiche], everybody is equal; whoever feels otherwise goes voluntarily into a madhouse" [TSZ/I/P/5]. Society and its members now lack, in effect, any values or ideals: losing their commitment to some practice's power, they lose that root interest in the world, which alone can support the concern that true values involve.

We might well share much of Nietzsche's distaste for this vision. But, we reply, surely it's not the only, inevitable alternative to his own (drastically hierarchic) ideal. Surely there are many other positions along the dimension opened up between these poles: many intermediate orderings of society, preserving some degree of competition and inequality, yet not to the brutal extreme he seems to wish. Surely our democratic-egalitarian principles can and do permit some 'tempering' of egalitarianism, and so would project a very different ideal from the one Nietzsche attacks.

So our natural reply is to (point out how we do) limit the respect in which persons are (or should be) equal: equal in political rights, equal in their right to the government's interest and resources. Perhaps the equality we believe in only arises in this 'public' connection. Why mightn't we continue to view persons as unequal in many 'private' respects, as better or worse at what they do, even as better or worse human beings? Mightn't one of our equal rights even be our right to compete, to try to be better than others in our private practices? And haven't we even a right not to be interfered with in this by the government?

To be sure, there are rules in these competitions, which players mustn't transgress, and this means we believe in equal rights to certain treatment not just by the government but by other persons: rights not to be stolen from or cheated or exploited in various ways. These are our very reasons for rejecting that hierarchic society Nietzsche prefers; the strong seem there to exploit the weak. But we're not even close to rejecting competition altogether nor to believing in a right never to suffer. Not all priority is exploitation, and not all suffering is undeserved. So it seems that the antiutopia Nietzsche attacks is a false target, having little to do with the democratic-egalitarian principles we in fact hold.

Clearly, we do so limit how far we wish everyone to be equally regarded or valued. And clearly it's possible to formulate principles that capture these limits and thus project a society that is only partially equalized; if this is our ideal, Nietzsche seems not to address it. Yet he thinks his envisioned extreme still bears against us; it just does so indirectly, by a route we don't expect. By his contextual point, he finds the very identity and value of our principles to lie not in themselves alone but in their psychohistorical role, in what they come from and lead toward. Thus even our (more moderate) principles are expressions of 'herd instincts' in us.[42] These principles lead on to that distasteful extreme; there isn't any sticking or resting point before there, at which their own logic will let them persist. If these tendencies (which are themselves societal practices willing their own power) maintain their grip on the world's societies, they'll gradually erode away the rest of our (already-attenuated) values. Because our principles are such halfway expressions of a social-historical movement that will culminate in that antiutopia, they must be judged (and rejected) as such.[43]

We feel strong doubts against this form of argument, however: if Nietzsche takes this historical line, he doesn't seem to have much of a point. It seems, first, a very open question whether that fully equalized society will eventuate; so the argument rests on a shaky long-term prediction. And second, even if that prediction were (to become) true, it seems not really to bear on our principles, in themselves, in the way we think a moral argument should. Shouldn't these principles be judged for their content, for the worth of the social ideal they themselves project? Why hold against them some different society that (let's assume) will follow after the one that ideal describes? Our ideal might still project the best society, so that our culture's inability to sustain it is a mere misfortune. For parallel reasons, I think, we're also doubtful of Nietzsche's 'psychologistic' attack on these principles for the personal motives or traits they might express.

But Nietzsche's historical point doesn't exclude a more direct argument; indeed, it even implies or involves one. He's supposing an inner, more nearly analytic connection between our principles and that future antiutopia; it doesn't just *happen* to follow after our holding them. (Nor need this antiutopia actually ensue, to reflect thus against our views.) Our principles bear in their very logic, as it were, the tendency toward

42. TI/IX/37: "'Equality', a certain factual growing-similar [*Anähnlichung*], which merely brings itself to expression in the theory of 'equal rights', belongs essentially to decline". TSZ/II/7 ("On the Tarantulas"): "To me you [preachers of equality] are tarantulas, and secretly vengeful!"

43. See how BGE202 insists on equating with 'anarchist dogs' even "the peacefully industrious democrats . . . and the brotherhood enthusiasts who call themselves socialists and will a 'free society'": "[They are] one in their tough resistance against every special claim, every special right and privilege (which means in the last analysis, against *every* right: for once all are equal nobody needs 'rights' any more)."

that extreme. This shows in the way our principles' weakest parts are the arguments in which they impose limits or exceptions on a more complete equality. It's there we find convolutions of epicycles appended to simpler, more forceful egalitarian thoughts such as utilitarianism, a central case. In contriving these epicycles, moral philosophers fight a retreating, rearguard struggle against the advancing logic of that core egalitarianism. An example will help make clearer how this might be so.

Consider how convincing an argument can be made that our ethical principles, when their absolute sense isn't qualified by contextual factors, dictate and preach a radical self-sacrifice. To be truly moral, I would have to commit all my own resources—money, property, time, and effort—to preventing the suffering of others. Each incremental sacrifice I make gives greater benefits to those much worse off than I am. All my arguments to resist this moral lesson seem ad hoc and hollow. They reflect, I might well confess, a background decision not to try to be as moral as I could. I (feel I) share with others this seldom-admitted 'pragmatic' loosening or weakening of morality's lesson; this half-secret agreement serves as the 'context' weakening the 'absolute' meaning of the moral terms we exchange. Acknowledging now this shared presumption, we see how it tempers a strict egalitarian thrust in our core moral values. And it's plausible to suppose that utilitarianism also imposes this leveling duty on its adherents, despite the denials contrived by (persistingly) middle- and upper-class utilitarians.

This strong egalitarian lesson can be traced back into some deep features of our valuative thinking. First, it's expressed in the good—'happiness'—our values chiefly intend. Isn't this at least the first thing to come from us when asked to name life's goal or good? And we half-deliberately form our notion of happiness so that it can be a democratic ideal.[44] We shape it to be a state potentially attainable by all, as we so feel it should be. Access to it mustn't depend on (more than a very minimal degree of) natural endowments, such as intelligence or physical vigor; we rebel against the thought that (in more than very rare cases) a person's inherent limitations might cut him off from 'the good for persons'. Thus, in a sense, all have an 'equal access' to this good: it's set at a low enough level to lie within the natural capacities of any human being.

Of course we do recognize distinctions between (as we differently state it) degrees or amounts or (higher and lower) types of happiness. But this has just the force of an afterthought; it's much more important that a person be (generically) happy than that he be extremely so. So the way we develop the thought about degrees, the way we conceive of its scale, itself reflects the egalitarian drive. We suppose that happiness rises

44. TI/IX/38: one who has become free "tramples upon the contemptible kind of well-being dreamed of by shopkeepers, Christians, cows, females, Englishmen, and other democrats."

or falls most steeply at the lowest, deficient levels: the 'distance' between starving and subsisting outstrips (nearly?) every interval between higher levels of happiness.[45] (By contrast, as we've seen, the Nietzschean good of power 'increases at the margin', grows ever more steeply at higher levels.)

That deep egalitarianism is even more importantly expressed in our views about persons' entitlement, or 'right', to this good. For in another sense all don't, of course, have an equal access to it, but (we feel) all *should*. All have an equal right to be happy. This deep conviction of an equal desert underlies our more elaborate views about citizens' political rights. Past generations believed that suffering or failure was justified by (appropriate to) one's class or race; we pride ourselves on seeing the irrelevance of these. What matters is our common humanity not anything less inclusive than this. Belief in the equality of 'moral persons'—that personhood is all or nothing and not a matter of degree, that each person counts as exactly one—underlies not just our political views but our valuative thinking quite generally. Even that thinking's effort to be 'objective' and 'impartial' might bear a logic that leads to egalitarianism.[46]

It might seem this goes too far and ignores ways we do think people differ in desert; we take it that they are responsible for some of their successes or failures.[47] For example, can't differences in ability or intelligence justify differences in success? Yet these criteria might not stand scrutiny: we're compelled to agree that the person himself isn't (fully) responsible for being smart or talented.[48] These are, as it were, just favored circumstances in which his metaphysical self is lucky to find itself. What should matter is only how hard this self works with

45. Connected with this is what Nagel (1991, 65) calls "the familiar fact of diminishing marginal utility", which in turn implies: "Transferable resources will usually benefit a person with less more than they will benefit a person with significantly more."

46. So Nagel argues (1979, 112) that "an assumption of moral equality between persons" is shared by all three "theories of social choice" common today—egalitarianism, utilitarianism, and rights theory; all three "attempt to give equal weight, in essential respects, to each person's point of view. This might even be described as the mark of an enlightened ethic." He goes on to defend the first theory's credentials; as he later (1991, 65f.) puts it: "I believe that impartiality is also egalitarian in itself. . . . [It] generates a greater interest in benefiting the worse off than in benefiting the better off". This follows from the Kantian project of trying "to view things simultaneously from everyone's point of view" (1991, 67); we'll see in § 4.5 that Nietzsche might agree to (a version of) that project, but hold that when all these viewpoints are so assembled, some will and should dominate.

47. So Nagel 1991, 71: "What seems bad is not that people should be unequal in advantages or disadvantages generally, but that they should be unequal in [those] for which they are not responsible."

48. Thus we're only at all comfortable using such criteria to justify access to higher degrees of happiness or the good: talent can make one deserve an unusual success, but the talentless, too, deserve to be happy.

whatever such tools it receives, because only in this do all get a fair, equal start. Thus our instinct tells us that society ought to remove those unequal constraints that make degree of effort fail to be mirrored by degree of success (of happiness). In the ideal world, equal efforts would accomplish what they deserve: equal results.

So rather than believing in a bare equal right to happiness, we believe in a right to 'an equal chance'. Thus, in an economic context, we think the person himself must take his fair opportunity by working hard. This shows how there's one criterion for deserving the good that we feel most confident in: we require of a person effort, a strength of will. Deficiencies in this, in how hard he tries, can limit or negate his claim to happiness. He's responsible for these defiencies and could therefore deserve any suffering it produces for him. Only a person's own greater effort can make him deserve any more than another, because only this effort really is 'his own'. In judging only by effort of will, we pride ourselves in being at the end of a historical contraction in what a person is held responsible for. Allowing only effort to count, we at last judge persons for themselves, for what they truly control.

Such beliefs also lie behind and condition our judgments of 'right' and 'wrong': a person (or his action) can only be better than another (and his action), if each was free to will the way that made him so. This shows how the notion of *free will* lies at our crux. Persons can be right or wrong, can deserve good or bad, only because they're all equally free to will as they should, to try as hard as they should. Thus our faith in free will gives a hidden expression to the egalitarian point. We only feel able to grant (that there can be) difference in worth, on the precondition that all are equal in their access to it. Free will is so important to us, because it secures this metaphysical equality. The supposition of an equal freedom stands at the ground of all our rankings of persons; unless all do start equal here, such rankings wouldn't (we feel) be fair.

Nietzsche argues that this web of metamoral beliefs isn't a stable one either. We eventually see through this dream of an equal freedom, as we see through the fictions of the (all-or-nothing) ego substance or soul atom on which it depends.[49] The truth increasingly presses itself on us that there's no metaphysical self to be the 'first cause' such freedom requires. The very notion mightn't make sense.[50] Psychology's advances suggest that even strength of will is something a person is shaped to

49. See § 3.5.2 for the attack on free will. WP765 [1888] attributes to Christianity the concept of the *"equality of souls before God"*: "In it is given the prototype of all theories of *equal rights:* first one taught humanity to stammer the proposition of equality in religion, later one made a morality out of it". See also KSA/13/11[156] [1887–88]. Nagel (1979, 126) derives equality's value from "the general form of moral reasoning", which involves stepping into others' perspectives. So it might be the way that perspectives (consciousnesses?) seem to have that all-or-nothing character that grounds our egalitarianism. When we finally confront Nietzsche's perspectivism—in chapter 4—we'll see how it denies any such perspective atoms.

50. See BGE21.

have; it's explained by causes other than any such free, deep self. And this realization must cancel the last criterion that could justify different deserts. What then will we say once we're fully convinced that a person is just an organism and that even lack of effort, the last failing we had allowed to justify anyone's suffering, isn't really 'his fault'?

This shows how ideas at the core of our valuative thought—our conceptions of happiness and of persons' entitlement to it—might express a radical egalitarianism, one that predictably *will* be driven by the facts themselves to renounce even those rankings of persons it now still allows. The egalitarian assumption is lodged so close to the core of our metamoral background beliefs that it must and will spin off, as foreign accretions, every inherited qualification to it: in the end, it must rule unfair every effort to rank persons. Thus the intermediate position we seek, between Nietzschean hierarchy and an utter equality, is at odds with our firmest principles (even though not yet recognized as such). Perhaps this is enough to give pause to our so-confident denial of Nietzsche's hierarchic views by making us see that our own democratic sentiments are also in play, also questionable.

Of course this falls far short of justifying Nietzsche's views; I must work next at this other end to make his alternative ideal less horrific than it seems.

3.3.2 For what type of inequality?

There's one general strategy for rendering Nietzsche's 'hierarchic'[51] ideal less threatening that will look inviting to any sympathetic interpreter. This is to limit the types of advantages the elite enjoy in his ideally structured society. And (as we anticipated in § 3.1.3) what Nietzsche says about power through spiritualization offers a familiar way to develop this line. Thus his defenders naturally suppose that his highest heroes won't be better ('better off') economically or politically but only 'spiritually'. Their spiritual preeminence won't be specially favored by society, in its distributions of economic goods and political power. Nor will this elite even pursue these goods with much interest or ability. This is because, these readers want Nietzsche to say, this elite owe their priority to drives directed intellectually; they pursue (and achieve) a *cognitive* dominance in preference to a crude economic or political rule. It's because these goods aren't even tempting to this elite that society won't try to encourage (develop) such persons by attaching material rewards to their type. And it's because they don't much care for these goods that they'll tend not to have them, even on their own and without society's special aid.

---

51. By 'hierarchy' I mainly mean any society structured into ranked classes. But inasmuch as Nietzsche's ideal will rank highest a class of philosophers—descendents (in spirit) of the priests—it will propose a 'hierarchy' in a narrower sense, too.

If indeed we can hear Nietzsche so—or even see this as a friendly amendment, consistent with the core of his power ontology—his 'elitism' might not worry us as much. This is some of the intent behind readings that stress the spiritual superiority of his ideal: it would ease our concern, much as it does to hear that Plato's elite will have no private possessions. Indeed, it's part of philosophy's tradition to palliate (the exclusiveness of) its ideal—its designation of just its type of person, the theoretical type, as best, as the finest fruit or flower of society—by rendering this ideal person as an ascetic; we all can better stomach an elite that doesn't care about worldly things. Does Nietzsche also take this line, if only in some idiosyncratic way?

We've already seen that Nietzsche indeed has a 'spiritual' dominion in mind in the case of the overman, the inventor of this new elite. By shaping (in some very general ways) the values and practices the new society trains its members into, this overman 'rules' all the generations so formed.[52] His superiority isn't economic or political, but ontological: his creative act gives those members (some basic aspects of) their identity, the 'meaning' to their practices and lives. Indeed, this might already amount to an intrusion or assault on these followers, even one more genuinely hurtful to them, by Nietzsche's own standards, than an economic subjugation would be. Mightn't it deny them the chance to 'create themselves'? Mightn't it amount to locking them into values and practices in which they (implicitly) mirror and glorify the overman? But we're probably not much disturbed by these points; we accept the sweeping influence of history's great creators.[53] If domination and inequality take only this ontological form, as in the overman, Nietzsche's social ideal won't seem badly unjust.

What, however, will be the manner of rule by that new elite in the society the overman founds? Will theirs also be a 'spiritual' dominion, and not economic or political as well? Some passages suggest this, as perhaps WP712 [1887]: *"high point in becoming* (the highest spiritualization of power upon the most slavish ground)".[54] Just what type of hierarchy does Nietzsche anticipate in his new society?

I think his clearest accounts of a social structure that he even might think ideal are in his treatments of the (Hindu) laws of Manu; the main passages are TI/VII/3; A57; WP145 [1888], WP143 [1888], WP142

52. Nehamas (1985, 28) stresses the importance of this type of power.
53. Though perhaps even Goethe, one of the most benign exemplars for Nietzsche's ideal, becomes a more disturbing figure if we see him as aiming at such power over his audience. And this worry applies to Nietzsche himself and to his own motives in addressing us: what type of effect on his readers does he want? We've already seen part of a (reassuring) answer: he wants to magnify himself precisely by having a magnifying effect on others—us. So he wants to bind us not just to his truths but to truths that free and inspire us to create ourselves in other respects.
54. WP957 [1885] attributes 'the highest spirituality' to the new ruling caste it advocates.

[1888]. His approval of these laws is most unequivocal in A57, which introduces them as opposite to (the archvillain) Christianity: "To set up a lawbook of the kind of Manu means to allow a people henceforth to become master [*Meister*], to become perfect—to aspire to the highest art of life." He claims that every healthy society recognizes three types: "Nature, *not* Manu, separates those pre-eminently spiritual, those pre-eminently strong in muscle and temperament, and . . . the mediocre—the last as the great number, the first as the select." This tripartite division obviously calls to mind Plato.[55] Like him, Nietzsche (implicitly) defends the inequality this division involves, using that argument from asceticism. He says of the elite: "asceticism becomes in them nature, need, instinct". Their pursuit of spiritual growth seems to turn them away from any material goods that would bring their interests into conflict with those of others.

Nietzsche goes on (in A57) to develop this argument, revealing the fuller strategy it serves. He stresses how the weak would not find the life of these elite more pleasant than their own: "Let us not underestimate the privileges of the *mediocre*. Life toward the *heights* becomes ever harder". He claims that the weak are happy in a society so structured: "For the mediocre, to be mediocre is a happiness; mastery [*Meisterschaft*] in one thing, the specialty—a natural instinct." This shows us the ultimate point to that citing of asceticism: if the best aren't better off in the weak's own terms, the latter seem to lack any motive for complaining of injustice. If, moreover, they get from this structured society just what they want anyway, that average happiness, then what injustice is done?[56] This fuller pattern to the defense of inequality is also natural and familiar to us; we find it elsewhere in philosophy's tradition, and every day whenever concrete inequities are being defended (including many that seem to us indefensible).

To be sure, Nietzsche also has complaints against these laws of Manu. So WP143 [1888] says that in them "the *spirit of the priest*, is worse than anywhere else"; WP142 [1888] attacks their use of the "holy lie". But he might just hope to replace these priests with (his new) philosophers, as rulers at the top of this same structure. Then we could supplement these passages with GM/III/5–10; these sections, in an essay on "the meaning of ascetic ideals", add details to that reassuring line.

55. By contrast, TI/VII/3 has the laws distinguish four castes; the lowest, leaving aside the casteless chandala, is the 'race of servants'.

56. Nietzsche also suggests that the rule of this elite is a culmination or fulfillment of the rule of the mediocre many themselves—that they have bred themselves into slaves in their instincts, and so made themselves suited for slavery in some further sense. WP954 [1885–86]: "And would it not be a kind of goal, redemption, and justification for the democratic movement itself if someone came who *made use* of it, by finally producing beside its new and sublime shaping of slavery—which the completion of European democracy will someday show itself as—that higher kind of masterful and Caesarian spirits . . . ?" See also BGE242.

They ask what these ideals mean when held by "a real *philosopher*" [5], the type that emerges as the essay's only hero (his competitors there are the artist and priest). Asceticism belongs to this philosophical type, Nietzsche says, because denial of the senses (the appetites) is "the optimum of conditions for the highest and boldest spirituality" [7]. A philosopher is formed by just such a dominating spiritual will or instinct, one strong enough to restrain all others in him. Thus he shuns wife, child, and even home, as well as "fame, princes, and women" [8], because all would interfere with his maximal expression (i.e., enacting) of that single drive.⁵⁷

This presents the philosopher's asceticism as a favorable exception, healthier than the priest's or his flock's. His denial of worldly goods isn't reactive, not the spiteful attack on something that can't be had and that one envies and hates others for having. Rather, he negates these only in consequence of a primary affirmation, lying in that stronger, spiritual drive's active willing. (Let's note but defer our suspicion of a certain dishonesty or self-ignorance in Nietzsche here: he seems not to have been either competent or successful enough at love or sex, for example, for us not to suspect that these drives were unsatisfiable longings in him.) This way of motivating asceticism may differ from traditional ones, which cite a reasoned insight into the unreality of this world and into our essence as immaterial souls at home in a different realm. But the result is the same: the ideal person still renounces worldly goods and pleasures for the sake of spiritual growth. If Nietzsche's new elite are ascetic philosophers, some of the most worrying types of injustice might not occur.

We still haven't specified how these ascetic philosophers do rule; society is organized in their interest, but just how do the others 'serve' them? Drawing on the hints just assembled, we can piece together, in Nietzsche's name, a somewhat less threatening political vision.

First, that 'enslavement' he mentions might lie mainly in the last humans' herd nature, in their unquestioning absorption in shared practices and values. They pursue by rote their material goals, busily spinning the wheels of industry, content with the comforts and pleasures their labor produces. Their democratized tastes let them value only these goods, and want them indeed to only an average, standard extent. So they're really, at the root, enslaved by their habits or customs and not by their rulers.

Second, the elite might then use these many, not by forcing them

---

57. GM/III/8: "In the end they demand little enough, these philosophers, their motto is 'he who possesses will be possessed'—*not*, as I must say again and again, from a virtue, from a meritorious will to frugality and simplicity, but because *so* their supreme master demands from them, shrewdly and inexorably: he has taste for only one thing, and gathers and saves up everything—time, force, love, interest—only for it." See also WP915 [1887].

into activities they don't themselves want but by skimming a (small) share from the productive labor they already prefer. So the many would 'support' the elite by providing material necessities, freeing the latter for a life of the mind or spirit.[58] Because the elite are ascetics, however, this support won't be to an extravagant or luxurious level; presumably, they'll want and get less of these goods than will the producers themselves. So perhaps WP764 [1883]: "The workers shall live one day as the bourgeois do now—but *above* them the *higher caste*, distinguished by their absence of needs! thus poorer and simpler, but in possession of power." We might then compare their maintenance to that for universities: society provides a livelihood to those who devote themselves to spiritual concerns.[59]

Third, this elite also need not have political power (preeminence), or not in any concrete way. It might guide society merely by persuading the other members: perhaps only by teaching them their basic values. These others would then freely give them that modest economic support. Some such background picture might well serve many more than (sometimes) Nietzsche, to reconcile with their egalitarian sentiments a faith in the superior value of spiritual persons (and belief that society should encourage their type).[60]

This is probably the least unjust political vision we can construct for Nietzsche. It may indeed still be disturbing to us. Yet such an 'enslavement' is at least much less onerous than we've expected; if Nietzsche means only this, he's not as violently cruel as he seemed. However, we can't really suppose he does mean only this. This relatively benign ac-

58. WP895 [1887] speaks of "preservation of the weak, because a tremendous amount of *small* work will have to be done". WP901 [1887]: "That which is free only to the *strongest* and *most fruitful* natures, for making possible *their* existence—leisure, adventure, disbelief, even dissipation—would, if it were free to average natures, necessarily destroy them—and indeed does. This is where industriousness, the rule, moderation, firm 'conviction' have their place—in short, the herd virtues: under them this average kind of human being becomes perfect."

59. Cf. Nagel (1991, 135–36), partly reconciling his socioeconomic egalitarianism with society's promotion of excellence in arts and sciences ("a mildly Nietzschean note"): "one might hope that creative and scholarly activities could serve largely as their own reward, under a more egalitarian system of compensation."

60. That 'slavish' base serves another way: it's crucial to the elite that there be a great gap between themselves and others. Because their own identity lies in their 'difference', in their struggle against opposite forces, they require the presence of the many, with its opposite ideal of averageness. So WP866 [1887] says that the higher man needs "the *opposition* [*Gegnerschaft*] of the masses, of the 'leveled', the distance-feeling in comparison to them; he stands on them, he lives off them." Also TI/IX/37: "the cleft between human being and human being, class and class, the multiplicity of types, the will to be oneself, to stand out—what I call the *pathos of distance*, that is proper to every *strong* age." And WP894 [1887]: "the continued existence of the rule is the presupposition for the value of the exception." But again, this 'gap' lies along a dimension not valued or even recognized by the many; it's not an inequity that disturbs them.

count depends on ignoring other things he says. Such a society of happy producers supporting thinkers and creators is far too pacific and innocuous a vision to be Nietzsche's; he favors a much rougher world. So we need to make several revisions in the story so far.

First, we've overstated the 'spiritual purity' of his elite. We can see so by now completing our reading of GM/III/5–10, broken off in midcourse above. This passage proceeds to a last point somewhat at odds with the ones we've reviewed: now [in 10] it turns out that the philosophical drive has adopted asceticism merely as a temporary disguise. In its weak beginnings, it has needed to appear in the form of "the *previously established* types of the contemplative human being", the religious. This drive (or practice) has grown inconspicuously and safely within this cocoon, but now (Nietzsche hints) it's strong enough to cast off this 'gloomy' disguise. So it seems that the new philosopher will cast off asceticism, too, unleashing drives that might make him want wealth and other worldly things after all.

Surely, part of the point of Nietzsche's correction in the laws of Manu—his replacement of priests with those new philosophers—is to establish a more multifaceted elite, one that accepts its 'animal' drives in a way the reactive priests can't do.[61] This suggests that Nietzsche's new rulers will be better (better off) not just 'spiritually' but also in all of those straightforward goods the many covet for themselves. It thereby undermines that argument from asceticism and even reveals it as part of the philosopher's priestly disguise: he (on behalf of his type) becomes socially acceptable by taking on the unthreatening pose of ascetic.[62]

Second, this point has a cousin at the social level. Recall that the laws of Manu provide for three classes: between the spiritual elite and the mediocre many are "those pre-eminently strong in muscle and temperament", a warrior-class. It turns out that these are the political rulers: "they are the watchmen of the law, the guardians of order and security, the noble warriors, and above all the *king*" [A57]. The philosophers emerge from this wider class by that process of spiritual growth; so

61. See how WP916 [1887] revises the Christian practices of asceticism and feasts. The ways Nietzsche's 'new philosophers' do and do not renounce asceticism are major topics in chapter 4.

62. Some of that argument's force might yet survive this point. Surely the new philosopher's interest in worldly goods will at least be moderate. His dominant project is spiritual, and although sensual drives aren't to be quashed for its sake, they're still to be mastered and guided by it. HH/II/304: "And if only this prosperity [*Wohlstand*] were true well-being [*Wohlbefinden*]! It would be less external and less of an incitement to envy, it would be more sharing, more benevolent [*wohlwollender*], more equalizing, more helping." And II/310: "Only one who has *spirit* should have *possessions*. . . . For the possessor who does not understand how to make use of the free time that his possessions could afford him will always *continue* to strive after possessions. . . . Thus in the end the moderate possessions that would suffice one with spirit are transformed into genuine riches—as indeed the glittering result of spiritual dependence and poverty."

WP978 [1885]: "The new philosopher can arise only in connection with a ruling [*herrschenden*] caste, as its highest spiritualization."[63] Even if the philosophers rule by persuasion, it seems clear that the caste they emerge from, these 'warriors', do not. They are the 'masters of the earth' [*Herren der Erde*] politically, too, a dominion that seems to us inherently unjust. Moreover, there's even less reason to think they'll be ascetics; they'll enjoy an economic advantage besides, so that Nietzsche differs from Plato here.[64] Thus many of our earlier worries are reintroduced.

There's a third way that the argument from asceticism doesn't ring true. It presumes that will to power can be channeled into, and safely confined to, a spiritual project, in a way Nietzsche surely denies. Whether or not this can be achieved in the rare individual, it surely can't be for whole societies. The healthy society must be a swarm of competing drives, drives alive in the lives of hosts of people high and low. Even if Nietzsche's philosopher does give these drives a chiefly spiritual expression, he has them from a social reservoir of drives, within which they're acted out much more straightforwardly; this is true above all of that 'ruling caste' from which he emerges. So over whole societies, forces inevitably 'spill over' into their simplest, bodily expressions. This makes Nietzsche's ideal society a more seething, violent place than in that sanitized vision.

A fourth point further disrupts that placid vision. He stresses how crucially a drive's strength is developed by the dangers or challenges it faces; a person grows strong by struggling against nearly insurmountable obstacles. So a healthy society must spur its members by imposing hardships on them. There have to be hurdles, with steep (to be maximally effective) penalties for failure and rewards for success.[65] It's true that one most important such challenge is (softened by being) spiritual or psychological in type: it's the thought of eternal return, that I'll live every moment of my life again and again.[66] Nietzsche's new society will hang this thought over the heads of its elite, compelling them to live in

63. WP998 [1884]: "the highest human beings live beyond the rulers [*Herrschenden*], set loose from all bonds; and in the rulers they have their tools."

64. WP960 [1885–86] attributes to the new aristocracy a "preponderance of willing, knowing, wealth [*Reichthum*] and influence". WP898 [1887] hopes for "an *affirming* race that may allow itself every great luxury—strong enough to have no need of the tyranny of the virtue-imperative, rich enough to have no need of thrift and pedantry, beyond good and evil".

65. TI/IX/38 makes this relation conceptual: "How is freedom measured in individuals [*Einzelnen*] and peoples? By the resistance that must be overcome, by the trouble it costs, to remain *on top*. The highest type of free human being should be sought where the highest resistance is constantly overcome: five steps from tyranny, close to the threshold of the danger of servitude." Hence not under "liberal institutions", he continues.

66. WP862 [1884]: "A teaching is needed, strong enough to work at *breeding*: strengthening the strong, laming and destructive for the world-weary."

disturbing awareness of it; he thinks many will be 'crushed', psychologically maimed, by the weight of this demand. But we mustn't think this the only danger his society poses. Drives must be spurred up and down through all the range of levels of their enactment; they must struggle against obstacles in all the different ways they're lived. So BGE44: "hardness, violence, slavery, danger in the street and in the heart, . . . serves the elevation of the species 'human being' as well as does its opposite". The existence of a lowest, suffering class is itself such a danger: its misery serves society as a visible warning of what one might come to; it's a hazard spurring the rest to greater effort.

It's toward this lowest class—those whose sickness or weakness prevents them from serving even that mundane productive role of the herd—that Nietzsche's callousness is most clearly expressed. So TI/VII/3 describes how terribly those laws of Manu treat anyone who falls out of its castes altogether, "the unbred human being, the mishmash human being, the chandala". The laws aim to make him sicker and weaker still, even by the brutal device of allowing him only unhealthy food and bad water. Although Nietzsche's support for these laws is less clear here than in A57, enough other passages speak in this way. Society's bottom should be not just that herd with its average happiness but a subclass whose lives are misery and struggle. Nietzsche often encourages these sick to 'die off' and thinks that a healthy society will encourage this, too (in some unspecified way). In any case, those thus sick will certainly not be allowed to reproduce.[67]

Finally, we should note a revealing procedural point: Nietzsche sometimes, preemptively, dismisses that whole argumentative strategy I've offered for him, of showing that the ruled aren't really worse off. Even to argue so is to take too much account of the interests of the weak; it already accords them 'equal rights' when it bothers to speak to their point of view. Inconspicuously, it thereby assumes 'the equality of moral persons': each person's interest needs or deserves to be addressed by an argument that shows how its treatment is fair. By contrast, Nietzsche so belittles the value of the weak or sick that he often takes their interests not to come into play at all. Their point of view can be simply ignored. In this mood, he *does* say the interest of the 'slaves' is sacrificed for the

---

67. WP40 [1888]: "It is a disgrace for all socialist systematizers that they suppose there could be circumstances—social combinations—in which vice, sickness, crime, prostitution, *need* would no longer grow.— But that means condemning *life*.— A society is not free to remain young. And even at its best force, it must form refuse and waste materials. The more energetically and boldly it advances, the richer it will be in failures and deformities". A2: "The weak and the failures shall perish [*zu Grunde gehn*]: first proposition of *our* love of humanity. And one shall even help them to it." GS73 seems to commend infanticide (in some cases). WP734 [1888]: "Society *should* in numerous cases prevent procreation: to this end, it may hold in readiness, without regard to descent, rank, and spirit, the harshest means of constraint, deprivation of freedom, in some circumstances castration."

sake of the few elite; they could have had better lives if free from that rule.[68]

Where does this bring us? To a point, perhaps, at which Nietzsche's political views will seem impossible to accept. But there are still some last points to make in his favor. Let's end—as I at least must—inconclusively, by seeing how he might, once again, attempt to shift the axis of our appraisal around, in a way that can open the issue for us yet again.

Our assumption has been that an ideal society mustn't make the innocent suffer, because their suffering is bad for them. We strongly feel that no amount of benefit to others can justify such injury and won't really entertain Nietzsche's efforts to show what such use it might be. But first, he has in reserve yet another tack: to deny that their suffering is bad even for them. They take it to be so, but this just shows their lack of the 'tragic wisdom'. All of our humanitarian qualms are rooted in the same misconception, a failure to see that the true human good isn't untroubled happiness but the pathos of a struggling will. Suffering belongs to this pathos.[69] Nietzsche might say he wishes no worse for the weak than for his favorites, the strong; indeed, he wishes the latter to suffer worse.[70]

It's probably hard to see how this argument could carry us very far along certain scales of hardship: Is it good to suffer from tedious or unpleasant labor or from starvation? Would Nietzsche wish these on his strong? But second, we should bear in mind that even if he does reserve such 'unspiritual' hardships for the weakest, it would be in his nonstandard sense of 'weak'; he needn't prefer them for all or even most of those who now suffer from them. (Similarly, his defense of 'discrimination' is not a defense of how we discriminate now.) Above all, his position shouldn't be weighed in the vanity of assuming that we do or would belong to his elite. Other defenses of inequality can repel us because they address (what we feel is) an ugly instinct of self-justification, comforting us in possession of all our privileges. Nietzsche's position isn't 'conservative' in so self-serving a way; it defends inequality, but not this in-

---

68. BGE258: "[A good and healthy aristocracy] accepts with a good conscience the sacrifice of countless human beings who, *for its sake*, must be pushed down and reduced to incomplete human beings, to slaves, to tools." BGE61 says, "ordinary human beings . . . exist [*dasind*] for service and for the general advantage and *may* exist only so".

69. GS12: "what if pleasure and displeasure were so . . . tied together that whoever *wills* to have as much as possible of the one *must* also have as much as possible of the other". BGE225: "You will if possible . . . *to abolish suffering*; and we? — it seems indeed that *we* will to have it even higher and worse than it was!" See further § 4.4 on the good of suffering.

70. WP910 [1887]: "To those human beings *who matter to me*, I wish suffering, abandonment, sickness, mistreatment, degradation". See also GS19. Note, too, WP763 [1887]: "the individual, *each according to his* kind, [should be] so placed that he can *achieve the highest* that lies in his range."

equality.[71] We have to keep it open whether he might not wish such hardships precisely on us, who too little grasp at philosophy's problems with that penetrating intensity he attributed to his own physical miseries. Even illness or poverty could be helpful to us, could be the one thing that would help us most. We, too, might need to be stressed to an utmost effort by something that concentrates our emotive attention into a prolonged focus, that makes us at last take our problems with fullest seriousness.

3.4   Nietzsche's ethics

Loaded atop our aversion to Nietzsche's politics is another strong worry against his values: they seem not to offer us any acceptable ethics, any tolerable rules for behaving toward the individual others with whom we interact. This brings us back to our guiding question, what concrete advice his power ontology offers the reflective agent. And it brings us back to our worry, that a person unabashedly willing power would probably mistreat these (particular) others. Nietzsche's chief defenses against this worry are again his notions of spirit and *agon*. As with his politics, I'll again stress the first, trying to make clearer just what the route of 'spiritualization' involves. The point seemed not sufficient to humanize Nietzsche's politics. Does it serve any better here? Will it deter or temper his ideal agent from those 'material' expressions of aggression we most abhor as unjust? As this agent works to spiritualize himself, will he treat others better in his daily doings?

This makes our problem look too single or simple, however. Recall (from § 3.3.1) how Nietzsche disputes the 'equality of moral persons'; this suggests the importance, for him, of drastically varying one's behavior toward different others.[72] Of course even those 'moralities' he opposes allow and require differential treatment of others on account of their differing circumstances—as friends or family, as needy, as objects of professional responsibilities, and so on. But before and beneath these complications, each other person is equally important, simply by being a person. This makes it appropriate to state these moralities' lessons with a certain abstraction, as what we owe to, or how we should treat, any other human being. Because Nietzsche rejects this core equality, how-

71. WP758 [1883]: *"Slavery in the present:* a barbarism! *Where* are those *for whom* they work?—* One must not always expect the *contemporaneity* of the two complementary castes." KSA/13/25[1] [1888]: "what is today on top in society, is physiologically condemned".

72. Let's set aside for the moment a second way that this makes the problem too simple: in taking Nietzsche to be advising 'the *anonymous* reflective agent', it neglects the chance that he means different advice to different agents; I take this up in § 3.5.3. Let's suppose, for now, that he offers the image of a single life and character, to which he invites us all to aspire.

ever, such a formulation of his 'ethics' is much less fitting; he doesn't have an ethics if this is taken to mean rules for treating 'the anonymous other'.

Thus although the Nietzschean agent will, surely, manage all his relationships with a view to his power, he'll pursue quite different strategies in different cases. It depends on who this other is, on how he is met: in what role or under what description. It would be a job to catalog the main ways Nietzsche tends to think of the other as appearing, but among these would be the following: as friend or enemy, as equal or inferior, as man or woman. His agent will adopt different stances (comportments) to each of these. Our own reactions to this varied advice varies as well: some of these projected relationships trouble us less than others. Yet all will be in some way harshly flavored for us, on account of their common root in the power egoism. To weigh Nietzsche's ethics fully, we would need to experience and evaluate this multifarious harshness.

I focus on two out of this host of relationships, and the treatment of even these will be superficial. First, I'll look at Nietzsche's advice for our (in his view) most intense and important relations to others: those to our friends and enemies. It's natural to place special weight here, where his interest is most engaged and he's sketching his ideal; some interpreters have found his position quite attractive here. Second, I'll turn to another plane of relationship on which his views seem especially and distinctly nonviable: our relations to the other as male or as female, as same or different in this respect from oneself. Nietzsche takes my and the other's sex or gender to be factors that matter to how I behave toward this other. By seeing just how, we can face his unappealing remarks about women.

Before turning to these topics, however, there's another, whose omission requires excuse. In narrowing in on these two, I'm avoiding a third on which his position looks particularly dubious: how one behaves toward those worse (or worse off) than oneself. How will Nietzsche's ideal agent treat, in his concrete or personal dealings with them, the weak, the sick, and the mediocre, all of whom are condemned to a secondary existence in his politics?[73] It's here that the worry over injustice, which so absorbed us as we weighed his politics, finds its clearest expression in his ethics. Can I really shirk it, then? But the fact that this is so largely another expression of the same concern gives us a good reason not to dwell on it here again: let's avoid a tedious traversal of much the same issues. Still, we should quickly note some of the main ways Nietzsche's ethics does and doesn't mirror his politics on this point.

How might we expect it to? If his politics commends or condones a miserable life for society's sickest or weakest, it seems clear his ethics couldn't advise me to ease the suffering of those (of this type) I know of

73. This is the closest approximation to that abstract other-as-person: the anonymous other, the 'neighbor' (in a quite attenuated sense), the undifferentiated fellow member of my society or species.

or meet. Indeed, we'd expect it even to license me to prey on them further myself.[74] Why should I have qualms about causing them to suffer, if I think the healthiest society will include a class of people in just their plight? Nietzsche's politics cultivates struggle and welcomes a lowly bottom of losers, where this is a sign of (or spur to) a higher top of winners. Because the Nietzschean agent will surely aim at that top, won't he be willing and happy to use and abuse those 'weaker' ones further himself? This can give a disturbing concreteness to Nietzsche's talk about climbing over others as rungs on a ladder.

The main line of defense is obvious: Nietzsche's ideal agent is spiritually turned, and so cares little for the material goods he might get by mistreating others. He seeks power in a spiritual struggle, not an economic one. Because the great majority of others, the weak and the average, lack this spiritual turn, they're exempt from his aggressive interest: they're not fit subjects (or victims) of the type of rule he wants. The result, perhaps, is that disengaged politeness Nietzsche himself displayed in such everyday dealings.

We've seen that this argument fails to humanize his politics. This is mainly because (Nietzsche thinks) a spiritual elite can only flourish on a background of material struggle. A healthy society needs aggressive drives whose immediate, material objects strongly matter to most members, in order for the spiritual forms of those drives to flourish in a few. That material struggle is adequately vehement only when it forces down an underclass; it's this that rendered Nietzsche's politics so 'unjust'. But this still leaves open the hope that his ethics might invite us, as aspiring to that ideal spirituality, to turn our backs on that struggle. Might it thus avoid counseling us to personal injustices, beyond that unjust politics?

However, we also raised doubts whether even that Nietzschean 'spiritualized' agent would still renounce material goods, because we doubted he would still be ascetic. Moreover, even if he were, I think he would still look to us far from ideal. Politeness—disinterest, neutrality—seems not enough; we want from our 'ideal agent' helpful deeds. We feel that even a 'spiritualized' agent owes these helpful deeds, since he can never be truly independent of that concrete struggle; for all his efforts to turn his back on it, his life and activity depend on it. Those practical others serve him as tools, substituting for him in countless manual chores; he needs and uses the struggle (and attendant suffering) of those he's politely indifferent toward. We've seen that Nietzsche not only acknowledges this but proclaims it. But he counsels us to a certain hard-

74. The worry over injustice can take two forms: (1) the Nietzschean agent would inevitably or necessarily treat these others unjustly (because he aims at his own power, and power is dominating others), or (2) more weakly, he *might* treat these others unjustly, if it suits him (because he's bound by no detaining rules or principles).

heartedness here, most familiarly in his campaign against pity.[75] It's here that our doubts against his politics find their strongest expression against his ethics.

3.4.1 Friends and enemies

At the other extreme, what does Nietzsche recommend with respect to the persons I'm closest to, with whom I have my strongest and best attachments? What such involvements should I cultivate, and how should I treat those I'm thus connected with? This leads us to Nietzsche's account of friendship: "I teach you not the neighbor, but the friend. The friend should be the festival of the earth to you" [TSZ/I/16].[76] Initially, his position seems far more attractive here; his stress on friendship puts him in the comfortable company of more respectable philosophers, most familiarly Aristotle. But once again problems arise.

First are some reservations against giving friendship this priority. We might question how this choice disvalues (comparatively, at the least) relations in the family (to spouse, child, parent, sibling), as well as sexual (erotic) relationships—both of which might seem to have strong claims instead. Although Nietzsche thinks persons in the latter relationships can and should also be friends, even here he's taking the pattern of interaction typical of (nonkin, nonsexual) friendship to be primary; those other relationships become very adequate only when they take on friendship's features. And we have, of late, a new kind of ground for suspicion against this choice: we can sense here the workings of Nietzsche's expressed contempt for women (a ground in the Greeks' elevation of friendship, too, it seems) and for women's contrasting involvement in the family. I postpone this cluster of worries until the next section.

Quite another sort of problem arises in the way Nietzsche then describes this friendship, in how he breaks from that classical model. He seems to tell us to view our friends more as we have done our enemies: "In a friend one should have one's best enemy" [TSZ/I/14]. (Sometimes his point looks even stronger: it's enemies instead of friends I should seek for my most important involvements.[77]) As a will to power, my best

---

75. GS338, TSZ/II/3, GM/P/5, GM/III/14. Many but not all of Nietzsche's attacks on pity have mainly in view a pity for a spiritualized sickness and suffering; so these might not mean to mock a pity for poverty, etc. Note also A57 (a passage stressed by Kaufmann [1974, 370]): "When the exceptional human being handles the mediocre with tenderer fingers than himself and his equals, this is not mere politeness of heart—it is simply his *duty*".

76. GS61 begins: *"In honor of friendship.—* In antiquity the feeling of friendship was counted the highest feeling, even higher than the most celebrated pride of the self-sufficient and the wise."

77. We might find this shift enacted in the way Nietzsche's most esteemed friend, Wagner, became his enemy.

relations to others have to be aggressive: "I am warlike after my kind. . . . [A strong nature] needs resistance; hence it *seeks* resistance: the *aggressive* pathos belongs just as necessarily to strength as vengefulness and rancor belong to weakness" [EH/I/7]. Won't we count it against Nietzsche if he insists on introducing this aggression into even one's closest relationships? Don't we here insist on a sympathy and a sharing of purpose, with which such aggression is quite at odds?

Our qualms against this tap a rather different source than do our complaints over injustice; there our instincts rebel on behalf of the other persons he'd have us mistreat, whereas here they resist his having us forego (what seems to us) a positive good for ourselves. The argument from injustice involves stepping into the perspectives of the others our behavior would hurt; it appeals to pity, a type of empathy Nietzsche denounces as unhealthy and unproductive. By contrast, these new qualms originate in our own perspective, in our positive view of what's best for ourselves: we want to be persons who love and befriend. These positive instincts should have more credit, on Nietzsche's own account.

If we're to be reconciled to Nietzsche's position here, it must be by developing two ideas we've often met before: spirit and *agon*. By pressing them here, we'll at last see how to combine these major ideas, in a fuller account of how spiritual wills (should) struggle for power against one another.

First, Nietzsche's stress on the 'enemy' threatens less when we see that this other is opposed as in the *agon*. Recall the Heraclitean point from § 3.2: we're to think of a struggle in which one values and even abets one's opponent. The enemy must be esteemed. GM/I/10: "How much reverence has a noble human being for his enemies!—and such reverence is already a bridge to love.— For he demands his enemy for himself, as his distinction; he endures no other enemy than one in whom there is nothing to despise and *very much* to honor!"[78] This respect goes along with a shift in my project toward the other: I no longer aim at a (conclusive) victory that subdues him to me, canceling the foreignness of his will. Instead, I aim to draw out and develop our disagreeing; I single him out for this abiding relationship and in it want him all the stronger a voice on the other side. So HH/II/75: "What is love, other than understanding and rejoicing that another lives, works, and

---

78. EH/I/7: "every growth betrays itself in the search for a mightier [*gewalt-igeren*] opponent—or problem . . . . The task is *not* just to become master over resistances, but over such as require one to stake his whole force, suppleness, and mastery of weapons [*Waffen-Meisterschaft*]—over *equal* opponents". GS13: "An easy prey is something contemptible for proud natures; they feel good only at the sight of unbroken human beings who might become their enemies". It's the unsubdued other that's really most valuable. D431: "The perfect sage without willing it elevates his opponent into an ideal . . . a god with shining weapons".

perceives in another and opposite way than we? If love is to bridge these oppositions through joy it may not abolish [*aufheben*], not deny them." As we might paradoxically (and in low-Kantian) put it, the other can serve me as a most useful means only if I allow him to remain an end in himself.

In § 3.2 we saw how this even broadens the 'self' whose interest (power) I pursue. My competition with this other becomes a more elaborate joint activity that I share in and strive to maintain and develop. What I do now acquires a richer meaning or identity, through its role in the interaction between us: a behavior or viewpoint of mine is now also a reply to what the other does or thinks, a reference that enriches it all the more, the better my opponent does and thinks. I thus acquire an interest not just in what I do, but in the composite activity formed by the interplay between us. I want this interaction to rise to ever higher levels, and this requires that the other become stronger and more foreign still. At the same time, I also keep my allegiance to one side of the struggle; I do my own part, by pressing my difference from that other.

The comparison with Aristotle is helpful. He, too, tries to show how 'enlightened self-interest' motivates a person to enter into friendships, into persisting relationships that are grounded in the concern of each for the other and for the other's own sake. Through such concern, a person expands the boundaries of the self in whose fine activity he can take delight. Since he 'identifies' with the friend, the latter's excellence can please him as well as his own and can even let him better appreciate his own.[79] Moreover, this identification reflects a real matter of fact: through the interweaving of their activities (by their 'living together'), the borders of their selves really do overlap.[80] Nietzsche thinks points analogous to all of these; his disagreement is with Aristotle's further assumption, shared by Plato, that this other must, in as many ways as possible, act and value the same as oneself. Nietzsche of course wants some things the same: these 'friends' must share a terrain to struggle on and must have comparable strengths. But in most ways beyond this, they'll challenge one another by their differences. Instead of growing more alike, they'll grow more complicatedly dissimilar.

Second, we must add the point about spirit. Nietzsche clearly thinks of these (ideal) friendly animosities as (mainly) 'spiritual' relationships, which promises vaguely to temper them, too. But how does a will or a

79. Price 1989, 122: "in my own person, my projects are . . . transparent on to their objects, so that my focus is upon the objects, not my pursuit of them; but joining in those projects with a friend I become conscious of his pursuing them, and so conscious in a new way of pursuing them myself".

80. Price 1989, 106: "parts of lives can be shared: one and the same act may count as contributing, as a constituent and not a cause, to the *eudaimonia* of two persons. It is this possibility that grounds Aristotle's ideal of friendship. . . . [I]t dissolves the obstinate dichotomy between egoism and altruism".

relationship get spiritualized? So far we've considered this process, this dimension of growth, only for what it seems to leave behind: it gives up concern for material things, thus implying an unthreatening asceticism. But what is this process more positively, where does it head? Consider TI/V/1: "All passions [*Passionen*] have a time when they are merely disastrous, when they drag down their victim with the weight of stupidity—and a later, very much later time when they wed the spirit, when they 'spiritualize' themselves." Does Nietzsche really believe in anything like a 'spirit' that is somehow responsible for this process?

It's clear that this spirit could not be consciousness and that spiritualization can't be forcing an initially physical drive to enact itself in consciousness. We've seen Nietzsche's claim that drives mainly grow more corrupt as they come to be performed more consciously. Yet if we can't hear the terms that way, it's puzzling what they might mean.

I think an answer emerges as we recall that Nietzsche attributes an unconscious purposiveness to all beings (wills). Because will to power is 'directed activity', it has two basic aspects: the movement itself and its aiming. As directed at ends, even the most primitive wills 'intend' those ends and so exhibit an 'intentionality'; this includes both a view of a goal and a view of surroundings or circumstances in and through which that goal is being pursued. I suggest that Nietzsche's spiritualization is a certain intensification and predominance of this intentional aspect, at the expense of the concrete movement or enactment itself. The will grows ever more preoccupied with setting its course and ever less occupied with sailing it.

So, in the person, the drives become spiritualized as they hold off fulfillment and savor pursuit, savor keeping the goal in view before them.[81] Rather than simplifying and shortening their route to the end (as a simple pragmatics demands), they complicate and extend it. We might describe this in either of two ways. Either what had been a drive's intentional arm—what had held it (mostly beneath awareness) toward its ends, through surroundings interpreted as means—becomes a new will in its own right, which now tries to develop itself, even at the expense of the original drive. Or there occurs a shift in the aim of that drive: it acquires a second-order, reflexive aim, which becomes more important than the first. The drive now values its own directedness, its arc of effort toward the goal (which now recedes in significance). So it stretches out beyond its earlier episodic, spasmodic rushes to satisfaction

81. TI/VIII/6: "That is the *first* preschooling for spirituality: *not* to react at once to a stimulus, but to get in hand the inhibiting . . . instincts." So spiritualization is an act of cruelty: it denies the straightforward enactment of whatever drive or will it acts on. TSZ/II/8: "Spirit is the life that itself cuts into life: with its own agony it increases its own knowledge". Not doing the deed heightens intention—focuses attention—in part just because it hurts. In § 4.3, I discuss how this intentionality becomes a 'will to truth'.

and is woven across and into the rest of the person's life. It 'weds the spirit', then, by interweaving itself with whatever pursuits have already become such ends in themselves.

To bring this back to our business, how would such a spiritualization affect relations to others? Nietzsche's answer is in TI/V, which describes the spiritualization of these relations' root aggressiveness.[82] Here, too, the consummation—now victory or mastery over the other—is delayed or disavowed, and stress is laid instead on the striving, which gets stretched out and elaborated. This shows how the point about spirit might even generate the one about *agon;* in favor of this, notice how TI/V/3 presents the agonistic stance as emerging through a "spiritualization of *enmity*": this "consists in deeply grasping the value of having enemies. . . . The church at all times willed the destruction of its enemies; we, we immoralists and antichristians, find our advantage in this, that the church exists."[83]

Moreover, since this struggle is between two 'spirits', wills whose intentional aspects have taken possession of them, what's important to each is the power balance between their viewpoints. So theirs is a 'spiritual war': an argument in which each tries (on any topic at hand) to 'incorporate' the other's position into his own by reproducing it as an answered and accommodated element within his own fuller view. One argues not to convince the other—to defeat his viewpoint in a cruder way, by inducing him to give it up in favor of one's own—but to spur him to ever stronger replies, replies that will then challenge one's own view, to take in and control ever more. Such struggle is mispursued when one tries to establish one's viewpoint as uniquely true and to exclude the other's as simply false. (In § 4.5 I show how this belongs to Nietzsche's 'epistemology for perspectives'.)

Although this may seem to us an attractive way of having enemies, it

82. This stress on the spiritualization of aggressiveness—as a process that leaves it still aggressive, still 'against the other'—sets Nietzsche at odds with a conception of spirit quite natural to us. Drives in their 'concrete' forms aim at material goods, such as money, whose possession is exclusive, either by you or by me; this gives me a motive to take them from you. By contrast, we expect, spiritual goods have a different logic of possession: they're shareable, and perhaps there's even *more* for each when they *are* shared. Thus spiritualization nullifies and even reverses our old motives for opposing the other; there's a solidarity among the spiritual, who are co-contemplators of the same truths and beauties. In one form or another, allowing for very different ways of describing this spiritual turn, we find this view throughout the philosophical tradition. But for Nietzsche, spirits still conflict.

83. Later: "Our relation to the 'internal enemy' is no different: here too we have spiritualized enmity, here too we have comprehended its *value*. One is only *fruitful* at the price of being rich in oppositions; one remains *young* only on the presupposition that the soul does not stretch itself and desire peace. . . . One has renounced the *great* life when one renounces war" [TI/V/3]. The tempering of aggressiveness may have been lost by Nietzsche near the end: his late vehemence against Christianity, in [A], suggests a hatred that wills only destruction, not growth through the other.

might not appeal to us as an account of friendship. It seems a continual vaunting over the other, a game of one-upmanship; it seems to rule out the sympathy and solidarity we value in friendship. But this may be partly because we still haven't appreciated how the other's view is to be 'incorporated' here; this involves a much tighter engagement. It's not that when I hear him state *x*, I attack *x* and fix it as a defeated thought or position into my own scheme of things; I'm not simply a critical audience to his statements. Nor do I go beyond listening just by temporarily 'stepping into his point of view' and 'seeing as if through his eyes'; I don't just periodically relocate into a viewpoint external to me.

Rather, I acquire this friend/enemy's attitudes (his concerns) as my own; they come to be some of my own phases, or faces. If I'm truly to 'rule' his viewpoint, it must be as what it really is, under the power ontology.[84] So I must take his 'views' teleologically: they lie not in his (conscious) beliefs but in his directedness, his ways of aiming and valuing. I must rule them in this same medium: by willing so myself, yet under the control of my own, defining will. I can 'incorporate' his perspective only by weaving (some of) his cares and pursuits into my own, by living through some of my life as he does his.[85] Yet I also express my difference from him, by situating and subordinating these adopted attitudes and efforts within my original own; I adapt them to fit under my own. It's only in this final restraint that the 'situating' or 'criticizing' of him occurs, and thus occurs most genuinely, because it rests on a maximal appreciation of his intentionality (his spirit).

These lessons apply to friendships at many different levels of spiritualization, including the highest: friendships of philosophers. Nietzsche calls philosophy 'the most spiritual will to power', because in it the doing is most thoroughly subordinated to the aiming/viewing. He agrees with Plato that the best friends are those who interact by philosophizing, though not quite as Plato thinks. It's not that reason leads like-souled friends to agree on a common truth. Here, too, Nietzsche preaches difference against Plato's sameness: the friend should also be enemy.

We best learn his notion of this most spiritual relationship not from what he writes specifically about it but from his writings in general. These are the vehicles of his friendships, the acts by which he interacts with his friends. His remarkable self-confidence (which he felt of course only for the most part) let him think of Socrates, Plato, and others from philosophy's history as his only worthy enemy-friends; his relationships

84. WP769 [1883]: "Everything living grasps as widely about itself with its force as it can, and subjugates what is weaker. . . . The *increasing 'humanizing'* of this tendency consists in this, that there is an ever *subtler* perception of *how hard* it is really *to incorporate* the other; while a crude injury indeed shows our power over him, it at the same time *estranges* his will from us even more—and so makes him less subjugable."

85. GS323: "Destiny renders us the greatest distinction, when it lets us struggle for a time on the side of our opponents. We are thereby *predetermined* for a great victory."

to them are the ones he values most. This means that a project of this book—to detail his agreements with, and differences from, his predecessors—has amounted to a map of his friendships. We've repeatedly seen that the differences he proclaims are rooted in appropriations from them, not just of their 'views' but of whole sequences of thought. His metaphysical roots are the credit and honor he pays to his friends, the way he preserves them in him.[86]

Aspects of this 'highest' friendship may not appeal to us now for reasons other than its aggressiveness. It renders irrelevant all the concrete dealings we associate with that relationship. Can one's best friends really have been dead two thousand years? Can the best sort of friendship be so one-directional?[87] These doubts are reinforced when we see how this preference was played out in Nietzsche's life. He interacted even with contemporary friends largely by letters; he looked down on all of them, as not his equals.[88] More than their company, he really most preferred solitude. Thus in his theory and practice of 'the very best' he leaves behind much of what we value most—and that he values, too, except when he speaks of this highest extreme. Ironically, we now feel similar qualms, and at a similar point, to those that arise against the 'ascent of love' Plato describes in the *Symposium*.

3.4.2   Men and women

Probably most of Nietzsche's interpreters have found his remarks about women simply embarrassing, hence the common effort to dismiss them from the field of inquiry by branding them just personal idiosyncracies, lying quite apart from his philosophical thought.[89] We can't be content

86. EH/I/7: "attacking is in my case a proof of benevolence, in some cases of gratitude. I honor, I distinguish by connecting my name with that of a case or a person: for or against—that counts equally for me."

87. We should bear in mind, though, Nietzsche's metaphysical reasons for thinking that this relationship is not as one-directional as we think: his theory of becoming disperses Plato's 'being' temporally and allows Nietzsche to have a retroactive impact on him, by his enriching rejoinders to the Platonic position.

88. Middleton (1988, 87) speaks of "how absent Nietzsche was from his friends" and raises the possibility "that, to judge by his letters, this most dynamic cultural psychologist never really warmed to a single individual human being wholeheartedly enough to confide in her or him". GM/III/27: "for I still *know* of no friend". KSA/13/24[1] [1888] (a draft for EH): "Like anyone who has never lived among his equals, and who from this destiny has finally made his art and human friendship". See also TI/IX/25, EH/CW/4. BGE40 suggests that a 'deep spirit' "*wills* and sees to it that a mask of him walks in his place through the hearts and heads of his friends". BGE41: "Not to remain stuck to a person—not even the most loved—every person is a prison, also a nook." BGE27 belittles "'the good friends', . . . who are always too lazy [*bequem*] and think that as friends they have a right to be so".

89. Kaufmann 1974, 84: "Nietzsche's writings contain many all-too-human judgments—especially about women—but these are philosophically irrelevant."

with this. Nietzsche's claims about sexual difference[90] are close to his heart, tangled up with his most central views. To be sure, BGE231 qualifies the aspersions on women that follow as merely *his* truths. Yet because he will allow (or proclaim) this of all that he says, it can't be taken to show that his views about women lie apart from the rest. Indeed, he elsewhere claims special insight here: "May I here venture the surmise that I *know* women? . . . Who knows? perhaps I am the first psychologist of the eternally feminine" [EH/III/5].[91] Just as Zarathustra hides his truth about women [TSZ/I/18], so we might see Nietzsche as disguising how important these issues are to him, and so how crucial to us in assessing his thought.

Offhand, one might have expected that his own stress on spirit would have kept his power ontology from having any 'gender bias': where power is spiritualized and becomes something else than a matter of physical strength, of muscle mass, the struggle becomes one in which women compete as equals, at the least. Or so our own instincts prompt us. Of course that has rarely been the conclusion of Nietzsche's great predecessors either, despite their stress on mind before body. Although they've claimed that their accounts of the mind (and its proper state) are ideals for humans or persons, and not just for men, they've typically still supposed that women are less able than men to achieve these ideals.[92] So although Nietzsche's new ideal of power or activeness is more plausibly, and much more self-avowedly, 'masculine' than such traditional goals as rationality and understanding, this may only disguise a subtler affinity. In thus lessening women, he shows yet another point of allegiance to that tradition before him, one we're much inclined to blame him for.

Nietzsche disvalues women not as 'weak' in physique but as 'sick' in the way they will power, a defect that persists when this power is pur-

90. I take Nietzsche's position to be that the biological sexes typically have different innate tendencies. These differences are 'typical' rather than universal in that some men and women may not follow their types. These differences are only 'tendencies' in that they can sometimes be overridden by other factors. I use 'female' and 'feminine' interchangeably, as also 'male' and 'masculine'—all for these claimed typical tendencies.

91. See also a letter to Gast of 9 Dec. 1888 (F&S #157): "Strindberg . . . regards me as the greatest psychologist of *woman*''. That these thoughts are 'more his' might instead make them all the more central or basic for him, more expressive of his individuality.

92. Plato (*Rep.* V) might spring to mind as an exception, but inspection shows that although he breaks with prevailing custom by advocating that women be educated to enter his highest class, it's as weaker, less-effective members. The argument (455) by which he shows that women should share in every type of pursuit (in every way of life) is that they're less good at everything than men are; that they excel in nothing shows that they haven't an independent nature, one that would imply for them special pursuits. See also, however, *Laws* 802e, which names order and moderation as women's virtues.

sued spiritually. The crux is that women are typically reactive. By their nature, they're turned aside from their (and the world's) essence as will to power. They pursue power in an indirect, even distorted form, because they wish to grow not in themselves but in or through some other (a man or a child). So TSZ/I/18: "The happiness of the man is called: I will. The happiness of the woman is called: he wills. . . . And woman must obey and find a depth for her surface." And so GS68 has a 'wise man' say: "Will is the manner [*Art*] of man, willingness that of woman."[93] WP864 [1888] gives the whole picture: "Finally: *woman!* *One-half of humanity* is weak, typically sick, changeable, inconstant— woman needs strength in order to cling to it—and a religion of weakness that glorifies [*verherrlicht*] being *weak*, loving, and being humble as divine. Or better, she makes the strong weak—she *masters* when she succeeds in subjugating the strong. Woman has always conspired with the types of decadence, the priests, against the 'powerful', the 'strong', the *men*—. Woman brings the *children* to the cult of piety, pity, love—the *mother* represents altruism *convincingly.*'' The feminine seems flawed metaphysically, for Nietzsche's power ontology.

This position is unacceptable to us, but we need to choose which way we'll reject it. Will we dismiss the standard by which Nietzsche judges women, or only his claim that by this standard they (by their nature) rank so low? Will we attack the way he thinks men and women are different, or the value he puts on that contrast? He thinks his power ontology is inherently masculine in that its deepest value of activeness or power picks out a good that men are more naturally fitted than women to value and achieve. Will we argue that women are just as suited for the spiritualized power he most favors? Or will we instead accept that this value is 'masculine' but reject the value itself, perhaps even taking its (mere) masculinity to limit or discredit it?

These options parallel the positions taken by two different schools of feminists, stances they of course adopt not just toward Nietzsche's values but toward the (much less obviously male) values of his predecessors: that traditional package, prominently including reason, autonomy, and justice. So the distinction is made between (a) a 'liberal feminist', as one who accepts these values as gender-neutral and argues that women should be allowed to pursue them as equals, and (b) a 'radical femi-

93. GS363 says that women want their love to be 'perfect devotion': "Woman wills to be taken, to be taken on as a possession, wills to be absorbed into the concept 'possession', 'possessed'; consequently, she wills someone who *takes*, who does not give himself or give himself away, who on the contrary shall be made richer in 'himself'—through the accretion of force, happiness, and faith given him by the woman who gives herself." And BGE238 says a man with depth "must grasp woman as a possession, as property that can be locked, as something predetermined for service and completing herself in it." WP1009 [1887] calls those who are 'womanly', "the born subjects [*die Unterthänig-Geborenen*]". Cf. Aristotle *Pol.* 1260a: "the courage of a man is shown in commanding, of a woman in obeying".

nist', as one who takes these values to show male bias and so to be flawed.

A similar split shows up in feminist replies to Nietzsche. Some accept his values but deny his assessment of women, rendering his values gender-neutral despite him. His aspersions against women could then be discounted, perhaps, as rooted merely in a faulty extrapolation from the evidence of the (oppressed and hindered) women of his day.[94] By contrast, others find his values especially raw and revealing expressions of a much more pervasive male bias. Those aspersions then become an instructive reductio of a long history of bias against and animosity toward women, merely more disguised in the 'rational' ideals of his predecessors.[95]

The latter view has gathered force recently among feminists. It involves rejecting the goal of 'equality' with men—of equal access to those (male) philosophers' goods—and embracing a feminine 'nature' different from, and plausibly superior to, theirs. This strategy has some evident advantages over the other. It allows (or expresses) an extra degree of solidarity with generations of women before, with what 'woman' has so far been. More concretely, it doesn't rely on a prediction that past and present differences between men and women are not 'by nature' and can be overcome by 'leveling the field'; it's a surer strategy to change values to reflect women's past and present dispositional strengths. For such feminists, the challenge is then to identify these distinctive strengths, disentangling them from behaviors or dispositions that allow or reflect women's domination by men.

The accounts of these strengths coalesce recognizably around women as 'nurturing', women as adopting 'the care perspective'.[96] Here

94. Parsons 1973, 171: "despite his remarks, Nietzsche was no simple misogynist. His distaste for women was a distaste for the slavish character shown by nineteenth-century women. It was this slave morality in woman which the women's revolution hoped to overthrow." Presumably, we can also group Kaufmann here, and all the others who accept Nietzsche's values while decrying his words about women. Compare Baier (1987, 53) on Hume: his apparently sexist remarks are "a display of his social realism, his unwillingness to idealize the actual"; in what matters most to him, he "never judges women inferior".

95. Figes (1987, 127): "In Nietzsche the philosophy of Will becomes a hysterical shriek and we see the facade begin to crack. Too much emphasis on domination and superiority betrays fear and a profound insecurity." Of course, there's also a third option: rejecting both (denying that aggression is typically male, and also denying that it's 'the good'.) So perhaps Schutte 1984, 176ff.: Nietzsche treats sexuality in two conflicting ways, because from two different "models of the will to power"—one stressing recurrence and the Dionysian affirmation of life (in which male/female differences are subsumed under life's 'overflowing', whether in begetting or nurturing, so that this is a neutral, not a female, principle to Schutte), the other power as domination (which she seems not to take as inherently male, though it's a value associated with patriarchy). It will emerge why I shelve this option for now.

96. Gilligan (1982) contrasts female care values with male justice values. Choderow (1989) claims that women's experience renders them nurturing and rela-

feminists find what Plato could not: a realm in which women excel, a positive difference from men. Women are (i.e., tend to be) engaged cooperatively in the 'we', whereas men compete against one another over an 'it'. Hence women are more disposed toward sympathy and pity, are more inclined to enter others' perspectives, to see things 'from their point of view'. Most feminists doubt or deny that these strengths are 'by nature', rather than a product of socialization; it's women's social roles or practices that have rendered them more nurturing, and not vice versa. Nevertheless, it's this way that women have been and are, that men should come to be, too; these strengths might not be women's 'by nature', yet past and present distribution still justifies calling them 'female'.[97] This (radical) feminist account of male/female difference seems almost a mirror image of Nietzsche's. So striking and extreme a contrast as this promises interesting lessons. How does each side argue its case?

Nietzsche depreciates the female by depicting it as an unhealthy version of the male. Women have the same basic goal as men, power, but their characteristic weakness cuts them off from it. It turns them aside: (a) from straightforwardly competing for power into covert and indirect strategies (e.g., ruling through a man), and (b) from willing genuine power at all, into reactive, distorted cousins to it (e.g., the destructive projects of resentment). So their typical moralizing is just such an indirect strategy, as well as a weapon turned vengefully against a stronger other. Even their nurturing and their sympathy are deeply a devious aggressiveness.[98] This is why although Nietzsche's attribution to women of 'willingness' might seem to make them and men natural collaborators, he still thinks women and men are and must be in hostility or conflict: "Has one had ears for my definition of love? It is the only one worthy of a philosopher. Love—in its means, war; in its basis, the deadly hatred of the sexes" [EH/III/5].[99]

---

tional, whereas men strive for autonomy; she 'overturns' the evaluation of these poles. See, too, Ruddick 1987, 1989.

97. So Ruddick (1989, xi, 44) on 'maternal thinking': historically, (biological) women have most often been engaged in the attitude-activity of 'mothering'; although this practice can and should be more evenly shared (men, we're to hope, will come to act and so think and feel this way just as much as women), it always has most often been carried out by women, and so appropriately takes the feminine term (this shows how that appropriation of the sexual terms need not depend on claims about nature).

98. BGE145: "woman would not have the genius for finery if she did not have an instinct for a *secondary* role". GS66 suggests that women exaggerate their weakness, so as to make men feel guilty for their clumsiness: "Thus they defend themselves against the strong and every 'right of the fist'." GS361: "think over the whole history of women: *must* they not be actresses first of all and above all?" BGE148: "Seducing one's neighbor to a good opinion and afterwards believing faithfully in this opinion—who could equal women in this trick [*Kunststück*]?"

99. BGE238: "To go wrong on the basic problem of 'man and woman', to deny here the most abysmal antagonism and the necessity of an eternally hostile tension, to

This attack much resembles the opposite one that (some) feminists direct against the male. They diagnose men's aggressiveness as a desperate and frustrated reaction to women—as arising, for example, from feelings of inferiority for being unable to give birth, or from their difference as boys from the care-giving mother. 'Deep down' men want this, too, but they're twisted aside into all their extraneous struggles and games by their own incapacity for it. So here the care values replace those of struggle at the psychological base, and the latter are interpreted as sick and reactive, in very much Nietzsche's own sense.[100]

It's easy enough to extend this feminist critique to Nietzsche himself: we can see his views against women and the 'hyper-male' character of his stress on power and war as really reactions to feelings of frustration and inferiority in his dealings with women. Such a diagnosis finds many indications or evidences: his childhood in a household of women; his estrangements from his mother and sister; his crisis with Lou Salome; his apparent lack of any sexual experience; his inability to find a woman to marry him. Given such facts from his life, it's easy to hear his aspersions against women as expressions of hurt or rejection, even as efforts to appear more manly to them. The whole power ontology can take on a comic aspect in this light: just one man's effort to puff out his chest before indifferent women.[101]

Other feminists might point to Nietzsche's lack of anything like the experience of 'mothering' (i.e., parenting), that he never engaged in that (typically female) complex of doings and feelings involved in the care of a child. Indeed, he seems not to have played this nurturing role toward anyone else, either; he had no such specially favored students, for example. In view of this concrete ignorance, all his avowals of a 'spiritual pregnancy' that is more important than its physical counterpart can look forced and unconvincing. This gap in experience (apparently) shows how his viewpoint is crimped and partial, and in a way that discredits his values. Why should we take seriously his contempt for pity and his

---

dream here perhaps of equal rights, equal education, equal claims and obligations—that is a *typical* sign of flat-headedness". See also BT1's opening sentence.

100. Choderow 1989, 112: "the primary sense of gendered self that emerges in earliest development constantly challenges and threatens men, and gives a certain potential psychological security, even liberation, to women." Ruddick 1989, 134: "Standpoint philosophers are ready . . . to declare that dominant values are destructive and perverse and that the feminist standpoint represents the 'real' appropriately human order of life."

101. Figes 1987, 127–28: "Under the pose of the swaggering warrior one can see a lack of assurance about the real nature of masculinity, resulting in falsely exaggerated aggression. It is one end product of sexual role playing, the man who has to try too hard to be a man, whose dominance disguises a vulnerability he dare not reveal." Russell 1945, 767: "'Forget not thy whip'—but nine women out of ten would get the whip away from him, and he knew it, so he kept away from women, and soothed his wounded vanity with unkind remarks."

praise for suffering if he lacked acquaintance with this most relevant practice and perspective for judging in such human concerns? He seems to lack proper standing for presuming to answer these questions for and to us.

In this light, Nietzsche's viewpoint indeed looks remarkably narrow: hyperbolically male; lacking in appreciation of, or insight into, the female (with its motherly care). His inability to step fully into that other perspective is reflected in his own interpretation of the female as really a will to power, too, just a devious one. But his presumption that women must deeply want what males (more clearly) want, turns out to rest in mere ignorance. It's only his narrow horizons that make him think of the female as flawedly male. From this sequence of points, it looks as if his whole power ontology totters, vulnerable to a psychosexual diagnosis.

However, it's time to begin to reflect on the ways in which Nietzsche *does* both bear (in his person) and credit (in his thought) 'female' traits after all; unfolding these, we discover (in and for him) a second, quite different stance toward sexual difference.[102] Often he celebrates, against the grain, certain 'female' attitudes traditionally disvalued or denied; these can even seem to be his thought's most distinctive features. His appeal to some feminists is rooted in their sense that he introduces female views and values into the millennia-old, male-philosophical dialogue.[103]

When we look at how (radical) feminists describe the distinctively female viewpoint and values, we find frequent echoes of Nietzschean thoughts we've already reviewed. Some feminists, for example, explain women's care perspective as rooted in a better recognition of our contextual character and the way this broadens our self-interest, in contrast with the male illusion/ideal of the autonomous self or ego. Others say that (female) care values differ from (male) justice values in not invoking moral principles or rules, especially none that apply universally. And many of these radical feminists dispute the (male) philosophers' usual ideals of reason, impartiality, and objectivity. All of these are campaigns that Nietzsche fights, too. Even his emphasis on 'spiritual pregnancy', which we derided before, now shows itself in a different light: as a stress on the 'nurturing attitude' involved in the care values. (Notice how TSZ

102. Derrida (1979, 95–97) finds in Nietzsche "three fundamental propositions" about woman: (1) woman is condemned as figure of falsehood, (2) woman is condemned as figure of truth, (3) woman is affirmed as dissimulatress, artist, dionysiac ("anti-feminism, which condemned woman only . . . so long as she answered to man from the two reactive positions, is in its turn overthrown"). Later (1979, 101): "perhaps it must simply be admitted that Nietzsche himself did not see his way too clearly there. Nor could he, in the instantaneous blink of an eye. Rather a regular, rhythmic blindness takes place in the text."

103. Many of the papers in Patton 1993b reflect this feminist interest in Nietzsche.

in particular is permeated with images of propagation and procreation.[104]) Can these scattered points of resemblance be organized?

A crucial clue here is that Nietzsche was in fact exceptionally 'empathetic', that is, able to think himself out into manifold points of view.[105] This capacity makes possible the great diversity of penetrating psychological analyses and diagnoses, which (in his affecting statements of them) are so great a part of his grip on us. He was surely aware of this special strength; he elevates it into a virtue in some of his central views. Thus his doctrine of perspectivism demands this special ability, for a grasp of perspectival truth, as I argue in chapter 4. We can find his sense that this skill is female hinted at in his personifications of life and wisdom [TSZ/II/10, III/15] and truth [BGE] as women. Since life, the world, is contextual, the truth about it can be grasped only by someone with a female aptitude for empathy, for traversing the multiple, intersecting perspectives that constitute that reality.

To reach its highest level, this empathic ability requires (Nietzsche thinks) that one already bear an exceptional diversity of viewpoints, in the forces or drives that make one up. We've seen how the overman is distinguished by such internal complexity and how Nietzsche's growing sense of himself as an overman goes along with a growing sense of his own comprehensiveness. So when he claims that he sees especially well into women, we should hear him as acknowledging that he bears female traits himself. Above all, we should hear him claim that (female) empathic ability, which gives him sympathetic access to these traits, letting him step out of himself (his dominant stance) by stepping into minority viewpoints within.[106]

These new points project a second, very different view of the female, more subtly yet just as surely present in Nietzsche's thought. Instead of viewing it as inadequately male, he allots it a positive character (and an independent value) of its own. No longer is it merely 'the reactive', the negative pole on his value scale. Woman now has a (positive) nature of her own, of the sort Plato denies her. This lets us differently hear his attacks on 'women who would be men': they ought to be radical, not merely liberal, feminists. They should aim to develop what women are and have been; it's not that this project is 'safer' than the other (as above) but that it's *active*, in Nietzsche's own sense. When he grants to women these distinctive strengths, he gives them the task of developing these strengths—that is, of actively willing their own power.[107]

104. Again, see Parkes 1994.

105. Thiele 1990, 153n.

106. Cf. Jaggar (1989, 164–65), who argues that women are epistemically privileged by their access to "outlaw emotions", and because they "are relatively adept at identifying such emotions, in themselves and others".

107. Her assumption of male roles involves "a crumbling of feminine instincts, a defeminization", and hence her own "degeneration" [BGE239]; cf. also BGE233.

Of course, the suspicion might still arise that the nature Nietzsche grants to women is still just subservience (or 'willingness'), that he's really just asking them to embrace their role as secondary aids or supports, and not to resent it; this would undo all our optimism. Yet even his disquieting insistence on a lasting 'war' between the sexes shows that he doesn't mean this. Here again he thinks the Heraclitean point: not victory (or tyrannic domination) by male over female, but a balance of tension between these (types of) wills. He wants an agonistic competition between these principles, a 'combative marriage' of them, both in the world and in himself. Our essential clue here must be the culminating scenes in *Thus Spoke Zarathustra*. The wooing and wedding of Dionysus and Ariadne (or of Zarathustra and life), depicted in TSZ/III/14–16, shows the complementarity Nietzsche affirms in his metaphysical heart.[108]

Here again it's helpful to mark, for contrast, a feminist analogue. Not all who speak for a female nature and female values offer them as replacements for the male; some affirm the equal (or incommensurable) validity of both types. Some indeed think that a refusal to prioritize stances is one important part of the female view, that the opposite insistence on hierarchy is something male. They find this insistence even, or especially, in the notion of an absolute or objective truth, valid above and across perspectives. Affirming the female involves renouncing such claims to the priority (or unique adequacy) of one's own perspective or practice. We can see how such a feminist perspectivism might be a natural development of the female aptitudes for empathy and context, a theory of truth in line with those virtues.[109]

Such passages suggest a nature best held on to—as possessing an independent value of its own, not merely the deficient opposite pole to activeness, as reactivity has seemed. Derrida 1988, 168: "Can one not say, in Nietzsche's language, that there is a 'reactive' feminism. . . . It is this . . . that Nietzsche mocks, and not woman or women."

108. It's indeed appropriate to speak of 'marriage' here, to reflect the erotic or sexual force with which Nietzsche thinks the point. Here his own sexuality finds its spiritualized consummation: in wedding these traits in himself. Note that life is not thought of as a woman earlier in TSZ (II/12); only in the culminating overman truth does it take this sexual aspect. See especially Lampert (1986, 210–44) on these last scenes of TSZ/III.

109. See Ruddick's perspectivist reservations (1989, 135) to 'standpoint theory'. She quotes (1989, 128) approvingly from MacKinnon: "Feminism not only challenges masculine partiality but questions the universality imperative itself. Aperspectivity is revealed as a strategy of male hegemony." Conway contrasts a "postmodern feminist epistemology" (which renounces the claim to objectivity) and "feminist standpoint theory" (which defends that claim); he offers (1993, 123ff.) a Nietzschean critique of the latter. Inasmuch as this standpoint theory both denies any purely objective perspective yet claims that some viewpoints have epistemic priority over others (thus avoiding a flat relativism), it resembles the position I attribute to

This perspectivism sounds a lot like Nietzsche. But we're also able to mark some points of disagreement, some last, most deep-rooted ways his stance might still be 'male'. He agrees with those feminists that reality lies in a web of interpersonal perspectives (not in objects) and that understanding lies in traversing them (not in objectivity). But he thinks of this web quite differently: these perspectives are and must be in that *agonistic* relationship; their healthiest behaviors and viewpoints on one another are competitive rather than cooperative.[110] Moreover, the same is true, for reasons I explore in § 4.5, for the project of understanding these perspectives: it, too, must proceed not by equally welcoming each new one (as equally true and an equal member in one's growing democracy of views) but by testing, struggling with, and ranking these viewpoints, into a hierarchical system of views. So Nietzsche means his perspectivism not as a leveling relativism.

Thus his empathy is different from women's: it's competitive, diagnostic, ranking. We see this in the strongly critical slant to most of his empathic 'entries' (or experiments): he sees/feels vividly what this other point of view is like, but in a way that climbs past it, that situates and incorporates it. He understands the *agon* by recreating its struggles within himself, but not just by this, because he's not just a microcosmic enactment of this sociohistorical battle. He also tries to establish for (or as) himself a higher vantage point on this whole, by seeing into, but also seeing through and beyond, each of its constitutive viewpoints. He competes with them by diagnosing them, and his diagnoses promote him (he hopes) above them, to a higher rank.

Still, we must hold in mind that although Nietzsche thus proposes, even at his metaphysical core, values we might indeed count as male, these values themselves demand that one cultivate and incorporate female viewpoints and values as well. They express Nietzsche's own large share of female traits and his effort not to renounce or ignore them but to develop and employ them. We might then hear his most dismissive remarks against women as masking (to us and perhaps to himself) his share in what he attacks. They're said by a 'spiritual competitor', who deeply needs and so welcomes the other, and who expresses this welcome by adopting many of the opposite's traits, incorporating them under his own. To conclude (I'm afraid) in the banal, we find Nietzsche's stance to be a compromise or synthesis of male and female elements: his

---

Nietzsche. But this feminist theory grants priority to quite different viewpoints than Nietzsche does: to the oppressed and dominated (see, e.g., Harding 1991, 121ff., 150), perspectives Nietzsche thinks are distorted by resentment and reactivity. I pursue this contrast in § 4.5.

110. So the female and male principles are called to cooperate by the female, but to compete by the male—Pythagoras vs. Heraclitus. Each calls the other out of its own nature, even in its notion of the 'synthesis'.

sense of the 'spiritualized *agon'* puts him out in the middle ground between the extremes of a male aggression and a female pity.

3.5 The force of Nietzsche's values

We've examined how the 'content' of Nietzsche's values disturbs us and have explored the major strategies by which it can be directly defended. These arguments probably haven't done enough to settle our strong complaints. But there's another type of strategy for easing them still to consider: perhaps he doesn't mean this content with quite the 'force' we've presumed. Perhaps when we see better *how* he commends it to us, the sense in which he means it to be '(the) good', we'll be less distressed by it.[111] So we naturally turn at last to this matter of force, and now Nietzsche's metaethics comes to center stage.

When (in § 3.1) we restated his values in the format we felt any full fledged value theory ought to address—as advice to the anonymous reflective agent (ARA)—we were actually making certain decisions about this force. This format wasn't the neutral or transparent medium we assumed for stating his values' content. And because our accounts of his 'politics' and 'ethics' were both couched within this assumption, we've really heard them, too, as meant with this force, one we indeed adopt (I think) almost inevitably. Yet a crucial aspect of Nietzsche's 'revaluation of our values' lies in his refusal to speak with this force and in his effort to get us to mean our own values differently, too. Once we see how, we'll have to retune, retrospectively, our accounts of his political and ethical positions. Will this retuning help to persuade or reconcile us to them? Will we find that our doubts were due to mishearing how these positions are offered us?

We come here to the crux of Nietzsche's campaign against 'morality' [*Moral*], his 'immoralism'. Whereas this campaign includes attacks on many value contents (e.g., against peace, against pity), his main objections are metaethical ones: less to the good Christianity (e.g.) offers, than to how it offers this good—from what motives (from resentment) and as having what status (as God-given to all).[112] So we must ask whether our

111. Of course, I don't deny that Nietzsche's writings address us in many tones, in different passages or even in a single one. But although he tugs us in many ways in many directions, this all serves a broad and basic strategy. This issue ramifies into the topics of chapter 4: Nietzsche's views about truth and understanding, and the extent to which objectivity is possible. Until we settle these larger issues, we can't reach conclusions about the precise force with which Nietzsche recommends his values—or any of the rest of his views—to us. But it helps to make a start on this nexus.

112. Compare the analysis by Leiter (1993). Bergmann (1988, 34) distinguishes between the "content" and "modality" of (what he calls) "codes" and analyzes Nietzsche's term 'morality' as picking out a certain modality, involving "notions like freedom, responsibility, blame, and guilt and, on a deeper level, selfhood and agency".

format of 'advising the ARA' involves any of that 'moralistic' force that Nietzsche rejects.[113]

We begin by considering whether this mode of address fits with the valuative content we've by now laid out. Is it consistent with the 'power values' just sketched? If Nietzsche addresses us as these values tell him to, will or can it be to advise us as 'anonymous reflective agents'? We naturally suppose that he writes with the same interpersonal strategy as is most commended by *what* he writes, by his 'ethics': we presume that he cares about us his readers, just as those values tell him to. But do they counsel him to offer such generalized, benevolent advice, as I think we hear other 'ethicists' to do?

This question immediately raises again some familiar worries: Don't the power values generate a writer's strategy that is much less benevolent than we expect? It seems that Nietzsche's goal must be power over us, and his writings must be designed to impose his personal viewpoint on us, to rule us by having us mirror him. Then he doesn't really care for our good (for how well we pursue our own power); he even wishes that we not develop in our own directions but in his. So his values would be propaganda for his own perspective; even if he pitches them as favoring advice, this would be mere ruse and lie. And if he abandons the role of 'ARA adviser' in this way, the new force of his values, rather than easing our aversion to them, would reinforce it. Can we trust him not to be preying on us, even if only thus 'spiritually'?

Our recurring notions of spirit and *agon* give here again a Nietzschean answer to these doubts; these notions 'humanize' Nietzsche the writer just as they did his ideal agent. By eroding the borders between selves, the power ontology generates an interest in others' enhancement. It gives Nietzsche himself the interest of surviving in the readers he affects, of sharing in their growth or power. This survival, to be worthwhile, must be in worthy descendents, and worth (for him) lies precisely in self-creation, in radically reshaping whatever one finds or receives. His views will be most enriched by being appropriated into something individual and different, and not by being copied, just as Plato's are best enhanced by Nietzsche's own struggles against them. Thus his true self-interest, as a will to power, allows and even requires that he want his readers to will their own power more actively and effectively than they have. Thus he can, after all, aim at the sort of benefit to his audience that we standardly expect of a philosopher, if only for the nonstandard reason that he wants them to be better enemies.

However, there are other respects in which Nietzsche does abandon that traditional role of ARA adviser. Or rather, as I try to show, he

---

113. The role of 'ARA advisor' already leaves behind some of what 'morality' connotes for Nietzsche, inasmuch as its focus is not on retrospective judgments (where resentment and revenge fixate) but on prospective advice. I return to this distinction in § 3.5.2.

stretches or recasts that role, while still in basic respects performing it for us. I distinguish three crucial ways he attacks and revises the force of traditional philosophical ethics, each bearing on one of the terms in that notion of an 'anonymous [§ 3.5.3] reflective [§ 3.5.1] agent [§ 3.5.2]'. These are also the main metaethical points in Nietzsche's attack on 'morality' and the main ways he pitches his own values differently to us. But, I also try to show, these novelties in the force with which he offers his values do not allay our 'humane' doubts about their content (in both political and ethical domains). So we can't any longer let his power values 'off the hook' by vaguely supposing that he 'doesn't really mean them that way'.

3.5.1 Against reflection?

The first of these revisions emerges in Nietzsche's depreciation of consciousness. We've so far thought of his values as directed toward a *reflective* agent: one consciously weighing how to act and looking for advice or guidance in deciding what to do. It's as thus reflective that we ourselves read value philosophers, and we hear them to mean to address just such an audience as we. But this assumption is at risk in Nietzsche's case. How can he mean to be addressing such when he strongly attacks reflection or consciousness? Indeed he does so in two rather different ways: he argues that so far as successfully practicing his values is concerned, such reflection is either *ineffective* or *corrupting*.

At the other extreme, many philosophers have of course identified reflection as itself the good we should practice and not merely a way to find out what's good.[114] But for Nietzsche my good is a condition of my drives, and not of my consciousness. So WP711 [1887–88]: "*not* increase in consciousness is the goal, but enhancement of power".[115] What really matters is not what I think but the implicit effort of the drives I comprise, and whose interplay shapes all my behaviors. For this purpose, my 'values', the ones I really need to improve, aren't those I'm conscious of and able to speak. They're the ways my world is polarized for me by those preconscious drives, especially the 'dominating committee' among them. It's in how these aim that I need to 'learn' his new values, Nietzsche thinks.

Not only is improving my thinking on values not itself the good, but

114. Aristotle *NE* 1103b27–29: "for we are inquiring not in order to know what virtue is, but in order to become good, since otherwise our inquiry would have been of no use"; but it turns out for him, too, that knowing is necessary and sufficient for the highest good (*NE*/X/7; the point is, of course, disputed).

115. WP707 [1887]: "If we willed to establish a goal broad enough for life, it could not coincide with any category of conscious life". This is part of the point of his attacks on hedonism (whether explanatory or prescriptive): pleasure, a mere epiphenomenon in consciousness, can't be the end.

it's apparently not very effective even as an aid to that good.[116] All my conscious resolution and effort can have little effect on my drives, which are more or less impervious to its demands. Indeed, my consciousness and what happens in it are little more than superficial expressions of the workings of those preconscious forces themselves. WP478 [1888]: "everything of which we become conscious is an end-appearance, a conclusion—and causes nothing".[117] So even my sense of control over my thoughts and deliberate decisions is illusory: "a thought comes when 'it' wills, and not when 'I' will" [BGE17].

But beyond this, Nietzsche also argues that consciousness is corrupt, that it's more likely to both *show* and *make* one sick than active. So, first, reflection is a sign of decadence: "every perfect deed is unconscious and no longer willed; consciousness expresses an imperfect and often sickly personal state" [WP289: 1888]. It's only the effete, whose drives don't enact themselves with a healthy straightforwardness, who look for theories of value to decide for them what to do. WP423 [1888]: " 'How should one act?' — If one considers that one is dealing with a sovereignly developed type that has 'acted' for countless millennia, and in which everything has become instinct, expedience, automatism, fatality, then the *urgency* of this moral question seems wholly comical. . . . [T]he appearance of moral scruples—in other words: the *becoming-conscious of the values* by which one acts—betrays a certain *sickliness.* "[118]

Moreover, reflection tends to lead one further astray. It interferes with the smooth running of the drives; in bringing those drives' values to consciousness, it steps somewhat out of them. Self-consciousness detaches from one's drives, though not to a stance of pure objectivity. Rather, it stands back from the drives to view them (in the main) from one's society's standpoint. The words it uses to express values, and in which they come to awareness, are themselves the product and property of the herd. To be common coin, they have to refer to what's shared within the community that speaks them. Thus, as we think with these words, we align ourselves with the herd's ways of willing and valuing

116. By contrast, Aristotle *NE* 1094a22–24: "Will not the knowledge of [the chief good], then, have a great influence on life? Shall we not, like archers who have a mark to aim at, be more likely to hit upon what is right?"

117. WP523 [1888]: "Consciousness in a secondary role, almost indifferent, superfluous". In WP666 [1886–87] and WP291 [1888], conscious purposes are 'epiphenomena' [*Begleiterscheinungen*]. See also WP676 [1883–84].

118. WP434 [1888]: "To the extent that it is willed, to the extent that it is known, there is no perfection in doing of any kind." TI/VI/2: "The most general formula on which every religion and morality is founded is: 'Do this and that, refrain from this and that—then you will be happy! Otherwise . . .' "; but instead, "a human being who has turned out well . . . carries the order that he represents physiologically, into his relations with other human beings and things." WP439 [1888], WP68 [1888], WP440 [1888].

and further lose sight of the goals and feelings distinctive and proper to ourselves.[119]

This two-pronged attack suggests that for Nietzsche the two parts to philosophy's usual goal might diverge or conflict: knowing what's good might be counterproductive for achieving it. A person who directs himself by a theory that names power as the good might be less likely to secure it than one whose sights are fixed on some concrete goal, some narrower personal project. Strongly willing some x—being wrapped up in some specific enterprise—is the best way to power; the ethicist's step back to the question 'what to do?' is either irrelevant or damaging.[120] But then how could Nietzsche intend his valuations—all his praisings and belittlings and rankings—as advice to readers reflecting what to do? How could he mean for these readers to take from him any guiding rules or goals (which we've taken an ethics to be)?

Because this critique of reflection itself expresses or presupposes those power values—it attacks reflection as *reactive*—it seems not to show that Nietzsche doesn't really think them true or think them best for us. If that critique swept away those values, it would sweep away itself as well. Instead, he must want us to cleave to that content 'beneath' consciousness, in our drives. This renders his proposing and praising of those power values puzzling: we can't tell why he bothers to say them, if not to make us conscious of them and to teach us to pursue them consciously. Why indeed does he say them even to himself? What's odd now isn't that he so rarely (for a philosopher) states his values but that he makes them explicit even as rarely as he does.[121]

So it seems that if Nietzsche does want to help us, it must be by bypassing our conscious or rational faculties and working directly on our preconscious drives. He must aim at a noncognitive, 'emotive' impact on us, and not at instructing or informing us. This takes on a sinister cast when we recall how he allows, and tries to explain to our discredit, that when we do reflect we'll probably disagree with his view of our interest. Once again, for new reasons, his writing seems meant as manipulating

119. See especially GS354: "My thought is, as one sees: that consciousness does not genuinely belong to the individual-existence of a human being, but much more to his social and herd nature; . . . and that consequently each of us, with the best will to *understand* himself as individually as possible, . . . still will always only bring to consciousness the not-individual in himself, his 'average'". See further § 4.3.1.

120. This question runs parallel to one familiarly raised about hedonism: mightn't the conscious pursuit of pleasure interfere with securing it? An analogous question has been posed for utilitarianism (and has helped motivate 'rule utilitarianism'). TSZ/III/12/5: "one should not *will* to enjoy! For enjoyment and innocence are the most bashful [*schamhaftesten*] things: both will not to be sought."

121. Nietzsche's motives for keeping his power values implicit are related to those he has for suppressing his power ontology; in both cases they help explain why the majority of the most direct statements are in the *Nachlass*.

propaganda, even if now for a benevolent cause: what *he* takes our good to be. If we disagree with that good, we'll dislike still more his efforts to persuade us toward it by appeals to our unreason.[122] So this finding—that the power values aren't 'advice to an anonymous *reflective* agent'—seems again to redouble our qualms about their content.

I think that at least this further worry can be answered, by two main points. First, insofar as Nietzsche's writing does appeal to our drives, this is not (he thinks) to a brute irrationality but to viewpoints with reasoning and discriminating powers of their own. Second, his writing appeals to us also as conscious reflectors, in a way that circumvents the objections just made against (what turns out to have been just a type of) reflection.

I think the 'emotive' character of Nietzsche's prose does indeed express his interest in addressing our drives. He tries, with all his hyperbolic gradings and degradings, to fan our competitive fires and to engage and involve us in particular contests and disputes; he even tries, with his images and dramas of truth as woman, to attract (some of) us erotically to his project. (In § 3.5.2, I touch on his efforts at a religious appeal.) But we should reconsider how 'irrational' his address to us must therefore be: that we decide in our drives needn't mean that we decide poorly or ill-judgingly. As Nietzsche deflates consciousness, he inflates the powers of the drives.

He attributes to the drives a 'reason', a power of discernment, that makes them more trustworthy judges than we'd thought.[123] In particular, they're better judges of that essential valuative dimension of health/sickness than reflection tends to be, because they themselves are the active forces from which reflection steps back reactively. If anything in us is active, it must be some among our drives. Moreover, these drives are also more educable than we'd thought. Indeed, we can recognize all of Nietzsche's diagnoses—his unrelenting exposures of weakness and resentment in so many psychological types—as efforts to educate our drives: to cultivate a better 'taste'—or, as he often puts it, better (sense of) 'smell'—in our preconscious instincts and habits. These drives themselves take valuing viewpoints on the world; the 'sight' involved in their preconscious caring can be improved by stimulating and thus exercising that caring in a certain way. So Nietzsche tries to render more acute our drives' ability to recognize sickness and reactivity in ourselves and others. And he submits and trusts his position as much to this judgment in our drives as to that in our explicit thought.

But this isn't to say that he doesn't speak also to that consciousness,

---

122. Perhaps the clearest and most worrying case in which Nietzsche appeals to our unreason is *The Antichrist* and its hyperemotive appeal for a holy war to the death against Christianity.

123. WP387 [1887–88]: "as if every passion did not have in itself its quantum of reason".

nor even that he doesn't speak mainly to it. To suppose otherwise conflicts with something plain in the way his books address us: How could he not mean us to reflect (dwell consciously on) what he says, both in his general claims about (such matters as) will to power, resentment, and eternal return, and in all his detailed diagnoses of specific psychological-cultural stances (e.g., the Christian)? Isn't his medium, writing, one that inherently depends on two bringings to consciousness—first in the writer, then in the reader—even if it also engages other parts to both? If Nietzsche were as opposed to reflection as all that, why would he stick with writing and philosophy, as (plainly) his self-defining activities?

A key to his subtler view about consciousness lies in reorienting those complaints about its harmfulness. These complaints don't mean that all should avoid it; indeed (in Nietzsche's warping of pragmatism) the strongest should pursue it, as a proof and incitement for their strength. It's peculiarly difficult to maintain health in one's drive base while growing ever more self-aware, because this awareness means seeing through ever more of the illusions that sustain one's care and commitment: only the strongest can stand the explicitness of things. So Nietzsche prides himself in being able to bear the most acute self-reflection. Because this reflection especially exposes weakness and reaction, it is a step to that 'great health' that is won from sickness (§ 2.5.3). Nietzsche thinks he applies this therapy to a 'self' that has been enriched to include the main wills and attitudes of his society and culture. So he thinks that in him this cultural thought web achieves a degree and breadth of self-reflection and self-healing never instanced before. He means his writing in this spirit: to spur in his readers a dangerous self-scrutiny, which is also their chance for best health.

I examine Nietzsche's conception of a healing reflection much more closely in chapter 4 (esp. §§ 4.4–5), as well as his idea of how this reflection must be accompanied by a 'knowing' in the drives. But this is enough to show that his attacks on consciousness don't mean that he appeals propagandistically to our unreason and that they don't prevent him from still addressing us as reflectors and spurring reflection in us. So when we specify just how he departs from this traditional format of 'advising a reflector', we discover him still close by, in the same (conceptual) neighborhood.

3.5.2 Freedom and fate

Our conception of values as 'advice to the anonymous reflective agent' is flawed in a second way for Nietzsche: in its notion of the agent. In § 3.2, I reviewed his attack on the very existence of any ego or self and concluded that it left still enough of an 'agent' as an entity to which or whom this advice could be addressed; we saw that his point was not that there's nothing there but that what's there is complex, a tangle of drives. But we didn't consider a more particular way he disputes that notion of the agent: by denying that what's there can 'act' or 'will' in such a way as to be a suitable addressee for advice, a thing that can receive, consider, and (especially) choose to act on such advice. If not, why give advice? But Nietzsche denies there's any *free* agent. Freedom of the will requires the *causa sui*, which is, as BGE21 begins, "the best self-contradiction that has been thought up so far, a kind of logical rape and unnatural-ness".[124]

To be sure, Nietzsche is mostly struck by the impact his denial of freedom has not on this attitude of offering (prospective) ethical advice but on that of making (retrospective) moral judgments. He most often stresses how that denial implies that persons aren't 'responsible' [*verant-wortlich*], as these judgments presume them to be. So WP786 [1887]: "moral judgments in general relate only to one species of aims and actions, *the free*. But this whole species . . . is purely imaginary".[125] These judgments want us to be free, because they want us to be responsi-ble, which they want, in turn, because they issue from resentment, and want to blame us. So TI/VI/7: "Wherever responsibilities are sought, it is usually the instinct of *willing to punish and judge* [*Richten*] which seeks them. Becoming has been stripped of its innocence".[126] So when we see through freedom, the whole practice of judging seems undermined.

Nietzsche also marks how his denial of freedom threatens the project of ethical advising. So, TI/V/6 says, it's not just that one shouldn't give the same advice or ideal to all: "even when the moralist addresses him-self only to the single [human being] and says to him, '*You* ought [*soll-test*] to be such and such!' he does not cease to make himself ridiculous. The single one is a piece of *fatum* from the front and from the rear". Again we lack a responsibility for our actions, without which it's not sensible for the moralist to advise us. But if people aren't free to change themselves on the basis of proffered values, how could Nietzsche be proposing his own to us, in that traditional spirit we've supposed?

Before we can decide this matter, however, we need to notice how

124. Bergmann (1988, 34) counts the notion of freedom a part of the "mo-dality" of moralities for Nietzsche. See also Schacht 1983, 304–9. Hunt (1991, 146–52) addresses the seeming inconsistency between Nietzsche's 'immoralist' critique of 'ought' and responsibility, and "his own ethical views".

125. TI/VI/8: ''*No one* is responsible, that [a human being] is there at all, that he is constituted so, or that he is in these circumstances or in this environment. The fatality of his essence is not to be disentangled from the fatality of all that has been and will be." This lesson is linked with that against consciousness; so WP676 [1883–84]: "We learn to *think less* of all that is conscious; we unlearn making ourselves responsi-ble for ourselves, since *we* as conscious, goal-positing creatures are only the smallest part of us."

126. WP765 [1888]: "the pessimism of indignation *invents* responsibilities in order to create an *agreeable* feeling for itself—revenge".

he sometimes seems to take an opposite view of both freedom and responsibility: he sometimes favors and preaches them. So WP975 [1885–86]: "On this road lies the future of the highest human beings: to bear the greatest responsibility [soon glossed as *'belief in one's right* and one's *hand'*] and *not to be broken by it''*.[127] In this mood, he diagnoses slave morality as avoiding or fleeing the responsibility for choosing or acting, by passing it off on an authority for values, God or conscience or reason or society: "One wants to *get around* the will, the *willing* of a goal, the risk of giving oneself a goal; one wants to shift away responsibility (one would accept *fatalism*)" [WP20: 1887].[128] This 'existential' line, this stress on 'choosing for oneself', would seem to fit better with Sartre's championing of freedom; it looks at odds with Nietzsche's insistence on 'fate'.

How can we reconcile these seemingly opposite views? Two routes offer themselves; the choice between them hangs on whether we take Nietzsche to commend belief in freedom as true. Is it that he thinks freedom and responsibility are illusions, but illusions we (or the best) need to believe (in a certain way)? Or does 'responsible' have different meanings in these two groups of passages, so that what the higher men embrace isn't slave morality's illusion after all and doesn't presume ('metaphysical') free will?

Perhaps Nietzsche thinks that although we're not free or responsible, there are ways we need to believe we are; what matters is where or why one accepts this illusion. So he commonly shifts attention to one's motives for believing in freedom or determinism, as in BGE21: "the 'unfreedom of the will' is taken as a problem from two wholly opposite sides . . . : some will not to let go at any price their 'responsibility', their belief in *themselves*, the personal right to *their* merit (the vain races belong to this class); the others, on the contrary, will not to be responsible for anything, or guilty of anything, and out of an inner self-contempt, desire to be able to *shift* it somewhere from themselves." Perhaps what counts for Nietzsche is whether one's faith in freedom takes a healthy form. Perhaps, taking up that earlier distinction, he wants us to stop assigning responsibility in our (retrospective) judgments but to assume it all the more while we're (prospectively) deciding and acting.[129] So he

127. GM/II/2 speaks of the "proud knowledge of the extraordinary privilege of *responsibility*, the consciousness of this rare freedom, this power over oneself and over fate."

128. WP243 [1887] diagnoses *''fatalism*, our current form of philosophical sensibility'', as a remnant of Christian faith in divine providence.

129. Compare this with Nagel's distinction (1986, 111–12) between the "problem of autonomy" and the "problem of responsibility"; he later argues (1986, 137) that although the objective view can be "reengaged" with action, it can't be with our "judgments of responsibility". Nietzsche might seem to preach a strong lesson here: to forego that stance of judging altogether and cleave to the viewpoint of a will now determining what to do. Isn't the latter the crux, for an active will to power? In

wants to disrupt our faith in free will whenever we're judging, even when we're judging ourselves. But for the sake of (or by virtue of) good health, he wants our stance in willing to be insulated from that insight, somehow ignorant or forgetful of it. We need to think ourselves free as we value and chase our ends; our effort would be too disheartened if we became 'fatalists' even there. On this account, what matters is *how* one believes this falsehood.

But I think Nietzsche's dominant view is, instead, that the 'freedom' and 'responsibility' we should presume as we act are different from those that corrupt our blame-laying judgments. Whereas the latter are indeed false, the former are true, so that we don't, at our best, still have to cultivate an illusion here.[130] We should apply this new type of responsibility in our judgings, too, which rids them of the 'moral' force they have usually had. This type of freedom we can have is consistent with an inevitability in all that happens, a new type of determinism, which this best health must also recognize: its *amor fati*. Hence Nietzsche's position is a version of compatibilism: it works by accepting but re-describing both sides of the freedom/determinism opposition; specifying new senses for each, he shows how both can be true in the world of will to power.[131]

By contrast, in the senses he attributes to reaction and resentment, both freedom and determinism are false. What type of freedom does resentment want? A freedom that reinforces and justifies its obsessive animus against the strong. To better focus its rage, it takes over and builds on a mistake already embedded in our grammar: the illusion of the subject as a single source of actions.[132] It shapes this subject to serve as an ideal target for its rage: it wants to hang all the blame for its suffering on (a) distinct targets, on isolable and sufficient causes, and on (b) final targets, on causes that are first or free, in the sense that in them

---

judging, we abandon the perspective of improvement, to stand as a third-party critic on past or present—a stance that is beside the main point. But although Nietzsche might indeed shift emphasis here, (I argue that) he by no means renounces judging altogether.

130. Cf. Williams 1994, 242f.: "But the first-personal consciousness which an agent necessarily has does not in itself have to lead to the kind of picture that Nietzsche attacks; action does not necessarily involve this understanding of itself."

131. Nietzsche often connects freedom and necessity. TSZ/III/12/2: "where necessity was freedom itself, that played blissfully with the sting [*Stachel*] of freedom". EH/TSZ/3, describing his own experience of inspiration: "It all happens in the highest degree involuntarily [*unfreiwillig*], but as in a storm of a feeling of freedom, of being-unconditioned, of power, of divinity". See also BGE213. Stack (1992, 177ff.) stresses Nietzsche's effort to reconcile freedom and fate, and shows the view's ancestry in Emerson.

132. GM/I/13: "the affects of revenge and hatred exploit this belief [in the subject] for themselves and basically maintain no belief more fervently, than that *the strong is free* to be weak, and the bird of prey to be a lamb—for they thereby gain for themselves the right to hold the bird of prey *accountable*, for being a bird of prey".

explanation (and accountability) ends. In these free agents, blame can come to rest and not, frustratingly, get passed along and diffused ever beyond them, to what caused them. Resentment wants its enemies (who might include itself) to be free, because this makes them maximally culpable.[133]

Resentment, as it passes into a nihilist phase, can also inspire a seemingly opposite view, a mechanistic determinism. Here the basic aim is to demean and diminish those enemies, by denying them that freedom and responsibility. Resentment now blames in a subtler way: by denying that anything is (even good enough to be) blamable. It revenges itself on the world, for giving it so frustrated a life, by flattening everything into dead and aimless atoms and forces. It reduces persons' behavior to the operation of mechanical causes, and not at all their purposive wills; it nullifies those wills, by counting them for nought in its explanations. In this way, this determinism adopts part of the free-will story for its new attack: it still thinks in terms of discrete causes. It's this notion it shares with that story that is Nietzsche's own favorite target when he attacks them together.[134]

Both sides of this dispute get wrong the world as will to power. In particular, they miss the contextual, part-whole structure of this world, as we sketched it in chapter 2; it's this aspect of Nietzsche's metaphysical vision, I think, that bears most decisively against both free will and determinism, in their standard forms. Both views carve up becoming into sequences of discrete causes and effects, atomizing process into parts complete in themselves. They separate the cause from the causing, the effect from the being effected, whether they treat these as substances or states of affairs.[135] But when we see that the world's real 'parts' are willful processes defined by their power relations to one another, we see that there are no self-sufficient parts and that things 'condition' one another in an even more penetrating way than determinism had supposed; we learn a new form of that thought, a new fatalism. Yet we also

133. So again TI/VI/7: "Human beings were thought 'free' so that they could be judged and punished—so that they could become *guilty*: consequently, every action *had* to be thought as willed, and its origin as lying within consciousness". See also WP288 [1888]. Cf. Williams (1994, 243ff.) on "the target of blame".

134. So BGE21: "Suppose someone comes thus behind the boorish simplicity of this famous concept 'free will' and strikes it from his head, then I beg him to drive his 'enlightenment' a step further and also strike from his head the opposite. . . : I mean the 'unfree will', that amounts to a misuse of cause and effect. One should not mistakenly *reify* 'cause' and 'effect' as the natural scientists [*Naturforscher*] do . . . according to the ruling [*herrschenden*] mechanical doltishness, which lets the cause press and push until it 'effects'". Elsewhere (e.g., WP671 [1883–84], TI/V/3) he focuses his attack on the notion of 'will' and seems to embrace mechanism. But I think his objection is against any 'personal will': against attributing behavior to something both single and conscious, rather than to the many implicit drives that steer our conscious choice; see § 1.4.

135. Schacht (1983, 179) makes this distinction. See, respectively, WP552 [1887] and WP551 [1888], and WP633 [1888].

see how these power relations of command and obedience give the basis for a new kind of freedom and responsibility, now not as the equal inheritance of all subjects but as an ideal form of command that some wills may achieve.[136]

Take first the new form of determinism. Nietzsche's 'fate' [*Geschick*] is the Spinozistic necessity of every part for the whole, and of every part given the whole, expressed in that predecessor's insistence that we're all modes of the same substance. Nietzsche understands these parts as perspectival wills, and the relations that bind them together as the ways they command and obey. Wills 'condition' one another—and so give and take their contextual identity—not by (the usual) causality but by the ways they rule and are ruled.[137] It's these power relations that lock each part in place in the whole and make the whole leave a place for just the part that's there. Taking away any one will, one perspectival angle of command, would change the 'look' to all the rest, change how it obeys. Given the whole, we must be as we are; recall from TI/VI/8: "One [*Man*] is necessary, one is a piece of fatefulness [*Verhängniss*], one belongs to the whole, one *is* in the whole". This means, Nietzsche goes on here to say, that "there is nothing that can judge, measure, compare, condemn our being", so that "nobody is [to be] held responsible any more", which is *"the great liberation [Befreiung]*—by which the *innocence* of becoming is established once again". This freeing embrace of necessity is of course *amor fati*.[138]

As this already suggests, such a fated world still has room for a new sort of freedom and for another way of judging. Indeed, this new freedom is really just a developed form of the commanding that helps bind up that world. Although all wills must be as they are, they differ (and along an essential dimension) in whether they chiefly command or obey. Some wills are (shaped to be) nodes and initiators of meaning:

---

136. Danto (1965, 33) connects *amor fati* with a "nihilism" he attributes to Nietzsche: "it is an intoxicating fact to know that the world is devoid of form and meaning"; by contrast, I think Nietzsche counts himself not a nihilist because (with his power ontology) he does find meaning in the world, as well as the chance for a freedom consistent with fate.

137. So Nietzsche's fate differs from a causal determinism (a) in making the 'elements' of the process (the constrainers and the constrained) wills, and so intentionalities, and (b) in then thinking of these wills as contextually interdefining, and hence not strictly elements at all.

138. GS276: "I will to learn more and more to see the necessary in things as beautiful—so I shall be one of those who make things beautiful. *Amor fati:* from now on let that be my love!" EH/II/10: "My formula for the greatness of a human being is *amor fati:* that one wills to have nothing otherwise, not forwards, not backwards, not in all eternity. Not merely to bear the necessary, still less to conceal it . . . but to *love* it". TI/IX/49: "Such a spirit [as Goethe] who has *become free* stands amidst all with a joyous and trusting fatalism, in the *faith* [*Glauben*] that only the single is loathsome, and that all is redeemed and affirmed in the whole—*he does not negate any more*". See also NCW/E/1.

they contribute to the sense of all by putting forward a perspective and project of their own. Other wills mainly respond, either by copying or opposing. At its root, Nietzsche's new freedom is just that activeness: a will's ability or tendency to cleave to its own viewpoint, to press and develop what distinguishes it, and not to be (in the main) swayed or jostled away from this by other forces, whether these impinge on it with physical pains or with tempting alternatives to its own point of view. Freedom is strength or health of will, and it is quite consistent with no will being ('metaphysically') free to will in this way.[139]

Nietzsche means by freedom something more precise than activeness, however. Freedom is the form activeness takes in the 'individual': a type of human being feasible only recently, after long social engineering by an 'ethics of custom', a process the second essay in *On the Genealogy of Morals* recounts. A familiar passage describes an early, masterly form of this freedom: "the human being with his own independent long will. . . . This one who has become free [*Dieser Freigewordne*], who really *may* promise, this master of a *free* will" [GM/II/2]. When the human drive synthesis is trained to discipline its exceptional complexity of parts and to subordinate them to a long-term and unifying project, it achieves a new kind of command, vividly reflected in its ability to make and keep promises. A common will now stretches itself backward and forward and through many activities and efforts, and knits these all together into a shared project, and hence a *self*, in the sense in which there really can be one.[140]

The (Nietzschean) freedom this individual enjoys rests crucially on the way he combines the stances of ruler and ruled. It's by being at once, in the same act, both commander and obeyer that this individual achieves a new awareness of commanding, which is our primal experience of 'freedom'. So, from BGE19's extended analysis of this experience: "'Freedom of the will'—this is the word for that manifold pleasure-state of the willer, who commands and also counts himself as one with the executor [*Ausführenden*]". There must be a ruling project or passion but also an allegiance to the competing forces subjected to it;

---

139. See especially TSZ/I/17: "Free from what? What does that matter to Zarathustra! But brightly your eyes should inform me: free *towards what* [*wozu*]?" TI/IX/38: "For what is freedom! That one has the will to self-responsibility. That one holds firm the distance that separates us. That one becomes more indifferent to trouble, hardship, privation, even to life itself. That one is prepared to sacrifice human beings for one's cause, not excluding oneself." See how WP720 [1885–86] equates 'freedom' with the drive for power; see, too, GS98, 347; GM/II/2; GM/III/10. This sense of 'free' is also at work in Nietzsche's notion of the 'free spirit'. This contrasts with Nagel's account of the freedom we can have, as an (essentially incomplete) objectivity (1986, 127); Nietzsche rather wants us to better embrace our individuality (subjectivity), free from (able to resist) the temptations or compulsions of other viewpoints.

140. In § 2.3, I developed the temporal aspect of this synthesis.

one must still take the point of view of those subordinated drives. This multivalency equips such a person to recognize the interpenetration of forces, which we saw is missed in the assumption of an atomistic causality. By identifying with both sides, he witnesses at vivid first hand the essential cleavage in the world, between ruler and ruled, and the mutuality of these parts. It's this persisting allegiance to all the drives and viewpoints he subordinates that generates the free individual's responsibility. This is the burden he takes on, in disposing of these multiple forces (and allegiances) to his single point: the challenge to bring them to a worthy culmination.

It's the philosopher, Nietzsche thinks, who experiences this freedom and responsibility to the greatest degree, by virtue of commanding, and becoming responsible for, the *most* such parts. He imbibes 'in spirit' the main elements in his society's structure of attitudes and remodels that structure. By thus subordinating the social and shared to a personal project, the philosopher achieves a freedom from that 'ethics of custom', from conventional views and values that others can't distance themselves from, and so can't help but obey. He experiences a grand spiritual freedom in reshaping this mesh of attitudes *his* way, but he experiences as well a great weight of responsibility, for all the cultural voices (present and past) he presumes to subject to his new meaning.

Nietzsche aspires to play this role better than previous philosophers have: to shape these cultural attitudes into a healthier structure than ever before. By seeing more clearly the sickness near the heart of philosophy or theory itself—its links to the practice of the priest—he (thinks he) can improve the philosophical eye and equip it to notice critically a general sickness in his culture that still gripped his predecessors. By healing the philosophical truth project (as we'll see in §§ 4.4–5), Nietzsche thinks he can proceed to heal his culture more generally and to redeem [*erlösen*] the deficiencies of its present and past. He aims to show the point of our millennia-long Christian sickness (what it will turn out to have been a preparation for), by accomplishing a fundamental turn, the revaluation of values, that brings it to a higher health. In this act, he thinks he achieves the fullest freedom: free now from that deep reactive bias that has most inhibited freedom itself.

He thinks also that the very 'lightness' of his freedom (how many viewpoints he commands) makes him also bear the 'greatest weight' of responsibility to the wills he subjects.[141] He commands these reactive forces in a spirit of allegiance to them, while still (also) taking their points of view.[142] This is why he cares to redeem them. Identifying with the weight of sickness and suffering in his culture's history, he feels the

---

141. EH/TSZ/6: "how the spirit bearing the heaviest destiny, a fatality [*Verhängniss*] of a task, nevertheless can be the lightest and most surpassing [*jenseitigste*]".

142. EH/TSZ/6: "How [Zarathustra] grasps even his adversaries, the priests, with gentle hands, and suffers with them of them!" See also BGE284.

burden of finding a meaning grand enough to make even that long Christian error have been worthwhile. Indeed, he pushes this redemptive aspiration and burden from a cultural to the cosmic level, in his thought of eternal return: his life, even each moment of it, must be such that all the world could hinge on it, or find fruition in it, as the 'great noon'.[143]

Let's set aside Nietzsche's presumption to be this culmination, as either an embarrassing self-delusion or a claim we can judge only after we make our final judgment on the truth of all he says. But let's notice an apparent contradiction in his very conception of this ultimate freedom: this stance 'says Yes' to every being (and as good in itself, not just instrumentally), but it also diagnoses these beings quite scathingly and finds most of them sick and weak enough to need redeeming. (How can Nietzsche, so penetrating and unrelenting a critic of just about everyone and everything, claim also to be the great *affirming* philosopher?) The answer once again lies in the way this stance 'incorporates' the viewpoints it attacks. The ascent to the culminating view involves 'saying No' to, seeing the inadequacy in, all other wills: it claims to rise past them. But it does so while retaining them as cares of its own, and for this reason (and not just because they were means to it) it 'says Yes' to all it goes beyond. Each part is perfect in itself, but only *for* the perspective of the whole, which experiences itself as making it perfect by its synthetic act.

Is the possibility of this new sort of freedom enough to rescue that project of 'ethical advice'? If our Nietzschean goal is to become free in his new sense—to will actively, for a start—but this is not something we're free in the old sense to do, or even to (choose to) attempt, how could he be advising us to become so? Doesn't this traditional mode of address depend on the sort of freedom and responsibility that Nietzsche rejects, rather than on the type he affirms? I think two points show that he can still address us in much of that familiar way.

First, Nietzsche doesn't hold that we're altogether unchangeable. To be sure, his denial of freedom is connected with a skepticism about whether certain great changes, or changes in type, are feasible. In particular, he thinks many who are sick (in will or spirit) just can't become healthy; their condition is settled by their physiology. Free will promised the accessibility of (ethical) goodness to all; Nietzsche denies not just this

---

143. GM/II/24 anticipates "the *redeeming* human being of great love and contempt . . . this bell-stroke of noon and of the great decision, who makes the will free again, who gives back to the earth its goal and to humanity its hope". As fated for this epochal role, Nietzsche thinks he has a 'destiny' [*Schicksal*]. EH/IV/8: "The *uncovering* of Christian morality is an event that has no equal, a real catastrophe. He who enlightens about it, is a force majeure, a destiny—he breaks the history of humanity in two pieces. One lives *before* him, one lives *after* him." Again, this expresses Nietzsche's will to be a god; see § 1.5.3.

magical route but that any route can carry some persons to his good (an active complexity). However, he still thinks some types of improvements are feasible. (1) Even if there can't be great positive transformations, there can still be incremental improvements along the value scales of activeness and complexity: the sick can become less sick, or less harmfully and miserably sick. (2) Whereas most of these sick can perhaps never be healthy, the healthy are very prone to becoming sick and can be helped not to.

Second, Nietzsche's denial of free will needn't prevent him from hoping to help us in either way, by teaching his values to us. It just changes the way he aims them at us: not to guide our free choice but to add a new stimulus to our multiply-constituted wills, a stimulus that quickens our healthy instincts and inhibits our sick.[144] Such stimuli, for example, are his numerous diagnoses of resentment: he 'advises' us away from it—not by asking any free and ultimate self to choose not to resent but by arousing and improving the taste of our drives themselves, of our constituting attitudes. He builds in these, as well as in our consciousness, an alertness to the signs of reaction. These appeals can still be argument, and good argument, even if we leave out any ultimate self that's free to attend to this argument, or not. This is not a drastic break, I think, from the way we already think of everyday or even philosophical advisers. Here again, I think the traditional format of 'advising the ARA' is still substantially in play.

Finally, does any of this ease our worries about the content of Nietzsche's values? Perhaps it helps in this slight way: we might be a bit less disturbed by his insistent rankings of persons when we bear in mind that they do not imply the sort of blaming of those they rank low that moral judgments might. Still, I think this doesn't affect our main qualms against Nietzsche's hierarchism. If anything, it might disturb us all the more that his inegalitarian politics and ethics so disvalue those who aren't free to be otherwise.

3.5.3   Rank order

The third amendment to my schema of 'advice to the anonymous reflective agent' concerns the 'anonymity' (or interchangeability) of the agent I've presumed that any—hence Nietzsche's—value theory must address. I've assumed that he offers a single, quite general lesson to everyone alike, to any human being.[145] But I could do so only by willfully ignor-

144. WP394 [1888]: "We do not believe that a human being becomes another, if he is not it already: i.e. if he is not, as often enough happens, a multiplicity of persons, at least of starts at persons. In this case one brings it about, that another role steps into the foreground, that 'the old human being' comes to be pushed behind."

145. This point is linked with those about consciousness and freedom: only seeing ourselves in these guises can we suppose we're all equal enough to be addressed in that 'anonymous' format.

ing his great stress on difference, including at this very point. People are so unlike one another, he often says, that quite different values are best for their different cases. All values, that is, are tied to specific perspectives and can be best only for them. 'Moralities' go wrong by preaching the same good for all, by addressing a single lesson to all. So he objects to Kant's categorical imperative: "A virtue must be *our* invention, *our* most personal defense and need; in any other sense it is merely a danger. Whatever is not a condition of our life *harms* it" [A11].[146] So how could he himself be offering a single lesson to all?

It's this third assault on the formula of 'advice to the ARA' that most promises to allay our doubts about the content of Nietzsche's power values.[147] It does so by suggesting, roughly, that he speaks these values as 'just true for him' and doesn't want us his readers, nor society in general, to accept them, too. If they have only this private and local status, we may be more forgiving of them than if they presumed to set public policy, and ours. We might feel ourselves invited, in particular, to purge these values of their antiegalitarian bent, as just Nietzsche's bias and idiosyncrasy, while preserving other parts we more approve of. On the other hand, this 'relativizing' move calls into question what relevance or importance to us any of Nietzsche's values could have. If they're indeed no truer or better than any other values, why should we attend to them at all?

So far I've tried to deflect or limit this undermining move, by my two-level strategy, which insulates the power ontology (and the values bound up in it) from the perspectivism. This line suggests that we hear Nietzsche's perspectivist attack as directed only against the too-great *specificity* of moralities' goods: moralists fail to see how the true good is 'formal', the activeness or power of whatever activity 'content' distinguishes one person from others; they try to press the same concrete activities on everyone alike. By avoiding such preaching of 'content', Nietzsche can still offer values meant to be good for anyone: activeness and power, goods he indeed presumes in those very attacks (such as A11) on too-specific values. When he proclaims the 'relativity' of values, it's because different things are needed for the survival and flourishing of different wills; hence it's on the supposition of these, his metavalues.

One large piece of evidence against that insulating move is that Nietzsche sometimes seems not to want all to adopt his value of activeness. "My philosophy is directed at a rank order: not at an individualistic morality. The sense of the herd should rule [*herrschen*] in the herd— but not reach out beyond it: the leaders of the herd need a basically

146. TSZ/III/11/2: " 'This—is now *my* way—where is yours?', so I answered those who asked me 'as to the way'. For *the* way—that doesn't exist!" See also BGE221. Bergmann 1988, 37: "Part of what makes a code moral, in our eyes, is . . . that it judges us *equally* as *equal* human persons." See, too, Foot 1973, 166.

147. But I'll be much briefer on this topic, because of the way it opens into the issues of chapter 4.

different valuation for their own actions, as do the independent, or the 'beasts of prey', etc." [WP287: 1886–87]. So even at the (supposed) meta-level of activeness or health, it seems he doesn't want the same for all, doesn't advise the same to all; in at least these two senses, he thinks some 'should' be reactive. This is better overall; they let activeness be itself, by opening up a difference from it. Nietzsche wants only that their reactive values take a form not tempting and damaging to 'the independent'.[148]

This last point, however, shows how he might still want everyone to hold values as (nearly) active as possible, which would make his break with the traditional schema much less extreme. This tempering of reactivity, so that it not infect the healthy, could amount precisely to making it less reactive. What Nietzsche wants, after all, is to lessen the resentful effort by the sick to destroy or corrupt the healthy, to impose their values on those others. The priest tries to do so by redirecting that resentment back onto the sick themselves; but Nietzsche decries the poisoning consequences of such a cultivation of guilt.[149] When he speaks of 'breeding the perfect herd-animal', he has in mind an alternative less banefully reactive: he hopes for a partial cure even among the worst. Perhaps, we might say, he wants ingrained reactors and obeyers to at least embrace their reactivity actively: to develop it as their own and worthy as such, not something that's a second best for them and for which others (or themselves) are to blame. This suggests how Nietzsche might aim his values even to (and for the benefit of) the many he thinks are incurably sick.

Whether or not he wants to benefit everyone, Nietzsche's insistence that different values are best for different persons doesn't 'relativize' them in the way we might think. Even if his perspectivism applies to those metavalues, too, it isn't a flat relativism that brings active and reactive into equality *as* perspectives. We have to hear the perspectivism as tuned by his thoughts about *rank order*: viewpoints aren't all on an equal (epistemological or valuative) footing. They stand in a hierarchy, and with them their suiting values; of course, the active/reactive distinction is the chief criterion in this ranking.[150] So even if Nietzsche doesn't offer his values to everyone, he thinks they still take the measure of everyone. And although he doesn't think that everyone is able to learn his lesson, he thinks each would be better if he could. He thinks that if

148. GM/III/14: "That the sick should *not* make the healthy sick . . . should indeed be the supreme viewpoint on earth".
149. Contrast GM/III/15's apparent approval for the priest's strategy, with the account of its eventual effects, in /21.
150. WP857 [1888]: "I distinguish between a type of rising life and another type of decay, disintegration, weakness. Can one believe, that the question of rank between these types still needs to be posed?" Deleuze (1983, 60) says of 'hierarchy': "It signifies, firstly, the difference between active and reactive forces, the superiority of active to reactive forces".

different values than his are best for some reader, it's because that reader isn't good (strong/active/rich) enough for his. So he speaks his values not with the relativist force of a Sophist but much more with that of tradition-founding Plato, who also projected a hierarchy of values for a hierarchy of psychosocial types. This means, I think, that our qualms about the 'content' of Nietzsche's values remain in full force and must be confronted for themselves, not deferred vaguely by gesturing at some novel 'force'.

This notion of a perspectivism that ranks perspectives raises large puzzles, however—puzzles best addressed with respect not to values but to truth.

4

TRUTH

We come now to the crux: whether Nietzsche means his claims to be true. I've tried to show how these claims, so seemingly chaotic, might still be gathered around and into a certain system or framework, a network of essential questions and decisions. I've mapped his main routes of thought and noted how he most often turns at their crossings. I've allowed that he often makes the opposite choices on these issues; that this system is *his*, therefore lies not in its being a single view to which he's unrelentingly loyal, but in his being preoccupied along this network of questions and mostly inclined to decide them as I've sketched. Nietzsche is surely uncommonly able to step out of his dominant perspectives and claims, but this doesn't mean that some aren't indeed quite dominant for him. Certain views are recurringly convincing to him, though he often skirmishes against them and forces progressive adjustments in them.

But we can't rest content with so prosaic a lesson. We must entertain certain more radical explanations for all Nietzsche's self-reversals and self-contradictions, which (to be honest) have seemed to trip up my project at every turn. I have to confront how the main alternative reading of Nietzsche interprets these: as reflecting a drastically different intent in all these claims I've culled from him. Other philosophers avoid self-contradiction, because they mean their claims to be true; what if Nietzsche doesn't mean his remarks as 'claims' (in this sense) at all?[1]

1. De Man (1979, 116) develops "the fundamentally ironic and allegorical nature of Nietzsche's discourse". Kofman (1993) suggests that Nietzsche's words (in particular 'will to power') are metaphors, not concepts.

Immediately, this seems to explain more simply and plausibly his un-usual tolerance and even delight in reversing himself. If he doesn't really care about truth, if he doesn't pursue it in what he says, my whole program of showing the system in what he says would seem to go quite astray.[2] So perhaps I've been hearing every one of his remarks in a subtly mistaken sense: my ears just haven't been tuned to his speech.

Nietzsche indeed raises major doubts about truth and often presses these as attacks on it. First, he calls the value of truth into question, most conspicuously, near the start of *Beyond Good and Evil*: "We asked about the *value* of this will [to truth]. Suppose we will truth: *why not rather untruth? and uncertainty? even ignorance?*" [BGE1]. He continues: "And can one believe, that it finally wants [will] to seem to us as if the problem had never even been posed so far—as if we were the first to see it, fix it with our eyes, and *risk* it."[3] Second, he sometimes doubts the very possibility of truth. So WP539 [1888]: "Parmenides has said 'one cannot think of what is not'—we are at the other end and say 'what can be thought of must surely be a fiction'."[4] He thinks that this doubt, too, distinguishes him from preceding philosophers.

Strictly speaking, of course, earlier philosophers *have* 'addressed these issues'. They often discuss the value of truth: they typically claim it's of highest value for us, that the best life is one of knowing or under-standing. Often they've argued this, adducing reasons 'why not rather untruth'. They've also considered, and even pressed, various arguments against the possibility of truth (or of knowing it). The positions of skepti-cism and relativism are familiar voices within the history of philoso-phy, and minority voices, too, in most individual philosophers. So are Nietzsche's claims to novelty grossly overstated?[5] But he thinks (and I try to show) that he stands before these doubts about truth in a different way—that its value and possibility are open for him in some new re-spect. He labels this different stance his *perspectivism*, a viewpoint com-plexly and subtly unlike those traditional precedents of skepticism and relativism. My major task in this chapter is to explain that stance, which lies at the root of his various doubts against truth.

So far, in accordance with my opening procedure, I've treated this perspectivism as subordinate to the ontology of will to power. I've

2. However, note that this needn't rule out my claim of a Nietzschean system; even if he means his remarks not as true but as helpful, for example, this might still depend on their hanging together that way.

3. His reservations are later stated in a 'saying': "'Where the tree of knowledge stands, there is always Paradise': thus speak the oldest and the youngest serpents" [BGE152]. He also claims priority in raising this issue in GM/III/24: "Consider on this question the oldest and the youngest philosophies: all of them lack a consciousness, how far the will to truth itself needs a justification".

4. WP616 [1885–86]: "there is no 'truth'".

5. Cf. Ellis's attack (1989, 38n) on de Man's suggestion that Nietzsche was the source for deconstruction's central theory of meaning.

shown how the power ontology can generate or support a perspectival lesson, but one that doesn't extend (or strike) back to undermine that ontology itself; this was my 'two-level' account of the relation between these teachings. (Put a bit more concretely, power is enrichment of some content; although a content is good only for a perspective, that enrichment is, really or objectively, the essential end of all wills.) However, there's too much evidence to ignore, that Nietzsche refuses thus to 'insulate' his views about will to power from that perspectival attack. In the familiar ending to BGE22, he says of his power view: "Supposing that this also is only interpretation—and you will be eager enough to object this?—well, so much the better."

However, we also can't lightly allow that the power ontology is itself 'just a perspective, not really true', as would seem to be the critical lesson of perspectivism. This would make it puzzling what claim to our attention all those descriptions of us and the world as will to power could have. Why should we believe them or pay any attention to them if Nietzsche himself doesn't think they're true? What reason does he then give us for looking at things his way? The readiest reply to this, that thinking this way might 'benefit' us, seems itself to depend on claims about what our ends are and should be; at the least, it depends on its being (probably) *true* that these teachings are helpful to us. Wouldn't any way of commending them to us have to depend on some claim's truth? Moreover, the perspectivism also makes its own status puzzling: in renouncing the power ontology, it undercuts the foundations it rests on. The reasons Nietzsche has given us for accepting perspectivism have been his accounts of ourselves and the world as will to power; if these weren't really true, mustn't we withdraw our assent?[6] So it's hard to detach these two teachings from one another, despite the strong tension between them.

My purpose here is to resolve this issue more satisfactorily than did my opening 'two-level' account. I keep the basic logic of that account: beginning with the power ontology, proposed to us as true, and generating from it a perspectivism that doesn't (in central respects) take back that truth. But the two-level device for protecting this truth from perspectivism was artificial and unconvincing, and it needs to be replaced. The 'limits' to perspectivism have to arise from the logic of that view itself. In fact, by fleshing out just what perspectivism the ontology actually does imply (not resting content with the simplest version of it, as announcing 'no facts, only interpretations'), we find how it can be compatible with the power ontology after all.

6. It seems we should reject the image of 'kicking away the ladder' (applied to Nietzsche by Habermas 1990, 86): the *reasons* for choosing perspectivism are more than just a route that ends at it—or more than Nietzsche's autobiographical report of how *he* got there; they're his reasons why we should follow him there. So Schrift (1990, 182–84) underestimates the problem.

Our route to this resolution lies through the notion of truth. I begin (in § 4.1 and § 4.2) with a preliminary survey of Nietzsche's explicit doubts about truth, over (in turn) its possibility and its value. As we weigh these skeptical arguments, which seem to make so utter and sweeping a denial, we find flaws or paradoxes in them, which lead us to wonder whether Nietzsche means them quite as we'd thought. We are challenged to investigate what truth is for Nietzsche. As always, this means (trying) to state and locate it within the terms of the power ontology: truth is essentially the object of a certain type of 'will', of that 'will to truth' whose historical and psychological developments he so often treats. Thus we look next (in § 4.3) at the 'genealogy' of the will to truth. This brings out the background intent to all those arguments against truth: these attack a historical phase of that will and what 'truth' is *for it*. This redescription of these arguments' target helps us resolve the doubts and puzzles we felt over them, by showing better their limits. We then see (in § 4.4) that, despite these attacks, Nietzsche deliberately (though often covertly) joins in the cause of that will, elects it as his most central drive. His attacks really aim to refashion the goal of truth in such a way that that will comes into its health and maturity, 'becomes itself'. It does so in the 'new philosophers' he anticipates. On the ground of all this, we finally see (in § 4.5) how this reconceived truth allows and even involves a perspectivism.

4.1 Against truth's possibility

We look first at Nietzsche's arguments that truth is impossible. Here, as also with the arguments against its value, his attack presupposes that truth is correspondence and therefore divides on two sides: into an intentional attitude and what it is 'of'. The traditional goal of truth describes (requires) both a certain state of the 'subject' or 'knower' and a condition of the 'object' or 'known'. The first must rise above all interest or bias, so that the latter can appear 'as it is in itself'. But Nietzsche's power view of the world rules out how each side would have to be in order for these standards built into the notion of truth to be met. It does so by making both of them wills to power. The redescription of the subject as a will to power, hence as a perspective viewing the world in relation to its idiosyncratic projects, threatens the way truth is supposed to be detached. And the redescription of the 'object' as also will to power, hence as becoming and as lacking clear boundaries either in or through time, denies that it 'is' any way 'in itself' for that attitude to grasp. These are the two clearest ways he argues the impossibility of truth: the knower can't match, and the world can't be matched.[7]

---

7. Cf Magnus's distinction (1988a, 153) between 'epistemic' and 'ontological' versions of perspectivism.

In the previous paragraph, and for the most part in the following discussion, I treat truth and knowledge more interchangeably than might seem right. I speak as if any truth believed is thereby known, thus ignoring the usual further requirement of an 'account' (a reason or justification). I proceed so because of the nature of Nietzsche's main epistemological doubts: these dispute our knowledge claims not as lacking proof or justification but as indeed false. Hence his usual skeptical arguments are not the Cartesian sort, which cite alternative possibilities as gaps in the knower's justifications, ways things might be otherwise. Nietzsche's is (in intent) a stronger skepsis: it's not just that we might (for all that our evidence and arguments show) be wrong; we *are*.[8] This means that for him the claim to know is chiefly the claim to true belief; this is the principal target of his two-sided attack. This permits a simplified vocabulary for most of the following discussion.

4.1.1   Becoming can't be known

We begin with the objective route to this skepticism, why the world is intrinsically 'unmatchable'. Nietzsche often argues that truth or knowledge would require (would have to be of) a stable reality persisting beneath or behind the change visible around us. It depends on there being lasting things, but there aren't: "Constant transitions forbid us to speak of 'individuals'. . . . A world that becomes could not, in a strict sense, be 'comprehended' or 'known'" [WP520: 1885].[9] We dwelt on this connection in chapter 2: we tested accounts of Nietzsche's theory of becoming for their ability to explain his sureness that a world that becomes could never be known.

This claim was initially puzzling to us, because it seemed there could still be truth and knowledge about 'constant flux', a comprehensible 'fact of the matter' about movements or changes, as also about their momentary states. Does the claim show any more than that we need to date our descriptions of the world—that is. specify the time at which they were/are/will be true? Thus a scientist might be quite undisturbed that the molecules composing things are continually rearranged and changed; it just gives him the task of describing these very changes. Surely such scientists are precisely the ones best acquainted with this constant flux; if they're not shaken from the effort to know it, their judgment has weight.

---

8. And even, that we must be; recall WP539 [1888]: "we . . . say 'what can be thought of must surely be a fiction'." See also TL [P&Tp86: 1873]. Nietzsche partly inherits this view from Schopenhauer, who (following Kant) claims not that we can't know whether time, space, and causality are true of the thing-in-itself, but that we *can* know they're *not*.

9. Note how WP560 [1887] associates "the apparent *objective* character of things" with their being relatively enduring. See also WP585 [1887].

This puzzle was resolved with our more radical sense for 'becoming'. This involved, first, a new point about 'process': no longer the claim of a flux of momentary states but the denial that there are such states, that they're real (or ontologically primary). It's not merely that no state persists because change is continual, but that such states are incomplete or partial 'in themselves'. A state 'is' its role in a process, or rather its roles in the multiple processes that intersect through it. Second, we saw how this relational point applies through 'space' as well: a thing's identity lies in its relations to its other cotemporals. Together, these claims make up what I called the 'context point', the non-self-sufficiency of every part.[10] Nietzsche claims that a world with this contextual being could never be known.

We can easily feel the trouble he has in mind: the ways such a world would resist the kind of discovery or insight we want. How could we hope to know or understand what anything is if its identity thus spills out beyond it, ramifying open-endedly into what its (spatial and temporal) neighbors are? How could we ever make a start on understanding the world, if there's nothing complete in itself with which to begin, if we can never establish any small and single facts but must always expect these very things to be re-understood, as we (or others) move to a wider view? Truth, we might easily think, requires the unit, the thing or moment complete in itself; this is the first main aspect of that goal or ideal attacked by Nietzsche.

As I tried to show in chapter 2, even in this stronger form, the point about becoming is (not merely consistent with ontology, but) indeed an ontology itself, it just describes a different reality. So Nietzsche isn't really an (ontological) nihilist, and his argument against knowledge isn't simply that nothing can be known because there's nothing really there. Rather, he thinks it's the nature of reality that it can never be mirrored or matched.

But this then raises major problems for this whole 'objective' line of argument. First, its attack on truth seems itself to depend on a claim to truth, to a grasp of the world's real nature. It depends on a different, albeit very abstract or unspecific, account of reality—as 'contextual process', becoming—an account that claims our attention only by purporting to correspond to what's really there. But this seems at odds with the denial that truth is possible. Second, it also looks very inadequate as a knowledge claim, if we now reintroduce that Cartesian demand for a justification. Why should we accept this contextual ontology? Why must all beings be their roles in processes? Nietzsche's few supports for these claims probably carry much less weight with us than do those concrete (everyday or scientific) beliefs they purport to dislodge. And now his

10. I take this (positive) context point to stand behind Nietzsche's denial of the thing-in-itself, so that the latter plays a less fundamental role than Clark (1990, 22) supposes.

disinterest in that Cartesian concern may look like a pernicious weakness in him.

An independent ground for dissatisfaction is that this argument is clearly incomplete; it needs to be supplemented with some story about the 'subject', explaining why this could never 'mirror', hence know, such a contextual reality. Because one might otherwise think that beliefs could be adapted to correspond to this different world (as we've tried to do ourselves just now), it needs to be spelled out just which features of the would-be knower rule this out. This brings us to the other side of Nietzsche's point.

4.1.2   Knowing can't be detached

This second, subjective route to skepticism seems far more important to him: he mainly argues against what the notion of truth requires the knower to be, that this is impossible. Familiarly, it requires 'detachment', or, in the analogy we've just been using, the smoothness to 'mirror' reality without distortion. Often, we think, the involved or interested character of our experience distorts or colors how things are presented in it. We believe that to know, one needs to annul or suspend such interest, to put out of play all the personal idiosyncrasies marring that smoothness. It's against this requirement that Nietzsche mainly wields his perspectival point: we can never know, because we can never escape the bias of perspective.[11]

His simplest way of denying that this is feasible is to recite his ontology: we *are* wills to power, and hence inevitably interested. It's not just that we 'bear' those drives, we *are* them; it's not merely that consciousness is altered or interfered with by these drives (in ways we might hope to avoid), it's a product or expression of them. So GM/III/12 warns against "such contradictory concepts as 'pure reason'", which "always demand that one should think of an eye that is quite unthinkable, an eye that has no direction at all, in which the active and interpreting forces, through which seeing first becomes a seeing-something, are tied down, are lacking; so they always demand of the eye something absurd and inconceivable."[12] Intention or meaning, a viewpoint, arises only

11. PTAG11p83 [1873]: "It is unconditionally impossible for a subject to will to see and know something above and beyond itself, so impossible that knowing and being are the most contradictory of all spheres."

12. Already in UM/III/6: "the scholar consists of a tangled network of very different impulses and stimuli, he is a thoroughly impure metal". D553 asks whether philosophies "are all together nothing other than the intellectual detours of . . . personal drives?" BGE3: "most of the conscious thinking of a philosopher is secretly guided and forced into determinate channels by his instincts. Behind all logic . . . stand . . . physiological demands for the preservation of a determinate kind of life." See also D539, BGE6 again, and WP423 [1888]. Besides arguing that viewpoints must always be interested, Nietzsche argues that if there were a disin-

through a willing. We see from this the 'space' these perspectives vary within. Although the spatial image—of seeing a thing from different distances and directions—is our inevitable first grip on the point,[13] we need to translate it into Nietzsche's alternative 'space' of wills. Seeing x 'from a different angle' is chiefly differently caring about x.

This bare and simple form of the argument can hardly persuade, however. Even if we agreed that we are such wills, why should willing power rule out the type of detachment needed for objectivity? It's easy to imagine ways a deeply self-interested person or drive could still 'step back' as needed to grasp objective facts. Grant that one's judgments of value might be compromised. Still, self-interest seems to allow (and even require) that one treat certain circumscribed matters 'of fact' in a detached or objective way, holding one's interests in temporary abeyance. Even a person who cares and worries about money more than anything else can still truly count the coins in his pocket. Besides, (we've seen that) Nietzsche thinks will to power our 'essence' in quite a loose sense, allowing that we often 'fall away' from it and fail to will power itself. Then why couldn't we deviate from it in that other way, too: into disinterestedness?

Sometimes Nietzsche himself allows that we can. His wavering on this issue, his willingness to state his opposition to truth while either allowing for detachment or not, is evident in BGE6. He begins by saying that it's "the basic drives of human beings" that guide or produce a philosopher's claims and not some "drive to knowledge". But he continues, "Of course, among scholars who are genuinely scientific human beings, . . . there may really be something like a knowledge drive, some small, independent clockwork that, once well wound, works on bravely *without* all the rest of the scholar's drives essentially taking part." Elsewhere he allows that this detachment can achieve the truth and knowledge it thus purely pursues.[14]

It's important that this allowance, when Nietzsche is willing to make it, grants the possibility of truth only for insignificant matters, which lie apart (and serve to distract) from the life issues with which we're humanly concerned. Because philosophy deals with the latter, it's inelim-

---

terested viewpoint, it would also be disinterested about truth; so HH/II/98: *"for a purely knowing being [Wesen] knowledge would be a matter of indifference."*

13. The spatial image is developed well by Magnus 1988a, 152f.; see, too, Clark 1990, 145ff.

14. So P&Tp19 [1872–73] allows knowledge of quantity, though not of quality (so that the forms of intuition are excused, and only concepts are accused of distorting): "Only [while] *calculating* and only in the form of space, does the human being have absolute knowledge; i.e. the last borders of all that is knowable are *quantities;* he *understands* no quality, but only a quantity." KSA/9/11[65] [1881] says that the 'impersonal', i.e., the weakly personal, can be useful in some branches of knowledge, e.g., mathematics.

inably perspectival; science can carve out a space for objectivity only by avoiding the field of those human concerns, hence only at the sacrifice of relevance. So Nietzsche concedes the possibility of truth only when he has that second attack, on its value, in reserve.[15]

Even so, this allowance is a minority move in him; he mainly denies that even this scientific 'clockwork' can be fully objective. His preponderant view is that science's claims are still 'mere perspectives', in a way that precludes their being true. The argument that most convinces him here is the one that deconstruction so much acclaims: the argument from language, what we might call 'conceptual relativism'.[16] As he puts it, *"we cease to think when we will to do so without the constraint of language. . . . Rational thought is an interpreting according to a schema that we cannot throw off"* [WP522: 1886–87].

This argument appears in a simple form in the early TL [1873] (and the notebooks of this period), where it's so often cited by deconstructionists.[17] It occurs there as part of a broader attack. Truth as correspondence is impossible, because reality can be 'viewed' by the subject only through a 'representation' [*Vorstellung*], a stand-in for the object, in the subject. But the translation into this other realm inevitably changes and distorts. Nietzsche lists a series of steps by which this transformation proceeds: the object becomes (is grasped through) in turn a nerve stimulus, an image, a name, a concept. Each is a 'metaphor' that warps it further. In these earlier steps, we've already gone wrong even before we carve things up with our concepts.[18]

15. BGE10 allows that a will to truth could be at work in "single and rare cases", but that "this is nihilism and sign of a despairing, deathly tired soul". BGE207 says that the scientist, the "objective human being", has "lost seriousness [*Ernst*] for himself". P&Tp13 [1872–73] speaks of "the unfettered knowledge drive . . . which *judges* ever more according to the degree of sureness, and seeks ever smaller objects. . . . [T]he *small* should also be eternal, *because it is knowable.*"

16. Schacht (1983, 61) states this as a dependence on "domains of discourse", as "D-relativity". Breazeale 1990, xxx: "one of the most remarkable and significant features of Nietzsche's theory of knowledge is his grasp of the transcendental function of semantic unities and syntactical categories, their constitutive contributions to human understanding and the world we would understand."

17. De Man 1979, 110; Derrida 1982, 178.

18. Most abstractly, TL [P&Tp86: 1873]: "it seems to me that the correct perception [*Perception*]—which would mean the adequate expression of an object in the subject—is a contradictory impossibility [*Unding*]: for between two absolutely different spheres, as between subject and object, there is no causality, no correctness, no expression". And earlier in the essay, P&Tpp82–83 [1873]: "To begin with, a nerve stimulus is carried over into a picture! first metaphor. The picture, again, is imitated in a sound! Second metaphor. And each time a complete overleaping of one sphere, into the middle of a wholly other and new [one]. . . . We believe that we know something about the things themselves when we speak of trees, colors, snow, and flowers; and yet we possess nothing but metaphors for things, which correspond not at all to the original entities [*Wesenheiten*]." Cf. Clark's argument (1990, 77ff.) that "Nietzsche does not base his denial of truth in TL on an insight concerning language".

In later years, Nietzsche continues to find such a layering of biases and distortions, occurring 'before' or 'beneath' any way we consciously ('personally') view a thing.[19] But now he reinterprets these steps in the power ontology's terms: each is an 'appropriation' of the object by one of the many 'prepersonal' wills to power that constitute each of us. Our personality and consciousness are built on a substructure of archaic wills, the living remnants of our society's and species' past. Thus sensation is the work of a primitive will embodied in our human sense organs, whereas our logic and language express the wills of ancestral societies.[20] So even if that scientist could manage to 'still' or 'suspend' all his personal interests, these unconscious biases will still shape all that he sees and says. Above all, in order to think, he needs words, which always express such interests, whether or not he (consciously) 'means' them as he speaks. Language is a sedimentation of biases.[21]

This interesting story is still far from a proof. How can Nietzsche show us that words always express interests and always distort? His commonest strategy is to show it in individual cases, and his imagination in finding, and power in conveying, such biasing interests even where they're least expected must carry considerable weight.[22] It may even be easy to feel that by following his example we could go on ourselves to uncover such biases in any concepts he hasn't addressed. But besides thus detailing cases, he also has one favorite general argument how concepts do, and why they must, distort: by their very generality of application (which is what distinguishes them from names), they group as 'equal' [gleich] things that aren't really so.

This argument, too, takes an early form: "every word at once becomes a concept, if it serves not as reminder for the one-time, quite individual ur-experience to which it owes its arising, but must also fit countless, more or less similar [ähnliche]—i.e., strictly speaking never equal and quite unequal—cases. Every concept arises from the setting equal of the not equal" [TL/P&Tp83: 1873]. It's our interests that impose this distortion: they need the world to be calculable, so they frame our

19. As Schrift (1990, 132) points out, the same sequence is reviewed in BGE268 and WP506 [1884].

20. GS57: "You still carry about with you the assessments of things that have their origin in the passions and loves of former centuries!" BGE20: "the spell of determinate grammatical functions is ultimately the spell of *physiological* value judgments and race conditions."

21. Nietzsche partly shares/takes this overall argument from (Kant but especially) Schopenhauer; there it is already applied both to preconceptual 'sensation' and to concepts (the categories, especially causation). One of Nietzsche's most striking developments is his far wider (and more psychologically subtle) diagnosis of the *ways* concepts are ideal/perspectival; rather than harping on time, space, and causality, as Schopenhauer did, he finds complex particular interests—human but also cultural—injecting particular values into concepts.

22. For example, see how BGE14 and 22 diagnose a plebeian instinct at work in physics, showing it 'bad interpretation'.

words to name things (and types of things) that can be counted, as well as counted on to last (to be equal or identical to themselves through time).[23] We need thus simplified conceptions of things to work effectively on them.

Nietzsche eventually gives this pragmatic story a metaphysical basis or supplement: this making equal is really just the primal effort of will, to grow by incorporating the other: "All thinking, judging, observing as *comparison* [*Vergleichen*], has as its presupposition a *'setting equal'*, still earlier a *'making equal'*. This making equal is the same as the incorporation of appropriated material in the amoeba" [WP501: 1886–87].[24] Our classifications aren't just a means to better dealing with things, they're intrinsically a mastering of those things, an assimilating of them to our past experience, hence to ourselves.

Why must these 'makings equal' always be wrong? Why can't some things be 'equal' in (enough of) the sense our concepts make them so? With this, it seems, we arrive at the limits of the entire subjective line of argument, where it must always fall back on claims about the object. Despite Nietzsche's greater stress on the subjective attack, it can never make as strong a point as the objective, as arguing the (intended) object of knowledge to be unknowable. Whereas the latter shows (if it works) that our beliefs are false, the former only weakens our confidence in their truth. It shows that our motives for believing what we do are epistemologically weak or useless: we're really aiming at different things than truth, so how can we be justified in claiming to have hit it?

But as I've said, Nietzsche is very seldom satisfied with this weaker form of skepsis, this doubt that attacks not the truth of our beliefs but whether we can adequately support or defend them. He says not that our beliefs might be false, but that they are.[25] Yet with the subjective point, he can never close the chance that we've stumbled on the truth about things despite our deeply corrupted (non-truth-seeking) motives. Given that our concepts divide up the world with a view to assorted interests, and not to truth, their divisions might still happen to match the world's true types. Even if truth isn't what we're hunting, it might still be what

23. P&Tp51 [1872–73]: "All the knowledge that advances us is an *identifying of the not-equal*, of the similar, i.e. is essentially illogical." This point persists later on; so WP515 [1888]: "only when we see things coarsely and made equal do they become calculable and manageable for us". See also WP521 [1887].

24. WP511 [1885–86]: "the spirit *wills* equality, i.e. to subsume a sense impression into an existing series: just as the body *assimilates* the inorganic. . . . [T]*he will to equality is the will to power*. — [T]he belief that something is thus and thus, the essence of *judgment*, is the consequence of a will that as much as possible *should* be equal." See also WP499 [1885]. There are already suggestions of this in the early notes: TL [P&Tp88: 1873] speaks of "That drive to metaphor forming, that fundamental human drive"; see Breazeale 1990, xxxi n27. When Nietzsche sees this as the real root to our 'making equal', he views practical considerations as checking rather than producing it; see WP510 [1886–87].

25. Cf. Clark 1990, 91.

we hit. To close this possibility, Nietzsche inevitably needs to say something about the (intended) object of knowledge.[26]

Thus the subjective attack on 'making equal' has to fall back on claims about the object: things are never equal, so any way we count them so must be false. Our concepts invariably distort, because there are no real likenesses, no real types.[27] With this we return to the cluster of points reviewed in § 4.1.1, each of which gives a part of Nietzsche's reason for denying that things are ever equal. The continuum argument calls attention to the microscopic (indefinitely small) differences it presumes there will always be between two things. The context point makes these things' identities depend on their situations, which Nietzsche expects to be macroscopically dissimilar. But this also reintroduces all of the problems we saw with this objective line, at the end of § 4.1.1.

Even apart from this way that the subjective argument leans back on the objective, it looks suspect because it seems itself to involve certain claims about reality; most broadly, that these wills or perspectives—with all those features that are supposed to bar them from truth—themselves belong to the inventory of the world. This argument presumes that the 'subject'—that is, the will that tries to know—is itself something real and something that can be known. Hence the argument suffers in its own right from the problems at the end of § 4.1.1. First, its own ontological presumptions seem to contradict the skeptical argument they belong to: How is it that *these* (Nietzsche's) truths about things aren't undermined by the distorting work of his interests?[28] Second, these presumptions are again apt targets for the Cartesian doubts. Why should we believe their claim that the would-be knower is essentially a will to power, a system of drives?

4.2 Against truth's value

I have raised a number of doubts about Nietzsche's arguments for the impossibility of truth. But we've seen that he keeps in reserve a different kind of attack: if, or so far as, truth is possible and achievable, it may not be worth our pursuit. It's not in our interest to have it or even to pursue

26. The boundary between these arguments is often concealed in the expressions Nietzsche uses, as when he speaks of our concepts as 'simplifying' the world for pragmatic reasons: he means both a point about the subject (it aims at simplicity) and one about the object (nothing is so simple). WP536 [1888]: "Everything that is simple is merely imaginary, is not 'true'. But whatever is real, whatever is true, is neither one nor even reducible to one."

27. P&Tp51 [1872–73]: "The *overlooking* of individuals gives us the concept and with this our knowledge begins: in *categorizing*, in the setting up of *kinds*. But the essence of things does not correspond to this". See n.52.

28. Cf. Taylor (1986, 94) on the incoherence of the 'Nietzschean' program in Foucault: "The idea of a manufactured or imposed 'truth' inescapably slips the word in inverted commas, and opens the space of a truth-outside-quotes, the kind of truth, for instance, which the sentences unmasking power manifest, . . . (a paradox)."

it. Like the doubts against truth's possibility, this, too, struck him early on; for example, it's expressed in the attack on 'Socratism' in *The Birth of Tragedy* and in the complaints against history in *Untimely Meditations*.[29] But the point comes into special prominence in *Beyond Good and Evil*. So BGE4: "The falseness of a judgment is for us still not an objection against [it]. . . . The question is, how far it is life-promoting, life-preserving, species-preserving, perhaps even species-breeding. And we are basically inclined to claim that the falsest judgments . . . are the most indispensable for us".[30] It's these indispensable falsehoods that we have always called true: our 'truths' aren't true, but helpful. (Oddly, it's such remarks that both encourage and disprove the suggestion that Nietzsche holds a pragmatic theory of truth—that is, that he means by 'true' what's useful instead of what corresponds.[31])

29. BT18 already speaks of the use of illusion: "It is an eternal phenomenon: the greedy will always finds a means, by an illusion spread over things, to hold its creatures firm in life, and to compel them to live on." UM/II/1: "Forgetting belongs to all acting". Breazeale (1990, xxxiv) says that (early) Nietzsche "wished to find out what knowledge *is* primarily in order to find out what it is *worth*".

30. BGE34: "It is no more than a moral prejudice, that truth is more valuable than appearance; it is even the worst proved assumption there is in the world. One should admit at least this much: there would be no life at all if not on the basis of perspectival assessments and appearances". In fact, Nietzsche seems to think this his more distinctive claim, judging from the way the opening of BGE stresses the question of truth's value. And see GM/III/24: "The will to truth needs a critique—let us determine our own task—the value of truth must for once be experimentally *called into question*".

31. The pragmatic reading is associated with Danto (1965, 80), who qualifies it, however: "Although [Nietzsche] had developed a pragmatic theory of truth, he often spoke in an idiom more congenial to the *Correspondence* Theory of Truth which he was trying, not always and perhaps not ever in the awareness that he was doing so, to overcome." But that latter idiom seems far more common. Indeed, many of the passages one initially hears in favor of the pragmatic reading turn out on inspection to say merely that things either are or should be *taken* for true on pragmatic grounds, not that those grounds give the analysis of truth (this is still correspondence). He's finding, and sometimes even recommending, a certain *mistake* in what we *believe* to be true. WP487 [1886–87]: "But that a belief, however necessary it may be for the preservation of a being [*Wesen*], has nothing to do with truth, one knows e.g. from this, that we must believe in time, space, and movement, without feeling compelled [to take them as] absolute". See also GS265, BGE11, WP483 [1885], WP507 [1887], WP455 [1888]. Nehamas (1985, 53) argues so against Danto, and Westphal (1984, 351–52) similarly against Wilcox. And see n.103 in this chapter. When Nietzsche does use 'truth' otherwise, it can often be heard as ironic shorthand (sometimes flagged by quotes) for 'what has always passed for truth'. WP493 [1885]: *"Truth is the kind of error* without which a determinate kind of living creature [*Wesen*] could not live." And WP584 [1888]: "The 'criterion of truth' was in fact merely the *biological usefulness of such a system of fundamental falsification;* and since a species of animal knows of nothing more important than to preserve itself, one might in fact speak here of 'truth'." As we'll see in § 4.3, Nietzsche's 'inconsistency' here reflects his readiness to use the term with any of the several senses—or in any of the several contexts—it has historically been appropriate in.

Nietzsche's most common way of denying truth's value is different from what we expect. Instead of dwelling on the harmful effects of having or pursuing the truth, he mainly attacks the psychological source of this project, its 'genealogy'. He diagnoses the theorist's motives for wanting the truth and finds these to be 'bad', unattractive or shameful. The will to truth manifests a reactive and unhealthy form of the will to power.

Why does the theorist (typically) pursue truth? He needs that detachment or objectivity, that stilling or forgetting of his drives; he needs it because he can't (successfully) enact these drives themselves, directly. He watches and talks about life because he's frustrated in his efforts to live it straightforwardly. Who else, after all, would choose so indirect and 'at-second-hand' a route, and a life? Such a person suffers from these frustrated drives and seeks the rest and stability of detachment as an escape from their unsatisfiable demands, indeed, even as a form of revenge against those drives. Moreover, the effort to conform one's beliefs to an external reality is a way of evading the responsibility for choosing and creating one's beliefs oneself. So WP585 [1887] asks "what kind of human being" mistrusts and disvalues becoming and seeks an unchanging, uncontradictory "true world", and answers, "An unproductive, *suffering kind*, a kind weary of life. . . . 'Will to *truth*'— *as the impotence of the will to create''.* [32]

We probably distrust such a 'psychologistic' attack on truth and would answer with something Nietzsche himself says elsewhere: "About the knowledge of truth what matters is that one *has* it, and not from what impulse one sought it or by what route one found it" [HH/I/225]. We value its possession apart from its motives. Even if we've come to this state or condition by a misguided or unsavory route, it's still a good place to be. We value it, presumably, as a fine or as a useful thing, as a thing that is good now and in itself or good for what it can bring. Setting aside for the moment the question of truth's intrinsic worth, we turn to Nietzsche's argument that (pursuing) it has harmful effects.

---

32. P&Tp7 [1872–73]: "The measureless, unselective knowledge drive, with its historical background, is a sign that life has become old." See how TL [1873] argues that all reflection or cleverness is a device adopted by wills unable to act directly; intellect evolves among the creatures too weak in claws, etc., to otherwise survive; it therefore involves simulation. GS344: "'Will to truth'—that might be a concealed will to death." BGE229: "every deep and basic grasp is an assault, a willing to hurt the basic will of the spirit, which unceasingly wills for the apparent and superficial— in every willing to know there is a drop of cruelty." WP608 [1886–87]: "'Wisdom' as the attempt to get *away* from perspectival assessments (i.e., from the 'will to power') [is] a life-opposing [*lebensfeindliches*] and dissolving principle, a symptom as among the Indians etc. of the *weakening* of the appropriating force." WP444 [1888] asks whether "a tendency toward such *generality* is not already a *symptom of decadence; objectivity* as *disintegration of the will* (to be *able* to stand so *distant*)". See also BGE253, GM/III/25. Cf. Gemes 1992, 51.

Part of his point here is something we've just seen: we need to believe certain untruths—that is, those falsifying 'categories', the concepts and logical rules that allow our simplest physical copings with our environment. We must organize our experience as being of objects that last and that fall into various types—that is, objects that are equal through time and to one another. To attempt persistently to view one's surroundings as an unstructured chaos of becoming, which it actually is, would be suicidal. We're able to act and set a course for ourselves in the world only by structuring it some way, but this is always a distortion of reality, which is inherently structureless.[33] Moreover, concurrently, we depend on a false self-conception: the notion of oneself as a single and simple ego or self, who will abide or persist through the actions or projects one undertakes. Absent this illusion, such projects would never be adopted or sustained.[34]

This argument has an obvious weakness or limitation, however: it seems only to rule out the effort to carry this truth of becoming over into all one's daily life. It seems one might still, in occasional but always-reenactable episodes, see and think this truth about things without injury. Why should we be surprised or worried by an inability to grasp this truth constantly? A physicist needn't wish to bring his subatomic analyses of matter to bear in all his handlings of things, nor a physician his knowledge of flesh/bone/blood into his relations to spouse or child. Why mightn't Nietzsche's different truth about the world also be useful, or at least not harmful, as long as it is grasped episodically, in speculative moments?

This seems to fit with Nietzsche's stress on the value of 'forgetting', which we easily hear as a 'voluntary' state, revokable at will. We hear it, that is, on the model of Plato's (and Aristotle's) distinction between having and using knowledge, between knowing in its potential and actual forms.[35] Thus indeed in UM it seems one can wield forgetting as a tool, while still enjoying moments of truth, which direct that forgetting. So, too, in HH/I/P/1 Nietzsche describes how he himself "knowingly-willfully closed my eyes" and adopted certain temporary illusions; he stresses "how much cunning in self-preservation, how much reason and higher safeguarding, is contained in such self-deception".[36]

33. BGE4, quoted above, goes on to make such points: "without accepting the fictions of logic, without measuring reality against the purely invented world of the unconditional and self-equal, without a continual falsification of the world through numbers, human beings could not live". See also BGE11 and GS111, 121.

34. Already in UM/II/1: "Think of . . . a human being who did not possess the force to forget, and who was condemned to see everywhere a becoming: such a one no longer believes in his own being, no longer believes in himself . . . : like the true [rechte] student of Heraclitus, he will in the end hardly dare to raise his finger."

35. Cf. the Theaetetus's image of the aviary. For Aristotle see, e.g., DA 412a22.

36. See how GS/P/2 presents the philosopher as experimenting with sickness, "as a traveler does, who resolves to wake up at a determined hour and then calmly

But for the most part, Nietzsche seems not to think that the truth is so easily 'stored': we need (and are naturally liable to) a more inured and irredeemable way of forgetting it.[37] Indeed, it's not just that we need to forget that truth of becoming in our daily doings, but we need to believe falsehoods—perhaps a more difficult thing to practice in that 'voluntary' way. Moreover, we need to believe false things not just about those abstract, 'categorial' matters mentioned before but even about the detailed contents of our experience. To live (or live well), we have to embrace illusions about our own identities, our pasts and our projects, and about those of the persons we deal with.[38]

Perhaps the crux for Nietzsche here is his conviction that motivation is corrupted by becoming conscious: the self-knower, bringing his own drives and intentions up into consciousness, robs them of their natural momentum or vitality, in the familiar way we know behavior can be vitiated by being overly 'self-conscious'.[39] Our drives or guiding wills must show a mask to consciousness, a false face of official-but-illusory motives and character traits; only this way can they keep their healthy obscurity or unreflectedness. HH/I/82: "As the bones, flesh, intestines and blood vessels are enclosed in a skin, which makes the sight of a human being bearable, so the agitations and passions of the soul are covered up by vanity: it is the skin of the soul."[40]

Moreover, it's not just that what happens to be true is harmful, but it's harmful *as* the truth. That is, even the bare logical structure of truth imparts a reactive and damaging aspect to the project and possession of it. The goal of truth is a certain passive state: to 'mirror', or correspond to, how things already are, and not to make them a particular way. Instead of creating one's own viewpoint, one has it prescribed from outside. (So, too, the search for 'objective values' is an abdication of

---

abandons himself to sleep". HH/I/154 says of the Greeks: "When their understanding speaks, how bitter and cruel life appears! They do not deceive themselves, but they deliberately play about life with lies."

37. See how D126 touches this point: "That there is a forgetting, is still not proven; what we know is only that the remembering-again does not stand in our power. We have provisionally set into this gap in our power that word 'forgetting', as if it were one more capacity in the register."

38. WP609 [1884]: "It is necessary for you to grasp, that without this kind of ignorance life itself would be impossible, that it is a condition under which alone the living [thing] preserves and develops itself". WP492 [1885]: "all self-reflection of the spirit has its dangers, in that it could be useful and important for one's activity, to interpret oneself falsely."

39. WP440 [1888]: "All becoming-conscious expresses a discomfort of the organism: something new must be attempted, nothing is quite right for it, there is trouble, tension, overstimulation—becoming-conscious *is* all this— Genius lies in instinct; goodness too. One only acts perfectly, so far as one acts instinctively." See also § 3.5.1, esp. nn.117–18.

40. See also HH/I/36, GS8.

one's responsibility to create one's own values; one has them otherwise determined.) To renounce all that is idiosyncratically one's own, to better allow the status quo to appear in oneself, stifles precisely what we most ought to cultivate. So A20 speaks of "an all-too-great 'objectivity' (that means weakening of the individual interest, the loss of a center of gravity, of 'egoism')".

This broad argument—that pursuing or having truth is harmful—is at least more clearly relevant to our estimation of truth than was Nietzsche's more prominent attack over motives. Yet it's still far from convincing enough to make us stop valuing truth. In part because it's still so abstract, it leaves us too many glimpses of ways these deleterious effects of truth might be avoided or outweighed. He still hasn't shown that insight into the world and oneself can't be insulated from that motivational core he claims it corrupts. Or such insight might bring benefits outweighing this rather obscure damage he claims it does. And doesn't his account of this damage rest on weakly supported empirical-psychological claims? Doesn't it rest besides on a conception of our proper interests—in power, in individuality—with which we might well disagree?

Moreover, this argument is subject to a charge of self-contradiction, related to the ones we considered in § 4.1. This attack on the value of truth seems to presume itself to be a higher-level truth, which it *is* of value, at least to us theorists, to hear: it helps us to avoid the harmful effects of pursuing truth elsewhere or more generally. Here again, it's not just the bare claim that 'truth is harmful' that seems subject to this difficulty; it's also all those grounds Nietzsche gives us for accepting this claim, in particular his psychoanalyses of various types of knowers, and the value standards by which he judges their cases. Aren't all of these implicitly treated as truths that it's valuable and improving for to us to hear?

Thus we find, in this first survey of Nietzsche's two main arguments against truth—against its possibility and its value—grounds for dissatisfaction and puzzlement. We have reason to hope and seek from him a more convincing account of truth, and one more consistent with his own grounds for it.

4.3   The genealogy of the will to truth

Our discussion so far has been, in a certain way, naive. We've failed to take adequate account of what truth really is for the power ontology. When we do, we discover how our approach needs redirection.

Truth is the goal of a particular will or drive, which Nietzsche so often calls 'the will to truth'.[41] This drive has that temporal spread we

41. He saw things this way from very early on; throughout the notebooks excerpted in P&T, his focus is on the 'knowledge drive' [*Erkenntnistrieb*]. We should keep in mind that with this drive, too, there's no 'doer behind the doing', so that our

saw typifies will to power. So, to begin with, the will to truth is a historical process that projects an 'evolving' conception of truth as its goal. Thus Nietzsche doesn't use the word for a single and settled notion. It has for him a historical resonance and can refer to (the goal of) any or all of the different phases in a long development. More radically, these senses are not just sequential but are 'layered into' any present, for reasons we will shortly see. So even right now, truth has multiple aspects, some given to it by its past, others by anticipations of its future, just as we saw (§ 1.4) in the case of the concept or practice of punishment (as Nietzsche treats this in GM/II).

This means that we can't expect any simple or single definition for 'truth'; we're after a more elaborate 'analysis' than philosophers are accustomed to give. This is why, I argue, Nietzsche both rejects and embraces (the will to) truth: he distinguishes different such aspects, or different historical (and psychological) phases or roles. This shows the importance of detailing his genealogy for truth.

Whereas Plato makes reason an autonomous agent with origins that are vague because divine, Nietzsche tries to explain it naturalistically, as a construction from our drives. He has an elaborate and interesting story to tell about the formation and development of the will to truth (or rather, we can piece such a story together from his splintered accounts of the topic and from his parallel handlings of other phenomena).

Macroscopically, this story runs at a cultural or societal level, describing (and predicting) a slow historical shift. Here the will to truth occurs less as a drive in individuals than in or as certain institutionalized practices—the language, theoretical disciplines—in which whole generations of individuals are trained. These practices gradually shift in how they predominantly will truth. Yet, by the nature of practices, past forms of this will aren't left fully behind but are preserved as 'strata' in what's currently done, as, for example, our words and even our grammar are crystallized remnants of past ways of willing truth. Individuals take on this complexly stratified, multivalent will to truth when they take on those practices: that will takes root in them as a drive in competition with their other drives. So it takes a life in this psychic arena, besides that social one. Thus Nietzsche's story runs 'microscopically', too, describing the ways this will to truth most typically develops in individual psyches (i.e., drive structures); he offers us psychobiography as well as history.

At both levels, this story has the same overall plot we've traced before; truth has a common sort of 'temporal logic'. Nietzsche tends to think of a (successful) will as passing through three main phases: its distinctive activity begins in subjugation to other forces, then achieves a

---

real topic is a certain type of willful activity, not an agent or faculty to which this activity is due. Indeed, the absence of a doer forces us to rethink the nature of the activity: "'Thinking,' as the epistemologists posit it, simply does not occur" [WP477: 1887–88].

reactive independence by opposing those forces, and then matures into an active willing of its own ends. These phases correspond roughly to the "three metamorphoses of the spirit" described in TSZ/I/1: the camel "that would bear much", the lion that "wills to struggle for victory against the great dragon", and the child who "wills *his* will". Nietzsche expects (hopes for) a similar evolution in the practices basic to our culture: these were first shaped under the dominion of quite different practices/values (the early masters'), then successfully asserted themselves in a slave revolt against these old rulers, and have now the potential to develop themselves more positively or actively. We find these same three phases in the will to truth, which is indeed a decisive strand in that overall cultural sequence. Thus Nietzsche's railings against 'truth' are directed against only the reactive form the current will toward it takes; here, too, he hopes the practice will grow into healthy maturity.

A doubt arises, however. Mightn't this will to truth play a more culpable role? Perhaps it's inseparable from the reactive stage of that process, so that Nietzsche's hope is precisely that we'll leave it behind. This is one way of posing the main issue of this chapter, and indeed of this book. I try to show that in fact he views the activity of thinking or reasoning, with its goal of truth, as not intrinsically reactive. He thinks it bears the potential for a healthy and active development and, as such, even gives it pride of place in human life, much as the line of philosophers before him did: his ideal life is once again the philosopher's life. More precisely, he values truth so much in his own maturity, because the story he tells about that will has a history itself; it gets different endings at different times in Nietzsche's life. In § 4.3.3 I quickly chart his development into his own mature view.

4.3.1   As a tool of the drives

The will to truth's ultimate ancestor or source is the intentional aspect of will to power itself: any will must have an implicit view of a goal and of surroundings as means or threats to it; only this way can it aim at that goal (see § 1.2 and § 3.4.1). So a primitive perspective belongs to each drive already. And Nietzsche often supposes that these implicit viewpoints already involve a 'believing' or 'thinking', so that he attributes to us bodily beliefs, beliefs embedded in our drives or instincts. So GS354: "the human being, like every living creature, thinks continually [*immerfort*], without knowing it".[42] Of course, this perspective inherent in any will is chiefly valuational: in each case, it 'interprets' beings as helps or hindrances to the drive it serves.

By a many-sided development, this aspect of any drive or will gets

---

42. Recall WP314 [1887–88]: "Our most sacred convictions, the unchangeable in regard to our supreme values, are *judgments of our muscles.*"

spun off as an 'organ' or 'instrument', separate from the drive but still subservient to it. Or, rather, it gets spun off not from the individual drive but from a 'ruling committee' of the organism's most powerful drives.[43] These delegate the task of 'viewing' the world to a single functionary. More precisely—because here again we're to avoid turning process into thing—they delegate this viewing to a certain new activity that now crowds in among those characterizing the drives themselves. I'll call this activity 'thinking' (using the term more narrowly than we've seen Nietzsche sometimes does).

From the start, this thinking is more than merely a tool of the drives. It's already itself a way of taking control over things. By seeing what can be done with them, by bringing into view their possible uses (or risks), this thinking organizes them into an environment it (and through it the organism) 'controls', even before that view is in any way acted on. Thinking already 'secures' things, by assimilating new experiences into its patterns. So GS355 says that what both "the people" and "we philosophers" want in knowledge, is "something that no longer disturbs us", "the reachieved feeling of security".[44] This way in which thinking is already a mastering can help to suit it for the independence it now gradually achieves.

This new activity increasingly wills to continue and develop itself, and so emerges as a drive in its own right.[45] (Presumably, it's some such process of specialization that spins off every new will in Nietzsche's psychobiology: every practice first takes shape as a subpattern of preexisting practices, a tactical step that then takes on a life of its own.) Yet this thinking practice's first independence remains incomplete: it still finds its identity and point in serving those primary drives and practices. The growth and development it wants is in becoming an ever-better servant; the truth it wants is as an ever-more-useful viewpoint. Hence it acts in

43. See here GS333's account of knowing as the result of "justice and a contract" among several different drives—a way of calming their struggle by finding all their viewpoints right; so knowing (*intellegere*) "is only a *certain relating of the drives toward one another.*"

44. Elsewhere Nietzsche stresses less defensive forms of mastery; see TSZ/II/12. HH/I/252 gives three reasons knowing 'is bound up with pleasure': "First and above all, because one thereby becomes conscious of one's force. . . . Second, because in the course of knowledge one goes beyond former representations and their advocates, and becomes victor or at least believes oneself to be. Third, because through a new [piece of] knowledge, however small, we become superior to *all* and feel ourselves as the only ones who here know correctly." WP423 [1888]: "The so-called *knowledge drive* is to be traced back to an *appropriation* and *subjugation drive*". WP455 [1888]: "the methodology of truth was *not* invented from motives of truth, but from *motives of power, of willing to be superior*".

45. WP504 [1886–87]: "*Consciousness* . . . at first most widely distant from the biological center of the individual: but a process that deepens and intensifies itself, and draws constantly nearer that center."

the interests not simply of itself, not simply of the drives, but of its own way of aiding the drives. It remains (in this way) *pragmatic*.

Either from the start or soon, this new practice takes on two decisive features: it becomes *conscious* and *linguistic*. Although that viewing intrinsic to any drive is preconscious and preverbal, the separated organ or activity is now an aware (explicit) speaking. Nietzsche (in GM/II especially) has an interesting story to tell about how these arise together; we can judge it by whether it helps at all to make this advent (of consciousness in particular) seem any less miraculous. (Of course, the step is already less dramatic to Nietzsche, because he finds intentionality already present in the stuff consciousness will appear in.)

He thinks this development was (if not initiated, then) accelerated by human beings' entry into social and (especially) city life. The sudden constraints this placed on behavior meant that the drives could no longer be allowed, or allow themselves, the free and direct enactment they had enjoyed. In these early societies, persons are punished, and with a cruelty Nietzsche makes vivid, if they forget or lose sight of the rules.[46] Under this great stress, the drives cede authority to that thinking organ, as what will remember the rules, or as what can keep (and so make) promises—that is, can commit itself to behave itself. So its 'thinking' is at first just referring to past and future, to rules and consequences, in a pause before acting. To play this role, those ruling drives appoint this new organ as acting captain, responsible for the interests of themselves, the passenger drives. It has authority to restrain them where necessary and to arrange for their safer expression.

This guiding viewpoint remembers the rules by becoming conscious, of those very rules above all.[47] These rules—which of course are not just the laws but all of a society's unwritten standards for comportment with others—are couched in the society's language: to grasp and follow them, the viewpoint must think its thoughts in the society's words, especially because much of this proper comportment is itself a matter of saying the right things. The societal person also needs consciousness and language, because he needs to be able to mark his needs and desires and communicate them to others. So GS354: "he *required*, as the most endangered animal, help, protection, his equals; he had to express his need, know how to make himself understandable—and for all of this he needed

---

46. GM/II/3: "With the help of such pictures and procedures one finally keeps five, six 'I will not' 's in memory, in relation to which one has given his *promise*, in order to live under the benefits of society—and really! with the help of this kind of memory one finally comes 'to reason'!"

47. GM/II/16 describes (ceding control to) consciousness as a dangerous experiment that was forced on human beings when they were pressed into a social existence with one another, and had to give up "their former leaders . . . , the regulating, unconscious and surely-leading drives—they were reduced . . . to their 'consciousness', their poorest and most mistaken organ!" See Schacht 1983, 291ff.

consciousness first, to 'know' himself what he lacked, to 'know' how he felt, to 'know' what he thought."

This means that, in ceding control to this conscious 'subject', those ruling drives employ a tool not wholly theirs, not faithful to their interests alone. The first and most pressing role of this new will is to 'look to the rules', to see that these are complied with. Its instinct is thus *reactive:* it takes its cue from 'outside', not just outside itself (from the drives) but outside the organism as a whole.

More seriously, with the language this subject speaks, the organism is infiltrated by societal forces, whose viewpoints are built into the words and grammar of that speech. Our concepts embody societal interests and perspectives, so that even our own desires get distorted, by being stated in the 'generic' terms of our language. *What* we think depends on the words we think with and on the meanings these words have in the social practice; describing and becoming conscious of our experience in these terms, we press it into society's molds or patterns.[48] In its early form, the will to truth, this thinking activity, remains unaware and uncritical of this aspect of its words; hence it is not just pragmatic but *conventionalist:* its truth is not just what helps but what conforms to tradition or authority.

However, we also mustn't overstate the threat this reactive and societal consciousness poses to the drives. At least in this early stage, they see that this organ is still too primitive an experiment, too unreliable, to be allowed unsupervised control. So GS11: "Out of consciousness stem countless mistakes that lead an animal or human to perish sooner than necessary"; we only survive at all because "the preserving association of the instincts" still "serve on the whole as a regulator", not ceding full authority to consciousness. And so WP524 [1887–88]: "It is *not* the director [*Leitung*], but an *organ of the director*''. Its reactive, even poisonous potential is thereby held in check.[49]

To apply this story to our chief concern, is this early thinking as yet a 'will to truth'? We've seen that its guiding aim is still to help the drives preserve and enhance themselves: ''*The utility of preservation, not* some abstract-theoretical need not to be deceived, stands as the motive behind

48. GS354 tells how consciousness arises so that the individual's thinking and feeling can be put into words and thereby communicated to others; as a result, consciousness expresses 'the perspective of the herd'; its viewpoint aims at common or herd utilities: "we 'know' (or believe or imagine) just as much as may be *useful* in the interests of the human herd, the species". (But see the qualification that follows.) See also BGE268.

49. See Nietzsche's many remarks on the 'impotence' of consciousness, on its 'purposes' as not the real causes of our actions; so he sometimes thinks of it not as 'acting captain', but as a mere figurehead, an ornamental wheel that turns nothing. GS113 discusses how the many different 'forces' that now comprise scientific thinking were originally 'poisons' and had to be separately developed.

the development of the organs of knowledge" [WP480: 1888].[50] This early thinking wants whatever view of its environment will let the drives operate most effectively. Or, as we saw, it wants whatever befits the rules and viewpoints of society. It wants these, and not (directly) the view of things as they are in themselves. So is it not yet a will to truth? Or, if it is such a will, is the pragmatic-conventionalist theory true for this first phase? Did 'true' then mean 'useful and proper'?[51]

The situation is already more complex. Although this early thinking is indeed deeply pragmatic and conventional, it already pursues a form of truth as correspondence, if only as a means to those ends, and within the scope of their projects. It takes on the goal of corresponding from both its pragmatic and its conventional roles.

First, although thinking can be of pragmatic service only by accepting certain 'categorial' or 'transcendental' lies (e.g., cause and effect, the equality of similars),[52] it still pursues an 'empirical' truth 'internal' to those presuppositions: what would be true if they were true. The false metaphysics is needed, because it sets up this 'internal' truth, which is itself so useful to have. So granted a general simplification and falsification of things (from a world of becoming to one of being), it 'is true' that certain plants are nourishing, others poisonous, and it's important to learn this truth. Granted parallel distortions about myself, it 'is true' that I am hungry and must answer this need; my organism must get this right, too. It's by securing just such 'empirical' truths that this early thinking serves the drives.

Second, although thinking begins in a deep allegiance to convention (to what *has* been thought), it still wants to 'get it right' both what those rules or conventions are and how they apply to the cases before it. Here, too, thinking is driven to pursue an 'internal' truth. Indeed, the very project of conformity and convention depends on the openness and truthfulness of its participants: they can align and meld themselves into a herd or collectivity only by each showing the others what it is and

50. See the important GS110, titled "Origin of Knowledge": "Over enormous stretches of time the intellect produced nothing but errors"; some of these were useful and were passed on "and finally became almost the basic human endowment, for example these: that there are enduring things; that there are equal things".

51. TL [P&Tp81: 1873]: "In a similarly restricted sense the human being also wills only the truth. He desires the agreeable, life-preserving consequences of truth; he is indifferent toward pure knowledge with no consequences, he is even hostilely inclined toward truths that are perhaps harmful and destructive."

52. Nietzsche inherits part of this point from Kant and Schopenhauer: time and space, and the categories—especially substance and cause—are not true of things-in-themselves. More distinctively his is the argument against equality or sameness. GS111: "Those . . . who did not know how to find often enough the 'equal' in regard to nourishment or . . . hostile animals, those who subsumed too slowly, who were too cautious in subsuming, had a lesser probability of survival than those who immediately guessed all similars as equals. But the prevailing tendency to treat

grasping what they are; they need accurate comparisons to copy one another successfully.[53]

In these ways, truth as correspondence is already on the scene, as a goal internal to these other projects. Yet so long as the will to truth serves them, it finds only an internal truth, which is really (transcendentally) false.

4.3.2   As ascetic opponent to the drives

Theoretical activity can change its own status. It can win a further degree of independence from the drives by setting itself up in opposition to them, as a practice or will that ignores or rather denies them. Instead of letting them dictate its goal, it now struggles to set its sights for itself.[54] Under the banner of this new goal, consciousness tries to wrest control of the organism away from the drives.[55]

When Nietzsche speaks of 'the will to truth', he usually has in mind this second phase: thinking now trying to view itself as an end in itself, by casting off the pragmatic and conventionalist criteria that had ruled it. It achieves autonomy, in its intent at any rate, because of course it still must struggle and compete with the drives. But now it articulates a new ideal or value, which it opposes to theirs. This ideal is expressed in a 'faith' [*Glaube*] GS344 attributes to science: " 'there is need for *nothing more* than truth, and in relation to it everything else has a value of the second rank'. . . . Thus—the faith in science . . . cannot have taken its origin from such a calculus of utility, but much more *in spite of* how

---

the similar as equal, an illogical tendency—since in itself there is nothing equal—first created all basis for logic." WP513 [1887]: "The inventive force that composed categories labored in the service of [our] needs, namely for security, for quick understanding on the basis of signs and sounds, for means of abbreviation: 'substance' 'subject' 'object' 'being' 'becoming' have nothing to do with metaphysical truths." See also WP503 [1884], WP507 [1887], WP480 [1888], WP515 [1888].

53. P&Tp27 [1872–73]: "The human being demands truth and accomplishes it in moral interchange with [other] human beings; on this rests all living together. One anticipates the severe consequences of reciprocal lying. From this arises *the duty of truth.*" See also P&Tpp34–35 [1872–73].

54. This shift is related to the movement of spiritualization, touched on earlier (§ 3.4.1); this is the way any drive's intentionality can become an end in itself, a self-referential diversion from the drive's straightforward enactment.

55. Nietzsche often takes Socrates to represent this step; so BT13p88: "While with all productive human beings instinct is indeed the creative-affirmative force, and consciousness behaves critically and dissuasively, with Socrates instinct becomes the critic, consciousness the creator—a true monstrosity per defectum." KSA/9/11[243] [1881]: "Reason is a support organ [*Hülfsorgan*] that slowly develops itself, that for enormous periods fortunately has *little* force to determine human beings, but works in the *service* of the organic drives, and emancipates itself slowly *to equal rights* with them—so that reason (belief and knowledge) fights with the drives, as itself a new drive—and late, very late [comes] *to preponderance.*" See also WP687 [1887].

the disutility and dangerousness of the 'will to truth', of 'truth at any price' is constantly proved to it.''[56]

It's important that in this new independence, truth becomes valuable in a certain spirit, from certain motives. As Nietzsche thinks typical of rebellion, this will is obsessed with opposing or negating what it struggles to free itself from.[57] Its main instinct is to deny and cast off the criterion of use, this emblem of its subjection, and it embraces truth (here at first) only as a ready alternative. Truth, so far a subordinate element in thinking's goal, is selected as something different from the drives, which can now be adopted as its own, raised as a standard in a war against these others; hence the passion for objectivity. In this spirit of opposition to the drives that had ruled it, the will to truth becomes something 'moral'; it expresses the 'ascetic ideal', a crucial aspect of its second phase.

Nietzsche supports this diagnosis by sketching the types of persons he thinks are most fitted for, or impelled toward, this rebellion: thinking is most able to assert itself against the drives where the latter are weak or where they're chaotic or where they're unactable and hence frustrated. These are the three chief species of (reactive) thinkers, the types Nietzsche most often diagnoses: the passionless, the sick, and the suppressed. Thinking's subtle and indirect way of mastering things, by explaining them, can (at first) satisfy only those cut off from power's more concrete forms.[58] Whereas Plato attributes the philosopher's ineptness to disinterest—the thinker could be a doer but prefers something finer—Nietzsche finds a rooted disability, at healthily harmonizing or enacting the drives. It's the sick or weak who turn aside from doing and embrace the project of truth. As typically adopted by those barred from these enjoyments of the drives, thinking now typically denies and fights the drives resentfully. So Nietzsche often speaks of the cruelty of this will to truth:

56. GS344 goes on to suggest that we understand science not as "the will *not to let oneself be deceived*", which would make of it "a long-range prudence, a precaution, a utility"—i.e., something still subordinate to other drives—but rather as "the will *not to deceive*", not even oneself.

57. Cf. TSZ/I/1's image of the lion.

58. Nietzsche on (1) the passionless: "Physiologically, too, science rests on the same [*gleichen*] ground as the ascetic ideal: a certain *poverty of life* is a presupposition of both—the affects become cool, the tempo slowed down" [GM/III/25]; "*objectivity as disintegration of the will* (*to be able* to stand so *far*) . . . this presupposes a great indifference against the strong drives" [WP444: 1888]; on (2) the sick: Socrates and his contemporaries needed reason because "no one was any longer master over himself, the instincts turned *against* one another. . . . When one has a need to make *reason* a tyrant, as Socrates did, the danger cannot be small that something other will make a tyrant" [TI/II/9–10]; on (3) the suppressed: philosophy expresses "an *unsatisfied* soul that perceives the tamed state as a torture" [WP461: 1888]. Cf. Plato at, e.g., *Rep.* 517d–18b, *Tht.* 173c–76a. We saw in § 2.2 that Nietzsche diagnoses Plato as of type (2): as needing an alternative to 'over-strong' drives; by contrast, he thinks (1) is our own typical flaw. See GS372.

how it wants to hurt the drives or instincts, by denying comforting illusions—that is, the illusions on which those drives depend (first of all, faith in the value of what they pursue).[59]

We should note how these points reveal, how (according to Nietzsche) this new will to truth doesn't reach full or genuine independence (autonomy) after all; it hasn't yet 'become what it is'. This will has, to be sure, cast off its service to the drives, so that its goal is no longer a 'pragmatic truth', that empirical or phenomenal truth useful to the drives. Similarly, it works to purge its reliance on tradition and convention. It now tries and claims to cleanse its truth goal of these (distorting and biasing) foreign influences and intrusions, to make truth its own end in itself. Its very motives and manner in thus rejecting the drives, however, warp and pervert its conception of truth in a different way. Its redefined truth, which it raises as a standard against those drives, bears the marks of its resentful, reactive rejection of them.[60]

Let's distinguish the three main elements in this new truth goal and note how they reflect this ascetic denial.

First, and centrally, truth is a correspondence to something else. But (I think Nietzsche thinks) we need to work to see this as surprising. Why should the rebellious thinking activity, this self-asserting linguistic consciousness, choose correspondence as its defining good? Granted that this will needs something to replace the goal of usefulness to the drives, there are other noninstrumental 'goods' than this mirroring that are available in viewing or reflecting on things. Why didn't it settle instead on one of these? Let's consider especially the alternative Nietzsche himself has mainly in mind: Why didn't (or doesn't) thinking aim at the view of things that most *beautifies* them, instead of at that which matches them as they are? Just as "the problem of science cannot be known on the ground of science", but rather "on the ground of *art*" [BT/ASC/2], so we can best grasp the motive or spirit of the will to truth by contrasting it with an *aesthetic* orientation, which is also feasible for thinking.[61]

Thinking-at-beauty can also free itself from pragmatic service to the drives. The artist's way of seeing and depicting the world needn't be any more practical than the theorist's: we recognize 'art for its own sake' as well as 'pure science'.[62] But (Nietzsche thinks) the artist, unlike the

59. See n.101.
60. TI/III/6: "To divide the world into a 'true' and an 'apparent' [world], whether in the Christian manner or in the manner of Kant . . . is only a suggestion of decadence—a symptom of *declining* life."
61. On the opposition between truth and beauty, WP812 [1888]: "The inartistic states: those of *objectivity*, of mirroring, of the suspended will"; WP822 [1888]: "Truth is ugly". See also GM/III/25. Cf. Heidegger 1979–87, 1:142ff.
62. Like truth, beauty has its roots in the pragmatic. WP804 [1887]: "To this extent the *beautiful* stands within the general category of the biological values of the useful, beneficent, life-enhancing: but in such a way that a host of stimuli that only distantly remind of and are tied to useful things and states, give us the feeling of the

scientist, is typically strong and healthy in his drives.[63] Although he prizes his art above these drives, he's glad when this art also pleases them; he bears no ill will toward them. He simply finds, in his creative acts, a way of channeling these drives to a much fuller form of personal growth and power than is involved in merely pleasing his drives. Indeed, because each artist aims to create beauty of his own, art's beauty goal is in special alignment with the essential end of power itself.

By contrast, the will to truth aims at correspondence: a passive mirroring of the world. In effect, the theorist tries simply to match his surroundings, not to act on or alter them in any way; such passivity is chosen, in the main, from incapacity.[64] The theorist wills not to create, not to impose anything peculiarly his own on that other-to-be-understood. Indeed, he wants to reflect reality so undistortingly that any other true consciousness of it would be just the same; he wants not a distinctive viewpoint but one generally or commonly available (and desirable). This amounts, the theorist might even proclaim, to a renunciation of self; his individuality is a bias to be suspended. In such ways, the goal of truth as correspondence is a reactive opposite to the artist's goal of beauty; it seems even at odds with the essential end of power itself. An eventual issue for us will be whether Nietzsche doesn't simply want the will to truth replaced (or overpowered) by this alternative, aesthetic will, whether he doesn't give up truth as a good, for beauty.

Second, it seems only slightly peripheral to this new concept of truth that the correspondence be achieved through *detachment*, by a stilling of the thinker's passions, emotions, and personal concerns. It's here that the will to truth's campaign against the drives shapes its new concept most directly. Not only are these drives not to be served or pleased, they're not even to be used in the effort at truth; they must indeed be canceled: they're so hated that they're denied even a supporting role. Once again, this stands in clearest contrast with the aesthetic-creative will, which (Nietzsche claims) involves 'intoxication' [*Rausch*]—that is, a heightening, an overstimulation of the senses and appetites. So WP800 [1888]: "artists should see nothing as it is, but fuller, simpler, stronger:

---

beautiful". WP815 [1888] shows how the artistic will uses and feeds on the passionate drives, rather than serving them; despite the artist's sensuality, he is "in fact a moderate, often even a chaste human being. His domineering instinct *wills* this of him"; see also WP814 [1887].

63. WP800 [1888]: "artists, if they are worth something, are strong (in body too), impetuous, forceful animals, sensual; without a certain overheating of the sexual system a Raphael is unthinkable". So WP812 [1888] says that what seem to be *morbid* conditions in the artist aren't such for one with his higher level of strength.

64. WP585 [1887]: "The *philosophical objective-look* can therefore be a sign of will- and force-poverty. For force organizes the nearer and nearest; the 'knowers', who will only *to establish* [*fest-stellen*] what is, are those who cannot settle [*festsetzen*] *how it should be*.''

to that end, their bodies must have a kind of eternal youth and spring, a kind of habitual intoxication."

Third, and still less centrally, yet also still typically, the new truth concept requires this detached mirroring to be a stable or persisting state. Those who want truth value it as something constant, in contrast with the shifting struggle of their drives. Hence truth is something that can be possessed: thinking tries to fix the world in beliefs or theories that can then be constantly present or available to the knower. Indeed, the very goal of correspondence itself involves a preserving and continuing of the understood object in the knower himself. Once again, all of this stands in sharp contrast with the aesthetic-creative urge, which essentially wants to change things as they are.

Not only does this thinking want stability in itself, it wants it in its object; it expects, it insists on finding, a certain sort of *true world:* one of lasting things, of beings instead of becomings.[65] Whereas we might take this to be not a part of the concept of truth at all (but rather a separate assumption about what happens to be 'out there' to be matched), Nietzsche thinks this expectation is a strong part of the force 'truth' has (so far) had, a usual, if implicit, criterion for something's being true. So, in the extreme case, Plato insists that reality could only be eternally unchanging. Nietzsche finds a similar temporal bias more subtly at work in the tradition's persistent discovery of substances, objects, and other such well-bounded things, indeed in those same 'categorial lies' we saw were required of thinking by its pragmatic service. It turns out that thinking's new phase is misled, by its reactive denial of the drives, to concur in some of the same lies and illusions imposed in the service it now casts off.

These three—correspondence, detachment, and stability—are the main elements in the new truth concept and the ways it reflects this will's campaign, in the soul and body of the thinker, to deny the drives. We've noted, however, that Nietzsche's 'genealogy' of the will proceeds not just at the psychic but at the social level. So we must go on to see how this new will to truth develops historically, in the institutions and practices of a society. Here again our main story will be how this will is initially put to use by other social forces and adapted to serve their purposes, and how it then gradually achieves a reactive (and so faulty) independence from them.

In § 4.3.1 we saw how the will to truth was first given social status— first institutionalized, as a virtue in a custom or practice—because of ways it thus serves very basic societal needs (needs of the group). So we saw that part of the very sense of 'truth' was initially 'what's accepted', the traditional or conventional: it was (and partly still is) settled almost

---

65. WP585 [1887]: "Contempt, hatred against everything that passes, changes, alters—from whence this valuing of the stable [*Bleibenden*]? Obviously the will to truth is here merely the demand for a *world of the stable.*"

by definition that the society's grounding beliefs and values are true. Hence inculcating the will to truth, teaching the value of truth, serves directly to bind the society together: allegiance is strengthened by a shared presumption that just these things, what we believe, are true and that foreign and competing customs and presumptions are ignorant and false. Moreover, the cohesion and efficiency of a society also depends on a certain 'truthfulness' in its members. They must mainly keep their promises to one another. And they must mainly be honest about their preferences, both to one another and to themselves; only so can they efficiently and stably adapt to, and fit, with one another. Yet this is an honesty that finds and reveals only simplified and herdlike aspects of each, what can be communicated and named with common words.[66] So 'truth' is here also (as part of its sense) 'what's shared', and the will to truth trained into members for the sake of this social need again aims askew from 'truth itself', from what it will maturely be, as it learns to cast off its service to these needs.

There's another way this will to truth is given an institutional status, one more crucial for its development. This lies not in its inculcation through all the society's members but precisely in its establishment as a 'specialization', pursued 'professionally' by a class or caste. Thinking is spun off as a separate organ in the society, just as happened in the psyche; it acquires a 'house' or 'vehicle' in a body of specialist practitioners, who transmit their discipline down through generations.

On the one hand, this 'housing' of the will to truth can help free it, in some obvious ways, from its pragmatic service. The thinker is relieved of the effort to procure his own food, to take a simple case; his thinking can float free from at least *these* practical problems. Moreover, this social support and recognition of the practice of thinking can also help free it from its dependence on reactive incentives to attract all its adherents. Some adopt the practice because they are born to it, or because of its professional rewards or social prestige, and not just because they're unfit for straightforwardly acting their drives. So thinking can acquire new practitioners, besides the sick and weak.

At the same time, this 'housing' of the will to truth also imposes new constraints on it, making it play just that role of the class or group it is assigned to, and play by the rules of that group's practice. Different societies 'house' the will to truth in very different such groups, with different social functions. We must simplify drastically here, by focusing (as Nietzsche himself mainly does) on Western, Judeo-Christian society and by falling back on the extremely schematic history for it that we've already sketched (in § 1.5.2 and § 2.5.2).

It seems natural that when society first finds a role for a class of 'thinkers', it should make use of the specific sickness of those typically

66. See again GS354 (and n.48).

inclined to the practice. So often, as in our society, the thinker is first employed as a minister to the sick and suffering, as a priest. Because of the stresses involved in the 'taming' of persons for social life, there are multitudes of sick and suffering. And because the thinker is sick and suffering himself, he's especially suited to comfort and sustain these sufferers and to redirect their resentment away from those better off. It was to play these roles, Nietzsche thinks, that a class of theorists was first tolerated and indeed cultivated. Truth grew up here, because the priest's main claim (the source of his nonphysical authority) was to possess the decisive truth.[67]

It's clear how playing this social role would reinforce all the reactive tendencies we found in the 'personal' will to truth. The thinker wants a true world not just to comfort himself but all those he ministers to as well. This purpose is reflected in the doctrine in which each new practitioner is trained: the elaborate account of God and his heaven, the slighting of earthly life by comparison. Such teachings tempt and corrupt even healthy beginners but strike a chord in the sick especially, and so are most developed and refined by them. This doctrine—the 'truth' of the priests—is in fact a lie, a 'holy lie', and is even known to be such by those who construct it. So, in its priestly form, the will to truth claims to have the truth, but hypocritically.[68] This choice of appearance reveals the priest as a (countertypically) sick artist: "Piety . . . would appear as the subtlest and last offspring of the *fear* of truth, as an artist's worship and drunkenness before the most consistent of all falsifications, as the will to the inversion of truth, to untruth at any price" [BGE59].

Thinking doesn't always have only the priest as its vehicle. Familiarly, an alternative emerges in the figure or role of the scientist, and here we follow some of the familiar Enlightenment story: Nietzsche agrees that a 'freeing' does occur here (though he thinks the scientist remains bound in other ways). Of course this new type and role are separated from the priest's only very gradually: Descartes and those after him still stand partly in the priestly role, as is most conspicuous in their proofs of God. But slowly the will to truth finds a vehicle that doesn't require it to pledge allegiance to the God illusion, and it is able to lift off its 'mask' of priest. It casts off its duty to the 'holy lie' and can, in this respect at least, pursue truth as correspondence more unreservedly, and less hypocritically. Now it begins to undermine and erode that edifice of

67. Nietzsche's main account of the priest as first incarnation of the will to truth is GM/III; e.g., /15: "We must count the ascetic priest as the predetermined savior, shepherd, and advocate of the sick herd: only thus can we understand his enormous historical mission." WP140 [1888]: "The *philosopher* as a further development of the *priestly* type". See also A12. WP139 [1888] describes the priest's way of claiming preeminence: "*Means: truth* exists. There is only one way of attaining it: to become a priest."

68. The holy lie is fashioned in "the most cold-blooded reflection" [WP142: 1888]; cf. also WP172 [1887].

theological-metaphysical suppositions, sedimented into thinking by the priests.[69]

In this new vehicle—which is less the empirical scientist than a certain sort of 'scientific philosopher', for Nietzsche—the will to truth frees itself by casting a critical eye over an ever wider field of its former assumptions. Its conclusions grow ever more skeptical and nihilist: nothing can be known, nothing even 'is'. It exposes more and more comforting lies, not only the priest's but also those deeper categorial lies, acquired in thinking's most primitive, pragmatic phase. GS110: "Thus knowledge became a piece of life itself, and hence a continually [*immerfort*] growing power—until finally knowledge collided with those primeval basic errors. . . . A thinker is now that being [*Wesen*] in whom the drive to truth and those life-preserving errors struggle their first struggle". The insistence on an unchanging 'true world', once even a part of thinking's concept of truth, is now cast off (while the goals of correspondence and detachment are retained). The objects around us are desubstantialized, first into swarmings of atoms, then more radically still; because belief in these objects is deposited in our senses, it turns out that our very eyes and hands tell us lies; because it's also deposited in our words and grammar, thinking learns to be suspicious of these.

Even more important, the scientist's objective eye finds no truth, either, in any of the values it focuses on: not in the priest's, not in society's, not even in those involved in the scientist's own drives. This new will to truth undermines faith in the worth of goals, just as much as of theories. So as this new will, this 'unrestricted knowledge drive', becomes dominant in a society, its saps away its cultural strength; its ever-firmer grip on our own society is a main element in our long slide or drive toward nihilism. Indeed, this withering effect is just what this new will deeply intends: it resents its former service so much that it wants to hurt and spite the social forces that have subjected it (and kept it from its truth), by exposing their founding lies.[70]

Nietzsche thinks this process has a logic that brings it to a certain culmination: eventually this will to truth turns its hypercritical eye back on itself, in a stage he took himself (in one of his aspects or phases) to epitomize. In particular, this will to truth now calls into question the value of truth itself. This step is partly encouraged by the increasingly obvious conflict between the will to truth and other personal and social

69. Nietzsche has doubts whether this independent science was reached by the Greeks: "In antiquity . . . even among [science's] most eager disciples, the striving for *virtue* stood first. . . . It is something new in history that knowledge wills to be more than a means" [GS123]. EH/D/2 calls the philosophers "*concealed* priests". GM/III/10: "the *ascetic priest* provided until the most recent time the repugnant and gloomy caterpillar form, in which alone philosophy could live and creep about".

70. P&Tp156 n.9 [1869–70]: "The goal of science is world-destruction." P&Tp46 [1872–73]: "Our natural science is heading for *ruin* [*Untergang*], in [pursuing] the goal of knowledge. Our historical education [is heading] for the death of every culture. It struggles against religions—and by the way destroys cultures."

values. But it also belongs to the 'logic' of this unleashed will that it should eventually turn its attention back on itself, to investigate its own nature and status, including its own conviction in the coherence and indeed highest value of the goal it pursues.[71] Shouldn't it include itself within the domain it explores? So GM/III/27: "And here I again touch on my problem, on our problem, my *unknown* friends (for I still *know* of no friend): what sense would *our* whole being have if not this, that in us that will to truth comes to consciousness of itself *as a problem?*'[72]

What does this will to truth, in Nietzsche incarnate, discover when it examines and evaluates itself? It discovers itself as a will, a species of will to power, but also a reactive and sick will. It discovers itself to be still 'ascetic', still guided by resentment against the drives, in all its aims and ambitions: its own love for the objective view is a hatred of their interests; its skeptical and nihilist lessons are ways of hurting and spiting the drives. So GM/III/24 argues that the denial and skepticism of 'free spirits' expresses "as much asceticism of virtue as any denial of sensuality (it is basically only a mode of this denial)".[73] The will to truth discovers, in the end, that there remains a deep kinship between scientist and priest, ultimately refuting that Enlightenment story's boast of independence. In these and other ways, the will to truth finds grounds for dissatisfaction with itself. Where will these critical insights take it?

4.3.3   In its active maturity

Saying what follows, in this Nietzschean genealogy of the will to truth, is the strategic crux of this book. When the scientific will to truth, in the person of Nietzsche himself, casts off all the categorial errors and hon-

71. HH/III/43 remarks on the paradoxical nature of this: the thinker, qua thinker, views everything as discussable and "is thus a man without [a sense of] duty", who questions even the duty of truth. "But is the consequence of this not that the thinker's machine will no longer work properly . . . ? Insofar as here the same element appears to be needed for *heating* [the machine], as is to be investigated by means of the machine." Cf. Foucault (1982, 219) on the difficulty the will to truth has in understanding itself.

72. Recall from GM/III/24: "The will to truth needs a critique—let us determine our own task—the value of truth must for once be experimentally *called into question*." And recall how BGE1 announces this problem: "Suppose we will truth: *why not rather* untruth? and uncertainty? even ignorance?" BT/ASC/2 says that BT's issue "was the *problem of science* itself—science for the first time grasped as problematic, as questionable."

73. On science's self-cruelty, BGE55 presents loss of God as a last form of religious sacrifice: "Did one not finally have to sacrifice whatever is comforting, holy, healing, all hope, all belief in hidden harmony, in future blisses and justices?" D/P/4: "we still feel ourselves akin to the German integrity and piety of millennia, even as its most questionable and last descendents, we immoralists, we godless ones of today—indeed, on a certain understanding, as its heirs, as the executors of its innermost will, a pessimistic will . . . which is not afraid to deny itself, because it denies with *pleasure!* In us there is accomplished—supposing you will a formula—the *self-sublimation* [*Selbstaufhebung*] *of morality.*"

estly understands and judges itself, how does this affect it? When it discovers that truth has no more intrinsic value than the ends of any other will or drive and that its reactivity may mean it has less (because taking truth as one's goal both expresses and furthers weakness), what lesson does it draw? (This is the decisive part of a more general puzzle: what Nietzsche hopes will come out of, or after, nihilism.) We can distinguish three plausible answers: (1) that this *cancels* or smothers the will to truth, so that persons 'erase' this desire from themselves once they've learned how it discredits itself; (2) that it *demotes* this will in the 'politics' (the drive structure) of the person, making it renounce the primacy or mastery it had claimed; or (3) that it *reforms* this will to truth, revising once again its conception of its end, and so fitting it at last for that role of dominance. I argue for the last.[74]

Nietzsche preaches, and thinks he achieves, a culminating development of the will to truth in which it comes at last to a healthy independence. Thinking now refashions its defining end of truth, to cleanse it of aspects laid into it reactively. This will thereby casts off its "mask" [BGE/P], its "gloomy caterpillar form" [GM/III/10]. But this change preserves enough of what's central to the traditional goal for its descendant to take the same name. The will to truth reorients itself; it's not canceled and replaced by something else, as in (1). Indeed, by overcoming its resentment, it now comes 'into its own', to its active maturity.[75]

Of course, this change in its intent affects in turn this will's bearing toward the (other) drives in the thinker's inner 'politics'; it now seeks and finds a different (less ruthless) place in the system of interests that make up the person. But this tempering doesn't mean, as in (2), that the will to truth becomes so tractable that it's now recaptured by the drives and returned to the status of a tool, as in its first phase. It retains its aggressive intent, *as* a will to power; it still wants to dominate the other drives but now sees this domination aright: not as lying in suppression or obliteration but in a certain way of using the drives, by collaborating with them. Nietzsche still wants the will to truth strong, indeed dominant, but not omnipotent or exclusive.[76]

74. Kaufmann (1974, 359) and Danto (1965, 191) argue whether Nietzsche 'still has faith in truth'; I side with Kaufmann. Schacht 1983, 95: "Nietzsche conceives of the possibility of a further, somewhat related but importantly different way of thinking of significantly greater epistemic import, which he considers to find exemplification in his own thought". Cf. Habermas 1990, 86: Nietzsche "renounces a renewed revision of the concept of reason and *bids farewell* to the dialectic of enlightenment." Clark (1990, 196ff.) claims the will to truth is retained but subordinated to a new ideal. Nietzsche's decision among these options aligns him (I suppose) with Heidegger and Gadamer, against Foucault and Derrida.

75. KSA/13/18[17] [1888] (a chapter title in a plan for "The Will to Power"): "The will to truth (first justified in the yes-value of life)".

76. D507: "I do not know why it should be wished that truth have sole mastery and omnipotence; it is enough for me that it have a *great power*."

My claim is that this *becomes* Nietzsche's principal view of these matters. Particularly in his earliest writings, but occasionally later as well, he describes this 'next stage' of the will to truth differently; he gives a different ending to his story about it. Before examining the mature position more carefully (in § 4.4 and § 4.5), I sketch the evolution of Nietzsche's endings, how what he wants to happen to this will changes. Given how personally he took this issue—he knew the strength of this will in himself and had an abiding worry about whether he wasn't pursuing truth at the expense (or to the detriment) of life[77]—this philosophical development reflects important shifts in his self-conception.

Early on, Nietzsche's verdict lies chiefly *against* the will to truth (though we'll see that even here, strong undercurrents favor it). Among the options given, his position is chiefly (2): he wants the will to truth subordinated to other drives (or social forces). This is a major theme in the early notes, especially those of 1872–73—many gathered by Breazeale in *Philosophy and Truth*. In those years, Nietzsche planned a book, to be called *The Philosopher*; his notes for it champion philosophy as what uses knowledge to 'restrain' [*bändigen*] the 'knowledge drive' [*Erkenntnisstrieb*]. That is, philosophy carries out that self-critique of the will to truth sketched in § 4.3.2, and so teaches that will to be 'selective'. *"The highest worth of philosophy shows itself here, where it concentrates the unrestricted knowledge drive and restrains it to unity"* [P&Tp9: 1872–73].[78] This is above all a cultural unity; Nietzsche's interest lies chiefly in the societal benefits of this step and not in its personal aspect. So another projected title for the book is *The Philosopher as Cultural Physician*.

In that period, Nietzsche was especially occupied with art as an alternative will or practice to which science—that inherently unrestricted knowledge drive—must be subordinated: "The *restraining of science* happens now *only* through *art*" [P&Tp12: 1872–73]. Following that lesson drawn by philosophers, the artists fashion certain saving illusions, which the scientific will is barred from examining.[79] Society learns to treat these illusions as more important than truth and as off-limits to that (debunking) will to truth. The scientist is prevented (in the best case, by his own trained aversion) from criticizing and disrupting these artistic-metaphysical illusions. He's confined to studying the 'phe-

77. This is expressed most dramatically in TSZ's two 'dancing songs' (II/10, III/15).

78. P&Tp92 [1873]: "Truth as an unconditional duty [is] hostile and world-destroying." P&Tp12 [1872–73]: "The knowledge drive, arriving at its boundaries, turns against itself in order to proceed to the *critique of knowing*. Knowledge in the service of the best life."

79. So he considers as a subtitle for that book "The Philosopher," "Reflections on the Struggle between Art and Knowledge" [KSA/7/19[98]: 1872–73]. P&Tp8 [1872–73]: "The philosopher should *know what is needed,* and the artist should *create* it.' WP853 [1888] says the author of BT knows "that art is *more valuable* than truth". P&Tp92 [1873]: "Everything good and beautiful depends upon illusion".

nomena' arising on their basis; he's limited to an 'empirical truth', one that of course is not really true. In this way, the societal will to truth embedded in the discipline of science is mastered (hemmed in) by a will to illusion.

Something similar occurs 'microscopically', too, in the philosopher himself, in the politics of his drives. He limits his own scientific element. He makes and believes in illusions, too, and so becomes artist as well as knower, as in BT's vision of an 'artistic Socrates'.[80] Now the philosopher takes over the glory of the artist: he aspires to create the basic cultural images (embedded with social lessons), then to be embroidered and disseminated by others (as perhaps Nietzsche himself intended the images of Apollo, Dionysus, and Socrates, projected so forcefully in BT). But in this aspiration, the philosopher seems to sacrifice his allegiance to truth, priding himself now more in his illusions.

On a closer look at this tale Nietzsche tells against truth, we find that even here he covertly values it, even gives it priority. The skeptical or nihilist insight is not abandoned or forgotten but indeed preserved as a crucial element in the 'artistic' way these illusions are embraced. So, at the social level, they're believed as the Greeks of the (sixth to fifth century B.C.) 'tragic' age believed their poets' stories: as illusions, as necessary comforts in the face of the chaos and suffering of becoming. The myths are believed not 'historically' or 'religiously' but in the same spirit as by the poets who invent them, somewhere between a full seriousness and a full playfulness.[81] Still more, for the philosopher himself; his artistic delight in his own fabrications is underlain by recognition that they're false, and false because of a deeper insight, which he communicates besides (and in) his stories.[82]

So in society, and especially in the philosopher, these illusions are underlain by an abiding grasp of a pessimistic and transcendental truth; they don't replace that truth, they make it livable. BT15: "When he sees to his horror how logic coils up at these boundaries and finally bites its own tail—there breaks through the new form of knowledge, *the tragic*

80. See BT14, 16. P&Tp17 [1872–73] says to ask about a "philosophical genius", "What *remains* when his system has been destroyed as science? But this remainder must be just what *restrains* the knowledge drive, therefore [it must be] the artistic in it." This higher estimation of art—and of music in particular—is of course tangled up with Nietzsche's own larger (than later) musical aspirations in this period, and with his self-subordinating fascination with Wagner.

81. P&Tp11 [1872–73]: *"The restraining of the knowledge drive—whether in favor of a religion? Or an artistic culture,* should now show itself; I stand on the latter side."

82. P&Tp11 [1872–73]: *"The philosopher of tragic knowledge.* He restrains the unleashed knowing drive, [but] not through a new metaphysics. He sets up no new faith." P&Tp19 [1872–73]: *"The natural description of the philosopher.* He knows, in that he creates [*dichtet*], and creates, in that he knows." P&Tp29 [1872–73]: *"Truthfulness of art:* it alone is now honorable [*ehrlich*]."

knowledge which, merely to be endured, needs art as a protection and remedy." Although Nietzsche most stresses this truth in the Schopenhauerian mood of BT and gives the richest content to it there (filling it out with a vision of the world as will), it remains in the sparer logic of P&T, now as a formal, skeptical-nihilist truth.[83] This basic insight is still the justification and point for the artistic lies: these are valued because they let one live with that truth. So even in this early, romantic and hypercritical phase, Nietzsche's will to truth finds a (half-hidden) place in him, from which it indeed still rules his other concerns.

As is familar, Nietzsche's position changes by the time of *Human, All Too Human* (its first part written 1877–78). For reasons perhaps more personal than conceptual, he passes into a 'positivistic' phase in which he reaffirms truth and science against art, and hence against metaphysics, as the art-philosophy.[84] In this spirit, he rewrites the story about philosophy, art, and science: art is preferable to (metaphysical) philosophy, but only as a stage toward science [HH/I/27]; "The scientific human being is the further development of the artistic" [I/222].[85] *Daybreak* shows a similar allegiance to the goal of scientific truth.[86]

As I try to show, this choice of self then abides with Nietzsche, as when he much later writes that whereas Wagner was a "genius of the *lie*'", he himself is "a genius *of the truth*'" [F&S #147: 1888]. To be sure, his sense of this truth evolves, so that it gradually becomes less easy to call it 'scientific'. This development is forced by an obvious instability to this stance in HH and D—so obvious, that we might agree with Nietzsche's account of these books as self-therapies. In this period, he reinvigorates his will to truth by temporarily suppressing other forces in him and by stilling certain skeptical doubts against truth. Then, as this

83. Inasmuch as the philosopher takes this insight as knowledge, he is not a skeptic after all; so P&Tp12 [1872–73]: "For the tragic philosopher, it completes the *picture of existence* that metaphysics appears merely anthropomorphic. He is not a *skeptic.*'"

84. HH/II/P/5: "it was then that I conducted with myself a patient and tedious campaign against the unscientific basic tendency of that romantic pessimism to interpret and inflate single personal experiences into universal judgments, indeed into condemnations of the world". See HH/I/3. The great biographical event here is the break with Wagner: in this crisis, Nietzsche cleaves to the will to truth in himself, against the will to illusion of 'the artist'; he does so in his self-conception and in the philosophy that partly then mirrors, partly just *is*, this self-conception. This personal, resentful element in his own turn against art and toward truth presumably became later a datum for him, an access to that larger resentfulness of the will to truth. Cf. Nietzsche's own accounts—in HH/I/P, HH/II/P, EH/HH—of this struggle back to health.

85. HH/I/223 anticipates the death of art.

86. D544 attacks those who try to do philosophy 'intuitively', 'artistically', nonlogically. D45 suggests that 'the knowledge of truth' is the one goal worth sacrificing humanity to (showing that he remains aware of how truth requires a sacrifice). D490 speaks of giving blood for "little truths".

chosen identity regains health and strength, he can reintroduce those competing voices, challenging the will to truth with them. Thus Nietzsche reenacts his own story from P&T, of philosophy as the self-critique of this will. But he does it from a more settled allegiance to that will, hence always seeking the best way to reaffirm truth in the face of those doubts.

Already in HH and D, 'science' means something specific: a new method in psychology. "All we require, and that can be given us only now that the single sciences have reached their present height, is a *chemistry* of the moral, religious, and aesthetic representations and perceptions" [HH/I/1].[87] But *The Gay Science* (1881–82), as the title suggests, brings this method to the fore. The allegiance to truth abides: "But what is goodheartedness, refinement, or genius to me, when the human being with these virtues tolerates slack feelings in his beliefs and judgments and when he does not count *the demand for certainty* as his inmost desire and deepest need—as that which separates the higher human beings from the lower!" [GS2]. Nietzsche sees how his psychological studies can be developed into a method for reaching a new kind of truth, one more consistent with art and the drives. So GS113 anticipates "when the artistic forces and the practical wisdom of life join with scientific thinking, so that a higher organic system is formed". And GS324: "the great liberator came over me, the thought that life could be an experiment of the knower. . . . *'Life as a means of knowledge'*—with this principle in one's heart one can live not only boldly but even *gaily''*.[88]

The details to this method will be treated in § 4.4 and § 4.5. But its capstone is the thought of eternal return, announced at the end of GS's first edition. This 'discovery' gives Nietzsche a culmination and nexus for all those specific psychological insights; it ties them up into a new kind of truth that escapes those skeptical doubts. *Thus Spoke Zarathustra* (1883–84) dramatizes the discovery of this nexus. It shows the return of art and its associates, but also an abiding affirmation of truth. To be sure, truth is subordinated to life, as in TSZ/ II/10 ("The Dancing Song"): "Basically I love only life—and truly, most of all when I hate it! But that I am good to wisdom, and often too good, that is because she reminds me so much of life!"; and in TSZ/III/15/2 ("The Other Dancing Song"), just before Zarathustra marries life: "But then life was dearer to me than all my wisdom ever was." But wisdom is not renounced in this marriage; it's his knowledge of eternal return that has made him fit to marry life (as he proves by whispering eternal return to her). Wisdom makes possible the best life.[89]

87. So Foucault (1984, 78) says the "characteristically Nietzschean" analyses begin with HH.
88. GS11 announces the *''task, to incorporate knowing* and make it instinctive''.
89. We should note an ambiguity here: does 'life' refer to other activities than thinking (and to different drives than the will to truth) or to an overall activity in

We may note just two highlights from later works. One conspicuous passage is the penultimate section of *Beyond Good and Evil* (1885–86), which caps all of that book's hard questioning about truth by anticipating the philosopher-god Dionysus, whom we might praise for "his explorer and discoverer courage, his daring honesty, truthfulness, and love of wisdom", even though he would abjure such labels. (The god's reason for denying them, a scorn for leaning on the emotive push to such virtue terms, is often Nietzsche's, too, and shows how he might overstate how far he breaks from truth.[90]) Second, the autobiographical announcements in *Ecce Homo* (1888) are of clear importance. EH/IV/1: "the truth speaks out of me. — But my truth is *terrible;* for so far one has called *lies* truth. . . . I was the first to *discover* the truth by being the first to experience—to *smell*—lies as lies." EH/IV/3: "Zarathustra is more truthful than any other thinker. His teaching, and his alone, has truthfulness as the supreme virtue".

4.4 The new philosophers

We now begin a more thorough look at Nietzsche's mature hopes, how the will to truth will evolve. What characterizes those 'new philosophers' whom *Beyond Good and Evil* so anticipates?[91] We get a useful intuitive view of this change, if also (I'm afraid) a loose and emotive one, by considering the *health* of the new will to truth. In § 4.5, I analyze more closely its defining notion of truth; avoiding this for the moment, I first map the periphery, taking only orienting glances at the central point. How can this drive, in person or society, achieve a healthier relation to competing forces? As it matures into activeness, what replaces its old resentful hostility toward them? I first note the general logic of this 'becoming healthy', then show how it is reflected in the new virtues embraced by this will to truth.

At the core of this development, the will to truth learns to will power over others in a different way, or it learns to will power of a different sort. It no longer campaigns to 'negate' the other drives, in any of its old spectrum of modes—ignoring, condemning, putting out of play, or extirpating—all incited by resentment. It ceases to be 'unconditional', to

---

which thinking can be part? If the latter, then life's priority doesn't rule out the will to truth's preeminence among the drives.

90. BGE230 renounces the "beautiful, glittering, jingling, festive words: honesty, love of truth, love of wisdom, sacrifice for knowledge, heroism of the truthful". See also GM/III/8, WP465 [1888].

91. The book's subtitle is "Prelude to a Philosophy of the Future". BGE42: "A new species of philosophers is coming up . . . philosophers of the future". The book is expressly addressed from and to the "free spirits" who are "heralds and precursors" of these coming philosophers; cf. BGE44. See also BGE203, 210, 211. Cf. Nehamas 1988, 58: "The future, therefore, is the time with which genuine philosophers are concerned, not the time when they exist."

demand ultimacy or exclusiveness, in the drive politics of the person. It finds its best success not in a cloistered autonomy from the drives but in mingling with them. To be sure, it still wants preeminence; and Nietzsche still wants that for it. And these others are still enemies it tries to master. But it has learned (better) what power or mastery is, in that lesson about friendship and animosity from § 3.4.1: the best relation to the other is that of the spiritual *agon*. Thinking-at-truth now applies this lesson in its stance toward all those 'subjective' viewpoints occupied by its drives.

The will to know wants neither to obliterate these other drives and concerns nor to turn them from themselves, into tamed servants of itself. It wants these other forces even stronger, and even more different from it, so that it may better enrich itself, by (a certain) interplay with them.[92] So it's eager and alert to find and institute games with these drives; this agonistic stance tempers its opposition to them. As in any game, the struggle is limited by the rules and objectives: the power goal gets specified as winning the game, by agreed-on means. But more than this, the very constitution and observance of those limits serve to unite the behaviors of both players into a common practice in which they participate as moments. To an extent, they now find their identity partly in this interaction; a share of their allegiance passes to the game they together constitute.

So the will to truth now looks for a mutually accommodating practice, or interplay, in which it grows by the very growth and self-expression of the other drives. But it does not sacrifice to this game its identifying interest in truth; it wants a competition in which it learns.[93] The game the new philosopher finds is this: he cultivates and spurs his drives toward a certain 'spiritualized' competition, bringing them into critical argument with one another, a debate through which he knows them (their perspectives, their relations, and their rank order). Insofar as he can thus embody and witness the rich range of viewpoints of his society, he diagnoses and knows it as well. He thereby even knows the gist of all reality, as a world of just such wills (most much less complex than the human).

Hence the new philosophy is (a new sort of) *psychology:* "psychology is now again the path to the basic problems" [BGE23]; "[T]hat a *psychologist* without equal speaks from my writings, is perhaps the first insight reached by a good reader" [EH/III/5]; "[T]here was no psychology at all before me" [EH/IV/6].[94] This new psychology is grounded

---

92. WP820 [1885] wishes for "an ever greater spiritualization and multiplication of the senses".

93. BGE284 describes the use of the drives: "To have and not to have one's affects, one's For and Against, at will; to condescend to them, for [some] hours; to *seat* oneself on them as on a horse, often as on an ass—for one must know how to use their stupidity as well as their fire."

94. Sometimes it is physiology that is so elevated: KSA/13/25[1] [1888].

in an *autopsychology:* in a certain access to drives or forces in oneself. The philosopher reproduces his culture's forces in himself and then studies the chemistry of their interactions. He can do so only because he welcomes these attitudes in himself and incites them to ever-stronger statement and reply. Self-understanding depends on such 'play' with the drives; the will to truth could never so 'see into' them while it was resentfully fighting them.[95]

These points can be illustrated, still very schematically, by returning to the case of the art drive, and the will to truth's relation to it. Among all the other drives, this may be most contrary to that will, because its aim is to create the 'beautifying illusion', a partial view that so pleases and captivates that it fixes us in its partiality and consequent falseness. Both early and late, Nietzsche stresses the 'discordance' between truth and art.[96] Familiarly, Plato also stresses this opposition and preaches the suppression of art in favor of truth.[97] By contrast, Nietzsche's extravagant praise for art makes us expect—and interpreters argue[98]—that he reverses this Platonic choice and wants that aesthetic drive to master or displace the will to truth.

In § 4.3.3 we saw that this was indeed an element in his early view. But we also saw that even then there are countervailing themes. First, Nietzsche already holds the Heraclitean point and favors 'discordance' as Plato does not. So he mainly wants the will to truth limited, not suppressed. He values the tension between it and the will to illusion and doesn't want their conflict resolved by the victory of either side. Second, even when he does favor the side of the art drive in this conflict, it's because it serves a deeper truth, that 'skeptical insight' into becoming and the impossibility of (any other) truth. It's in allegiance to this bare truth—sometimes elaborated with the Schopenhauerian world-as-will view—that he grants the will to illusion its priority.

My claim is that Nietzsche finds, in his maturity, a way of unfolding that single skeptical-nihilist truth into a wide new field of truths, to be

95. KSA/12/6[4] [1886–87]: "My writings speak only of my own experiences [*Erlebnissen*]—fortunately I have experienced much". See how TSZ/III/12/7 links truth with 'hearing' oneself and says the good are incapable of this, because they sacrifice themselves in their obedience. I take the opening of GM/P to regret that "we are not 'knowers' for ourselves."

96. WP822 [1888]: "It is disgraceful for a philosopher to say: the good and the beautiful are one: if he adds 'also the true', one ought to beat him. Truth is ugly". See also n.61.

97. *Republic*, III, X. But in the *Phaedrus*, Plato makes love of beauty serve truth: the beautiful sensuous leads us toward the true nonsensuous.

98. Heidegger seems to read Nietzsche so; but note that the 'truth' that is so judged is "fixation on an apparition" (1979–87, 1:217)—it is, in fact, a 'truth' that's not really true (for either Nietzsche or Heidegger). Implicit in the notion of art as 'perspicuous' (as will to power's most transparent form)—which Heidegger's reading of Nietzsche stresses (1979–87, 1:69)—is that art is a means to a truer truth.

explored by a novel method. While once the will to truth's self-critique taught it to submit itself it to the art drive, now it learns how to use the latter as its best tool in its new truth method. The philosopher no longer molts into artist, but he cultivates that impulse in himself, as his best clue to reality: "The phenomenon 'artist' is still the most *transparent*—to see through it to the *basic instincts of power*, of nature, etc.! Also of religion and morality!" [WP797: 1885–86]. In the artistic act, the creative-destructive urge of will to power itself appears 'least veiled'; so the new philosopher must especially spur and study *this* drive.

Again, I delay until § 4.5 the fuller logic or method of this 'auto-psychological' study and the type of truth it finds. Here, continuing to dwell on the health of this new will, we can make this vivid in another aspect by noticing the two chief virtues this new will adopts, once it takes that positive turn: the character traits it most praises and promotes in itself, as those that best fit it for finding truth.[99]

A first new virtue, and one clearly relevant to truth, is honesty [*Redlichkeit*]. Broadly conceived, this is the defining virtue of any will to truth: its mere persistence in seeking (thinking) truth, in the face of (unspecified) obstacles or temptations. But Nietzsche mostly has in mind something more specific: the honesty of a culminating phase of this will, in which it faces certain especially basic and pervasive temptations to lie. This is an honesty not so much by a person about himself as by the will to truth about itself: a recognition of its own drive nature, and of how this 'perspectifies' all its theories. This honesty exposes how each 'truth' expresses drives and interests; it shows this not in an abstract distance (in such summary tags as 'all judgments are perpectival') but down into the details of biases in one's firmest, founding views.[100] So this honesty

99. D556 and BGE284 offer rather different lists of 'the four virtues'. The former names honesty, bravery [*Tapferkeit*], magnanimity, and politeness; the latter gives courage [*Mut*], insight, sympathy [*Mitgefühl*], and solitude (after reclassifying polite-ness as "that roguish and cheerful vice").

100. This honesty is an openness toward, of course oneself and not necessarily others; to them one may well show masks. D456 says that honesty "occurs among neither the Socratic nor the Christian virtues: it is one of the youngest virtues, still little matured, still often misjudged and misunderstood, still hardly conscious of itself—something becoming, which we can advance or obstruct as we see fit." D556 lists it first among the cardinal virtues; an opposing vice is described in D543. BGE5 complains that philosophers are "not honest enough. . . . They all present them-selves as if they had . . . reached their genuine opinions through the self-development of a cold, pure, divinely untroubled dialectic . . . : while at basis it is . . . most often a wish of the heart that has been sifted and made abstract, and is defended with reasons sought afterwards". (This is indeed the 'dogmatism' attacked in BGE/P.) BGE227 says honesty is the only virtue left to free spirits, but BGE284 omits it from its list of four virtues; BGE295 attributes it to Dionysus, although he would deny it (for reasons BGE230 mentions, too; see n.90). Gemes (1992, 52) says that in Nietzsche's genuine philosophers, will to truth recognizes itself as will to power. On the difficulty of this, cf. Foucault 1982, 219: "True discourse, liberated by the nature of its form from desire and power, is incapable of recognizing the will to truth which pervades it".

is especially a skill for unmasking and diagnosing—for unsettling convictions by showing them rooted in interest and partiality; hence it's also a sort of cruelty against our urge to simplicity and all our straightforward acceptances.[101]

A second Nietzschean virtue, courage [*Mut*], is closely related to the first. That new honesty requires a new courage, where it was never pressed before: the courage to bear up against the honesty's cruelty, in exposing the partialities of all one's views. "How much truth does a spirit *endure*, how much truth does it *dare?* More and more that became for me the genuine measure of value. Error (belief in the ideal) is not blindness, error is *cowardice*'' [EH/F/3]. And "precisely as far as courage *can* venture forward, precisely according to that measure of force one approaches the truth" [EH/BT/2].[102] This new courage dares the psychological experiments in 'reversing perspectives', which alone give the type of truth Nietzsche believes in.

Reflection here helps clarify the 'pragmatics' of truth. To begin with, it counts further against assigning a 'pragmatic theory of truth' to Nietzsche that he thinks truth hard and dangerous, damaging indeed to most persons. It's only those 'truths' that are really lies that he thinks are of practical use.[103] This also shows how the new will to truth is still ascetic—and the extent to which Nietzsche embraces asceticism, despite his many mockings of it. The new truth drive must not just enter, but also 'cut into' the drives, reversing their perspectives and so seeing their partiality. "One has had to wrestle for truth at every step, one has had to surrender for it almost everything to which the heart, to which our love, our trust in life, cling otherwise. That requires greatness of soul: the service of truth is the hardest service" [A50].[104]

---

101. Note BGE230: "*This* will to appearance, to simplification, to the mask, to the cloak, in short to the surface—for every surface is a cloak—is worked *against* by that sublime tendency of the knower, who grasps and *wills* to grasp things deeply, manifoldly, basically: as a kind of cruelty of the intellectual conscience and taste". See also BGE229 and GM/III/12.

102. EH/IV/5: "this kind of human being that [Zarathustra] conceives, conceives reality *as it is*, being strong enough for this". TSZ/IV/15: "But courage and adventure and pleasure in the uncertain, in the undared—*courage* seems to me the whole prehistory of human beings. . . . *This* courage, finally become refined, spiritual—".

103. BGE39: "Something might be true even though it was harmful and dangerous in the highest degree; indeed it could belong to the basic constitution of existence, that full knowledge of it would destroy one—so that the strength of a spirit could be measured by how much of the 'truth' it could still endure". D45 says the ultimate human self-sacrifice would be to truth: "the knowledge of truth would remain as the only tremendous goal commensurate with such a sacrifice, because for it no sacrifice is too great." I here take 'practical' and 'pragmatic' to refer to an everyday sort of benefit; of course I claim Nietzsche attributes a nonstandard, 'spiritual' benefit to the effort at (proper) truth.

104. BGE229: "the knower, in that he compels his spirit, *against* the tendency of the spirit and often enough also against the wishes of his heart, to know—i.e., to

These points trump the attacks on truth in § 4.2: that we need illusions, because truth harms us. Nietzsche thinks the strongest persons will and must endure this harm; they make and show themselves strong by not needing these illusions. Thus, his critique of the will to truth as 'against life' is 'taken up into' his principal point: this will is also, overall, the most empowering of drives, and precisely by virtue of facing the greatest dangers, by enduring the greatest harm. For not just truth but power is found above all through suffering [*Leiden*]. "The discipline [*Zucht*] of suffering, of *great* suffering—do you not know that only *this* discipline has created all elevations of human beings so far?" [BGE225]. This suffering that truth involves, is one of Nietzsche's main grounds for holding that the will to truth is the highest form of will to power.

4.5   Truth with perspectivism

So far we've merely circled the periphery of Nietzsche's new truth project. I've sketched it in its aspect as 'healthy' and described its chief virtues: the character traits it cultivates. Now I must analyze the project itself, as a certain method for or toward a certain end. I must map this new will's 'telic logic': its new goal of truth and the strategy by which it pursues it.

We must weigh this analysis against this book's guiding issues. Most decisively, we must see whether the new truth project avoids the two horns to my basic dilemma. Does it retain enough of the old sense of 'truth', correspondence in particular, to let Nietzsche, by claiming this truth, avoid the self-deflation and contradiction afflicting a Protagorean relativism? Does it also preserve enough of the force of his strongly held perspectivism to still be called 'Nietzschean'? Does it give us, in short, a truth as correspondence that is still deeply perspectivist?

In chapter 1, I provisionally reconciled these apparent inconsistents by my two-level, insulating strategy: truth at the ontological-transcendental level of will to power, perspectivism in the ontical-empirical domain this opens up. This allowed us to give to his power analyses the credence they need to support his perspectivism as he intends. It also let us accommodate Nietzsche's avowals of perspectivism, albeit by limiting their scope (their field of application) to that empirical domain. But this strategy is unsatisfying in several respects. It has little textual basis: one would expect so simple a division to be stated at least sometime explicitly, and perhaps to be reflected in one or more recurring pairs of contrast terms (as, for example, the active/reactive distinction is, in such pairs as healthy/sick and ascent/decline). The strategy also seems un-Nietz-

---

say no where he wants to affirm, love, adore—works as artist and transfigurer of cruelty". See also GS/P/3.

schean in a general way: by contrast with that other opposition, the transcendental/empirical bifurcation looks supernaturally sharp, not two directions along a polar continuum but separate 'realms', divided distinctly, not grading toward one another. Nor, probably, do we expect any such border to survive a closer study; the strategy is embarrassed by such questions as 'how much *can* be said in specification of our will to power essence, and why just this and no more?' Abandoning this stopgap, artificial insulation, I must now try to sketch a perspectivist truth.

We must see how Nietzsche's perspectivism is not just a new truth content (i.e., something he claims to be true) but a new truth form (an account of a new way of being true). This new form shows us *how to get* such contents, including itself, a circle we can hope is benign. This lets us situate, most schematically, the perspectivism's differences from its more familiar look-alikes, skepticism and relativism. It's not skepticism, because truths are achievable; it's not relativism, which also redefines truth, because perspectivism's new truth form is more substantial than a relativist truth and avoids those dilemmas the latter is subject to.

This new truth form is developed by Nietzsche precisely out of his critique of truth, as a lesson learned from all the challenges against it that I cataloged in § 4.1 and § 4.2. The type of truth he can want is one fashioned to evade the sharpest of his attacks on truth, making them turn out to apply only to what truth has been *so far*. Indeed, our best access to his new truth is along this same route: what must truth become to escape his critique of it? In § 4.4 we saw how it might avoid or trump the charge (developed in § 4.2) that pursuing truth is sick and harmful. By seeing how to avoid the arguments (in § 4.1) that truth is impossible, we now get at its inner logic.

The main points in § 4.1 were that correspondence isn't possible because (a) the would-be 'object' is a contextual process and (b) the would-be 'subject' is an interested viewpoint; so context and interest are the two main obstacles for any (positive) Nietzschean theory of truth. My tactic is to turn these vices into virtues, by turning them toward one another: because reality is thus contextual, our interestedness isn't a bar to grasping it after all but indeed is just what makes it possible. As exceptionally complex wills to power ourselves, we're ideally fitted to 'mirror' reality, in a way that involves a privileged sort of insight into it.

Thus I develop a certain obvious way we might expect any 'perspectivism' to make room for truth: how could it not posit (that there are) perspectives, and so allow for a truth *about* these perspectives, by somehow representing or reproducing them within oneself?[105] So for Nietzsche, because wills to power are what there is, understanding re-

---

105. Nor does this positing of (the reality of) perspectives seem to be merely an inconvenience in stating the view. What 'view' is there at all, absent such a positing?

quires 'incorporating' them a certain way, learning to see and feel and will from their points of view. Although no beings can be subject and object to one another, their common nature as wills lets certain ones still 'mirror' others, in a way that preserves most of the sense our cognitive terms have had.

One reason this avenue to perspectivist truth is often either denied or ignored is the conception of perspectives as 'incommensurable' and the allied notion that they're 'unbridgeable'. If each viewpoint speaks an untranslatable language, if people are so different it's impossible to 'see from another's point of view', then there looks to be no way a perspective could grasp anything but itself; its truths could never be more than single, personal ones, on a footing with each singular other's. But this stress on incommensurability is quite at odds with Nietzsche's own procedure; his interest is always in the ways schemes or perspectives interact, attract, convince, corrupt, and incorporate one another. Other persons and points of view are far from inaccessible, far from being 'closed books'.[106] Nietzsche chiefly thinks them accessible in his power ontology's terms: by a person's bearing these other interested viewpoints as occasional or adoptable attitudes of his own; by his being able to inhabit or occupy these viewpoints. This inhabiting is a step or stage in grasping or understanding these viewpoints.

4.5.1   The new truth method

The most important part of Nietzsche's new method is the nature or *quality* of that 'grasp' of perspectives. But before we dwell on this crux, we can get an orienting view of the method as a whole by unfolding a simpler result about *quantity*.

4.5.1.1   *Knowing more*

This notion of truth requires a breadth of empathic studies, an ability to see (or a having seen) from many perspectives. This is the ultimate point to all Nietzsche's praise for internal multiplicity: encompassing all this, one understands hosts of others, seeing what they see, and more.[107] So

106. Cf. Gadamer 1991, 292: "we do not try to transpose ourselves into the author's mind but . . . into the perspective within which he has formed his views. . . . The task of hermeneutics is to clarify this miracle of understanding, which is not a mysterious communion of souls, but sharing in a common meaning." I take Nietzsche's truth method to share some ground with Gadamer's hermeneutics; I note some connections in the notes below.

107. GS301: "For one who grows up into the heights of humanity the world becomes ever fuller; ever more fishhooks of interest are cast at him; the number of his stimuli is continually growing, as well as the number of his kinds of pleasure and displeasure". GS382: "Whoever has a soul that thirsts to have experienced the whole range of values and desiderata so far . . . , whoever wills to know from the adventures of his ownmost experience how a conquerer and discoverer of the ideal feels [*zu Muthe ist*], and also an artist, a saint, a legislator, a sage, a scholar". KSA/13/25[6]

one extends the part or share of the world of perspectives one grasps. This demands the inclination and ability, which in § 3.4.2 we saw he conceives as feminine, to approximate toward the viewpoints of others, to see as if with their conceptions and concerns.

Such diversity is good not simply because one knows more if one has more 'bits' of knowledge. It's indeed because there are no such (independent) bits for knowing to accumulate.[108] Because wills (in their being or identity) are themselves contextual, to know another is not just to see from its viewpoint but to see it from a (suitable) range of other viewpoints. Hence knowing grows, as it were, not just cumulatively but exponentially, when one multiplies (in a certain way) the perspectives one takes. Hence dogmatism, the insistence on a single viewpoint, is so calamitous an antimethod for Nietzsche. So GM/III/12: "There is *only* a perspectival seeing, *only* a perspectival 'knowing'; and *the more* affects we allow to speak about a thing [*Sache*], *the more* eyes, different eyes, we know how use to observe the same thing, the more complete will our 'concept' of this thing, our 'objectivity', be."[109]

Each part is, as it were, a balance of tension between interests—its own and others'. Understanding it requires not just a single step into it but shifting or rocking back and forth across that balance, thus experiencing the inter-interpretation of perspectives. Only in this way does one properly 'inhabit' this site, as a nexus among the world's wills. It follows from this that a will doesn't immediately, naturally, or inevitably understand itself; it can't, except by passing out of itself in a certain way, in

---

[1888]: "I have the greatest comprehensiveness of soul, that any human being has had." See also HH/I/P/4, 6. The goal is mentioned from early on; so P&Tp22 [1872–73]: "[The philosopher] tries to let all the notes [*Töne*] of the world resound [*nachklingen*] in himself, and to set forth out of himself this total sound [*Gesammtklang*], in concepts." Schrift (1990, 155ff.) gathers many passages relevant here.

108. WP530 [1886–87]: "A single judgment is never 'true', never knowledge, only in the *connection* [*Zusammenhange*] and *relation* [*Beziehung*] of many judgments is there a surety [*Bürgschaft*]."

109. WP560 [1887]: "That things have a *constitution in themselves* quite apart from interpretation and subjectivity, is *a wholly idle hypothesis*: it presupposes that *interpreting and being-subjective* are *not* essential, that a thing freed from all relationships is still a thing." KSA/9/11[65] [1881]: "Task: to *see* things *as they are! Means:* to be able to see them out of a hundred eyes, out of *many* persons!" WP556 [1885–86]: "A thing would be designated [*bezeichnet*] only when all creatures [*Wesen*] had asked and answered their 'what is that?' about it. Supposing one single creature, with its own relationships and perspectives towards all things, were missing: and the thing is still not 'defined'." WP616 [1885–86]: "that every *elevation of the human being* brings with it the overcoming of narrower interpretations, that every achieved strengthening and power-expansion opens new perspectives and means believing in new horizons—this [idea] runs through my writings." Cf. Schrift (1990, 184) on 'interpretive pluralism'; he seems to make multiplicity the ruling value: "interpretations which enhance the text insofar as they open the text to further interpretive activity are 'better'".

regarding itself from contrasting views. Thus Nietzsche rejects the self-containment of Descartes's subject: both the (self-sufficient) being his ontology assigns it and the (from-the-beginning) method his epistemology commends to it, as the way it can know. No such immediate self-presence or self-understanding is available to it.[110]

Hence an important tactic of this method is to reverse perspectives.[111] No view is allowed to stand firm and unchallenged. Against any now-dominant attitude, one stirs up and marshals opposing viewpoints, which deny and (above all) diagnose it.[112] This is a painful policy—wounding whatever concerns are uppermost—and requires (as we saw in § 4.4) courage as well as honesty. It's enacted in Nietzsche's most typical aphorisms and passages: taking some viewpoint we recognize from ourselves, he subjects it to surprising and disturbing attack. He sets it 'in play' in a way we hadn't done.[113] Of course, these exercises are models to us of how to begin to disturb ourselves by persistently practicing just such a reversing and undermining move.

The back-and-forth in Nietzsche's alternative method is (much like) the hermeneutic circle; it's the type of knowledge feasible for a world of becoming. Indeed, this circle is demanded not just by the contextual aspect of becoming but by its process-being, because what's required is movement through this circle (not, as it were, a view of it from above). The old truth goal demanded an abiding view of persisting structures,

110. HH/I/P/5: "he was *outside* himself, there's no doubt. Now for the first time he sees himself". Cf. Gadamer 1991, 306: *"understanding is always the fusion of these horizons supposedly existing by themselves."* Hence the hermeneutic intent to understand a text better than its own author. I and the other are not two languages untranslatable, but elements in a single language, sides to a dialogue; I can know my side, what I say and am, only by knowing the other, too—by harboring the other as a minority point of view in myself.

111. EH/I/1: "Looking out from the optics of the sick at *healthier* concepts and values, and again, conversely, looking down from the fullness and self-certainty of a *rich* life, into the secret work of the decadence instinct—this was my longest training, my genuine experience; if in anything, I became master [*Meister*] in this. Now I have in the hand, I have the hand for, *reversing perspectives:* the first reason why a 'revaluation of values' is perhaps possible for me alone."

112. GM/III/12 speaks of the intellect's "future 'objectivity' . . . as the ability *to have under control* one's For and Against, to put them on and take them off: so that one knows how to make precisely the *difference* of perspectives and affect-interpretations useful for knowledge." Scheiffele (1991, 32) says "a primary feature of Nietzsche's perspectivism" is *"the 'estranging' of what is one's own by questioning it from behind [hinterfragen], from the perspective of the foreign"*; he contrasts the (familiar) movement of incorporating the other with that of viewing oneself from foreign positions, thereby "letting what is 'obvious' appear as something *strange."* (See D523, entitled "Hinterfragen.")

113. Gadamer (1991, 298–99) describes how we can 'foreground' our prejudices, by encountering a text as distant from us; the text makes us not set aside our prejudices, but put them into play: "In fact our own prejudice is properly brought into play by being put at risk. Only by being given full play is it able to experience the other's claim to truth and make it possible for him to have full play himself."

but now both knower and known are processes. Hence we should read the multiplicity of Nietzsche's positions as reflecting his view that knowing lies in shifting perspectives, in this way of moving through time.[114] This is how we must hear his stress on questioning, investigating, experimenting, and the like: these aren't merely means to an end, not the routes his philosopher travels to reach the true goal, an abiding insight or belief. Rather, it's in those very activities that his truth occurs.[115]

This reading of Nietzsche's perspectivism has to answer several challenges. It seems, to begin with, an implausible position: How could chasing across perspectives advance one in knowing? Without any account of a 'logic' to this movement, it seems a mere random wandering that would build no understanding at all worth having. Indeed, we haven't yet been told a method concrete enough that we can see just how we would put it in practice. Is the point just to gather ever more perspectives—any new ones, it doesn't matter which? Moreover, the 'sum' of perspectives at which this effort apparently aims—the totality of views, WP556 [1885–86] seems to insist—looks unachievable, or even incoherent.[116]

The position also seems not to be Nietzsche's. Doesn't he explicitly rule out any such truth? WP540 [1885]: "There are many kinds of eyes. Even the sphinx has eyes: and consequently there are many kinds of 'truths', and consequently there is no truth." It also seems at odds with other stances he takes. Doesn't he argue it a mark of decadence to sympathize with other perspectives? Isn't the healthy will the one that imposes its own perspective on others, rather than being seduced into the views they take? And aren't his new philosophers supposed to value their 'truths' as (distinctively) their own?[117] It seems Nietzsche would denounce that perspective-explorer's lightness of commitment to his own viewpoint; this gets too much sacrificed, in all his experimenting with others' viewpoints.

4.5.1.2 Knowing better

I think we can answer these objections by developing the strategy by which the new philosopher will inhabit and study these many perspec-

114. HH/II/19: "A becoming [Werdendes] cannot be mirrored in [another] becoming as [something] firm and enduring, as a 'that' [Das]." Cf. Gadamer (1991, 291) on "the movement of understanding". Cf. Heidegger (1979–87, 1:213–14) on truth as fixity/persistence of a perspective.

115. D432: "There are no scientific methods that alone lead to knowledge! We must deal with things experimentally, being now evil, now good towards them, and having in turn justice, passion, and coldness for them." See also GS51, BGE42, BGE210 ("Versucher").

116. Cf. Magnus 1988a, 152ff.; and Clark 1990, 145ff.

117. Cf. BGE43. And throughout BGE, Nietzsche speaks of 'our truths', 'our virtues', etc.

tives. Nietzsche's ideal isn't a perspectival chameleon, constantly randomly varying his viewpoints, with allegiance to none in particular. Nor is he the 'spiritual nomad' described in HH/II/211.[118] Merely taking multiple perspectives doesn't ensure genuine insight into any one among them; there might just be chaos. To counsel merely multiplying and mixing perspectives, as in (1), projects what we might call a *polymath's truth;* Nietzsche's knower aspires to more. What must we add? What is, as it were, the dialectical logic to that 'hermeneutic circle'? This will be, in Nietzsche's (self-preening) vocabulary, the masculine aspect to the method, the 'form' it imposes on that empathic ability.

Note what's at stake in this step. The polymath's truth project, with its criterion of quantity, is easier to defend than the qualitative criteria we now must add. Given (by Nietzsche's metaphysical hypothesis) that perspectives are what is to be known, the polymath's truth goal is to *know more* of these than he did before, than others do. In the clearest case, X knows more than Y when X knows (can take) all the perspectives of Y, and more perspectives besides. That there can be such quantitative difference, that perspective knowers can be ranked this way, is hard to deny. And it seems more compatible with (what we take to be) 'perspectivism' than does a qualitative distinction: even a relativist might allow one perspective to 'know more' in this way. By contrast, it seems harder to justify a criterion by which one perspective *knows better* than another, to defend a qualitative difference in grasping even the same (number of) viewpoints.[119]

Nietzsche takes our very preference for a quantitative standard to reflect a democratic or leveling taste he condemns (see § 3.3.1): it rests on the assumption that each atomic perspective counts equally, so that improvement can only lie in adding more and more of them. Against this, he asserts several interconnected qualitative standards, which together constitute his epistemic method, the specific strategy in gathering and diagnosing perspectives that he thinks lets one know them best. With this method, Nietzsche pursues a *constructive* project of understanding, by contrast not just with the polymath's additive one but also with a merely critical, diagnostic, or deconstructive project, which aims just to lay low each pretension to a privileged truth.[120] His method of

118. Cf. Deleuze 1985 on Nietzsche's 'nomad thought'.

119. It's clear that Nietzsche does rank perspectives. I claim (a) that he does so *epistemically,* by how well and truly they see (and not just, e.g., by how 'nobly'); and (b) that this epistemic priority lies in more than just quantity or breadth. His frequent talk of 'nook' and 'frog perspectives' (e.g., BGE2) and of perspectives 'from a height' implies the epistemic priority of some views. And although the basic image of the view from above stresses a quantitative gain—in sweeping or scanning a broad expanse—Nietzsche thinks this view must sweep with method and focus.

120. These two truth strategies—the additive and the deconstructive—are partly conflicting, partly reinforcing; they seem to me near the heart of 'postmodernism' (at least in its commonest forms).

'reversing perspectives' has the point not just of adding a supplementary view, nor just of deflating, showing the partialness of, that first or uppermost view; it has the *dialectical* intent of constructing out of their conflict a new and better view. By virtue of following this method, Nietzsche thinks that he knows better than others (his predecessors) have.

It will help, in developing Nietzsche's version of this method, to compare it with another philosopher's. My choice is Aristotle, who employs a dialectic in examining 'the appearances', the opinions of 'the many and the wise', with which his arguments so often begin. His philosophical problems arise from conflicts among these views; he enters and studies these conflicts to resolve them. He uses this method more obviously in his ethics and metaphysics, but arguably means it even in the detailed sciences. Arguably, it's those common and learned opinions or appearings that Aristotle counts generally as his data, as the basic evidentiary 'experience' in his empiricism, which all his conclusions must do justice to.[121] So understood, Aristotle's dialectic, his way of handling these opposing 'appearances' (*phainomena*), is enough like the method I attribute to Nietzsche to make the differences interesting.[122]

Two crucial differences should be noted at the start: unlike Aristotle, Nietzsche treats perspectives not merely as data but as what's to be understood, and he treats perspectives as wills to power and as needing to be understood *as* such. Whereas Aristotle examines opinions and arguments *about* the topics he's concerned with, Nietzsche's interest is in these opinions themselves, as expressing certain willful viewpoints. Whereas Aristotle's attention is on these opinions' 'content', Nietzsche cares about the content mainly for what it shows about the ways these viewpoints *will* or *care*.[123] In these basic ways, his method is shaped by

121. Aristotle most obviously uses the method in his ethics; cf. *NE* 1145b2–7. Owen (1961) argues its presence in the *Physics* and the *De Caelo* but holds that in other scientific contexts (biology, meteorology) Aristotle's grounding 'phenomena' are perceptual data. Nussbaum (1986, ch. 8) shows how Aristotle might count even the scientist's observations as among those opinions, as part of 'what we say'—a part indeed privileged by the scientist's expertise, but only because this expertise is itself accredited by 'what we (generally) say'. I try to show how both Aristotle and Nietzsche rest their positions in such (local or partial) 'appearances'—yet how both also aspire beyond them and their warrant.

122. They are interesting in a different way than the comparison with Plato, stressed in chapter 2: there we saw how Nietzsche's presentation of himself as polarly opposed to Plato, although indeed marking important reversals (of being, of other-worldliness), misrepresents his break by ignoring a great web of continuities. Here we see that even those reversals were partly anticipated by Aristotle, which renders yet subtler (but not less worthwhile) what is new in Nietzsche's view.

123. To be sure, in Aristotle's ethics and politics our viewpoints and values *are* more the topic to be understood, and here his procedure swings nearer to Nietzsche's. I therefore focus on his ethics and politics in what follows. Like Nietzsche, he relies on metaphysical premises in treating these topics; cf. Irwin 1988, 358. The differences between their methods follow from the different ways their ontologies conceive these viewpoints to 'be'.

an anticipated ontology of the general sort of reality this method must bring to light. Indeed, his claim that his method lets him 'know better' (and not simply more) depends on the claim that it better suits the sort of world that's there. So the basic ways his method claims to accomplish a qualitative epistemic improvement in viewpoint follow from some by-now-familiar elements in his power ontology. I think we can distinguish three broad impacts on that method by the ontology, reflecting the ontology's three main aspects, as developed in my first three chapters.

A first nexus of reasons Nietzsche thinks he knows better (e.g., than Aristotle) lies in the lessons he draws from his ontology of us as perspectival wills, as sketched in chapter 1. These concern more importantly the 'manner' of his dialectical method—where (to what kind of 'dialogue') its rules are applied—and less what the rules are. The different reality the Nietzschean knower pursues requires that he 'place' this dialectic differently in himself, that he carry it out with a different set or mix of cognitive faculties. His aim to know viewpoints less as theories than as ways of willing requires of him a fuller way of 'experiencing' these viewpoints, and a more severe way of 'suffering' their conflicts, than Aristotle intends.

Whereas Aristotle maintains a theoretical distance from the conflicts he explores, Nietzsche tries to inhabit the opposing attitudes, the better to learn what drives them.[124] His knower collects viewpoints not as inert specimens but as living factors in his thought; he incorporates them into the web of wills he himself is. Rather than being mere passive objects of study, these viewpoints acquire an autonomous potency, as self-asserting voices in his ongoing debate: he's inclined, partly or sometimes, to see and value things so. Nietzsche's dialectic is the cross-criticism of such minority wills in himself, which he effects by rocking back and forth across the tension of conflict between them.

This different 'site' of Nietzsche's method is determined not only by his different notion of what's to be known but (of course) by his different notion of himself, as knower. The method itself involves this revised self-interpretation of the one who carries it out: the interpretation of this

---

124. Or wheras Aristotle 'reports' on view conflicts, Nietzsche 'enacts' them; this is the 'existential' aspect to his dialectic. The difference is subtle, because Aristotle does 'step into' the argumentative positions he's considering and makes their cases for them. Nussbaum (1986, 247) infers from Aristotle's comparison (*Met.* 995a31–33) of the mind's puzzlement to bondage that he (by contrast with the Greek skeptic) "found the experience of dilemma anything but delightful". Nussbaum connects this with Aristotle's deep allegiance to the principle of noncontradiction and famous defense of it (against Heraclitus and Protagoras) in *Met.* IV/3–6. I consider in what follows whether Nietzsche, despite so suffering from these view conflicts, still welcomes or tolerates them in a way that means abandoning that principle and embracing the contradiction that Aristotle denounces.

knower (and his knowing) in the power ontology's terms.[125] Take first the contrast in Aristotle. His method is framed to be carried out by a mind (*nous*), with the general capacity of reason (*logos*) and the crowning ability to intuit universals and first principles. One applies Aristotle's method by identifying with this part and exercising its conceptual talents to examine and judge the dialectical conflicts in 'what we say'. Hence one 'steps into' only the discursive or conceptual positions of the opposing sides, severed from their roots in willing; one must even be purposely blind to these (because to judge by them would be unfairly ad hominem).

Against this, Nietzsche thinks of his method as applied by a 'will to truth' whose special capacity is precisely its ability to intuit wills as wills: to see how they will power. One becomes such a will to truth by learning this method: how to manage the conflicts between viewpoints on the basis of that special insight (or angle of attention).[126] This insight elevates that debate by 'bringing it to the point', by enabling each side to see the other as it is (by the power ontology). Each side makes more telling points, and the debate makes better progress.

So in this debate, each viewpoint frames its critique of the other on the basis of a recognition of that other as a will. And this changes the type of critique or attack these viewpoints mainly make: they direct against one another not chiefly the Aristotelian logic's demands for conceptual clarity and consistency but a certain genealogical-diagnostic attitude, which looks for weakness or self-contradiction less in the content of a view than in this content's relation to the power will that holds it.[127] They hunt for inadequacies in why or how an opposing view is willed. This *diagnostic* attitude is their chief weapon against one another: their

---

125. It seems that any method must involve some self-interpretation, to be adopted while performing it—that a method is incomplete without specifying what type of thing I'm to take myself to be, as I carry it out. It's not just that 'a person' must perform it, but a person in a certain attitude or using a certain faculty.

126. HH/I/P/6: "You should obtain control over your For and Against, and learn to know how to hang them off and back on their hinges [*sie aus- und wieder einzuhängen*], for the sake of your higher goal. You should learn to grasp the perspectival in every value assessment—the displacement, distortion and apparent teleology of horizons, and everything else that belongs to the perspectival".

127. This new angle of attack makes Nietzsche critical (as Aristotle is not) even where opinion seems uniform. He brings to the opinions of both 'the many and the wise' a distrust: they're the data, but data that must be reinterpreted. These opinions are true but not in the way they suppose—not in their own terms. Nietzsche's diagnosis of 'the wise' will be especially important below; so TI/II/1: "About life, the wisest of all ages [*Zeiten*] have judged the same: *it is worthless* [*es taugt nichts*]. . . . What does that *prove*? What does that *indicate?*—Formerly one said . . . : 'Here at least something must be true! The *consensus sapientium* proves the truth.' . . . 'Here something at least must be *sick*' — *we* answer". From here on I use GM/III's diagnosis of the wise as sick with the ascetic ideal, to expose more of Nietzsche's new truth method.

cross-criticism is chiefly cross-diagnosis. Nietzsche thinks his own dialectic is especially truth revealing, because it so stresses this form of critique.[128]

Some of the most distinctive features of Nietzsche's works lie in how they report (or even consist in) these cross-diagnoses among the many viewpoints he includes. Because he has collected these viewpoints mostly from his readings, his 'incorporation' of them is reflected in the striking frequency with which his phrases and sentences are simply *assembled* from the books he reads;[129] Nietzsche means not to quote others but to speak with their voices himself. He gives unusually free expression to minority (and even fleeting) attitudes in himself, which begins to explain the 'chaotic' or 'contradictory' character of his writings. His aphoristic style is partly a device for allowing these many viewpoints each to have a say. Because these minor voices are woven through his works, the latter express much less consistently, if at all, the 'official' position of a single or unified self, which we expect of philosophers.

Again the comparison with Aristotle helps: his dialectic of viewpoints is typically confined to an opening phase of inquiry, then closed and resolved by the presentation of his own synthesizing position. This is true at both macro- and microlevels: the dialectic is concentrated at the start of works, and at the start of treatments of specific problems; Aristotle then gives main space to presenting his solution to the disagreements. Moreover, even where these conflicting attitudes are expressed, they are usually not given voices of their own but are reported in the even tone of the inquirer himself.[130] So not only do the debating views take the stage only in prologue, but even there they are under close direction, by a supervising view that goes on to tell a separate story of its own.

Although this account of Aristotle ignores subtleties of his procedure, I think it captures its main spirit. And it sets up what will be an ongoing issue for us: whether Nietzsche also *closes* his dialectic, by culling and collecting his minority elements into a 'self' with a viewpoint of its own, in which they find no separate expression (a viewpoint that answers the problems they debated and so renders their debate obso-

128. To be sure, Aristotle practices a sort of diagnosis himself; his dialectical treatment of common and learned opinions includes the task of explaining why a false view is held (*Phy.* 211a9, *NE* 1154a22). But his diagnoses focus on failures at conceptual distinction or reasoning, and not on the emotive or willful motives that Nietzsche mainly seeks.

129. See Blondel 1991, 19–20.

130. Of course, the dialogue format—used by Plato famously, but by Aristotle, too, in works we don't have—has an obvious aptness for presenting dialectical conflicts between viewpoints: it purports to give the sides dramatic voices of their own. We can also study in Plato's case the different ways and degrees this format can be used 'undialectically'—to develop a single view against only token opposition.

lete). Does he, like Aristotle, aspire to resolve and remove the contradictions between appearances? It seems that Nietzsche might in some way avoid such 'closure', but it's harder to say just how.

It's clear that his works, even the 'aphoristic' ones, are not mere anthologies of multiple viewpoints diagnosing one another. Each work draws lessons from these cross-critiques it includes; it deploys them in service of a broader story, told from a perspective that arches over the work as a whole. So each of Nietzsche's books speaks also (if not only or consistently) with a dominant voice, the voice of one carrying out a larger diagnostic program, in which all of those cross-critiques are data (or 'experiments'). This viewpoint earns its dominance precisely by diagnosing better and more widely than those it supervises. This dominant voice is, I take it, the voice of Nietzsche's dominant will, his will to truth. So this will not only steers the debate among other attitudes but also offers a diagnosis of that debate, a higher view 'on' it. (Does it thereby 'close' their dialectic?)

It's in these overarching diagnoses, the longer stories he tells, that we best see Nietzsche's method at work; let's choose one as our ongoing example. Probably the clearest, the most focused and explicit, such story is the diagnosis of 'ascetic ideals' that occupies GM/III. And this case is all the more useful because it helps advance our comparison to Aristotle, who, on the one hand (*NE* VII/11–14, X/2–3), offers a 'critique of ascetic ideals' himself, in his arguments against his predecessors' denials that pleasure is good, but who also (*NE* I/5) condemns pleasure lovers, in a way that may seem to express asceticism. Does Nietzsche's critique of 'ascetic ideals' apply to Aristotle, and if so does this diagnosis indeed let Nietzsche 'know better' than he? I address these issues as I go on to map the further features of Nietzsche's method, seeing how they arise from other basic claims in the power ontology.

A second nexus of reasons Nietzsche thinks his diagnoses truer (more revealing) lies in how they take up the lessons of chapter 2. They proceed on the basis of the insight that the world 'becomes': they recognize the viewpoints they critique as contextually defined, both temporally (as stages in processes) and 'laterally' (as roles or functions in persons and societies). They see that these viewpoints mustn't be treated as if fully constituted by their presence here and now. So just 'inhabiting' a viewpoint, or just scrutinizing its occurrences, can't be enough to know it. Diagnoses must try to place viewpoints within larger personal, social, and historical stories. They must try to give, at each of several levels, *genealogies* for the perspectives they critique. We'll see that Aristotle seldom makes this contextualizing, genealogizing move—a second main weakness of his examination of 'appearances' (in Nietzsche's view).

To begin with, diagnosis must locate a view within the drive psychology of persons: Who (what type of person) thinks this way, and why? How does this view sit among his other views? Thus GM/III pursues the "meaning of ascetic ideals" into the separate cases of several personal types—'the artist', 'the philosopher', 'the priest'—and indeed into many subtypes and instances of these. The text stresses from the start that these values have very different significance in these different cases. Only in the priest do they help define or constitute the type itself, and so here the diagnosis concentrates. By contrast, Aristotle's critique of predecessors who deny pleasure focuses on their stated arguments and makes no effort to go 'behind' these to any typical motives.[131] Moreover, where he does distinguish types of persons by their psychic stances toward pleasure (NE III/10–12, VII/1–10), he pays no attention to undervaluings of pleasure (as rare and even nonhuman), focusing exclusively on the vice of excess.[132] Although we can read Aristotle's ethics as disavowing Plato's ascetic denial of worldly pleasures and pursuits, we find no account of why Plato or others might take that stance.

Nietzsche thinks those personal types are themselves only comprehensible in their social contexts. So GM/III tries to identify the main social function of the priest type: the priest 'serves life' by tending the multitudes of sick, by easing their suffering and redirecting their resentment. Because he does so precisely by preaching the ascetic ideal, he is really only a vehicle for that attitude, which indeed has a social presence far beyond individual priests. Nietzsche's diagnosis ascends to the level of this social will, to treat it in its own right. By contrast again, even where Aristotle does catalog different personal types—of hedonists but not ascetics—he treats them in abstraction from any social setting: he looks for no larger role their attitude might play. Although he elsewhere suggests a social-contextual view,[133] he doesn't pursue this suggestion by developing social meanings for those types, so that self-indulgence, for example, could mean different things in different social contexts; the vice is the same vice wherever we find it.[134]

In widening contrast with Aristotle, Nietzsche's study of the social will takes on a historical dimension: he examines how the ascetic ideal is

131. Note the suggestion, though, at NE 1172a30 that some who say pleasure is completely bad intentionally overstate their point, in order to counteract people's overly strong attraction to pleasure.

132. The temperate person (sophron), who desires and chooses bodily pleasures to the proper degree, is intermediate between the self-indulgent person (akolastos), who values such pleasure excessively, and one who values it too little, a type we so rarely meet that it hasn't even a name (NE 1119a6). So, too, in the related distinction between the controlled (enkrates) and uncontrolled (akrates) persons: both suffer the defect of having 'strong and bad appetites' for bodily pleasures (so neither is temperate), and both try to control these appetites (so neither is self-indulgent), but only the former can; the possibility of an excessive, ascetic control doesn't arise.

133. Generally, Pol. 1253a18: "And by nature the city is prior to the household and to each of us. For the whole is necessarily prior to the part." See also 1337a27.

134. Here, by and large, Aristotle's substance ontology prevails; vices and virtues are determined for the species human being and apply uniformly to individuals whatever their social setting.

itself in process, evolving by an inner dynamic from ancestral to descendent forms. He must attempt a social genealogy of this will not just because it means something different at each stage in its development, but because its meaning at each stage depends on those before and (especially) after. So his project reflects, once again, his 'temporal contextuality', which we find (only) partly anticipated by Aristotle.[135]

Most important for Nietzsche, to say what the ascetic ideal now means, one must say where it's heading; genealogy must try to predict the future of this will. Nietzsche bases this prediction precisely on his own dialectical studies, on his enactment in himself of his society's basic conflicts and *aporiai*.[136] He tries to locate and activate in himself his society's dominant and institutionalized views; by cultivating these basic cultural tensions in himself, under the hothouse conditions of his critical discipline, he tries to hurry them through their natural dialectic, to the conclusions that society as a whole will draw only much later. And by anticipating, through these self-experiments, where the prevailing values are heading (what they're becoming), he understands them in a privileged way. He is, in this further sense, too, a 'philosopher of the future': he sees the present partly *from* the future it's becoming.[137] Because this future is also the upshot of that intercritical work, it 'knows better' than the present from which it emerges.

The culminating stages in Nietzsche's story about the ascetic ideal have a special relevance to his method. He describes how this social will finds expression as a will to truth, a moralistic 'Christian truthfulness' that goes on to undermine Christian dogma and eventually turns against even the Christian morality that it itself involves [GM/III/24,27]. His diagnosis of asceticism finally hangs on the question of what will ensue when this will to truth turns back on itself to discover its own asceticism. The answer is not explicitly given. But it is, I think, that this will adopts precisely the method we are now analyzing. Nietzsche's new truth method is not only what allows this ascetic ideal to be adequately understood; the method takes its distinctive features *from* that (developing) self-understanding. Nietzsche shapes his method as that proper to the will to truth once it sees its own asceticism. By contrast, Aristotle's inability to notice the asceticism at work in his own truth project is linked

---

135. Perhaps Aristotle moves most toward Nietzsche wherever his ontology shifts its weight from substance (understood as the persisting thing that acts) to actuality (understood as the acting). Yet his 'actuality' still seems at odds with the process point. Its defining exclusion of 'potentiality' shows that it crucially claims self-sufficiency: actualities are not to be understood in relation to anything further, but in themselves.

136. WP/P/2–3 [1887–88]: "What I tell, is the history of the next two centuries." He speaks "as a spirit of risk and experiment who has already gone astray in every labyrinth of the future; as a prophetic spirit [*Wahrsagevogel-Geist*] who *looks back* when he tells what will come". GM/III/27: "what has [the problem of the *meaning* of the ascetic ideal] to do with yesterday or today!"

137. So the phrase has also the sense stressed by Nehamas (1988, 58); see n.91.

to the defects of the method he employs for truth. To see this, we must turn to the valuative aspects of his and Nietzsche's methods.

A third basic feature of Nietzsche's dialectic is its reliance on the values intrinsic to the power ontology, and developed in chapter 3. He hunts especially for the ways a viewpoint is active or reactive, healthy or sick. He directs, mainly, a 'masterly' eye on the dominant views and values of his society, and he diagnoses and *ranks* them accordingly.[138] In setting them into this new rank order, Nietzsche's dialectic 'heals' the system of views, renders it healthier. He takes this health-improving reranking of these viewpoints, his 'revaluation of values', to have epistemic rewards: activeness involves both a truth and an honesty, and so is another part of his method to 'know better'.[139]

Of course the sick slave will likely know more than the healthy master, in ways Nietzsche stresses;[140] indeed, we've seen (§ 4.3.2) how the will to truth was crucially developed among the sick. Yet the healthy still know better at an essential point: they aim aright (and true) at power itself; they 'know what's good for them' (in their essence) as wills to power. This core insight gives a ramifying strength to their position, in debate with the sick: it allows them an honesty and self-consistency that the slave must lack. The latter's attacks on the master conceal and depend on a primary envy and preference for his life; even the slave 'knows what's good for him'—the drive-enhancing activity of the master—but he knows it defectively or deficiently: he (feels he) can't enact it, so he buries this preference beneath an opposite ideal he constructs in its place. His position is a lie, his elaborations of it aimed as much to convince himself as the master.[141]

---

138. GM/I's concluding note identifies "the future task of the philosopher" as being "to solve the *problem of value,* . . . to determine the *rank order of values"*. CW/F: "a self-discipline was necessary for me: to take sides *against* everything sick in me, including Wagner, including Schopenhauer, including the whole modern 'humaneness'". See also BGE212.

139. The epistemic aspect of the revaluation of values emerges in EH/IV/1: *"Revaluation of all values:* that is my formula for an act of the highest self-reflection of humanity, that has become flesh and genius in me. My lot wills, that I must be the first *decent* [*anständig*] human being, that I know myself in opposition against the mendacity of millennia". EH/IV/6: "Nobody yet has felt the *Christian* morality as *beneath* him: that involves a height, a far view, a formerly quite unheard of psychological depth and abyssalness."

140. GM/I/10: "A race of such human beings of resentment will necessarily in the end be *cleverer* than any noble race". See also TI/IX/14.

141. GM/I/10: "While the noble human being lives in trust and openness with himself . . . , the human being of resentment is neither upright, nor naive, nor honest [*ehrlich*] and straightforward with himself." GM/II/11: "The active, grasping, encroaching human being is still a hundred steps closer to justice than the reactive; for it is not at all necessary for him to evaluate his object falsely and with prejudice, as the reactive human being does and must do." See also GM/III/14. BGE26: "And nobody *lies* as much as the indignant."

Nietzsche's new knower must work to overcome in himself such motives for falsifying. He must apply 'the viewpoint of health' in his major diagnoses, and bring to them its truth and honesty. So in GM/III, as Nietzsche places the ascetic ideal in personal and social context and process, he constantly judges both it and its associates in this essential dimension. His critique exposes not mainly inconsistency, but sickness in this will's motives and tendencies. He judges it with a masterly eye and finds it, in the main and the crux, something bad.[142] Hence, when he discovers this ascetic ideal at the heart of the will to truth, this calls it into question as never before.

On the one hand, and speaking very broadly, I think Aristotle shares with Nietzsche this 'viewpoint of health' and reflects it throughout his system, particularly as this differs from Plato's. His ontology replaces the Forms with individual substances, especially living organisms; his psychology replaces a soul seeking release from the body with a soul that's precisely a capacity of the body; his ethics replaces Plato's anti- and postcorporeal goals with the ideal of an active life here and now. Moreover, Aristotle like Nietzsche credits himself as healthy and credits his health as a ground of his truth. Yet although he thus rejects the life-denying asceticism of Plato's system, he doesn't (as we've seen) diagnose that tendency in Plato. Nor (we now add) does he notice its subtler presence in his own truth project.

Nietzsche's further revisions in Aristotle's method are the lessons he draws from his own disturbing self-diagnosis—of his defining truth project as sick with asceticism. But his overall lesson is not, as we might have thought, to remove (or eliminate) the asceticism but rather to control it, to turn even its negativity into service of a dominantly affirmative project. That 'master's truth' is itself just a stage or part in an 'over-man's truth' that supplies the real principle for Nietzsche's dialectical method. He wants (see § 2.5.3) not the 'pure health' that would come from renouncing and purging himself of asceticism, but a 'great health' that bears even this poisonous, life-denying will.[143] So we can distinguish, in Nietzsche's method, the ways it retains and even heightens attitudes of rejection and denial but also how it shifts the broader project these serve into an active mode.

The new philosopher still makes crucial use of ascetic denial. His

---

142. On one side, *"the ascetic ideal springs from the protective and curative instincts of a degenerating life"* [/13]; on the other, this ideal is *"the genuine disaster* in the history of the health of European humanity" [/21].

143. Recall from GM/I/16: "today there is perhaps no more decisive mark of a *'higher nature'*, a more spiritual nature, than being divided in this sense and still really a battleground for these opposites". GS120 asks "whether . . . our thirst for knowledge and self-knowledge doesn't need the sick soul as much as the healthy". Nietzsche's acceptance of asceticism is suggested in the way he 'blesses' it as itself an expression or device of life as will to power [GM/III/13, 28].

'spiritualizing' of his drives denies them straightforward expression; his dialectic sets them into rigorous conflicts and cross-critiques; his diagnoses, by their new angle of attack, 'cut into' these drives with an especially knowing cruelty, paining them by exposing their worst. We saw in § 4.4 Nietzsche's insistence that one must suffer for truth. So when the new philosopher steps out from the "gloomy caterpillar form" of the ascetic priest [GM/III/10], he does not leave such suffering behind; he inflicts it on himself still more methodically. But he also discovers, as his still-priestly predecessors could not, a positive meaning and purpose for this suffering, *in* life and the drives themselves, and this is the hinted resolution to the plot and puzzles of GM/III (connecting section 10 with 28). The philosopher finds the positive values to replace the ascetic ideal by finding a new truth project that blesses his drives, even as it makes them suffer.

The new philosopher reflects this love of the drives in the several ways he brings them into his project. Although he still denies them a life of bodily expression, this is now with the explicit purpose not of excluding or nullifying them, but of shifting them into that 'spiritual *agon*', his dialectic, where they join in his truth project. So instead of seeking the objectivity that dishonors the drives by counting them as mere obstacles to its goal, the new philosopher tries to know in and through drives' subjectivities. And though he 'cuts into' these attitudes with his diagnoses, he does so with a deep delight in them and reflects this in the way he gathers their perspectives into his truth. Whereas the old will to truth was 'moralistic', in conceiving its truth in opposition to the partialness of the too-interested drives, the new will wants truth precisely in their partialities.

More deeply, that old will was 'moralistic' because, Nietzsche thinks, it improperly thought of truth and falsity as 'opposites'. It thought of them as if they excluded one another, as if a belief or proposition could be, must be, only one and not the other (if true, then not at all false; if false, then not at all true). Nietzsche's new method abandons this exclusiveness. When exposing views' partiality and falseness, he doesn't cast them away as epistemically null. He reembraces them as real appearances contributing to the sense of all; by mapping their partialities, he wants to know *which* parts they play. So, in parallel to that 'great health', Nietzsche wants a 'great truth' that incorporates lies as well, or that shows them not utterly false after all.[144] His 'universal affirmation' occurs epistemically, too; he credits everything with truth. WP259 [1884]: "this contradictory creature has in his essence a great method of *knowledge:* he feels many Fors and Againsts—he raises himself *to justice*—to conception *beyond good- and evil-esteeming.*''

144. BGE34: "Indeed, what compels us at all to accept that there is an essential opposition of 'true' and 'false'? Is it not enough to accept levels of apparentness, and, as it were, lighter and darker shadows and shades of appearance . . . ?''

This brings us back to our earlier questions of whether Nietzsche breaks with Aristotle in abandoning the principle of noncontradiction and in refusing to 'close' his dialectic. It now appears that he does both. Whereas Aristotle aims to remove conflicts between views, by showing that some are false (and so must be excluded from the system of science),[145] Nietzsche wants to preserve the opposing positions and to build his own viewpoint with, or out of, their contradictions. But this embrace of contradiction doesn't take a form that paralyzes thought: A and not-A can both be true when we allocate the claims to different willful views. Aristotle's insistence on the principle depends on the legitimacy of isolating these propositions from the viewpoints from which they're held. By contrast, my A and your not-A collide less intolerably to the extent that we see how these opposites are mine and yours. Yet this mustn't, on the other side, remove all contradiction between them, as would a flattening relativism. Either my A or your not-A can have *more* of truth; the point is to see better which part of truth each has, by advancing their conflict by the method described.

In sum: the polymath added perspectives unselectively, because he thought of 'simple' or 'atomic' views as all on a par epistemically, none knowing better than any other. By contrast, Nietzsche thinks some perspectives do 'know better', and not merely by encompassing others (and so 'knowing more'). He thinks we uncover such priorities by engaging these viewpoints in that dialectic of cross-diagnoses and genealogies. That's how we find which side has the stronger case, which side is better able to explain the other. By that dialectic, these viewpoints settle into a rank order that reflects how well they know.[146] The knower accomplishes in himself the real epistemic levels of these viewpoints: their power in him reflects how well they see.

Yet we must grasp aright the lesson that emerges in this rank order. The scenario Nietzsche has in mind is not that in ranking (say) x ahead of y, the philosopher counts x (epistemically) victorious, pronounces it true and y false, or renounces the latter and believes/asserts the former. Rather, he finds truth not in either alone but precisely in the continuing,

145. Aristotle shows his masterly way of rejecting the false as sick in *Met.* 1062b33: "To hold equally to the opinions and seemings of those disputing against one another is foolish, for clearly one of them must be mistaken. This is apparent from what happens in sensation; for the same thing never appears sweet to some and the opposite to others, unless the sense-organ and judgment have been corrupted and injured." But against this, see *EE* 1216b30.

146. See HH/I/P/6 on how the free spirit's study of perspectives must help him see "the problem of *rank order* . . . and how power and right and comprehensiveness of perspective grow into the heights with one another." Clark (1990, 141) argues that Nietzsche's perspectivism allows for one perspective to be "cognitively superior" to another, when it "satisfies more fully . . . the cognitive interests of the perspective constituted by all of the relevant beliefs the two perspectives agree on." See, too, Leiter 1994.

unequal dialogue between them, in which each progressively qualifies the other.[147] This synthetic understanding holds even lesser perspectives in their place, as parts to its comprehensive truth. Thus it ranks itself above both of them, because they see just parts of its whole. So WP259 [1884]: "The wisest human being would be *the richest in contradictions,* who has, as it were, antennae for all kinds of human beings—and in the midst of this his great moments of *grand harmony*".

4.5.2   The new truth goal

Using this new method, we can ask, what new type of truth does Nietzsche claim or aspire to achieve? We begin by focusing on what we saw (§ 4.3.2) was the crux of the old notion of truth: correspondence. Indeed, if Nietzsche's new goal involved no sort of correspondence, we might hesitate to call it still a truth goal. I try to show, however, that he retains but revises this key element in the traditional goal: he re-aims the truth will at correspondence of another sort.

My sketch of his method has already projected a type of correspondence: not by the 'intentional object' of consciousness or language (the idea or concept or proposition) but by the intentional structure of the knower's own viewing and valuing; not to a world of mere matter but to one of telic and perspectival wills. By applying that method, the Nietzschean knower tries to bring it about that his synthetic viewpoint matches or mirrors the larger structure of reality: his social-historical context in particular but also (what he hypothesizes to be) an essential bent or bias to all the world (as a world of such wills). So, generally, Nietzsche follows the classical correspondence model of a microcosm mirroring a (the) macrocosm, the part isomorphic to the whole.

To begin with, Nietzsche's knower tries to gather in himself the attitudes and values that are or have been dominant in his society, to gather them in their main conflicts and debates. He comprehends each attitude by inhabiting or experiencing it himself, 'from inside', and by directing competing attitudes on it, thereby viewing it 'from outside', from (the point of view of) its most relevant or neighboring opponents. By holding in synthetic view both stances (of it as 'subject', of it as 'object'), he knows it better than it knows itself and better than it can be known by any external view, including (to the extent even possible) the purely objective 'view from nowhere'.

---

147. GS373: "Above all one should not will to strip [reality (*Dasein*)] of its *ambiguous* [*vieldeutigen*] character". Gadamer (1991, 305) says that by putting ourselves in the other's place we rise to a "higher universality that overcomes not only our own particularity but also that of the other". So I think Nietzsche has an answer to the question by Clark (1990, 148): "But if one perspective is cognitively superior to another, why should the truth it makes manifest need supplementation by the interpretations of things from an inferior perspective?"

This project—of so mapping these social wills and values—pursues a type of correspondence that is unusual in important ways. The knower knows the part (a viewpoint or value) not just by including and mirroring it, but by matching its dialectical setting: he must correspond to the relevant whole—a certain tension among viewpoints—in order to comprehend any part. (This makes a certain type of systematicity particularly necessary in Nietzsche's truth project.) Moreover, this correspondence must be between processes, not states: it's the knower's performance of the dialectic, his cross-diagnosing of viewpoints, that is to match the main crosscurrents of his society. In this activity, he sees the dominant social forces and attitudes as they see themselves.

Our look at Nietzsche's method showed, however, that he aspires to more than this: he wants to see these social forces better than they see themselves. He wants to carry their dialectic ahead to a new attitude they don't include. He wants to see 'us', his contemporaries, by the time span he means, not just as we see ourselves but also as we look from a better future: better in its values, and better knowing. He presumes to know and judge us from this standpoint, viewing our social forces in their strengths and weaknesses, their potencies and hindrances for this advance. Only by taking this step ahead is he able to set our age in the 'historical context' necessary for understanding it.

The question is, does Nietzsche identify this 'better future' as just whatever happens by the internal logic of our attitudes and values, as wherever their dialectic goes by its own momentum (a momentum shaped, of course, by its experience)? Will 'the truth about us' just be however our future views us? In that case, Nietzsche would still only seek and claim an 'internal truth', internal to that dialectic of social views and values. He would not project his claims beyond the warrant of that dialectic; he would aspire to 'transcend' the ways we view ourselves, but only to the ways we *will* view ourselves (and not to a way we might be, apart from all of our self-views).

I think it's clear that Nietzsche does not base his judgments on a prediction that our history will so proceed: that 'better future' may never come. Our social dialectic might instead end in nihilism, but that nihilistic viewpoint would not judge or know us 'better than we know ourselves'. Nietzsche's conviction that his own 'revaluation of values' advances to a better view rests in no faith that our values *must* so evolve. But he thinks they now have the potential for this improvement, so that if nihilism instead ensues, this will be a failure at something possible for us (even though nihilism won't itself view it so). In this and many other ways, Nietzsche shows that he aspires to a truth that 'transcends' the warrant of our social dialectic, to an 'external truth'.

Indeed, Nietzsche is pressed to attempt such external truths by a basic conviction we've often noticed: the contextuality of perspectives. Our culture's dialectic of viewpoints hasn't a complete meaning in or by itself (any more than an 'individual consciousness' has); its relation to external views on it, the critique they do or would direct on it, are crucial determinants of its identity or character. I think Nietzsche is pressed by this contextualism to try to push always outward into foreign views, so that he aspires to ascend from the viewpoint of European culture to that of world culture, to that of all humanity, to that of all life. The broadest of these, 'the viewpoint of life', plays an especially important role in his estimations of us, because it's in that view that he purports to find the standard of activeness. Judged by that viewpoint, from the healthy values of other living things, we are 'the sick animal'; GM as a whole can be seen to (try to) carry out its diagnoses chiefly from this broad external perspective.[148]

Nietzsche aspires not just to match his society's view structure, even as it will be, but to improve it, and by a standard not just internal to those views themselves. He views himself not just as discovering and announcing a momentum in our ideas; he presumes to shift them, under the warrant of a transcending view. He aspires to see and judge his neighborhood—this perspectival locale—not just from inside but from a stance (by a standard) that is true for all life: by the essential value of power or health. He speculates that power is the basic aim of all wills, so that all are subject to a basic evaluation as healthy or sick; he hopes that any better view than his own—even from outside our society, even from outside our species—would concur in this standard he mainly employs. Indeed, I think Nietzsche aspires to a transcending view not just in how he evaluates social wills but in his framing conception of society as consisting of such wills. He expresses his external-realist intent in his claim to have caught our essence as that of perspectival wills.

In § 4.5.3 I examine more closely the status of this external or essential claim and whether Nietzsche really does (or needs to) make it. But first let me sketch how I think it again involves a correspondence: not to the detailed content of the knower's own neighborhood but to (what Nietzsche claims to be) a structural feature of all reality—its aim at power or growth. Here again we can distinguish two aspects of this essential claim: a 'master's truth' and an 'overman's truth'.

On the one hand, the new knower sees the essential priority of the active; he matches, in his dominant attitudes, this primary tendency of all wills—present even in the sick, but there suppressed—to develop themselves (rather than reactively denying others). Judging his society's values in this light, he regards them from an angle structurally basic to all reality (as a world of power wills). He aligns himself with that deep tendency and claims from it the authority to rank his society's values by a standard that transcends them.

Beyond this, the new knower achieves a 'great health' by the way he gives priority to the active. He ranks it above the reactive not in the

148. See also GS380.

master's exclusiveness but in the overman's comprehensiveness: he retains the reactive as crucial contributor. Here again Nietzsche thinks he matches a structural feature of the world as will in the way this will, in aggregate, deploys its sick and healthy parts: a world or a culture builds itself always through collisions between opposites, especially those structural opposites of health and sickness.[149] In this overman's truth, the knower 'realizes' essence both practically and epistemically at once; thus for Nietzsche, as for Plato and Aristotle, the highest human condition is also the best understanding. So EH/BT/3: "This last, most joyous, most wantonly exuberant Yes to life is not only the highest insight but also the *deepest*, that which is most strictly confirmed and supported by truth and science."[150]

Nietzsche expresses this higher way of corresponding in his thought about eternal return. Interpreters have debated whether he thinks it true that all things so return or whether he means the thought just as a useful test or aid (in ranking persons or guiding practice).[151] We can now see a sort of middle way here: the claim of eternal return may indeed be (merely) false but useful, yet useful by helping toward a genuine truth that lies not in the claiming but in the willing that everything return. This involves that universal embrace of life that approves even sickness, hence aligns one to that broad structure in will to power itself. This helps explain Nietzsche's insistence on the thought, despite how dissatisfying (to us and him) are all efforts to prove the 'cosmological' claim. But he can be agnostic or even skeptical about that claim, because his truth lies in loving opposites enough to *want* them to return.[152]

---

149. Inasmuch as the overman is the highest case of this creation, he might even be viewed as a 'new creature' in this dramatic sense: he accomplishes a synthesis between the basic viewpoints of life (in its background health) and the human (in our typical sickness).

150. Against this might seem to count BGE9's mockery of the Stoic attempt to live "according to [gemäss] nature": "Imagine a being like nature, wasteful without measure [Maass], indifferent without measure, without aim or regard . . . —how *could* you live according to this indifference? Living—is that not precisely willing to be other than this nature?" Yet, as so many of Nietzsche's pragmatic complaints against truth, this point reverses direction for us when we remember that the hardest things are welcomed as hurdles for the most powerful.

151. Magnus offers (1978, 116) a sustained argument against any 'literal', 'empirical', 'cosmological', or 'descriptive' reading of eternal return; he also argues (1978, 140) against a 'normative' reading of it, i.e., against treating it as an action-guiding device like the categorical imperative.

152. Nietzsche might think that many (or all) people need to believe that (cosmological) claim, in order to will return properly, because only when they believe things do return, do they take the thought seriously enough for their welcome and embrace of it to count. (Similarly, they need to have vivid experience of the sickness, suffering, and other key 'negatives' they affirm; their affirmation must overcome this.) If so, he would mean that claim as a 'holy lie', analogous (partly) to the Platonic and priestly lies he so often discusses: his new philosopher tells that lie—perhaps even to himself—as a help toward that metaphysical insight.

4.5.3   A Nietzschean metaphysics

To strengthen this account of the new truth as correspondence Nietzsche claims and proposes to us, I return at last to my opening questions: Does he have a metaphysics? And how can he, compatibly with his perspectivism? At the core to the introduction's definition of metaphysics was the account of it as offering 'a systematic truth about essence'. To what extent does Nietzsche offer or believe such a metaphysical truth himself? And insofar as he does, how does this fit with all his perspectivist attacks on (and denials of) any absolute truth? In particular, does this account of his truth goal let us improve on the artificial two-level strategy I've used to reconcile those basic but conflicting aspects of his thought?

Of course, I've pushed Nietzsche's views in a metaphysical direction from the beginning, and the upshot isn't in doubt. I've tried to show, in the analyses of § 4.5.1 and § 4.5.2, how he builds a metaphysics of and for perspectives. As he adjusts the traditional truth project to this task, he must radically recast it so that he retains its central features—system/truth/essence—only in unfamiliar and hard-to-notice forms. So as we've clarified his perspectivist thoughts, we've been mapping not only how he recasts metaphysics but also just where he retains those central elements, disguised but recognizable. In this last section, I first note three important ways Nietzsche's perspectivism affects his 'epistemology'. Then I return to the crucial question in § 4.5.2—whether he really wants or claims an external or essential truth. I conclude by summing up this 'perspectivist metaphysics' I read in him.

In adapting the truth project to suit a knower and world that are perspectival wills, Nietzsche imposes certain *modesties* on it; these crucially flow from his requirement that one must incorporate and synthesize perspectives in order to understand them. I distinguish three such modesties, which concern, as it were, knowing's past, present, and future: how his new knower thinks he *got* the truth (his truth method), how confident he is that he *has* it (this truth's transparency or presence to him), and how he *aims* this truth (the future he hopes for it, in collisions with opposing views). At each point, Nietzsche draws epistemological lessons that limit or reduce the aspirations by most metaphysicians before. Returning to our comparison with Aristotle, we again find that he partly anticipates these lessons. But although Nietzsche's epistemology broadly follows Aristotle's anti-Platonic model, he works coherent and distinctive changes in it.

1. Nietzsche's truth is—in how he gets it, in the past that gives him title to it—*empirical*, not a priori. The knower needs insight into a wealth of viewpoints, common and particular, in his society; his perspective must come to encompass these many others. Clearly there's no a priori route to this perspectival content, no way of deducing it by reason alone. The knower must begin by observing his society and its personalities, by

'taking specimens' of their attitudes and values. But this observing can still be chiefly an armchair activity, carried out by reading and by studying oneself (as largely shaped by those common values).[153] These experiences of viewpoints form the main 'data' Nietzsche's theories try to fit and explain. In § 4.5.1, I compared this type of empiricism to Aristotle's reliance (clearest in his ethics and politics) on the *phainomena*, the 'opinions of the many and the wise'.

But Nietzsche's knower 'observes' these viewpoints in a special way, and here we saw he breaks from Aristotle and offers an unfamiliar empiricism. He tries to look not just at these viewpoints but through them ('through their eyes'); for this purpose, he assembles (incorporates) these attitudes as living factors in himself, as ways he can and does (sometimes) view the world. When he does look 'at' these viewpoints, it's not from the disinterested eye of a pure objectivity but from competing interests, in the intercriticism analyzed in § 4.5.1. He studies these viewpoints by gathering them into himself and subjecting them there to that disciplined debate in which they grow subtler and stronger. He learns about them not merely by watching them in others but by subjecting them to tests and experiments within himself. This route or method by which he reaches his truths, this odd empiricism, is also his justification for them, the ground for his confidence in them.

2. This new knower's truth is—in its presence to him as he has it—*hypothetical*, not certain. It lacks the transparent sureness often claimed by metaphysicians: his theory might not (so far as he can tell) be true, after all. Because he has reached it empirically, it must lack the apodicticity associated with the a priori. Further, his peculiar version of empiricism brings him to his truths not along the straight road of demonstration but through an intricate dialectic among a multitude of voices or attitudes; in this dialectic, viewpoints are judged by standards much less evident than logical consistency. And instead of using this method to pile up a mass of specific psychological insights about these views, he extrapolates far beyond such details, to attempt grand rankings of the attitudes and values of his culture. These special features of his empiricism carry him beyond Aristotle's admissions of imprecision in his own ethics and politics.[154] Nietzsche repeatedly stresses that he offers his thoughts as attempts, conjectures, experiments.[155]

3. This new knower's truth is—in its aspiration to constrain future

153. The viewpoints this knower most needs to observe are (on the one hand) those so basic and general in his society as to be pervasively available, and (on the other) those great articulations against the common, found in history and literature (together with especially revealing portraits of the common).

154. *NE* 1094b12–27 and 1103b34–1104a10 suggest that this imprecision is inevitable because of (what we might call) the contextuality of the fine, the just, the good.

155. BGE42. See Kaufmann (1974, 85ff.) on Nietzsche's 'experimentalism'.

debate—*partial,* not absolute or complete. It does not presume that it could not be improved. Its truth lies in its synthesis of viewpoints; this truth is incomplete insofar as there are always viewpoints it fails to take in. A complete truth of perspectives would require including them all (seeing from all eyes), which is a more clearly unachievable ideal than that of objectivity. (We can plausibly aspire to a single best view on the whole, but not to combine all views.) Nietzsche's knower allows that his view can always be surpassed, by introducing further perspectives into the dialectic he offers us.

There's an obvious way in which Aristotle—indeed any theorist—would admit this partialness; nobody can hope to have all the facts. But Nietzsche's contextual point heightens this incompleteness by changing the status even of the part of the truth he has: in being ignorant of these foreign perspectives, he's partly ignorant, too, of his own, because this *is* also as they view it. Because the new knower's views about the part can never be 'the whole truth', they can't even be 'wholly true'; his truth has a different logic than the old, a more radical 'partialness'. The old knower aimed (misguidedly) at a reality complete in each part; his truth also had a logic of complete parts, of atomic truths that could be laid in place one by one. The new knower sees that any neighborhood he inhabits is not just as that nexus of wills sees itself but also as it looks to foreign eyes. He allows that some of these others may understand even himself better than he does.

This modesty does not, however, prevent Nietzsche from hoping that on some central points his perspective will not be annulled or reversed by such fuller and better views. Here (as not in his details) he aspires beyond partiality, to a truth that will or should survive and even prevail in our dialectic, should become a presupposition the parties then share and build from. He hopes this, I think, for his core ontological thought: reality consists of contextual perspectives willing power. And he hopes it for his evaluations (rankings) of perspectives by the standard embedded in this ontology: activeness or health. He hopes it, that is, for his judgments of essence, in which he aspires to speak not just for our viewpoint but for that of all life, as I've argued in § 4.5.2. These essential-external views and values guide and pervade all of his diagnoses; they are (as we've seen) *why* these diagnoses pursue an empirical, hypothetical, and partial truth.

This poses a puzzle about these essential-external claims: if these are premises that found Nietzsche's truth method, mustn't they be themselves outside it? Mustn't they be not just nonpartial but nonempirical and nonhypothetical, too? How can the power ontology be known the same way as all the findings of the method it founds? Mustn't it be established somehow a priori, and for certain, before that study can get under way?

The Aristotle comparison can help us set our sights here. Of course

Aristotle's treatments of human life, in his ethics and politics, are also pervaded and steered by metaphysical first principles (*archai*), those stating his ontology of substance, with its embedded value of actuality (as 'keeping-in-the-end' essential to substance). So a similar question arises for Aristotle as for Nietzsche: What is the epistemological status of these first principles? Two special routes to them are suggested: (a) Aristotle sometimes says that they're established independently of that dialectic, by *intuition*,[156] and (b) he might also, as Irwin argues, try to establish them by *transcendental argument*, as "features of reality that are necessary for it to be an object of scientific study at all".[157] Either route promises to improve on the empirical-dialectical method, by securing the certainty Aristotle demands for his first principles. Does Nietzsche think the power ontology is justified in either of these ways: by intuition or by a (Kantian) transcendental argument?

First, does Nietzsche rest his power ontology and values on some privileged intuition he thinks his dialectic brings him to, a self-validating insight into the viewpoint of life in general? Does he think that the will to power essence becomes transparently evident when one 'looks at it' the proper way, perhaps after peeling away the contingent accretions that had blocked it from view? I think it's clear that on the whole Nietzsche rejects any such 'immediate certainty' about anything at all.[158] He is, as we've seen, highly suspicious of consciousness and stresses that what it gives us 'inwardly' is also just appearances, not facts. His contextual point further suggests that no moment *could* be self-sufficiently reliable. For these reasons, he chiefly denies that there's any sure 'presence' of essence to us.

Second, does Nietzsche instead rely on a transcendental argument to ground his ontology, reasoning that it's a 'condition of the possibility' of experience that we and the world be wills to power? There are importantly different forms such an argument might take, and several can be traced in Nietzsche; it would be a large project to map them.[159] But it's very unlikely that he means, on the whole, to ground or justify his power ontology this way. He typically thinks of such argument, following Schopenhauer more than Kant, as showing that we can't help but think or experience the world *as it is not*; by contrast, he uses his power

156. An immediate and certain awareness of first principles seems to be the chief function of *nous*; *NE* 1143a35–b5, *PoAn* 100b5–17.

157. Irwin 1988, 19. Irwin argues that Aristotle's addition of such arguments to his earlier "pure dialectic" gives him a "strong dialectic" that better supports his external-realist positions.

158. See BGE16, 34, 281. Cf. Clark 1990, 213f.

159. For example, he sometimes suggests that we (humans) can understand something only by reading intention—hence will—into it. GS373: "But an essentially mechanical world would be an essentially *meaningless* [*sinnlose*] world!" See also WP619 [1885], WP627 [1885–86]. See Kaufmann (1974, 207) on the implausibility of such an argument for will to power.

ontology to suggest *how it is*, despite or behind the distortions inevitable in our thinking or experience.[160]

I think Nietzsche renounces such efforts to ground his claims independently of that dialectic. But he does not therefore retract the scope of his claims, to mean them merely true for that dialectic. He allows his aspiration to transcend the warrant of his past method and present certainty. He aspires beyond partiality toward external truth on his central points, while remaining empirical and hypothetical in his method and sureness.

So the empirical truth method does apply to the ontological claims as well: they are part of the systematic hypothesis, whose capacity to organize and explain the 'data of experience' is its title to truth. Those perspectival 'entries' serve as Nietzsche's evidence for both his content claims about society and selves and his essence claims about perspectival power wills; he hopes that this system of claims will fit and clarify this data better than other theories can. We can adopt here Quine's image of a web of beliefs, in place of the Cartesian edifice. The essence claims stand not as foundations (laid down first and a priori) but at the center of a web, providing the basic concepts and structures employed by all more particular views, including those 'at the periphery', that describe particular data. It is the web as a whole that adjusts itself to that data and gets credit for explaining it.

In their centrality, the essence claims are, in one way, at some remove from the experiential data: we're not to expect that any specific experiences could decisively confirm or disconfirm the power ontology. There's no experiment that could isolate that sector of the theory and put just it to the test. But in another way, these essence claims reach right out to the data and are (partly) confirmed or disconfirmed by all experiences: they propose basic concepts and structures for describing that data, and their aptness for this can be partly judged in every case. Does it clarify this experience to describe it under the will to power framework?

Epistemically, there's no sharp boundary between Nietzsche's claims about essence and about content, between his metaphysics and his particular psychological and cultural insights. Instead of two 'levels' to his truths, divided by a transcendental line, we find a continuum or range in generality, in how broadly, hence indirectly, they bear on experience. But even the claims that 'meet' experience most indirectly and loosely, by broadly structuring all more direct descriptions, are still subject to appraisal through experience. They, too, are empirical and hypothetical.[161]

Nietzsche expects that our dialectic (of our culture's will to truth) will tend to bring his method and theory to the top—but only if we carry

160. See, e.g., WP497 [1884], WP487 [1886–87], WP515 [1888].
161. BGE36.

out this dialectic in enough like the way described in § 4.5.1—which means with enough of his method to begin with. Given that we are perspectival wills, and given how our will to truth's history has prepared us to recognize this reality (§ 4.3.2), Nietzsche has hopes that our own views and values will lead us to his. But it's not inevitable that we will, and their truth does not depend on our cultural dialectic arriving at them. Thus he doesn't posit these truths as merely true *for* our social context, as an 'internal realism'. He guesses at essential-external truths, and his hopes for internal success depend on this: these truths will be progressively confirmed by experience, but only by an experience properly conceived and studied, because only then will we be 'led by the facts themselves'. Because he knowingly casts his claims beyond their warrant in this way—without a priori proof and beyond not just his own experience but all the experience of our culture—he offers them all the more hypothetically.

On these incomplete grounds, Nietzsche still aspires to completeness, in his central ontological claims. In radiating his other ideas out from these, he has still a metaphysics, an attempt at systematic truth about essence. Although he renounces the effort at a decisive, conceptual proof of these central claims, he still offers them as true in a sense (described in § 4.5.2) crucially continuous with the traditional one. He aspires to transcend his personal, our cultural, and even the human viewpoint, to that of all life.[162] He hopes that his gist would be true for any fuller or better view than his or our own, that a better view would still have to have something like the ontology of perspectival wills as a central and organizing thought.[163]

When we understand the metaphysics this way, we see how to overcome the dichotomy with which we began: between Nietzsche's perspectivism and all his positive claims, especially the power ontology. At our beginning, it seemed we could sustain both positions only by 'insulating' the ontology from the perspectival point. But now we see how Nietzsche can agree that his metaphysics is itself 'just a perspective' (as in BGE22) without giving up its claim to epistemic rank. We see how his perspectivism indeed adds certain modesties to his epistemology yet how he still aspires to a truth transcending the warrant of his and our experience.

We now know not to hear that perspectival critique ('only an interpretation') in the commonest way: as the relativist's challenge that reduces every view to an equal footing with others, each true for itself

162. He expresses this aspiration, I think, when he posits or imagines a god—Dionysus—as a most knowing being emblematic of the essential truth (and truth method) he proposes; see BGE295, WP1035 [1887], but also WP1037 [1887].
163. Nietzsche speaks of his aspiration to endure in TI/IX/51: "To create things on which time tests its teeth in vain; in form, *in substance* to try for a little immortality—I have never yet been modest enough, to demand less of myself."

alone. This is not how Nietzsche mostly and most tellingly carries out such critique (exposes a view as 'mere perspective'). Rather, he presses it in the form of often-elaborate diagnoses of specific psychological types, as misdirected by their typical motives. He invites us to learn to overcome these mistakes ourselves, thereby encompassing and rising above those types and tracking truth better than they. So his critiques presume that perspectives can become truer, in particular, by encompassing more perspectives, and by the self-clarity of (a for-the-most-part) health or activeness. Nietzsche replaces the bivalent notion of truth with a graded hierarchy of perspectives, ranked as they see more and better than one another. The question is not whether a perspective speaks, but which perspective.

Recognizing how Nietzsche's perspectivism ranks perspectives, we can hear his insistence that his thoughts are 'his truths' not as renouncing the claim that they're truer than others, but as boasting that nobody else is strong (honest and courageous) enough to see as much as he. So BGE43: "'My judgment is *my* judgment: another [person] does not easily have a right to it'—says perhaps such a philosopher of the future." Similarly, when Nietzsche denies that his truths are 'for everyone', his principal suggestion is not that others will have equal truths of their own but that others can't or won't bear so much truth, and such truth. Few could stand a truth that requires adopting such a multitude of viewpoints, sustaining so intense an intercritical struggle among them, but keeping an active or positive eye despite suffering these constant conflicts.

Nietzsche retains the 'cognitive' values of philosophy's tradition—only reinterpreting them, not rejecting them. The old goal of understanding, of 'being in the truth', still abides in his thought, despite his many famous aspersions against it. To correspond in his new way, to his new reality, is the highest form of will to power and the best human activity. Hence Nietzsche's ideal person turns out to be still the philosopher, the one who knows most and best, turns out indeed to be Nietzsche himself. Thus he remains deeply continuous with the tradition before him.

APPENDIX: A NIETZSCHEAN VOCABULARY

As described in the Preface, I have tried to translate Nietzsche's main philosophical vocabulary consistently, according to the following equivalences. I mark with an asterisk cases in which a single English word is used to render more than one German term. I have grouped the words into subvocabularies.

Metaphysics of Power

Macht [power]; *Kraft* [force]

stark [strong]; *Stärke* [strength]; *erstarken* [to strengthen]; *Verstärkung* [strengthening]

    schwach [weak]

Gewalt [control]; *Gewaltmensch* [controller]; *Überwältigung* [subjugation]; *Gewaltsamkeit* [violence]; *vergewaltigen* [to assault]

überwinden [to overcome]; *unterordnen* [to subordinate]; *unterdrücken* [to oppress]; *unterwerfen* [to subjugate]

einverleiben [to incorporate]; *aneignen* [to appropriate]

befehlen [*to command]; *gebieten* [*to command]; *Gebot* [command]; *regieren* [to rule]; *richten* [to direct]

    gehorchen [to obey]; *Gehorsam* [obedience]

Kampf [struggle]; *Wettkampf* [contest]; *Krieg* [war]; *Spannung* [tension]

Gegensatz [opposite/opposition]; *gegensätzlich* [opposing]; *Widerspruch* [contradiction]

Feind [enemy]; *Feindschaft* [enmity]; *feindlich/feindselig* [hostile]; *Gegner* [opponent]; *Widerstand* [resistance]

Becoming and Difference

Werden [becoming]; *Fluss* [flux]
  Sein [being]
Wandlung [*change]; *verwandeln* [to change]; *Wechsel* [*change];
  Veränderung [alteration]; *Bewegung* [movement]
Geschehen [happening]; *Prozess* [process]; *Entwicklung* [development]
  Augenblick [moment]; *Zustand* [state]
vergänglich [transitory]; *Übergang* [transition]; *vergehen* [to pass away]
  fortwährend [constant]; *beständig* [continual]; *Dauer* [duration];
  dauerhaft [durable]; *dauern* [to endure]; *fest* [firm]; *ewig* [eternal]
  Wiederkehr [return]; *Wiederkunft* [recurrence]
Verhältnis [*relation]; *Relation* [*relation]
  an sich [in itself]
Ganze [whole]; *Ergänzung* [*completion]; *umfänglich* [comprehensive];
  Einheit [unity]; *Vielheit* [multiplicity]
  Vollendung [*completion]; *vollständig* [complete]; *vollkommen* [perfect]
  Theil [part]; *theilbar* [divisible]
Verschiedenheit [*difference]; *Differenz* [*difference]
  gleich [equal]; *ähnlich* [similar]
  anders [other]; *fremd* [foreign]

Ascent/Decline

aktiv [active]; *Akt* [act]; *Aktivität* [*activity]; *Aktion* [*action]
  reaktiv [reactive]; *Reaktivität* [reactivity]; *Reaktion* [reaction]; *passiv*
  [passive]
  Handlung [*action]; *handeln* [*to act]; *agiren* [*to act]
  thuen [to do]; *Thun* [doing]; *That* [deed]; *Thäter* [doer]; *Thätigkeit*
  [*activity]; *Thatsache* [fact]
Gesundheit [health]; *Überfülle* [overfullness]; *Überfluss* [overflow]; *reich*
  [rich]
  Krankheit [sickness]; *Verarmung* [*poverty]; *Armut* [*poverty]
Aufgang [ascent]; *aufsteigen* [to rise]
  Niedergang [decline]; *niedersteigen* [to fall]
wachsen [to grow]; *Wachstum* [growth]
  Erhaltung [preservation]; *Bewahrung* [maintenance]
  Entartung [degeneration]; *Verdorbenheit* [corruption]; *décadence*
  (Fr.) [decadence]
schaffen [to create]; *schöpfen* [to produce]
vergeistigen [to spiritualize]; *sublimieren* [to sublimate]

Will and Psychology

Wille [will]; *wollen* [to will]

Trieb [drive]; *treiben* [to drive]; *Antrieb* [impulse]; *streben* [to strive]

Affekt [affect]; *Gefühl* [feeling]; *Begierde* [desire]; *Bedürfniss* [*need]; *Noth* [*need]

Glück [happiness]; *Lust* [pleasure]; *Freude* [joy]; *Wohlbefinden* [well-being]; *Zufriedenheit* [contentment]; *angenehm* [agreeable] *Leiden* [suffering]

Seele [soul]; *Geist* [spirit]

Mensch [human being]; *menschlich* [human]; *Übermensch* [overman]

The Social Order

Rangordnung [rank order]; *Grad* [degree]

Herr [master]; *herrschen* [to master]; *Herrschaft* [mastery] *Sklave* [slave]

vornehm [noble]; *Adel* [*aristocracy]; *Aristokratism/Aristokratie* [*aristocracy]

züchten [to breed]

Individuum [individual]; *einzeln* [single]; *Ausnahme* [exception]; *Auswahl* [select]

Heerde [herd]; *gemeinsam* [common]; *gewöhnlich* [ordinary]; *durchschnittlich* [average]; *mittelmässig* [mediocre]

Values and Moralities

Werth [value]; *werthen* [to value]; *Umwerthung* [revaluation]; *entwerthen* [to devalue]

schätzen [to esteem]; *Schätzung* [assessment]; *Wertschätzung* [evaluation]; *Abschätzung* [appraisal]

Moral [morality]; *moralisch* [moral]

Sittlichkeit [ethics]; *sittlich* [ethical]; *Sitte* [custom]; *gesittet* [civilized]

gut [good]; *nützlich* [useful]; *förderlich* [beneficial]; *Vortheil* [advantage] *schlecht* [bad]; *böse* [evil]; *schädlich* [harmful]

Tugend [virtue]; *Redlichkeit* [honesty]; *Mut* [courage]; *Tapferkeit* [bravery]; *Ehrfurcht* [reverence]

Laster [vice]; *Feigheit* [cowardice]

ressentiment (Fr.) [resentment]; *Rache* [revenge]

Selbstsucht [selfishness]; *Grausamkeit* [cruelty]

Mitleid [pity]; *Mitgefühl* [sympathy]; *Wohlwollens* [benevolence]

Schuld [guilt]; *verantwortlich* [responsible]; *strafen* [to punish]; *Gewissen* [conscience]

Unschuld [innocence]; *erlösen* [to redeem]; *rechtfertigen* [to justify]

Perspectives, Knowing, and Truth

Perspektive [perspective]

interpretieren [*to interpret]; *auslegen* [*to interpret]; *bestimmen* [to determine]; *bestimmt* [determinate]

wahr [true]; *Wahrheit* [truth]; *wahrhaftig* [truthful]; *richtig* [correct]; *entsprechen* [to correspond]

    falsch [false]; *Irrthum* [error]; *Fehler/Fehlgriff* [*mistake]; *Lüge* [lie]; *verlogen* [mendacious]; *Betrug* [deception]

wissen [*to know]; *(er)kennen* [*to know]; *gewiss* [certain]; *weis* [wise]; *Weisheit* [wisdom]; *Beweis* [proof]

    Unwissenheit [ignorance]; *Ungewissheit* [uncertainty]

Erlebniss [*experience]; *Erfahrung* [*experience]; *Empfindung* [perception]; *Anschauung/Intuition* [*intuition]; *Bewusstsein* [consciousness]

    Verstand [understanding]; *Vernunft* [reason]; *Urtheil* [judgment]

Sprache [language]

    Sinn [sense]; *Bedeutung* [meaning]; *Begriff* [concept]

    Satz [proposition]; *Grundsatz* [principle]; *Glaubenssatz* [doctrine]; *Lehre* [teaching]

BIBLIOGRAPHY

Primary Sources

For Nietzsche's German text I have relied on the *Kritische Studien-ausgabe,* ed. Giorgio Colli and Mazzino Montinari (Berlin: de Gruyter, 1980). Where I provide the German, it reproduces this edition.

Nietzsche's Published Works

The following are the near-standard English translations of the works Nietzsche completed for publication, arranged by their (approximate) years of *composition* (to facilitate comparisons with the *Nachlass* references). I cite these works by the codes given below, according to policies described in the Preface. For my revisions to these translations, see the Preface and the Appendix.

1869–71: **[BT]** *The Birth of Tragedy.* Trans. W. Kaufmann. New York: Vintage Books, 1967. (With CW.) Revised 1873.
  [/ASC] "Attempt at a Self-Criticism" written 1886
1873–76: **[UM]** *Untimely Meditations.* Trans. R. J. Hollingdale. Cambridge: Cambridge University Press, 1983.
  [/I] "David Strauss the Confessor and the Writer"
  [/II] "On the Uses and Disadvantages of History for Life"
  [/II/F] Foreword
  [/III] "Schopenhauer as Educator"
  [/IV] "Richard Wagner in Bayreuth"

1876–79:　[**HH**]　*Human, All Too Human.* Trans. Hollingdale. Cambridge: Cambridge University Press, 1986.
[/I] Volume I
[/II] Volume II, Part I: "Mixed Opinions and Maxims"
[/III] Volume II, Part II: "The Wanderer and His Shadow"
[/I/P], [/II/P] Prefaces to both volumes written 1886

1880–81:　[**D**]　*Daybreak.* Trans. Hollingdale. Cambridge: Cambridge University Press, 1982.
[/P] Preface written 1886

1881–82:　[**GS**]　*The Gay Science.* Trans. Kaufmann. New York: Vintage Books, 1974.
[/JCR] "Joke, Cunning, and Revenge"; Prelude in German Rhymes
[/P] Preface written 1886
—Book V [343–83] written 1886

1882–85:　[**TSZ**]　*Thus Spoke Zarathustra.* Trans. Kaufmann. In *The Portable Nietzsche* [PortN], New York: Viking Press, 1968.
[/I]–[/IV] Four parts
[/I/P] "Zarathustra's Preface" to Part I

1885–86:　[**BGE**]　*Beyond Good and Evil.* Trans. Kaufmann. New York: Vintage Books, 1966.
[/P] Preface

1886:　　　BT/ASC, HH/I/P, HH/II/P, D/P, GS/P, GS343–83

1887:　　　[**GM**]　*On the Genealogy of Morals.* Trans. Kaufmann and Hollingdale. New York: Vintage Books, 1969. (With EH.)
[/P] Preface
[/I]–[/III] Three essays

1888:　　　[**CW**]　*The Case of Wagner.* Trans. Kaufmann. New York: Vintage Books, 1967. (With BT.)
[/F] Foreword

1888:　　　[**TI**]　*Twilight of the Idols.* Trans. Kaufmann. In PortN.
[/F] Foreword
[/I]–[/XI] Eleven chapters

1888:　　　[**A**]　*The Antichrist.* Trans. Kaufmann. In PortN.

1888:　　　[**EH**]　*Ecce Homo.* Trans. Kaufmann. New York: Vintage Books, 1969. (With GM.)
[/F] Foreword
[/I]–[/IV] Four parts
[/BT], [/UM], etc. Subparts of [/III] on Nietzsche's earlier works; I cite these subparts by the codes for these works

1888:　　　[**NCW**]　*Nietzsche contra Wagner.* Trans. Kaufmann. In PortN.
[/E] Epilogue

Nietzsche's *Nachlass*

I use codes to refer to the following translations of notes, letters, and drafts not completed for publication (or that Nietzsche decided not to publish)—his *Nachlass*. When citing these materials I give in brackets the year of composition (according to the Colli-Montinari dates for the source notebooks). As described in the Preface, I cite *Nachlass* materials not found in the following translations by giving the volume, notebook, and entry number from the Colli-Montinari *Kritische Studienausgabe*, together with the year; for example, KSA/10/7[77] [1883]. This allows the text to be located as well in the *Kritische Gesamtausgabe* by the same editors.

[P&T] *Philosophy and Truth: Selections from Nietzsche's Notebooks of the Early 1870's.* Ed. and trans. D. Breazeale. Atlantic Highlands, N.J.: Humanities Press, 1979. (I cite this by page number.) Includes: [TL] "On Truth and Lies in a Nonmoral Sense"

[PTAG] *Philosophy in the Tragic Age of the Greeks.* Trans. M. Cowan. Chicago: Regnery Gateway, 1962. (I cite this by section number.)

[WP] *The Will to Power.* Trans. Kaufmann and Hollingdale. New York: Vintage Books, 1967. (I cite this by note number.)

[PortN] *The Portable Nietzsche.* Ed. and trans. Kaufmann. New York: Viking Press, 1968. (I cite miscellanea from this anthology by page number.) Includes: [HC] "Homer's Contest"

[F&S] *Nietzsche: A Self-Portrait from His Letters.* Ed. and trans. P. Fuss and H. Shapiro. Cambridge: Harvard University Press, 1971. (I cite this by letter number—e.g., F&S #20.)

Secondary Sources

References to secondary sources are to author, year of cited publication, and page number. I cite Plato and Aristotle with the familiar abbreviations of works, and with the standard (Stephanus and Bekker) pages and lines. I cite Heraclitus by the fragment number in Diels-Kranz; for example, DK10.

Alderman, H. 1977. *Nietzsche's Gift.* Athens: Ohio University Press.

Allison, D. B., ed. 1985. *The New Nietzsche: Contemporary Styles of Interpretation.* Cambridge: MIT Press. Orig. pub. New York: Dell, 1977.

Baier, A. C. 1987. "Hume, the Women's Moral Theorist?" In Kittay and Meyers 1987.

Barnes, J. 1982. *The Presocratic Philosophers.* Rev. Ed. London: Routledge & Kegan Paul. Orig. pub. 1979.

Bergmann, F. 1988. "Nietzsche's Critique of Morality." In Solomon and Higgins 1988.

Bergson, H. 1946. "The Perception of Change." Trans. M. Andison. In *The Creative Mind: An Introduction to Metaphysics.* New York: Philosophical Library. Address delivered in 1911.

Blondel, E. 1991. *Nietzsche: The Body and Culture: Philosophy as a Philological Genealogy.* Trans. S. Hand. Stanford: Stanford University Press. Orig. pub. as *Nietzsche le corps et la culture.* Paris: Presses Universitaires de France, 1986.

Bolton, R. 1975. "Plato's Distinction between Being and Becoming." *Review of Metaphysics* 29 (1):66–95.

Bostock, D. 1988. *Plato's Theaetetus.* Oxford: Oxford University Press.

Breazeale, D. 1990. "Introduction" and notes to *Philosophy and Truth: Selections from Nietzsche's Notebooks of the Early 1870's.* Paperback Ed. Atlantic Highlands, N.J.: Humanities Press. Orig. pub. 1979.

Burnyeat, M. 1990. "Introduction" to *The Theaetetus of Plato.* Indianapolis: Hackett.

Chappell, V. C. 1962. "Time and Zeno's Arrow." *Journal of Philosophy* 59 (8):197–213.

Choderow, N. J. 1989. *Feminism and Psychoanalytic Theory.* New Haven: Yale University Press.

Clark, M. 1990. *Nietzsche on Truth and Philosophy.* Cambridge: Cambridge University Press.

Code, L. 1991. *What Can She Know?* Ithaca: Cornell University Press.

Conway, D. W. 1993. "Das Weib an Sich: The Slave Revolt in Epistemology." In Patton 1993b.

Cornford, F. M. 1937. *Plato's Cosmology: The Timaeus of Plato Translated with a Running Commentary.* London: Kegan Paul.

Danto, A. C. 1965. *Nietzsche as Philosopher.* New York: Macmillan.

———. 1994. "Some Remarks on *The Genealogy of Morals.*" In Schacht 1994. Orig. pub. in *International Studies in Philosophy* 18 (2):3–15 (1986).

Deleuze, G. 1983. *Nietzsche and Philosophy.* Trans. H. Tomlinson. New York: Columbia University Press. Orig. pub. as *Nietzsche et la philosophie.* Paris: Presses Universitaires de France, 1962.

———. 1985. "Nomad Thought." Trans. D. Allison. In Allison 1985. Orig. pub. as "Pensée nomade" in *Nietzsche aujourd'hui.* Paris: Union Generale d'Editions, 1973.

de Man, P. 1979. *Allegories of Reading: Figural Language in Rousseau, Nietzsche, Rilke, and Proust.* New Haven: Yale University Press.

Derrida, J. 1976. *Of Grammatology.* Trans. G. Spivak. Baltimore: Johns Hopkins University Press. Orig. pub. as *De la grammatologie.* Paris: Les Editions de Minuit, 1967.

———. 1979. *Spurs: Nietzsche's Styles.* Trans. B. Harlow. Chicago: University of Chicago Press. Orig. pub. as *Éperons: Les Styles de Nietzsche.* Paris: Flammarion, 1978.

———. 1982. *Margins of Philosophy.* Trans. A. Bass. Chicago: University of Chicago Press. Orig. pub. as *Marges de la philosophie.* Paris: Les Editions de Minuit, 1972.

———. 1988. *The Ear of the Other: Otobiography, Transference, Translation.* Trans. A. Ronell & P. Kamuf. Lincoln: University of Nebraska Press. Orig.

pub. as *L'oreille de l'autre: Otobiographies, transferts, traductions*. Montreal: Vlb Editeur, 1982.

Ellis, J. M. 1989. *Against Deconstruction*. Princeton: Princeton University Press.

Figes, E. 1987. *Patriarchal Attitudes: Women in Society*. New York: Persea Books. Orig. pub. New York: Stein and Day, 1970.

Fine, G. 1988. "Owen's Progress: A Critical Notice of *Logic, Science, and Dialectic: Collected Papers in Greek Philosophy*. By G. E. L. Owen, Edited by M. Nussbaum." *Philosophical Review* 97 (3):373–99.

Foot, P. 1973. "Nietzsche: The Revaluation of Values." In Solomon 1973b.

———. 1994. "Nietzsche's Immoralism." In Schacht 1994. Orig. pub. in *New York Review of Books* 38 (11):18–22 (1991).

Foucault, M. 1982. "The Discourse on Language." Trans. R. Swyer. In *The Archaeology of Knowledge and The Discourse on Language*. New York: Pantheon. Orig. pub. as *L'ordre du discours*. Paris: Gallimard, 1971.

———. 1984. "Nietzsche, Genealogy, History." Trans. D. Bouchard and S. Simon. In P. Rabinow (ed.), *The Foucault Reader*. New York: Pantheon. Orig. pub. as "Nietzsche, la généalogie, l'histoire" in *Hommage à Jean Hyppolite*. Paris: Presses Universitaires de France, 1971.

Gadamer, H. G. 1991. *Truth and Method*. 2nd Ed. Trans. J. Weinsheimer and D. Marshall. New York: Crossroad Publishing. Orig. pub. as *Wahrheit und Methode*. Tübingen: J. C. B. Mohr, 1960.

Gemes, K. 1992. "Nietzsche's Critique of Truth." *Philosophy and Phenomenological Research* 52 (1):47–65.

Gilligan, C. 1982. *In a Different Voice: Psychological Theory and Women's Development*. Cambridge: Harvard University Press.

Guthrie, W. K. C. 1962. *A History of Greek Philosophy*, Vol. 1. Cambridge: Cambridge University Press.

Haar, M. 1985. "Nietzsche and Metaphysical Language." Trans. C. Welch and L. Welch. In Allison 1985. Orig. pub. in *Man and World* 4 (1971).

Habermas, J. 1990. *The Philosophical Discourse of Modernity: Twelve Lectures*. Trans. F. Lawrence. Cambridge: MIT Press. Orig. pub. as *Der philosophische Diskurs der Moderne: Zwölf Vorlesungen*. Frankfurt: Suhrkamp, 1985.

Harding, S. 1991. *Whose Science? Whose Knowledge?: Thinking from Women's Lives*. Ithaca: Cornell University Press.

Hayman, R. 1982. *Nietzsche: A Critical Life*. New York: Penguin. Orig. pub. New York: Oxford University Press, 1980.

Heidegger, M. 1979–87. *Nietzsche*, Vol. 1–4. Trans. D. Krell, J. Stambaugh, and F. Capuzzi. San Francisco: Harper & Row. Orig. pub. Pfullingen: Günther Neske, 1961.

Hunt, L. H. 1991. *Nietzsche and the Origin of Virtue*. London: Routledge.

Hussey, E. 1972. *The Presocratics*. New York: Scribner's.

Irigiray, L. 1991. *Marine Lover of Friedrich Nietzsche*. Trans. G. Gill. New York: Columbia University Press. Orig. pub. as *Amante marine: de Friedrich Nietzsche*. Paris: Les Editions de Minuit, 1980.

Irwin, T. 1977a. "Plato's Heracleiteanism." *Philosophical Quarterly* 27:1–13.

———. 1977b. *Plato's Moral Theory: The Early and Middle Dialogues*. Oxford: Oxford University Press.

———. 1988. *Aristotle's First Principles*. Oxford: Oxford University Press.

Jaggar, A. M. 1989. "Love and Knowledge: Emotion in Feminist Epistemology." In A. M. Jaggar and S. R. Bordo (eds.), *Gender/Body/Knowledge: Feminist Reconstructions of Being and Knowing*. New Brunswick: Rutgers University Press.

Kahn, C. H. 1979. *The Art and Thought of Heraclitus: An Edition of the Fragments with Translation and Commentary*. Cambridge: Cambridge University Press.

Kaufmann, W. 1974. *Nietzsche: Philosopher, Psychologist, Antichrist*. 4th Ed. Princeton: Princeton University Press. Orig. pub. 1950.

Kirk, G. S. 1951. "Natural Change in Heraclitus." *Mind* 60:35–42.

Kittay, E. F. and D. T. Meyers, eds. 1987. *Women and Moral Theory*. Totowa, N.J.: Rowman & Littlefield.

Kofman, S. 1993. *Nietzsche and Metaphor*. Trans. D. Large. Stanford: Stanford University Press. Orig. pub. as *Nietzsche et la métaphore*. Paris: Payot, 1972.

Lampert, L. 1986. *Nietzsche's Teaching: An Interpretation of "Thus Spoke Zarathustra."* New Haven: Yale University Press.

Leiter, B. 1993. "Beyond Good and Evil." *History of Philosophy Quarterly* 10 (3):261–70.

——. 1994. "Perspectivism in Nietzsche's *Genealogy of Morals.*" In Schacht 1994.

Lyotard, J.-F. 1991. *The Inhuman: Reflections on Time*. Trans. G. Bennington and R. Bowlby. Stanford: Stanford University Press. Orig. pub. as *L'Inhuman: Causeries sur le temps*. Paris: Editions Galilée, 1988.

MacIntyre, A. 1981. *After Virtue: A Study in Moral Theory*. Notre Dame: University of Notre Dame Press.

Magnus, B. 1978. *Nietzsche's Existential Imperative*. Bloomington: Indiana University Press.

——. 1983. "Perfectibility and Attitude in Nietzsche's *Übermensch.*" *Review of Metaphysics* 36 (3):633–59.

——. 1986. "Nietzsche's Philosophy in 1888: *The Will to Power* and the *Übermensch.*" *Journal of the History of Philosophy* 24 (1):79–98.

——. 1988a. "The Deification of the Commonplace: *Twilight of the Idols.*" In Solomon and Higgins 1988.

——. 1988b. "The Use and Abuse of *The Will to Power.*" In Solomon and Higgins 1988.

Mann, T. 1973. "Nietzsche's Philosophy in the Light of Contemporary Events." In Solomon 1973b. Address delivered in 1947.

McDowell, J. 1973. "Notes" to Plato's *Theaetetus*. Oxford: Oxford University Press.

Megill, A. 1985. *Prophets of Extremity: Nietzsche, Heidegger, Foucault, Derrida*. Berkeley: University of California Press.

Middleton, C. 1988. "Nietzsche's Letters and a Poem." In Solomon and Higgins 1988.

Nagel, T. 1979. "Equality." In *Mortal Questions*. Cambridge: Cambridge University Press, 1979. Orig. pub. *Critica* 1978.

——. 1986. *The View from Nowhere*. New York: Oxford University Press.

——. 1991. *Equality and Partiality*. New York: Oxford University Press.

Nehamas, A. 1975. "Plato on the Imperfections of the Sensible World." *American Philosophical Quarterly* 12 (2):105–17.

———. 1985. *Nietzsche: Life as Literature*. Cambridge: Harvard University Press.

———. 1988. "Who Are 'The Philosophers of the Future'?: A Reading of *Beyond Good and Evil*.'' In Solomon and Higgins 1988.

Nozick, R. 1989. *The Examined Life: Philosophical Meditations*. New York: Simon & Schuster.

Nussbaum, M. C. 1986. *The Fragility of Goodness: Luck and Ethics in Greek Tragedy and Philosophy*. Cambridge: Cambridge University Press.

Owen, G. E. L. 1953. "The Place of the *Timaeus* in Plato's Dialogues." *Classical Quarterly* n.s. 3:79–95. Repr. in Owen 1986.

———. 1957. "A Proof in the *Peri Ideon*.'' *Journal of Hellenic Studies* 77:103–11. Repr. in Owen 1986.

———. 1961. "*Tithenai ta phainomena*.'' In S. Mansion (ed.), *Aristote et les problèmes de méthode*. Louvains: Publications Universitaires de Louvain. Repr. in Owen 1986.

———. 1966. "Plato and Parmenides on the Timeless Present." *Monist* 50:317–40. Repr. in Owen 1986.

———. 1970. "Plato on Not-Being." In G. Vlastos (ed.), *Plato I: Metaphysics and Epistemology*. Garden City: Doubleday. Repr. in Owen 1986.

———. 1976. "Aristotle on Time." In P. Machamer and R. Turnbull (ed.), *Motion and Time, Space and Matter*. Columbus: Ohio State University Press. Repr. in Owen 1986.

———. 1986. *Logic, Science, and Dialectic: Collected Papers in Greek Philosophy*. Ed. M. C. Nussbaum. Ithaca: Cornell University Press.

Parkes, G., ed. 1991. *Nietzsche and Asian Thought*. Chicago: University of Chicago Press.

———. 1994. *Composing the Soul: Reaches of Nietzsche's Psychology*. Chicago: University of Chicago Press.

Parsons, K. P. 1973. "Nietzsche and Moral Change." In Solomon 1973b.

Patton, P. 1993a. "Politics and the Concept of Power in Hobbes and Nietzsche." In Patton 1993b.

———, ed. 1993b. *Nietzsche, Feminism and Political Theory*. London: Routledge.

Popper, K. 1963. "Kirk on Heraclitus, and on Fire as the Cause of Balance." *Mind* 72:386–92.

———. 1966. *The Open Society and its Enemies: Vol. 1. The Spell of Plato*. 5th Ed. Princeton: Princeton University Press. Orig. pub. London: G. Routledge, 1945.

Price, A. W. 1989. *Love and Friendship in Plato and Aristotle*. Oxford: Oxford University Press.

Rawls, J. 1971. *A Theory of Justice*. Cambridge: Harvard University Press.

Rorty, R. 1989. "Self-Creation and Affiliation: Proust, Nietzsche, and Heidegger." In *Contingency, Irony, and Solidarity*. Cambridge: Cambridge University Press.

Ruddick, S. 1987. "Remarks on the Sexual Politics of Reason." In Kittay and Meyers 1987.

———. 1989. *Maternal Thinking: Toward a Politics of Peace*. New York: Ballantine.

Russell, B. 1945. *A History of Western Philosophy*. New York: Simon & Schuster.

Schacht, R. 1973. "Nietzsche and Nihilism." In Solomon 1973b. Orig. pub. *Journal of the History of Philosophy* 11 (1973).

———. 1983. *Nietzsche.* London: Routledge & Kegan Paul.

———, ed. 1994. *Nietzsche, Genealogy, Morality: Essays on Nietzsche's "Genealogy of Morals."* Berkeley: University of California Press.

Scheiffele, E. 1991. "Questioning One's 'Own' from the Perspective of the Foreign." Trans. G. Parkes. In Parkes 1991.

Schrift, A. D. 1990. *Nietzsche and the Question of Interpretation: Between Hermeneutics and Deconstruction.* New York: Routledge.

Schutte, O. 1984. *Beyond Nihilism: Nietzsche without Masks.* Chicago: University of Chicago Press.

Simmel, G. 1991. *Schopenhauer and Nietzsche.* Trans. H. Loiskandl, D. Weinstein, and M. Weinstein. Urbana: University of Illinois Press. Orig. pub. as *Schopenhauer und Nietzsche: Ein Vortragszyklus.* Leipzig: Duncker und Humblot, 1907.

Small, R. 1989. "Absolute Becoming and Absolute Necessity." *International Studies in Philosophy* 21 (2):125–34.

Solomon, R. C. 1973a. "Nietzsche, Nihilism, and Morality." In Solomon 1973b.

———, ed. 1973b. *Nietzsche: A Collection of Critical Essays.* Garden City: Anchor.

Solomon, R. C. and K. M. Higgins, eds. 1988. *Reading Nietzsche.* New York: Oxford University Press.

Sorabji, R. 1983. *Time, Creation, and the Continuum: Theories in Antiquity and the Early Middle Ages.* Ithaca: Cornell University Press.

Stack, G. J. 1992. *Nietzsche and Emerson: An Elective Affinity.* Athens: Ohio University Press.

Stern, J. P. 1979. *A Study of Nietzsche.* Cambridge: Cambridge University Press.

Strong, T. B. 1988. *Friedrich Nietzsche and the Politics of Transfiguration.* Expanded Ed. Berkeley: University of California Press. Orig. pub. 1975.

Taylor, C. 1986. "Foucault on Freedom and Truth." In D. Hoy (ed.), *Foucault: A Critical Reader.* Oxford: Basil Blackwell. Orig. pub. *Political Theory* 12:152–83 (1984).

Thiele, L. P. 1990. *Friedrich Nietzsche and the Politics of the Soul: A Study of Heroic Individualism.* Princeton: Princeton University Press.

Vlastos, G. 1941. "Slavery in Plato's Thought." *Philosophical Review* 50:239–304. Repr. in Vlastos 1981.

———. 1957. "Socratic Knowledge and Platonic 'Pessimism.'" *Philosophical Review* 66:226–38. Repr. in Vlastos 1981.

———. 1965. "Degrees of Reality in Plato." In R. Bambrough (ed.), *New Essays in Plato and Aristotle.* London: Routledge & Kegan Paul. Repr. in Vlastos 1981.

———. 1966. "A Metaphysical Paradox." *Proceedings of the American Philosophical Association* 39:5–19. Repr. in Vlastos 1981.

———. 1981. *Platonic Studies.* 2nd Ed. Princeton: Princeton University Press. Orig. pub. 1973.

Westphal, K. R. 1984. "Was Nietzsche a Cognitivist?" *Journal of the History of Philosophy* 22 (3):343–63.

White, R. 1994. "The Return of the Master: An Interpretation of Nietzsche's *Genealogy of Morals.*" In Schacht 1994. Orig. pub. *Philosophy and Phenomenological Research* 48 (4):683–96 (1988).

Wiggins, D. 1982. "Heraclitus' Conception of Flux, Fire, and Material Persistence." In M. Schofield and M. C. Nussbaum (eds.), *Language and Logos: Studies in Ancient Greek Philosophy Presented to G. E. L. Owen*. Cambridge: Cambridge University Press, 1982.

Wilcox, J. T. 1982. *Truth and Value in Nietzsche: A Study of His Metaethics and Epistemology*. Washington, D.C.: University Press of America. Orig. pub. Ann Arbor: University of Michigan Press, 1974.

Williams, B. 1994. "Nietzsche's Minimalist Moral Psychology." In Schacht 1994.

NAME INDEX

This lists only names of philosophers and interpreters of Nietzsche. References are to page numbers in the main text (not including the Preface or Bibliography) on which these names, or their adjectival forms (e.g., Platonic or Cartesian), occur. A few of these names are also included in the subject index.

SUBJECT INDEX

References are selective, to pages at which these topics are most importantly discussed. "N." indicates "Nietzsche."

active, 39; as commanding, 42, 49; as freedom, 42, 213; whether good for all wills, 217–19; as knowing better than reactive, 276, 282–83; as life's own valuing, 282; loves past and present, 113; in master, 54–55, 130; in overman, 69, 137–38; as power ontology's basic value, 39, 149; 'realizes' will to power essence, 27, 43–44, 115; as self-command of person, 49–50, 119; its telic priority to reactive, 43–44; its temporal stretch and rhythm, 119–20; wills to enrich and redeem past, 114–15

aesthetic, 112–13; aesthetic drive vs. will to truth, 245–47, 259–60. *See also* art

affect, 37

agon, 30, 199–201; broadens self-interest, 162–63, 187; as friends' enmity, 186–87; as N.'s stance toward his readers, 202; as spiritualization of enmity, 189; tempers N.'s values, 156–57, 162–63; uses other's difference to grow, 157, 186–87; in will to truth, 258, 278. *See also* contest

altruism, 162, 187; attacked by N., 151–52

amor fati, 210, 212. *See also* fate

anonymous reflective agent: whether addressed by N.'s values, 147, 201–3, 207, 215–16, 218–19; against agency, 207–16; against anonymity of values, 216–19; against reflection over values, 203–7

Apollonian, 20; as lower form of activeness, 113–14, 117, 130. *See also* Dionysian; master

aristocracy, 54, 129, 166, 179. *See also* hierarchy

Aristotle: and ascetic ideal, 273–77; his dialectical method compared with N.'s, 269–79, 284–87; on friendship, 187

whether N. accepts, 4, 8, 223–
24, 226, 250–51, 255–56, 263;
N.'s strong form of, 224, 230
slave, 57; as 'interesting', 57–58;
Plato's view of, compared with
N.'s, 132–33; as reactive diversely, 40; as reactive in nihilism, 65–66; as reactive in resentment, 60–65; as reactive in
subjection, 58–60; rejects eternal
return, 71; as rich but poorly
synthesized, 58–59
slave morality: its judgment evil pre-
cedes judgment good, 61–63; as
product of resentment, 60–61;
its self-overcoming, 65–66
slave revolt, 64–65
slavery: whether advocated by N.,
59, 164, 175–77, 180; as subjection, 58–59
societies: differences between, 51; N.'s
ideal for, 67–68, 124, 163–64,
178–81; N. values less than persons, 52, 122, 126, 141; as syntheses of persons or practices, 50–
51; their temporal structure, 123
Socrates: N.'s assessment of, 75, 116,
133
spiritualization: fails to humanize
N.'s politics, 178–81, 184; generates *agon*, 189; as strengthening of intentional aspect of will,
188–89; tempers N.'s values,
156–57
strength: contrasted with power, 28;
how measured, 29–30
sublimation, 23; as higher form of
growth, 25. *See also* spiritualization
substances: reanalyzed as wholes,
84; ruled out by becoming, 77,
80, 83
suffering: discipline of, 130, 262; as
good, 181, 262; leveling society
tries to eliminate, 166–67; of
overman, 70, 137, 214; of slave,
59, 249; for truth, 270, 278
synthesis: in overman, 68–70, 136,
138; of drives in person, 45–47,

119–21; of practices in society,
50–51, 122–23; of wills, 44. *See
also* wholes
system: attacked by N., 8, 110–11;
implicit in N., 5–6, 8–9, 205,
220; required for N.'s new truth,
200, 281, 288; its role in metaphysics, 3, 7

teleology: attacked by N., 21; involved in power ontology, 21
things. *See* substances
time: as topic in N.'s thought, 73–74
truth: whether abandoned as goal by
N., 220–21, 252, 280; attacked
unconvincingly by N., 225–26,
230–31, 233, 236; endured by
strongest, 262–63; essential
truth, how known, 287–88; as
indefinable, 237; internal vs. external, 281–82, 286, 289; master's vs. overman's, 277, 282–
83; N. attacks possibility of, 221,
224–32; N. attacks value of,
221, 231–36; N. first subordinates to art, 253–54; N. later reaffirms, 255–57; as not atomic,
286; as not opposite to falsity,
278; as object of evolving will to
truth, 236–37; pragmatic theory
of, 232, 261; shared in by all
perspectives, 278–80. *See also*
correspondence; will to truth
truth method: as autopsychology,
258–59; orders perspectives with
dialectic, 269; studies many perspectives, 264–66. *See also* dialectic
two-level account: insulates power
ontology from perspectivism, 10–
11, 222. *See also* perspectivism

utilitarianism, 149–50, 158–59, 165,
170, 205

values: as aspect of will to power,
37; express some interest, 144;
whether N. means his as true,
145, 217; whether N.'s are un-

Printed in Great Britain
by Amazon